Builders of the Dawn

Community Lifestyles in a Changing World

Builders
of the Dawn

Community Lifestyles
in a Changing World

**By Corinne McLaughlin
and Gordon Davidson**

**BOOK PUBLISHING COMPANY
SUMMERTOWN, TENNESSEE**

ISBN 0-913990-68-X
Library of Congress Card Catalog Number: 89-29638

McLaughlin, Corinne.
    Builders of the dawn : community lifestyles in a changing world /
By Corinne McLaughlin and Gordon Davidson.
      p.   cm.
    Reprint. Originally published: Walpole, N.H. : Stillpoint Pub.,
1985
    Includes bibliographical references.
    ISBN 0-913990-68-X : $17.95
    1. Communal living--United States. 2. Collective settlements-
-United States. 3. Religious communities--United States.
I. Davidson, Gordon. II. Title.
(HQ971.M37 1990)   89-29638
307.1'4--dc20   CIP

9 8 7 6 5 4 3

This book is manufactured in the United States of
America. It is designed by James F. Brisson, cover art
of Arcosanti by Ginger Brown and published by
Book Publishing Company, PO Box 99,
Summertown, TN, 38483

Dedication

This book is dedicated to the *builders of the dawn*—the coura-
geous pioneers of the new communities who are inspiring us
with visions of a positive future for humanity.

Table of Contents

Foreword

This is a needed book. Having worked in adult education for many years dealing with such topics as the development of intentional communities and the relationship of such development to spirituality, personal growth, and human relations, I have long wished for a comprehensive book on these themes. That is what this book is. In fact, the authors have done such a complete job of covering this topic, there is little left for me to add.

This book appeals to a wider audience than those living in an intentional community or contemplating joining or creating one, for it is about much more than just community living. It is about empowerment and creativity. Specifically, it is about the power we all have, whether we express it through a community or not, to envision the future we want for ourselves and for humanity and to make a positive contribution to the emergence of that future.

As we come into the last fifteen years of the twentieth century, the dominant feelings for many people are fear for the future and helplessness to change what is seen as humanity's destructive bent. Clouded by the dangers of nuclear weapons, environmental pollution, and international tensions, the world's destiny appears bleak. Worse, there seems little that anyone, least of all the average citizen, can do to change the situation.

At a time when humanity needs clear thought and creative action, such helplessness can lead us either to violent actions born of frustration or to apathy. Either way, we diminish the chances we have to move successfully through the dangers of our time. We lose the sense of our capability to change. We lose our sense of power. We abdicate our potential to make a difference in the world and to affect the course of human history.

To me, this abdication of potential is our greatest threat, the one that can trigger disasters. It consigns our future to those whose vision is at best limited to images of survival and selfishness instead of growth and the well-being of all our world.

This book is about people who refuse to make such an abdication. That they do so using the community as an expression of their creativity and vision is in some ways a secondary issue. The true story is that they are rejecting fear and helplessness as guidelines for their lives. They invite the rest of us to do the same, whether through the medium of intentional community or through some other expression of our potential.

There are many reasons why people create communities. These include enhanced economic power, security, the pleasure of living together, a shared ideology. In the last twenty years, I have observed communities forming for the additional purpose of exploring and empowering options for a better future. Findhorn is one of these, and this book lists others.

Such communities often call themselves "new age," suggesting that they will be laboratories for researching and testing the inner and outer components of a new cultural vision. These communities often do not look for or expect permanent membership, other than having a body of "core" individuals who provide continuity. They are more like learning centers where people may come, live for awhile, and then return to the larger culture.

What do people learn in such places? What do they go away with? There are the traditional skills one can develop in community, such as enhanced understanding of the dynamics of human relationships. These skills are well described in this book. However, community members also learn the power of their intentionality: the power of their imagination, their vision, their will, and their love to create a new order, a new society.

In short, these communities become training places for creative participation in the unfoldment of the future. They are schools for change, for transformation, for the exercise of "voluntary history," as the authors of the book *Seven Tomorrows* put it.

Such "schools" or communities do not have all the answers. They are not the only sources of vision for an evolving society. But they are antidotes to feelings of helplessness. They demonstrate that people can do something to make the world a better place. Once people experience that fact as a personal reality, they are free to leave that specific community and continue to practice their creative work in the larger community of humankind.

Thus these communities nourish the power of intentionality itself. At their best, they offer us the realization that we can go beyond the boundaries of the familiar and explore new territory. We can innovate. We can be, in the wonderful word coined by Walt Disney, "imagineers."

As we learn this, we can move beyond the limits of our intentional communities and into the community of intentionality, the community of human and planetary aspiration and commitment towards the emergence of a healed and healing world.

David Spangler

Acknowledgments

We'd like to thank all those many community members whose spirit fills these pages for their time and patience in answering our questions and showing us around their communities. Without their openness and cooperation, this book would not have been possible. And our appreciation goes to fellow Sirius Community members whose dedication and hard work helped to create the context that gave us firsthand experience to write from.

We'd also like to thank Judith Bergman, Nancy Fisher, Cheryl Gray, Anna Hemingsley, Sue Kennedy, Tom Klein, and Katy Wolf for their help with typing and with collating community names and addresses for the Resources section. We're grateful to Peter Caddy, Jeff Fishell, Donald Keys, Michael Marien, Beldon and Lisa Paulson, and Mark Satin for reviewing early copies of the manuscript and giving feedback; to John and Libby Farr and Zell Draz for providing quiet places to work on the manuscript; and especially to Joshua Mailman and Richard Perl for finances and resources to enable us to visit the many communities and write about them. We thank John White, our agent, Caroline Myss and Shakti Reiner, our editors, and Jim and Chip Young, our publishers, for their invaluable assistance.

And thank you to all the communities that gave us additional photographs to use: Findhorn, The Pathwork, Sevenoaks (Tom Cogill) and Phoenicia, Chinook, Renaissance, High Wind, Living Love, Terre Nouvelle, Kripalu, Spring Valley, Yogaville, The Farm, The Bear Tribe (Tom Hammang), Esalen (Kathy Thormod), Twin Oaks, Arcosanti (Ivan Pintar), and Auroville. (Other photos were taken by us.) On the cover of the book is a drawing of Arcosanti, one of the communities featured in the book. And thanks to everyone who gave us support and encouragement while we were writing the book. We love you all!

Introduction

Know the new that seeks birth within you . . . The world moves into a new cycle . . . Come forth, you builders, and build the new heaven and the new earth.
—DAVID SPANGLER

    This book is based largely on our combined personal experiences of living in intentional communities for more than twenty-three years and visiting more than one hundred other communities over a fifteen-year period. The two of us have lived in everything from the hippie communes of Haight-Ashbury to radical political communes; from shared urban households of professionals to rural spiritual communities. For several years, we both lived at the Findhorn Community in Scotland, which had a particularly profound effect on us in our personal growth and in inspiring us about the effectiveness of community as a strategy for social transformation. In 1978 we co-founded Sirius Community on eighty-six acres in western Massachusetts as a non-profit educational center to communicate new ways to transform self and society.

From our perspective, intentional communities seem to catch glimpses of a positive future for humanity and then build new forms to express that vision. They stand on the edges of culture, watching the horizon, awaiting a new dawn.

These Builders of the Dawn are building not only new social structures, but, more importantly, new people. They are learning how to change fear, selfishness, and conflict into love, cooperation and sharing. These Builders are pioneering a positive response to societal ills and demonstrating the attitudes and values needed to restore a sense of community to our lives, wherever we live.

To us, the new intentional communities are one of the mapmakers for humanity's journey into the future. They function as research and development centers for society, experimenting with new approaches to problems of inflation, pollution, energy shortages, job alienation, unemployment, and rising health care costs. Many ideas and techniques being developed in communities are directly applicable to urban and suburban life, like reducing living costs while enhancing the quality of life and the sense of being surrounded by friendship and support.

The impact of the community movement today is not due to one particularly successful prototype of community but rather to the diversity of new communities and the strength of their combined innovations in so many areas of human life, from new techniques for conflict resolution and good communication to alternative forms of energy and health care. These workable solutions to real life problems have wide appeal.

To study communities is to examine in microcosm the problems, and some of the solutions, in creating a new social structure for humanity. Many different personality types live together in a given community, and they may even share certain values. The main task of community living is to create unity out of human diversity. Communities educate people in a cooperative way of life, with new attitudes and values, in an environment that enhances personal growth.

Living in these communities is a powerful training in the art of relationship: learning to live as an inter-related part of a whole system, balancing the needs of others with one's own. This "whole system" awareness is a much needed skill in today's world—in families, in businesses, and in international politics.

Learning to live as an interrelated part of a whole system

Community living teaches us firsthand the reality of the interdependence of all life. We learn to be good stewards in caring for things that belong to the whole community (or the whole earth) as we would care for our own possessions; we learn how to circulate resources and share with others less fortunate; we develop tolerance for differences and learn how to resolve conflicts peacefully; we focus on giving and producing, rather than on just receiving and consuming. It is this "community awareness," so often lacking in people today, which is needed to create a world that truly works for everyone.

Communities are thriving in the '90s and have a new maturity and sustainability, unlike the communes of the 1960s. Most communities are not manipulative, crazy "cults," as the media likes to label all non-mainstream religious groups. The majority are very down-to-earth and non-fanatical.

Each community is formed for a specific purpose—political, spiritual, educational, or scientific. Most offer a specific service to society and have a different atmosphere than do those that are focused just on meeting the needs of their own members. Most are working towards the creation of a better world and/or towards personal growth and development. Rather than being utopias, a "heaven on earth" where all problems have been left behind, communities are involved with an ongoing process of working to attain certain ideals.

Communal living is taking many forms today, from the simple cooperative households of urban areas, formed mainly to reduce costs, to the more complex and committed communities of

Working towards the creation of a better world

rural areas, where members share common values and goals. Today, most groups prefer to call themselves "cooperative households" or "communities," rather than "communes," to distinguish themselves from the stereotyped "hippie crash pad" image of communes of the '60s and to emphasize the return to the spirit of good neighborliness implied by the word "community."

Many diverse lifestyles and values are represented in the new communities. Some have a very communal focus, pooling all resources and living together in one house; others offer more individual space and resemble a new kind of village. Some communities follow Eastern spiritual paths; some follow a "new age" spiritual path; others follow no spiritual path.

Members of one community (Sparrow Hawk in Oklahoma) feel that seven different prototypes of communities (based on the concept of seven rays of energy) are being built today as models for the future: some are a new type of ashram, serving God's will; some are educational communities, teaching, caring, and supporting people; some are centers of philosophical experimentation; others are creative communities of artists and poets; others are technological/ecological; others are monastic in a devotional pattern; and still others are oriented primarily towards concepts of ownership and finance.

Community means different things to different people. To some, it is a safe haven where survival is assured through mutual cooperation. To others, it is a place of emotional support, with deep sharing and bonding with close friends. Some see community as an intense crucible for personal growth. For others it is primarily a place to pioneer their dreams.

Deep sharing and bonding with close friends

This book does not present an overview of all types of communities. We did not visit communities that are, in our opinion, highly authoritarian and manipulative and create an extreme dependence and passivity in their members. Nor did we include those that are mainly survivalist and very hostile to their neighbors, stock-piling guns for "protection," as these seemed to represent the worst aspects of society as it is today and were not an inspiring alternative.

We also did not visit the older traditional religious communities. We were drawn to those communities that share certain "new age" values like ecological concern, personal growth, and planetary awareness, which are discussed more in depth in Chapter 1. We have included only residential communities (where members share the same house and/or land), not groups who experience a strong sense of "community" through their shared work or values, as we found that actually living together creates a particularly strong focus for studying the areas we are interested in here.

We visited only those communities that are open to the public as demonstration centers of their way of life and are not afraid of publicity. Many of the urban communities are shared households that are not open to the public. Although the majority of communities in this book are rurally based, there are important exceptions, such as The Movement for a New Society in Philadelphia and the Institute for Cultural Affairs in Chicago.

While we could not include all of the new communities we would have liked to, we have presented a representative sample. We have concentrated mainly on American communities, as this is what we are most familiar with, although we have included a few examples of communities in other countries to give somewhat of an international perspective. Not all of the examples presented in this book would necessarily define themselves as "communities," but each consists of people living together for a common purpose, sharing certain values and resources, and cooperating with each other.

We focus several chapters on the innovative and interesting aspects of thirty different communities, but we don't give a complete description of any community individually. We hope this approach will give an overview of the fascinating range and depth of communities today.

Unlike bureaucratic institutions, communities often change rapidly from year to year, depending on who their members are. The information included in this book is accurate (to the best of our knowledge) only as of this writing (1985). We are not able to guarantee that someone will find exactly what is described here if s/he visits a community in the future.

Why study communities? Aren't they just "utopian dreams" or "the rebellion of society's misfits"? Far from drawing only misfits, today's communities include some very brilliant and creative people. Innovations being pioneered by community members are relevant to problems facing our world today. We'd like to communicate these new approaches to people in the mainstream.

The impetus to write a book on communities has come from several sources. We have strongly felt the lack of community spirit and good neighborliness in society as a whole, and we've wanted to help address that deep inner need for human connectedness by pointing the way to some solutions.

Also, for the last seven years, we've been presenting all over the country a slide show on thirty new age communities that we've visited. We've given a workshop for hundreds of participants on building communities and have repeatedly been asked by people to put all of our material into book form so it would be available to others.

When we did extensive research to locate textbooks for a course on Alternative Communities that we taught at American University in Washington, D.C., we discovered that almost nothing is available on communities of the late 1970s and '80s. Most books focus on the communes of the late '60s and contain nothing on how to start communities. There are few books written by those actually living in communities, perhaps because people are too busy actually living the experience to write about it! For us, trying to write a book in the middle of a busy community was a tremendous challenge.

Information on today's communities is lacking even in books with comprehensive overviews of the new consciousness today, such as *The Aquarian Conspiracy* and *Networking: The First Report*. Today's communities are a very well-kept secret!

In the last year, we have received increased requests for information about our community. It appears that as the world political and economic situation worsens, as pollution and poisoned wastes spread, and as people respond to a need for inner peace and spiritual growth, the interest in communities grows proportionally.

It is our sincere hope that this book will be useful to many kinds of people:

—those already living in communities could benefit both from the mistakes and successes of others in community and from the feeling of support and affirmation which this book might provide.

—people who are interested in starting communities might benefit tremendously from the chapter on "Guidelines for Building Communities," since it is based on interviews with many successful community founders and long-term community members.

—those who are studying communities in academic settings and public policy and corporate think tanks are interested in successful innovations in all sectors of society. Many communities, including our own, have been visited by college classes.

—those who like to stay informed of current trends on the leading edge of human activity can appreciate a comprehensive overview of communities today.

—most importantly, those people who are experiencing personal crisis, economic upheaval, or the need for inner change in their lives and who are searching for new solutions and alternatives to the mainstream approach will be inspired with the hope of a more positive future, both for themselves and for society, by seeing successful models of communities that express human caring and cooperation, as well as more economical living. This book will be helpful in selecting a community that matches a person's needs and interests.

—and finally, the general public has been given a lot of misinformation about communities by the media's labeling all alternatives as "hippie communes," or worse yet, "cults." The most extreme and controversial alternatives have been played up, and the more sedate and successful ones have been ignored. We hope to reduce the fear level about communities by providing helpful guidelines for distinguishing the true "cults" from the good work of honest communities.

This book offers a more personal, immediate, and firsthand account of what it's like to actually live in community and why it's such a powerful experience, eternally challenging on every level and deeply rewarding. As community members ourselves, we had the advantage of more honest and in-depth interviews with members of other communities than reporters and sociologists have been able to obtain. People trusted us, knowing we would understand them and accurately represent their thoughts. Many community members and founders we interviewed were friends we have come to know through our networking projects and through visiting their communities several times over the years. We believe that our "insiders' view" will prove more lively and insightful than the tedious reports of sociologists.

Whether or not you ever live in an alternative community, we hope the experience of these communities will be of value to you in your home and work life. They may help you to bring a greater sense of community and connectedness into whatever you're doing, to enhance the quality of your life, and even to live more economically.

Finally, we'd like to add that we understand the difficulty of trying to separate out our personal values and provide a scientifically objective study of human social systems. We are not presenting any absolute truth about our study of communities. Rather, we are offering a perception of a new social phenomenon as seen through the eyes of two of its participants who clearly share many of its values.

In particular, living in a spiritually-oriented community ourselves, we value the inner level of reality, consciousness, more than external forms, per se. In our own analysis of community problems and solutions, we are oriented towards changing the inner attitudes and values first, since we feel that energy follows thought. Our thoughts and beliefs create the reality we experience. (For example, we emphasize the importance of positive thinking, or faith in the goodness and abundance of the Universe, in dealing with financial problems.) Although the book focuses on the forms of community—economics, governance, relationships, alternative energy, etc.—we also include a more subjective, value-oriented analysis, especially in the chapters on Guidelines for Building Communities and on Problems in Communities.

1 The Human Yearning for Community

*The modern quest for community is a quest for one's
personhood...The essence of community is wholeness: the
opportunity...to co-create a livingness that meets my
needs and those of the greater whole of which I am a part.
Community is the deeper reality within which I move and
have my being. It is one of the names of God. Community
is the gift of myself that I give in endless participation
with my world.*[1]
—DAVID SPANGLER

The Meaning of Community

There is something in the human condition that eternally yearns for a greater sense of connectedness, yearns to reach out and deeply touch others, throwing off the pain and loneliness of separation to experience unity with others. In all times and all places people have consciously reached out to feel their connectedness with a larger whole. This is the experience of *community*.

The word "community" contains the word "unity" and, on the deepest level, community is the experience of unity or oneness with all people and with all of life. We can be in community with our family, our friends, our clubs, our co-workers, our neighbors, and with our fellow humans—as long as we are feeling a sense of connectedness and unity with them. Social researcher Daniel Yankelovitch describes community in this way:

> Community evokes in the individual the feeling that "Here is where I belong, these are my people, I care for them, they care for me, I am part of them, I know what they expect from me and I from them, they share my concerns. I know this place, I am on familiar ground, I am at home."[2]

Community is not a static structure; rather it is an ongoing process of unfoldment of the wholeness of a person on all levels — physical, emotional, mental, spiritual. Community is the context for actualizing potentials within the individual and between the individual and others, for connecting with others and experiencing oneness. It is a sense of brother/sisterhood, beyond separation, where we recognize ourselves in the "other." At times, this experience of unity bursts upon us spontaneously, revealing the wonder and mystery of life—a taste of the Divine. And yet we also can create a sense of unity consciously, building it patiently, step by step, as we get to know each other, revealing more of our deeper selves, trading vulnerabilities, developing trust, keeping our hearts open as we work out conflicts and differences. As this process extends beyond the human world, we develop a sense of community with all other life forms who share the earth with us.

Being in community with others means we consciously cooperate with them, as community member Ingrid Komar writes.

> Cooperation takes us beyond the narrow confines of our little lives. It leads us to the wealth of human resources all around us and opens doors onto sweeping cultural vistas we would otherwise never imag-

ine. To cooperate is to participate; and to participate is to end loneliness, helplessness. It is to be empowered, to be fulfilled. To live such a fulfilled life—living the dream—is the greatest gift we can leave to our children.[3]

Barn-raising at Sirius Community

The Decline of Tribes and Villages and the Rise of Alternative Communities

Throughout most of human history, community was the normal pattern. Our roots are tribal. Our lives used to be deeply connected to each other and to nature, and there was both intimacy and security in this. For centuries, people lived in large extended families or tribal networks. Small villages functioned like communities in the truest sense. Even today, much of the world still lives in these kind of villages. Until recently a true sense of neighborhood existed in most places in this country, as people helped each other in work projects like barn raisings and in times of crisis. They shared meals and child care. Only as our society has become more technological, with increased wealth and urban growth and transient patterns, have people lost touch with a strong community consciousness. They have greater individual freedom, but the cost has been social isolation.

"When we lack closeness to others, we do not become deep as human beings; we become shallow," according to Swami Kriyananda of Ananda Community. Perhaps because of this deep alienation in the modern industrial era, there has been a recent rebirth of the idea of alternative or intentional communities.

The Human Yearning for Community 11

A conscious community, as distinct from a neighborhood or town, is a group of people experiencing a common purpose in being together, with an agreement to cooperate and create a sense of unity together. Often the community shares resources such as land and/or housing.

These communities have always sprung up as a response to the ills of society, beginning with the first ashram communities of the East and the monasteries of the West, continuing through the early communities and colonial settlements of America, in the Utopian movement of the 1800s, the kibbutz movement in Israel, the hippie communes of the 1960s and the new communities of the 1980s. Historically, many ancient and modern cities were seeded from religious and pioneer communities. And communities often have served as the seedbeds of new cultures and ideas.

The new intentional communities of the 1990s are a conscious response to societal problems and are working to restore a sense of community in our neighborhoods and towns. Like the Christian monasteries of the Dark Ages, today's communities sometimes see themselves as preserving a spark of culture and human caring during the dark days of modern society. Lessons being learned in these communities may be of great value to all of us in the future, when we try to rebuild our society along more humane lines. As communities are demonstrating, we can blend the best aspects of our tribal roots and the feeling of closeness to others with the technological advances of modern times that save labor and hardship.

The Appeal of Alternative Communities

Why have alternative communities been so fascinating to mainstream society? Why has there been so much media attention? One answer seems to be that there is a deep yearning in the human psyche for the freedom they represent, for self-liberation, for loosening the fetters of the 9-to-5 grind, for getting back to nature and living life on our own terms. And in each of us a longing exists to build a better world, to live and work with loving friends, and to cooperate with others, instead of always competing.

Communities live this dream. They act it out for all of us. They step out of our narrowly-defined reality and dare to live the future. They build the new. They are a ray of hope for the future, beckoning to us with the promise of a better world and the triumph of the human spirit.

But communities both attract us and frighten us. We long

for and we fear the dream they seek to live. For if the dream is real and it works, it has important implications for our daily life. We might have to give up the security of our routine lives, which up to now have had a hypnotic hold on us. And it might be that the things we've worked so hard for are now outmoded, and we would have to change to catch up. It might be safer not to find out if the dream is really working.

And yet, deep down, we know that life has to be better than what most of us are experiencing. We feel so fragmented; our personal life, friendships, and spiritual values are often so separate from our work life that we feel schizophrenic. We drive hours per day across town to get from home to work to shopping center to entertainment to friends' homes, to church. Our life is compartmentalized, not whole. We feel alienated in our huge impersonal cities, suffering from the pollution, the noise, the crime. We feel the grayness of our urban/suburban lives.

'Living lightly' on the earth and needing less income

Community can offer a way out, a solution to our dilemma. In community we can live on less income by sharing resources and "living lightly on the earth." At the same time, we can be doing something to heal the environment by reducing our consumption of energy and caretaking the earth. With reduced living expenses, there is less need for work and more time for relaxation, hobbies, and self-development. Stress is reduced and personal growth is enhanced.

Community offers a safe, supportive, and loving environment of friends. There is freedom from loneliness, safety from

The Human Yearning for Community 13

violence and theft. Community doors are often left unlocked because there is a high level of trust. Some older communities even have their own complete cradle-to-grave social security for illness and accidents. And today there is a whole range of different lifestyles to choose from in different communities—something for everyone. We can pick one to meet our needs, from shared housing and land to individual housing and land.

In community we can feel the freedom to be creative and design a new life for ourselves, experimenting with new types of relationships, governance, and economics. We feel empowered, no longer a slave to some boss or institution.

In community we can continue our education. We learn new things: practical skills like gardening or solar building, techniques for overcoming negative emotions or healing a cold, as well as new ideas and values.

Community can become a kind of "social laboratory" where we can develop previews of a possible future and help to pioneer solutions for social problems through personal experience.

> [Communities] can provide the dying industrial sectors with genuine safety nets and viable bridges to the dawning planetary-aware cultures and communities of the Solar Age.[4]

The Community solution offers new options in the areas where modern society has clearly failed: national security, agriculture, energy, economics, and health care. Communities serve as a necessary outlet for creativity in society. And they are a comfort in reassuring us that we are indeed a pluralistic society, since we freely tolerate the diversity they represent. Communities also function as permanent peace camps with a dedication to solving problems non-violently and working on creating a state of inner peace within each person.

We will undoubtedly discover a deeper sense of fulfillment and meaning to our lives by living in community, as there is usually some kind of service or outreach offered to the world, such as healing or educating. And we will feel more of a sense of inspiration and hope for the future, as community tends to be a happy place with a positive vision of life and human nature.

Community living, sharing, and cooperating doesn't come easily to most Americans raised in an individualistic, competitive society. It takes patience and practice. But the deep, soul-expanding rewards of learning to live and work with others have accrued to those who have taken this road, and much can be learned by society today from these community experiences.

Today, unlike the '60s, there are people of different ages and lifestyles in communities

People in Communities

What kind of people live in communities? Today, unlike the 1960s, there are people of different ages and lifestyles. More mature and more professional people have been joining communities in recent times, according to reports from both urban and rural communities.

> As communities mature they attract more mature people. This is what has been happening at Findhorn. There are more people who have experience and have made their mark in the world, but realize there's something more. They may have got to the top of their tree in business or the church and they come to communities to go through a change of consciousness, a change of experience, and then to take that back into the world. I see people from all different walks of life, different professions, coming for a time to communities to help speed up the transformation of society.
> —Peter Caddy
> Co-founder of Findhorn

The majority of community members today are in their late twenties to mid-forties, but there are many over fifty in some communities such as Sunrise Ranch, Krotona, Findhorn, and Spring Valley. Most community members are from white, middle-class backgrounds, though an increasing number are from the working class. Most, but not all, are college educated. Unlike the '60s communes, which attracted many single people, about half the population consists of families in today's communities. Most community members tend to be carpenters, gardeners, and teachers, but there are also engineers, artists, and businesspeople. People who join communities are generally more freedom-loving and adventurous than the average person. They're less concerned with material security. They're often searching for a deeper meaning and purpose to life or wanting to help change the world in some way. Community members are generally more sociable people than average, enjoying the friendship and support of friends and willing to help others. On the darker side, communities also tend to attract those who have a hard time coping with life psychologically and are looking for an easier life with people to take care of them. These types don't stay long in most communities today, however, as more is asked of them than when they're on their own, and most find it too challenging to confront their own internal problems.

Community members tend to be more sociable people than average

The Growth of Communities

In the 1960s the American media was full of stories about hippie communes, but today people wonder what happened to them all. According to sociologist Benjamin Zablocki (who studied hundreds of communities in America over a twelve-year period), communities have experienced a rapid decline in newsworthiness as they've become less radical in their programs and less shocking in their behavior. This has led to the widespread impression that the popularity of community as a lifestyle has dwindled.[5] But in fact, from our extensive research around the country, we discovered that there are just as many communities today as in the '60s and probably even more. Researcher Judson Jerome found that

Interestingly, public attention waned precisely when the movement began to get serious and to grow, becoming more practical and more positive in its efforts to create a viable alternative.[6]

Over the years, the mainstream has adopted much of the alternative lifestyle that made communities unique and newsworthy in the '60s, from freer sexual values and non-marrieds living together to wholistic health practices, health foods, and solar energy.

Thousands of people have begun to explore some form of group living in the last decade, taking their first step into community. It's very difficult to get any accurate count of how many people live communally, but the 1980 U.S. Census found that 824,000 households (1% of the 82.4 million total) in America had 3 or more unrelated adults living together, and 216,000 (0.25%) had 4 or more unrelated adults.[7] (This figure includes roommate situations as well as true communal households, so there's no way of accurately knowing how many are communal.)

An extensive study done by Judson Jerome and his staff found

> [t]here was no area of the country without its complement of rural communes, i.e., at least one within a hundred square miles of wherever one happens to enquire...That implies some 30,000 in the U.S. (excluding most of Alaska), a figure that doesn't seem unlikely if the barren and low density areas are averaged with those of high commune concentration such as California, Oregon, New Mexico, Colorado and New England.[8]

The majority of communities shun publicity, so it's very hard to get an accurate count of how many there are. A fairly reasonable guess would be that for every public community, there are ten to twenty private ones.

In 1978, *The San Francisco Chronicle* estimated that there were 6,000 members of communal households in the city of Berkeley.[9] But the popularity of communal living is not limited to California. Even in more conservative areas like Washington, D.C., communal living is on the rise. In an article entitled, ''Capitol Living: Group Houses Gain New Respect,'' in the *Washington Post*, it was noted that in one Sunday paper in Washington there were 382 classified ads by people who were looking for people to share their house.[10] According to the article, most of the people using a popular house-mate-finding service in the area are professional people and government workers. (''The Community'' for example, is an urban community in the Washington, D.C. area whose members are all professionals who run a computer business.)

Group living is also becoming increasingly popular among the country's senior citizens. In Los Angeles, Alternative Living for the Aging has helped establish shared housing for seniors with funds from the U.S. Department of Housing and Urban Development in order to offer an alternative to institutionalization.[11]

Alternative communities of one kind or another can be found in every industrialized country in the world today. They are especially numerous in the United States, Israel, Canada, England, Holland, Denmark, Japan, and Germany. Denmark alone has about 10,000 communes and about three hundred state-funded communes for young people with social problems.[12] There are diverse and fascinating communities on every continent: Findhorn in Scotland, Auroville in India, Aiyetoro in Nigeria, The Quaker Monteverde in Costa Rica, Riverside in Australia, Beeville in New Zealand, and The Farm in the United States. Well-documented cases of urban intentional communities can be found in cities as diverse as Hiroshima, Mexico City, Washington, D.C., Geneva, and Budapest.[13]
Many countries such as Denmark have established successful communities for the unemployed as an alternative to government aid.

Criteria for Success

Are today's communities successful? In a well-known study of the communities of the 1800s, Harvard sociologist Rosabeth Kanter established criteria for a successful community based on longevity, noting that only a dozen of the ninety-one known groups lasted more than sixteen years, while nine lasted thirty-three years or more.[14] Most members of communities today would probably argue that the criteria for a successful community would more appropriately be based on the degree of personal fulfillment and growth the community provided for its members rather than on how long it lasted. To extend this argument further, there are many institutions and corporations in America that have lasted over a hundred years (for instance, our public school system), but would we want to call them "successful" just because they're still in existence and we haven't yet created anything better for mass education? Whether or not a community is successful depends on what you compare it to—society itself?—the nuclear family? If a family lasts over 16 years, does that mean it has been "successful"? This seems like a very crude measure focusing on quantity, rather than quality, as does much of American life today. And it provides one more reason why communities creating a better world are needed: to provide a better *quality* of life, not an increased *quantity* of things, of possessions that don't bring true happiness, or of longevity merely for its own sake.

But even based on this sociological criterion of "success," it is interesting to note that today there are at least as many active and long-running communities as there were in the 1800s:

1. Spring Valley, New York - *61 years*

2. Pendel Hill, Pennsylvania - *58 years*

3. Krotona, California - *50 years*

4. School of Living, Pennsylvania - *54 years*

5. Bryn Gweled, Pennsylvania - *53 years*

6. Koinonia Partners, Georgia - *47 years*

7. Sunrise Ranch, California - *45 years*

8. Koinonia, Maryland - *38 years*

9. Bruderhof, Pennsylvania - *36 years*

10. Yasodhara, British Columbia - *33 years*

11. Findhorn, Scotland - *27 years*

12. Heathcote, Maryland - *23 years*

13. God's Valley, Indiana - *22 years*

14. Lama, New Mexico - *22 years*

15. Twin Oaks, Virginia - *21 years*

16. Renaissance, Massachusetts - *21 years*

17. Auroville, India - *20 years*

18. Goodlife, California - *20 years*

19. Stelle, Illinois - *20 years*

20. The Farm, Tennessee - *20 years*

Utopias?

Modern communities have been no less successful than the mundane American dream, like having a successful marriage or a small business. We only judge them more harshly because they attempt to be more.[15]

When faced with the growth and popularity of the new communities today, historians are apt to offer a pessimistic view, commenting that utopian communities were tried in the 1800s and didn't succeed then, so they won't now. The use of the word "utopian" seems to indicate the creation of heaven on earth, a final destination place, rather than "a journey which fosters lessons useful for later stages on the path,"[16] as Susan Campbell describes the new communities. Communities today, she comments, have more of an "evolutionary perspective," viewing themselves as a cultural learning *process*, not a final goal.

Interestingly enough, most communities today do not refer to themselves as "utopian." Instead they prefer to call themselves "new age communities", "earth communities" or "planetary villages"—meaning that they live and work with a consciousness of the oneness of life and a concern for the whole planet. "Utopian" implies something unrealistic and unattainable. But to those who live in communities all over the world, and to the thousands who visit them, communities are a daily reality and their benefits are quite tangible.

Professor Donald Pitzer of Indiana State University, Director of the National Society of Historical Communities, points out that the word "utopia" means literally "no where." But he says we can move the "w" in this phrase over to the left, joining the "no" to make "now here"—creating utopia here and now.

Perhaps the tendency to avoid the word "utopian" today is in order to avoid the suggestion that human problems are strictly the result of the environment, as if bad social structures are to blame, never people themselves. The old theory was that if the right social structures were created, the problems would be eliminated and utopia attained. But today, community members emphasize changing themselves as well as creating new social structures. As Buckminster Fuller wrote, "The world is now too dangerous for anything less than utopia."

Fashioning from the dreams of tomorrow the reality of today

The Vision of the New Communities:

We're going through a time of change and transition on the earth, and therefore there is strength in unity. I remember in the early days of Findhorn taking a drive after a great storm. And trees that had been standing alone, were now flat on the ground. But where there were clumps of trees, they were still standing. In the days ahead, those who will pass more easily through this time of cleansing are those who are together in groups. It's much easier when there's a group of people with a similar vision, working for the same goals—the transformation of consciousness on this planet, which starts with each individual.

—Peter Caddy

The new communities are fashioning from the dreams of tomorrow the reality of today. They are creating centers of positive vision amidst the fear and crisis in the world, proving there is another way to live that is workable. The seeds of what could be a new culture and civilization, one more in harmony with the human spirit and with all of life, are being planted and nourished in the new planetary greenhouses of community life. As economist Hazel Henderson notes,

These "earth keepers" are creating webs or networks that enfold the crumbling institutions of the dying industrial age in the emerging, self-organizing planetary cultures of the solar age.

The Human Yearning for Community 21

These new "eco-villages" (ecologically in balance) are popping up like weeds in the cracks of the sidewalk, green living things amidst the concrete jungle.

Today's communities have a new record of sustainability; they're in it for the long haul. Unlike the communities of the 1960s, the new communities of the 1990s are providing for the basic necessities of their members without disturbing the ecological balance of the earth. And most importantly, they're providing for the spiritual and emotional needs of their members. Important lessons were harvested from the communal living experiences of the '60s that have helped build the solid foundations of the new communities of the '90s. The primacy of individual freedom—the rallying cry of the '60s—has been preserved as well as the magic that comes from inspired creation, building a new society to truly live their ideals.

While "living lightly on the earth" and reducing consumption are still important, the virtues of poverty are no longer extolled so adamantly as they were in the '60s. Experience has taught that poverty usually necessitates all energy being used for pure survival, with nothing remaining to help others or transform society. Members of most new communities have discovered a balance point between the extremes of hardship and waste. They are living a life of simple beauty, meeting their true needs through God's abundance, and working to restore the free circulation of that abundance throughout the world.

In these new communities there is a synthesis of nature and culture. Instead of just living a simple rural life close to the earth, they have often added some of the best aspects of modern culture: the beauty of art and music, the efficiency of technology. There is a new balance between concern for individual rights and the welfare of the group.

> The ambiguous status of communes somewhere between being private homes and public institutions may be an important element of their vitality and viability.[17]

Today's communities have the same pioneering courage and spirit of freedom and celebration that captured the imagination of a generation in the 1960s. Communities continue to be magnetic for those on the path of self-realization. Although not always ideal or easy places in which to live, these communities promote a strong sense of integrity and empowerment.

Most significantly, the new communities have realized that sustainable communities cannot be built around only the things that are rejected, as was the case in the 1960s, but must be built around common *positive* values. Some of these shared values are:

• A planetary awareness of the oneness of humanity and all life, with a corresponding conscious response to the global crisis;

• A commitment to personal change *and* social change, to psychological/spiritual growth and to service in society, where individual needs are balanced with group needs;

• An emphasis on cooperation and some form of sharing of resources and skills;

• A dedication to healing the earth and working in harmony with the forces of nature, rather than exploiting the land and its resources;

• An emphasis on "living lightly on the earth"—embracing appropriate scale technology (including tractors and computers) while reducing consumption, recycling resources, and using renewable sources of energy such as wood, solar, and wind;

Using renewable sources of energy at the Findhorn Community - solar panels for hot water

• Development of some degree of self-sufficiency in food and energy, but also developing interdependence with others through barter and business;

• A commitment to non-violence, world peace, and racial and sexual equality;

• A commitment to *process*, to facing up to interpersonal conflicts and working them out through some agreed-upon method;

The Human Yearning for Community 23

• A respect for the wholeness of the individual—body/emotions/mind/spirit;

• An emphasis on work as a type of prayer or meditation and on daily life as a teacher;

• A dedication to "thinking globally, acting locally"—working to create solutions to universal social problems in a chosen local field of focus.

• A commitment to the primacy of an individual's relationship to God, to the Universe (or to The Common Good, if the community is more secular in orientation) and a corresponding reverence for the Divine within all life—God immanent (or Life itself).

2 Benefits and Purposes of Community

When the banner of community is unfurled as a realization of necessity, then life will become winged in each day's action; as long as it is thought that the community is an experiment, so long will the community be found in the alchemist's jar. Only a firm realization of historic necessity will bring community to life.[1]

Communities offer valuable benefits to both individuals and society as a whole:

- **Reduced living expenses**—cutting costs by pooling resources.

- **Companionship and support**—extending one's "family" of natural affiliation, offering love, caring, and closeness to overcome the loneliness and alienation of modern society.

- **Spiritual and psychological growth**—helping to overcome personal problems and develop positive traits of tolerance, love, and cooperation.

- **Empowerment and freedom**—encouraging self-sufficiency and creating community institutions such as schools, government, work places, and health care facilities that meet the real needs of members.

- **Research and development**—pioneering new solutions and models for society; a place to dream dreams and see if they work by putting them into form.

- **Education for the future**—experiential, hands-on learning with a planetary awareness.

- **R and R**—places of rest and retreat for visitors from the cities who are on the front lines of social change.

- **Service**—giving a sense of meaning and purpose in life by working for a greater good and serving the needs of others.

- **Wholeness and synthesis**—creating whole people through the integration of mind/body/feelings/spirit, and developing unity out of diversity and conflict.

- **"Centers of Light"**—places of hope and positive vision in the midst of negativity, violence, and injustice in the world.

Reduced Living Expenses

Live simply, that others may simply live.
—Mahatma Ghandi

Live simply that others may simply live

In these times of national economic difficulty, with high unemployment and high interest rates, living in a community makes good economic sense. A simpler lifestyle consumes fewer resources and creates less pollution. Today, even many professionals in Washington, D.C. are living communally to beat the rise in living costs. The more that is shared, the cheaper it is to live. At Twin Oaks Community, for example, members live on only $250.00/month each. At the Findhorn Community, members eat three wonderfully plentiful and healthy meals for $1.50 a day per person. Approvecho Community members have reduced their home energy bill to $7.90/month total for six residents.

Some specific examples from our community, Sirius, will illustrate how we've reduced costs by sharing and cooperating. Two families in our community, for example, with four and two children each, share a three-story five-bedroom house, and each pays only $250 rent per month. Each family has a private bath and shares a third bathroom and the kitchen and living room. The trade-off in this arrangement is having less privacy, but the children love having playmates (and the parents have babysitters!), so it works out well.

Even those who build individual homes in our community pay a fraction of what a similar house would cost in the suburbs, since the land is shared and community members and visitors help with labor. Members often use recycled building materials and this cuts costs even further. Furthermore, because the cost of building is so greatly reduced, money often doesn't need to be borrowed, and a huge amount is saved from interest payments over the years.

Because we've organized our own food buying club (or "co-op") and buy our food in bulk, our cost for food staples (including grains and vegetables) is only $28.00 per month each (and this also pays two part-time gardeners who raise our vegetables). With additional food such as dairy items, the total food bill for an adult is between $40 and $90/month, depending on the person's dietary preferences. In another three years, we should be producing all our own fruit from orchards we planted.

In addition, we've pooled many tools and appliances and further cut our operating costs. Nearly all our buildings are heated with wood from our land, so we have no heating bills. Only labor is needed to cut the wood. This work is shared, so it's more fun. And because we eat home-grown organic foods and use self-help, wholistic health practices, we have very minimal medical bills compared to the average American.

Besides reducing our living expenses, living in community has enabled us to reduce the time we each would spend in cooking, cleaning, and household chores, as these are all shared. Each adult contributes eight hours per week to community work projects such as buying bulk food staples, growing vegetables, cutting firewood, building, repairing and cleaning community buildings. Child care is also shared some of the time, allowing more free time for parents.

Because we each need a lot less money to live on, we're not chained to permanent 9-to-5 jobs that most people do just to survive, even when they dislike their work. We've created our own cooperative businesses or work at part-time jobs in town, jobs we enjoy and which reflect our values. Since we need to work less than full-time to support our simpler lifestyle, this leaves us more time to pursue our deeper interests: spiritual growth, service projects, travel, hobbies, and education. To us and to most community members, the major attraction of reducing our living expenses is having time for self-fulfillment and things that really matter. In addition, having fewer possessions means that fewer possessions "possess" us and occupy our time and attention. So instead of focusing so much on things, we can focus on *people* and notice more of the beauty of the natural world all around us.

Companionship and a supportive environment

Companionship and Support

Communal orders [are] one of the roads to sanity that will reassert the dignity of humanity.[2]

On a week-long tour of six New England communities that we conducted for the public, one of the participants, Bill Bradley, a professor of Engineering at Western Massachusetts College, commented,

I'm convinced there's so much loneliness in the world. We've moved away from family and roots, so arranging ourselves into larger groups or intentional communities makes sense. I'd like to make a lifestyle change like this myself, once my son has finished college.

When people in communities are questioned about their reasons for joining, a popular response is usually something like "to be with like-minded people" or "companionship, security, a supportive environment." This is especially true if the community is not based around a larger purpose, like some kind of service to society, and people are merely sharing a household together in the city.

In the last twenty or thirty years, our society has become so restless and transient, our cities so large and impersonal, that most people feel fairly isolated and alienated in their neighborhoods and on their jobs. Gone is the spirit of the small towns and friendly neighborhoods of earlier days where you knew all your neighbors, and people were always willing to lend a helping hand. Gone are most of the small family farms and businesses where an employee would know everyone in the company. Gone too, for the most part, are the large extended families of earlier generations when aunts, uncles, and grandparents often lived with Mom and Dad and the kids under one roof or very close by. Today, families are scattered all over the country. People seldom know their neighbors. Friends are scattered all over the city, so visits are infrequent.

In his book *New Rules*, Daniel Yankelovich discusses surveys done by his firm which found that 80% of Americans are to one degree or another seeking new meaning or fulfillment through changing their values and lifestyles. Seventy per cent felt that they had few close friends, although many acquaintances, and they experienced this as a serious void in their lives. Yankelovich's firm measures a "Search for Community" social trend, based on the need to search for "mutual identification with others based on close ethnic ties or ties of shared interests, needs, background, age or values."[3] The number of Americans involved in the "Search for Community" according to Yankelovich increased from 32% in 1973 to 47% in 1980.

It is in this context that communities and shared households have been growing in popularity all over the country in the last ten to fifteen years. For many people, community offers the kind of family they never had: supportive, loving, understanding, and fun-to-be-with people who share similar interests and values. Communities are like most families in that members can always count on each other. No matter how difficult you can be at times, your family will usually stick by you, and eventually things get worked out.

But of course, if things get really difficult in a community, people will move out and the community will split up, just as families do. Still, community offers all the advantages of a caring family, without the loss of freedom often experienced in a blood family and without the authority and control often exercised by parents over children.

In a community there is always someone to talk to or someone to share your excitement with when something wonderful happens. There are people who will really help you out when you need them. If you're sick, there's someone to care for you. If your car breaks down, there's someone to give you a ride. If you want to go to the movies or a party, there's usually someone to keep you company. If you're single and afraid of living alone, there's the safety of the group. And there are always community social events, like parties and special celebrations, that create a sense of belonging and of closeness, and group work projects where everyone pitches in. For many who long to move to the country but are afraid of feeling lonely and isolated away from city life, a rural community offers the best of both worlds—the beauty of nature and lots of friends and social life.

In most communities, there is also some kind of structured personal sharing process where members can help each other with their personal problems. This fills a real human need for experiencing intimacy with others. On the deepest level, community offers a safe and loving environment to allow individuals to develop their full potential and to discover greater meaning to life. As Brian Lyke comments,

> Esalen is a very supportive community. It's a place where I found I could explore who I am without a lot of fear of judgment and with a lot of acceptance—basically, more than I give myself.

Spiritual and Psychological Growth

> Community for me has proved to be one of the fiercest fires of purification and, at the same time, one of the most satisfying and productive paths for growth.
> —Ram Dass

Community probably provides the most profound and intense experience of personal growth that is available anywhere, if a person is open to it. The ultimate purpose of community is self-

transcendence, going beyond our limited sense of self to realize our oneness with all others. A dream one of us had several years ago dramatized very powerfully and simply how the spiritual growth process works in community.

One of the fiercest fires of purification and one of the most satisfying and productive paths for growth

I dreamed I was in a large building where thousands of people had come to hear a young spiritual teacher I knew very well. They saw him as a guru and brought flowers and fruit to lay at his feet. His talk was very inspiring, but then it was as if I blinked and the whole scene instantly changed and we were sometime in the future, in a space-age building. I was hearing the same teaching, but this time there was only a fraction of the number of people as before, because the teacher was a black man instead of white. I understood that this was because people's prejudices prevented them from hearing the same truth from a different source. For some people it was their prejudice against blacks; for others it might be their prejudice against women; and for others, it might be prejudice against children or other religions. But then the most amazing part happened. I blinked again, and this time I was in an ordinary house, with only a handful of people present. And I understood that again I was hearing the same teaching, but this time there was *no* teacher present. *The teaching was the dirty dishes in the sink!* As the full meaning of this hit me, I remember

Benefits and Purposes of Community 31

feeling sick to my stomach and having to sit down on the bed and really think about it deeply.

It seemed as if the other people around me were just as upset as we each realized this simple truth: it's the way in which we do the most mundane tasks in our life that helps us grow the most spiritually. If we do things lovingly and well, keeping our attention fully in the present and on the task at hand, every experience can be transforming. In community there are always plenty of mundane tasks (like dishwashing) to do together, so there is always plenty of opportunity for growth!

Apparently, the old mystery schools of ancient times offered similar teachings. The story is often told of the student who would sit in what he thought was his classroom, waiting in vain for the great teacher to arrive. And then one day he suddenly realized that the broom that he tripped over each day in the dirty hallway on his way to his classroom was actually meant for him. The broom and dirty hallway were his real classroom!

> Everything we do here is a kind of Karma Yoga. Chopping wood or carrying water done in the right spirit is meditation. Simple tasks keep me focused, centered on what's real. We praise God by building domes.[4]
>
> —Barbara Durkee
> Lama Community

Modern spiritual communities have inherited this tradition from the old mystery schools and monasteries. Down through the centuries, in every culture, like-minded souls have banded together to deepen their spiritual life. Earth is a schoolhouse for souls and community is a most effective classroom! Living with so many different types of people and learning to get along together is a process for speeding up one's growth, if it is done consciously. Auroville Community in India calls this "accelerated evolution."

There's probably more personal growth possible by living in a community for even a month than there is from taking ten workshops in personal growth! Brian Lyke of Esalen Institute once commented that he didn't need to attend any of the growth workshops there because, "just living here is a workshop—365 days a year!" This process is often called "the greenhouse effect." When the energy of a place is strong enough, it is like the hot sun shining down on a greenhouse of plants packed close together and speeding up their growth. Or as Zen Master Sueng Sahn of the Providence Zen Center says,

Washing one potato is slow work. But when many potatoes are in the sink bumping up against each other, they get clean much faster!

The attraction/repulsion most people feel about the personal growth process in community was summed up very succinctly by one community member: "To live with others transparently, with no holds barred, is both a dream and a nightmare for most of us."[5] We desperately want to be close to others, but we are also deathly frightened of this closeness because of the separative nature of our ego. As Da Free John of the Dawn Horse Community notes:

> People resist entering into community because what is primarily wrong with people is a relational problem, the tendency to avoid relationship, to be self-contained, narcissistic, self-pleasurized, unwilling to enter into the discipline represented by other people, unwilling to overcome themselves in relationship. Obviously, there is a reluctance in the ego to create community.[6]

The only way through the impasse is to surrender to the growth process of community, to surrender control—"ego death," as it's often called. When we let go of our limited sense of self, our sense of separateness from others and from God, we are then re-born into our larger Self which experiences oneness with others and with God and feels at perfect peace. Robin Paris of the Renaissance Community comments:

> Community is a growth process, and you grow like hell. You get pushed up against yourself. You get things mirrored back to you constantly by living around many people. You're asked to let go of many, many things that it's hard to let go of. You're constantly being asked to help out. It really strengthens a person. The fruit of living in community is that people share deeply as they work all that stuff out, as they work off the rough edges.

Communities produce a kind of mirroring effect. We see ourselves more clearly in the effect we produce on others. We realize that everyone around us is reflecting back to us how s/he sees us. Rather than blaming someone else for a problem, we realize we must first turn within ourselves and see how we contributed to it. With this kind of environment, no one has to give us feedback directly. It's all there very subtly if we're willing to really look and listen to others, to see ourselves more clearly and honestly.

It's relatively easy to feel very spiritual when sitting in meditation by ourselves. It's much harder to put that spirituality into practice in our relationships with others. And it's often easy to avoid experiencing direct feedback on how we're relating to others if we only have a limited relationship to a couple of people, like one or two co-workers during the day and a husband or wife to come home to at night for a couple of hours. Community intensifies this process because it involves the totality of our being. We're usually relating to many different kinds of people all day, and not all of them may feel as sympathetic or forgiving as a husband or wife who understands us and has learned to put up with us.

In community we interact with the same people in different situations throughout the day, so there's no hiding our true self—positive and negative—in the way we can when we leave the office and blow off our anger by yelling at our husband or wife instead. Then only the spouse sees our negative side, and we return to work the next day with our public smile.

Community living gives us opportunities to play many different roles, not just ones we're confident or skilled in. This brings out different aspects of ourselves in relationship to others, and it softens our ego and aids our spiritual growth. We may be working in the garden in the morning, for example, where someone more skilled is teaching us what to do, and we have to learn new skills as well as humility. In the afternoon, we may be in the office showing a new member of the community what to do, and we have to learn authority, responsibility, and careful organization. In the evening, we may be cooking dinner with someone who is very slow and has a whole different style of cooking, so we have to learn patience and tolerance. Or we may work with the children's playgroup and have to learn how to be nurturing, playful and imaginative.

Lama Community members describe this growth process:

> Personal identities dissolve through Karma Yoga: building the barn, cleaning the outhouse, digging the truck out of the mud, backpacking vegetables through snowdrifts. The physics professor, the hitchhiker, the dancer, the Israeli soldier, the stockbroker, the political activist, the yoga teacher—all the same.[7]

Also, when we live and work with people in such close contact, we learn a great deal about them. We observe how they interact with other people and with various situations, and we see the feedback they get from life. This helps our growth because we can learn what to do and what not to do by observing. And we see how different personality types experience the world.

For example, in one community we know, there are two people who represent polarities in the way they relate to the world, both in their personality types and in their philosophical beliefs. One person is very gregarious and believes that caring for people and working on relationships is the most spiritual thing you can do. But he is always confronting difficulties he has with people and trying to work them through in a very aggressive way that often puts people off and creates even more of a problem. Another person is very introverted and believes her relationship to God is the most spiritual thing. She feels she must learn detachment from emotional involvement with people and only see the God presence within them. As a result people usually feel she doesn't like them or is mad at them, because she stays so aloof and distant. Now there's truth in each of these views, of course, but to see these two people put their beliefs into practice on a day-to-day basis in the community and to observe the results is a great teaching about the limitations of each approach when applied exclusively. Both approaches need each other for balance.

Of course, there's a balance to all this intense focus on personal growth and relationships. If we push ourselves into doing too many new things or having to relate to too many people all the time without enough personal space, then we can overdo it, not help ourselves grow at all, and merely burn out. Lama Community members advise humor and detachment from the ego in this often too-serious growth process:

> We call ourselves Lama Beans. Humor crops up like weeds between the plants we think we're so seriously tending. We're learning to stop clinging so desperately to privacy, vision, judgment, the ego trips that separate us. We are learning to open our hearts. We are learning that who we think we are and what we think Lama is, are just more veils between us and God. It is not our intention to create a definable, model community. We are here to become transformed.[8]

Living in community can be hard work because working on ourselves is a slow process. But the positive side to all this is the support of other community members, as Swami Kriyananda of Ananda Community notes.

> When you live in the world, and you have a big breakthrough, you're determined to change and be like this from now on. But when you go

back to your old friends, they just say, ''Oh, come on, get off it. That isn't you. Be your old self.'' And they keep pulling you down with their old expectations. But when you live in a community, they feed that change, they help you to change. They're all for change, while the world is all against change. And if you slip from the resolution you made to change, your fellow community members are the ones who help you get back into it.

Community provides the opportunity to learn about transforming society from the inside out, from personal experience first. We work on changing ourselves as we try to change the structures of society, so that a truly new society will grow out of a new way of being, as Chris Roberts of Sunbow Community remarks.

I feel we have been given a valuable opportunity to learn new patterns of behavior which are intensely needed for the human species to continue in a right relationship with the rest of the earth.

It is in our power to begin the world over again

Empowerment and Freedom

It is in our power to begin the world over again.
—Tom Paine

After living in intentional communities for years, I spent a few months living in Washington, D.C. to teach a course on communities. I'll never forget an overwhelming impression I had one day while walking down the suburban street where I lived. The houses seemed so desolate, so unconnected to each other, each one exactly like the other; neighbors hardly spoke to each other or cared about each other, each rushing off to separate jobs in separate cars. Through my eyes it felt like another country, another century. A very sad country. It hardly felt like an inspiring future for humanity. It was such a contrast to the experiences of connectedness and sharing I'd been having in community: growing our own food together, designing new solar buildings, laughing, singing, working, and meditating with people I really care about.

Perhaps the quality of communities that makes them so attractive to people is the freedom, creativity, and pioneering spirit they offer, and the opportunity to actually live the values you believe in.

> I'm getting used to doing the impossible. It's easy when you can find a dozen close neighbors who are willing to listen to you. Intentional communities provide an atmosphere where things become possible. I never did any construction work, but I ended up building a house. I never had any money, but now I have investments. Now I've written a book so I'm an author. My [fellow community members] are doing the work of contractors, architects, farmers and executives, all without being certified. We are turning dreams into reality. We are creating an environment in which all things are possible.[9]

Community members often withdraw legitimacy from existing institutions in society by simply not participating in them and creating an alternative instead. This is true empowerment—enabling people to feel in control of their lives rather than victimized. Corb of Twin Oaks Community expresses his experience this way:

> At Twin Oaks we are experimenting with appropriate technology, and all kinds of things I dreamed about wanting to do...On the outside I was just too busy to incorporate any of that—any solar, composting or gardening. Living in the suburbs and going to my job, I just never had the time. Here I feel I have an active part in a lot of these things. My life has political meaning, just by living here and doing what I am doing. It's a message, an example to people, something they can look at, come to visit, and talk to us and get inspired to change their own life. I don't see it as sheltered from the wrongs of the world. I feel much more aware of things that are going on in the world. I feel I am doing something about it rather than just riding on

the tide of America's temporary wealth. I was living on borrowed time and here I am living something that can be sustained an indefinite period of time.[10]

There must be outlets in society where people can explore new ideas and visions. Where there are no outlets, creative energy often becomes destructive instead. People are most fulfilled when they know they are empowered to shape their own destiny. Communities are a laboratory where we can work out all our ideas about society, our feelings about the way things could be, to create new institutions.

But as Ingrid Komar warns in her book on Twin Oaks:

> This lifestyle demands a great deal from all the participants. It calls for total commitment. Whereas it may be possible for those living outside community to be politically active on a sporadic or part-time basis, those maintaining and building a cooperative alternative are on duty seven days a week. Much more work is required to create the "yea" of a new society than it takes to merely say "nay," to adopt a critical stance regarding the old existing one.[11]

In the best of communities, people make a deeper discovery of their own creative power because they have the freedom to choose how they will contribute and what they will think. They also more consciously accept the consequences of their choices. They discover how powerful they are in creating their own destiny in a very real sense, for they see clearly the cause and effect relationship of their thoughts and actions on their surroundings.

Communities offer fertile ground for working out new social structures, new economic systems, new types of self-government. As Tom Olinger of Twin Oaks Community in Virginia puts it:

> Living at Twin Oaks you get a feeling that you can control different aspects of your environment. Of course, you're controlling it with sixty-nine others who live there too, so what you personally want may not always come through. But at least you have a chance of influencing it, rather than just being a political entity in a group of 10,000 or a city of 100,000 where your personal views will rarely be heard.

Besides giving people the space to experiment within the community, a united group of two hundred members or even twenty with similar views can make quite an impact on local politics. This can happen not only through voting but also by working as a team to organize other residents in support of a particular issue, such as preventing the dumping of hazardous wastes in the town, as Twin Oaks Community has done. Having developed good communication with each other and worked out interpersonal problems within the context of their living situation, community members are able to be more effective in political organizing than political interest groups who are often divided by in-fighting. In fact, some communities such as The Traprock Peace Center at Woolman Hill, Massachusetts and the Philadelphia Life Center (part of Movement for a New Society) are formed for the main purpose of developing better political organizers.

Most communities today, however, have not yet put their political power to use except for the community's own well-being, like helping to change archaic zoning, building, or health codes that discriminate unfairly against group living, against new forms of architecture like domes, or aginst more ecologically-balanced waste recycling such as composting toilets. In the future, communities may focus their energies more politically as they become larger, more cohesive and stable, and as the national political situation necessitates. Already some communities, such as Renaissance Community in Massachusetts, Terre Nouvelle Community in France, and Findhorn in Scotland, have members who are working on local town councils.

As communities reach out and unite with other communities, working together and forming regional networks, the potential for political effectiveness grows exponentially. Both through their ability to inspire and educate the public about successful alternatives that solve some of society's problems, and through direct political organizing, communities have tremendous potential power for transforming society, as may soon become evident.

Research and Development for Society

S/he who affirms the Community contributes to the hastening of the evolution of the planet...Pay attention to the history of the past; you will perceive clear jolts of progress; you will see graphically that these jolts coincide with manifestations of the idea of community—cooperation. Despotic states have been destroyed, attainments of science have been secured, new ways of labor have arisen, benevolent boldness has shone forth, when the banner of cooperation was unfurled.[12]

Clear jolts of progress are perceived when the banner of cooperation is unfurled

Communities sometimes function as a type of "research and development" center for society, often pioneering solutions to problems facing society: energy shortage, inflation, pollution, hunger, unemployment, rising health care costs. The importance of this pioneering work of communities was recently illustrated for us in the example of a friend of ours who started a community in the mid-1970s and is now applying his nine years of group dynamics experience in his work with the Harvard Negotiation Team, training mediation teams for Arab/Israeli and Russian/American disputes, and in his work with the mayor and city council of Malden, Massachusetts on conflict resolution. Another friend has applied his ten years of communal living experiences to his work with team-building and organization development as Director of Training at the National Institute of Health and at the Center for Cooperative Global Development at American University.

David Spangler describes the new communities as:

> ...colonies of the future—laboratories in which the spirit of a new culture can discover its appropriate shapes, and like any laboratory or colony, they have their share of failures as well as successes. In the best of their work, communities can provide us with previews of a possible future.[13]

Many of the institutions of society have become so large and bureaucratic that they have lost their ability to respond creatively to new situations and changing times. Often the vested interests who control large institutions are too busy protecting their own institutional security and status and profits. They feel threatened by any real change in the status quo. "Cultural creativity is always the province of minorities," Theodore Roszak observes in his book *Person/Planet*.[14]

The collectivities that have created or reflect major problems in society—governments, unions, the military, schools, churches, etc.—are all large groups which cannot easily be changed by an individual. But a transformed *group* can be effective in changing these larger collectivities:

> Group chemistry is far more complicated than individual chemistry, and the heart of a group needs to be spoken to by the heart of another group's being...When a group begins to serve selflessly, love endlessly, act in the calm of a great power...it penetrates like an arrow into the soul of every collectivity in the world, as an invasion of health might undo every wrinkle in the body of the earth.[15]

Peter Caddy adds:

A community is a living laboratory, a place of living and demonstrating. It is then up to the politicians, the psychologists, etc. to come and see what is happening at the community. A lot of Ph.D.'s have been written as a result of studying different aspects of Findhorn Community. And the principles that are lived there can be applied almost anywhere. For example, to learn the lesson of loving where you are, to love what you're doing, and to love whom you're with. If you just learn that, it will change your life.

Historian William Irwin Thompson calls some of these new communities "planetary demes." Geneticists use the word "deme" to describe small, isolated sub-populations that have a mutation in them. The species always sends out little tendrils from the major adaptation of where it is now, and these tendrils will explore new ecological niches. It is in these niches that mutations occur, Thompson explains.

As long as the mutation is in communication with the rest of the species, then there's a feedback into the species as a whole, and it will flow into the ecological breakthrough and will create the major adaptation for the future and then once again will fan out.[16]

Through communities, the species-preservation instinct of life can be seen responding to the self-destructive qualities of society today: the poisoning of the air and the waters, the economic crisis, the threat of nuclear annihilation. And the diversity of expression of different communities is perhaps Nature's way of ensuring the survival of the fittest of these expressions. Thompson sees communities as small groups of people who come together in periods of cultural change around new constellations of values and a new image of the future. They move to the periphery of society and begin to create models that can serve as guiding images for the rest of society. They seek to draw the best heritage of the past into the future, creating a synthesis.

David Wickenden and Sally Walton of Auroville Community in India explain the mutation and experimentation process in their community in this way:

In a place like Auroville, one feels caught occasionally in a strange twilight zone, straddling myth and reality: the daily problems, struggles, sweat and anguish are real enough, but because the process is

Benefits and Purposes of Community 41

symbolic of much larger concerns that must be worked out on the global level, the most seemingly insignigicant occurrences of daily life take on archetypal significance. And a place like Auroville really *is* symbolically, mythically, as well as actually, enacting on a small stage the drama of bringing a new civilization to birth. The significance of communities such as this lies not in their creation of cut and polished new structures...It's the exploration itself, not a finished product, that opens up channels for evolutionary growth.[17]

As sociologist Lawrence Veysey expressed it in his book *The Communal Experience*, "Every victory, however temporary, takes on great meaning, for these are efforts at cultural birth."[18]

Today's communities are "imagining" many beautiful new ways of living and working together and are actually living these new alternatives now. Renaissance in Massachusetts is researching forms of alternative energy to meet the current energy crisis and reduce their own fuel costs. They are developing the use of solar energy for heating homes, solar greenhouses for year-round food production, and windmills for production of electricity. Twin Oaks in Virginia offers a model of highly-efficient, cooperatively-organized agricultural and industrial enterprise with participatory decision-making and worker ownership. Shannon Farm in Virginia has developed a successful model on a smaller scale of cooperative business that is worker-owned and managed. It not only provides paid employment but also offers a more human, growth-oriented workplace, producing goods and services that are consistent with the values of the community, like energy-efficient solar home building. And by living close to the earth, avoiding chemical fertilizers, recycling resources, and consuming less, East Wind Community in Missouri helps to reduce another problem of society: pollution.

Communities have been experimenting with new forms of self-government, conflict resolution, and group decison-making that could be helpful to government and business. The use of group "attunement" (periods of silence and centering when there is disharmony in the group) has been very effective in creating more clarity and agreement. Consensus-building has been effective in overcoming the divisiveness of majority/minority voting, thereby creating a sense of empowerment for all parties, so that everyone feels identified with each decision and helps to carry it out. This has been used successfully at Lama Community in New Mexico, Movement for a New Society in Philadelphia, and Findhorn in Scotland.

New tools for building more harmonious relationships among people are being researched and developed. Spring Hill in

Massachusetts uses a process for "opening the heart" and Mettanokit Community in New Hampshire uses co-counseling techniques where peers help each other to "discharge" their negative emotions and create healing. Esalen Institute in California has pioneered techniques for personal growth for twenty years. Today their work is being used by top corporations in their management training and by governmental consulting groups that create dialogues between Arab and Israeli leaders. Esalen also established a Soviet Studies Center to apply psychological insights to improve American/Soviet relations.

New patterns of male/female relationships are being tested and experimented with in communities. "Open marriages," where partners agree to non-exclusive sexual relationships, are being explored at Stardance Community in San Francisco. "Co-creative partnerships," couples who work together equally on some creative project, are being developed at High Wind Community in Wisconsin and at Sirius Community. Communal child-raising, where children spend most of their time away from their parents in children's houses, cared for by a rotating group of parents and other adults, is being explored at Twin Oaks Community in Virginia.

Hohenort Hotel, a community of members of the Emissaries of Divine Light that has many communities around the world, is demonstrating how whites and blacks in South Africa can live together in peace and harmony. Likewise, Neve Shalom, started by Father Bruno in Israel, is a community of forty Arab and Israeli families living together peacefully, and Shantivanti is a community of Hindus and Christians living peacefully in India. Christiana, a community of 1500 members started by local hippies in the middle of Cophenhagen, has set up its own self-governing city and is showing it can take care of its own needs without police or taxes.

Social researchers who have recently observed the problems caused by the giant size of our cities, our businesses, and our government, have realized the need for decentralization of government. Communities of the 1960s were the pioneers of a new trend in self-reliance, small-scale Jeffersonian democracy, and a return to rural areas. Between 1970 and 1973, a net migration of over one million people occurred from the cities and suburbs to rural areas.[19] The increasing number of new rural communities continues to add to this number.

Communities are a microcosm of society with many of the same problems but with different ways of handling them. As they are in a smaller, simpler context, they are easier to study. By attempting to create new forms and institutions out of their own visions and ideals, community members begin to see more clearly the problems of society that are reflected in themselves, as they meet their own limitations, resistances, and negativity. They have learned in a direct and personal way that the problems in society all begin with what's inside each of us, and we have to ''clean up our own act,'' so to speak, right at home first. Many have come face to face with the *real* reasons things work or don't work in the world by tackling the problems themselves. For example, consider the problem of welfare and the issue of whether to share with those who could help themselves, but don't because they're not able to psychologically. On the one hand, community living teaches members to learn to truly give and to share what they have because they feel that ultimately, all of humanity is one and is deeply interdependent. So helping someone is really helping yourself. On the other hand, community members have learned that welfare sometimes actually hurts rather than helps a person, as it creates dependence and doesn't reward initiative and individual responsibility. So the community solution is to give in the way advised by the old proverb: ''Give a man a fish, and you feed him for a day. Teach him how to fish, and you feed him for the rest of his life.'' Communities work to help make people self-reliant.

Harvard sociologist Rosabeth Kanter comments:

> Utopian communities are important not only as social ventures in and of themselves but also as challenges to the assumptions on which current institutions are organized...
>
> The utopian community itself represents a model for a different kind of community organization, one from which community planners can derive a useful set of options.[20]

Education for the Future

If you can dream it, you can do it.
—Walt Disney

Communities may well evolve into the colleges of the future, with an experiential approach to learning and a planetary awareness. They may be training centers for the next step in human evolution. The new curriculum being developed in the communities and the new methods of hands-on learning might well become seed patterns for the education of tomorrow.

Evolving into colleges of the future

In community, "students" live in with "faculty." Students can continue dialoguing with teachers, and learning never ends. Most importantly, distinctions between learners and teachers begin to fall away, as each person has something important to teach, whether it's a specific skill, concept, or even a personal quality, like generosity. Education in the community setting becomes centered in the student's process, not in the teacher's lesson plan.

For example, Michael Lindfield feels that Findhorn's gift is not to tell members where to go or what to be but rather to offer them the learning environment where they can make contact with their own gifts, vocation, and direction and then freely choose how to develop these. Michael describes how the community's educational process approaches political issues.

Whenever we focus on a global issue such as nuclear disarmament in a seminar session, we find it absolutely vital to see how the patterns and principles involved in the drama on the world screen are being played out in our personal lives. We would ask each person to look at the roots of insecurity and the need to erect personal defense systems in his/her own life. We then explore how global disarmament can begin with a personal peace treaty and a willingness to dismantle personal defenses. This makes learning a very real event as it affirms the living link between the larger global situation and the personal process of searching and learning.

Benefits and Purposes of Community 45

People learn best by doing, and as mini-societies, communities provide the perfect settings for learning new skills—from solar energy design and building to financial management of cooperatives. Since most communities are open to visitors and welcome their help with community work projects, communities teach visitors as well as their own members these skills. Many visitors write to our community saying they want to live with us for a specific time in order to learn construction skills, cultivation of herbs, or meditation, for example.

By developing their own internal economic systems as well as setting up businesses for producing income, community members learn firsthand about bookkeeping, fiscal planning, capital investment, budgeting, marketing their products, etc. Some communities, like Alpha Farm and Sirius, teach people how to set up worker-owned and managed cooperatives.

By creating their own forms of self-government, community members learn about the use and abuse of power, leadership, delegation of authority, compromise, majority/minority voting or consensus-building, conflict resolution, etc. Many communities are developing creative and unique solutions to the age-old problems that arise in these areas.

In developing self-sufficiency, community members learn all kinds of practical skills for "living lightly on the earth," skills that are usually not yet taught at traditional universities. The Bear Tribe in Washington sometimes refers to their educational programs as "The College of the Earth."

Some of the wide range of skills taught at various communities include

- Composting, mulching, companion-planting in organic gardening (Findhorn)

- Food storage: drying, canning, freezing (The Bear Tribe)

- The use of herbs for medicinal purposes (Center of the Light)

- Soybean production and use as a cheap protein source (The Farm Community)

- Woodlot management for lumber and wood heat use (Sirius)

- Building "arcologies" (Arcosanti)

- Incorporating solar and energy-efficient design in building (Twin Oaks)

- Solar greenhouse design (Farralones)

- Production of ethanol fuel from corn (Stelle)

- Windmill use for energy production (Renaissance)

- Bioshelter construction and aqua-culture (High Wind)

- Vegetarian cooking (The Abode)

- Composting toilets (Temenos)

- Raising of chickens, cows, and goats for eggs and milk (Alpha Farm)

Many communities are even set up as non-profit corporations and offer classes and workshops especially for the public on

- Conflict resolution techniques (University of the Trees)

- Trainings in good communications and relationships (Living Love Community)

- Alternative forms of healing (Lama)

- Gestalt therapy and planetary economics (Esalen Institute)

- Bio-energetics therapy (Sevenoaks)

- Eurythmy movement (Spring Valley)

- Stress management (Himalayan Institute)

- Native American studies (Mettanokit)

- Awareness through movement (Koinonia)

- Wholistic health (Breitenbush)

- Polarity therapy, reflexology, Shiatsu (Kripalu)

- Creating a new economic order (Chinook)

- Leadership training (Green Pastures)

- Spiritual practices from the world's religious traditions (Ojai Foundation)

- Healing with herbs, crystals, and sound (Sunray)

- Sufi dance and prayer (Light of the Mountains)

- Bio-feedback training and Indian Ayurvedic medicine (Mt. Madonna)

- Yoga teacher's training (Yogaville)

Some communities are even beginning to offer credits

through established universities for their educational programs: High Wind Community with the University of Wisconsin, Chinook with Antioch College, Findhorn with California State University at Sonoma, The Himalayan Institute with the University of Scranton. Fourteen books published by the Himalayan Institute are used as textbooks in over 40 colleges around the country. Students at Dartmouth College received credit for attending a program at Auroville Community in India, Findhorn in Scotland, and Arcosanti in Arizona.

Some community members teach university courses based on their experiences and training in communities. Teresina Havens of Temenos teaches at the University of Massachusetts' Enquiry Program, John Saley of the Pathwork Community in New York teaches at Pace University, and we have taught courses on communities and social change at American University and Boston College.

Community members have also been invited into university classes for guest lectures on everything from wholistic health techniques to experiences with self-government. Sociology classes from various colleges often visit communities such as Twin Oaks to study their alternative structures firsthand. We've even had elementary school children visit Sirius Community to learn how we work in our forest and garden.

Professor Robert Kenny of George Washington University has taught courses on "Utopian Communities" in which students live together in a community for three months to study it. Downeast Community is actually set up as a three-month-long community in Freedom, Maine, where students live together for a semester of credit from Manchester Community College in Connecticut. Instructor Jay Stayer sees the community course giving the students "a chance to learn by doing, to know from their guts, rather than from their heads, some of the facts of life."

A new idea for something called "The University of the Future" has been developed by High Wind Community in Wisconsin, Sirius in Massachusetts, and Findhorn in Scotland. Students get a full semester of undergraduate or graduate credit from the University of Wisconsin for an alternative "semester abroad," spending a month living, working, and studying in each of these communities. Included are classes like The Role of Art and Creativity in Communities; The Re-definition of Work in a Changing Economy; Global Issues and the Politics of Place; Local Ecology and Self-Sufficiency. According to Professor Beldon Paulson, Director of the program,

Some of these alternative communities might be considered harbingers of an emerging culture...embodying a combination of philosophical values, workable technologies, and a day-to-day living process that, in retrospect, may have historic significance. If, indeed, a new culture is emerging, we need to be educated and to educate for a new era, with useable visions and tools.

In addition to the concepts and practical skills taught at communities, there is also a new approach to learning that is different from traditional education. Experiential education emphasizes

  • Drawing wisdom and information out of students rather than just pouring it in

  • Learning *how* to learn, how to ask good questions, how to draw one's own conclusions

  • Encouraging both right and left brain activity, intuitive as well as rational thinking

  • Valuing the affective domain—feelings, dreams, intuition, imagery—since building good relationships with people is as important as learning facts

  • Valuing Eastern as well as Western approaches to life—being, as well as doing; the good of the whole, as well as the importance of the individual

  • Encouraging planetary awareness and appreciation of other cultures

  • Seeing purpose and values as equally important as skill and knowledge

  • Using spontaneity and flexibility to aid the learning process.

Most communities include their children in work projects, teaching them how to garden, how to build, how to cook, etc. Large communities generally have experimental schools, based on their values and philosophy, for their children. Esalen's Gazebo school is based on experiential learning, and the community is the classroom. Ananda, Mt. Madonna, University of the Trees, and the Abode communities all have schools for their own children as well as for local children.

One of the most impressive of the community schools is Green Meadow Waldorf School in Spring Valley Community, New York. It is based on the philosophy of Rudolf Steiner and has three hundred students from pre-school to high school. It uses the usual curriculum subjects to aid the development process of the child. Subjects are taught in a sequence attuned to Steiner's picture of the stages of a child's inner growth. Every subject, including math and the sciences, is taught in an artistic fashion. Of the five beautifully-designed school buildings inspired by Steiner's architecture, one is devoted entirely to music and art. The object is to stimulate not only the students' minds, but also their hearts and hands. Physics is demonstrated by playing musical instruments. Counting skills are developed by teaching students to knit. The key learning ingredient at the school is relationships: teacher to students, students to teacher, students to students. The same teacher stays with the student through all 8 grades to develop continuity and a deeper understanding of each student.

Also of special interest is the children's education program at Stelle Community. In its "Motherschool," mothers come to school for four hours a day with their children (newborn to six years) and act as primary tutor for their child on a one-to-one basis. Stelle members feel the mother/child bond is essential in these early years, and by following this program they find that children can read by age three, write by age four, and work at a typical third grade level by age six. Emotional development is stressed, and Stelle teachers have found that the more physical contact a child has, the less violent s/he is inclined to be. There are no grades given at Stelle, but students must demonstrate mastery of the material before moving on. Stelle also has a Montessori classroom which teaches character development and independence to the two- to six-year-olds. An atmosphere of beauty is created. Body movement, drama, and dance are used to help teach subjects, as the physical body retains information easier than the mind at this age, they feel. By focusing on new and effective approaches for educating children, communities are helping to create a more positive future.

R and R Centers

It is our utopias that make the world tolerable to us: the cities and mansions that people dream of are those in which they finally live.
—Lewis Mumford

Many communities (but not all) serve as places of rest and retreat for visitors to unwind and be refreshed. Rural communities, of course, provide the fresh air and healing power of nature

Places of rest and retreat, to unwind and get refreshed

to calm jangled nerves and renew the spirit. Visitors often work in a community's garden, and such work can be very grounding and healing. Ponds for swimming and nature trails for hiking are available in most communities. But even urban communities—especially the spiritual ashrams such as Sivananda Ashram in Washington, D.C. and the Sufi Community in San Francisco—provide an oasis of calm in a frantic world. The peaceful feeling of these places is often created through the use of meditation and spiritual practices as well as by the usually positive and joyful consciousness of the members.

Communities also serve as "de-toxification" centers for visitors, places to purify their systems of the poisons accumulated through living in stressful, polluted environments, eating unhealthy foods, etc. Often programs of specific diets, exercises, meditation techniques, and Native American sweat lodge ceremonies are designed for this de-toxification process, as at the Center of the Light Community in Massachusetts. Some communities even have special retreat programs for corporate leaders. Many communities such as Lama, the Abode, and Sirius have set aside special cabins in remote parts of their land where visitors can have a time of silent retreat, and these are increasingly in demand.

Communities also serve as way-stations for those in transition or crisis, helping to heal the spirit of those who have just left a marriage or a career and are searching for something new. Communities offer supportive places to reflect, consider options, explore new possibilities, and unfold new potentials.

Benefits and Purposes of Community 51

Service

Those among you who will be really happy are those who have sought and found how to serve

I don't know what your destiny will be; but one thing I do know: the only ones among you who will be really happy are those who have sought and found how to serve.

—Albert Schweitzer

To be fulfilled on the deepest level, people need to experience a sense of meaning and purpose in life: serving a greater good, helping other people, helping society in some way.

Once you've had a taste of serving, you won't be able to leave it. Because there's joy in serving others...And when others support you in serving, as occurs in a community, you gain more incentive for it and you find the joy of it. It brings spiritual progress. People find over the years that the more they live that way, the happier they are. The less they live that way, the less happy they are.

—Swami Kriyananda
Ananda Community

But in order for a community to last more than a couple of years, it needs to be focused on more than the immediate survival, benefit, or happiness of its own members. Otherwise too much individual or group self-centeredness is fostered, and inevitable quarrels about whether each person is getting her/his due seem to arise and split the group apart. When a community is able to turn outward and serve the needs of society, it lifts the whole group and thereby helps the growth of its members. True service builds for the future, for future generations, and for the future well-being of our earth.

When communities only come together because of convenience or common interests, sooner or later that breaks down. It's not a cohesive reason to be together and to go through all the dynamics of close living. To be successful you've got to have something vastly more important at your core than common interest, or even the "common good," which is what most people think of when they think of community. You must participate with a concern for something larger than yourself. I think personal growth is a matter of service. We grow through service.

—Jim Frid
Emissary Community

Most ongoing communities have service projects to help society in some way. The Center of the Light in Massachusetts and The Himalayan Institute in Pennsylvania are healing centers. The Abode Community in New York gives instruction in meditation and organic gardening. Camphill Community in Copake, New York helps retarded people. The Community for Creative Non-Violence feeds the poor of Washington, D.C. in soup kitchens. Approvecho Community in Oregon is working on solutions to global firewood scarcity and training Peace Corps volunteers in alternative technologies. They've also taught Third World peoples in Kenya, Mali, Senegal, China, and Mexico how to build efficient clay stoves and other appropriate technologies. Farm Community members in Tennessee work as volunteers for Plenty, their international relief organization, teaching medical and agricultural skills to Third World peoples and running a free ambulance service in the South Bronx. Stephen Gaskin commented:

> These two aspects of Farm purpose, self-growth and global outreach, provide the tensions and the balance that make the Summertown Community such a lively place...If the members there did not have the purpose of doing good for others and instead concentrated all their energies on making their own material lives and environment better, in time the Farm would become complacent and probably extinct. The dedicated at-home work makes the outreach possible and the outreach gives that at-home work an important reason for continuing.

Communities are the most effective and most loving situations for helping the retarded, the handicapped and the emotionally disturbed. As communities mature and stabilize over time, they will undoubtedly take on more of this function for society.

When communities relate to each other and to the larger world so as to provide each other with the maximum opportunity for development, then true service is being offered. Individuals can truly receive no more from their own community than that community is willing to give to the world.

Creating Wholeness and Synthesis

> [These groups] are an experiment which has for its objective, the manifestation of certain types of energy which will produce cohesion, or an at-one-ment, upon the earth.[21]

Creating synthesis -
embracing diversity in a
unified whole

The highest goal of community life is to overcome the fragmentation caused by society and to create *whole* people, integrating mind/body/feelings/spirit so that all parts of the self function harmoniously. The greatest challenge of community life is to create synthesis, embracing diversity in a unified whole, resolving differences with the healing spirit of love and dedication to the good of the whole.

As Sociologist Rosabeth Kanter observes in her intensive study of communities, past and present,

> The underlying theme that has been stressed from Plato [in *The Republic*] to the present, despite variations in style or ideology, is wholeness or integration. Communes are social orders designed to counteract the fragmentation of human life in some kinds of society. They are seen as vehicles for bringing fragments together into unity, for making connections between people and parts of life, for developing the "whole person"...The various kinds of integration communes have attempted to bring about are: between values and practical everyday matters; between work life and family life; between people and nature; between people and God; between members of the group; between adults and children; between the roles of men and women; between education and life.[22]

Historically, a major theme in community has been the creation of unity through the union of opposites—in other words, synthesis. "Learning to deal with conflict is in fact why God created intentional community," according to Danaan Parry, cofounder of Earth Stewards in Washington. He comments:

You may think that your community exists solely to provide wheat grass juice for the world, or to channel Light from the Pleiades, but what is more correct is that you and your companions have been cleverly drawn into a set-up to help you move beyond your limited view of "what I can deal with now." Conflict isn't going to fade out when you all get it together, because learning from conflict is a primary reason for the existence of community.[23]

As Rick of Alpha Farm put it simply, "All we have to do is to get along. If we do that, it's revolutionary."

Like the ideals of our pluralistic society, most communities support diversity and the freedom of the individual to pursue her/his own highest good within the context of the agreed upon purposes and values of the community. And as a microcosm of the larger whole—all of life on earth—the work of community is to bring together many types of diverse elements. Different human personalities need to be blended. Human and non-human kingdoms—plants, animals, minerals—must work in harmony. Divergent values and philosophical issues struggle to be resolved—hierarchy vs. democracy, capitalism vs. socialism, the group vs. the individual, freedom vs. responsibility.

> By making the small human community into a microcosm of the planet, the community itself becomes a "yantra," an object of contemplation for insight into universal processes of evolution and transformation. What MIT was to post-industrial society, [the new communities] will become for the new culture.[24]

The more diversity that a community can handle and still create a strong sense of unity, the more powerful it is. Lama Community in New Mexico synthesizes the best of many of the great religious traditions of the world: Hindu, Christian, Buddhist, Islamic. The Findhorn Community in Scotland unites people from many different countries and lifestyles, with an age range of newborn to eighty.

As Chris Roberts of Sunbow Community expresses it:

> Our main areas of commonality are our spiritual focus, Earth awareness, and the sharing of a common vision of wholeness and service...In all other areas we are richly diverse, having quite a wide variety of backgrounds, professions, experiences and perspectives. This diversity is a great gift for it has required each of us to become more inclusive and to honor one another's truths as well as our own.[25]

Benefits and Purposes of Community 55

Joan Halifax of the Ojai Foundation sees an important value in the diversity in their community.

> The purpose of our educational programs is to have teachers from every religious and philosophical tradition, and for people to eventually discover the underlying values, the unity in all the different paths...It's a micro-planetary culture in a way, in terms of the tremendous diversity within the staff and the programs. What binds it together is that unity of vision and of values. Within the crucible of the programs themselves, teachers have an opportunity to encounter each other from the other traditions. And there's a great alchemy of diverse elements metabolizing with each other and...releasing new energies, new forms. So the Lama loves to come here because he's always with Native Americans, and the Zen Master comes and he loves the Lama. It's just wonderful to see people see each other from the point of view of their own humanity.

But if a community takes on more diversity than it can really handle, without having strong processes for creating unity and synthesis, the result will be dispersion of energy and/or dissolution of the community as a result of too much conflict. On the other hand, too little diversity in a group creates stagnation, crystallization, and a dull conformity, as evidenced today in certain rigid religious communities.

Synthesis is a higher level of integration than mere compromise. Compromise is the blending or halfway place between two poles—it contains half of each. Synthesis on the other hand can be seen as the point equidistant from each pole *and* from the bottom level of the pole—in other words, a third dimension, height, or broader awareness, is brought in.

> Synthesis is brought about by a higher element or principle which transforms, sublimates and reabsorbs the two poles into a higher reality...The method of synthesis which is analogous in a certain sense to a chemical combination, includes and absorbs the two elements into a higher unity endowed with qualities differing from those of either of them.[26]

Rather than a compromise between two extremes, synthesis is that which holds the key to their relatedness. As Einstein once said, "You can't solve a problem on its own level." We must take it to a higher level and see it from a broader perspective.

The task for each individual in community, as for each individual in society (ideally), is to overcome the personal problems and negativity that create conflict with others. The diversity of personality types found in communities is essential for creating spiritual power and for the type of service which communities offer to the world. When an old disciple of Sri Aurobindo's at his ashram in Pondicherry, India complained about the mixture of people in the ashram and the "impossible" people he found there, Sri Aurobindo observed that this mixture was of utmost necessity in the kind of transformation work undertaken there. Aurobindo saw the community as a laboratory where each member must confront the "impossible point" in himself, the major problem in life which he has in common with a particular segment of the population (for example, arrogance or fear). By transmuting this problem in himself, Aurobindo said, the person contributes to the progress of the collective evolution of earth, as we are deeply connected to each other on a subconscious and superconscious level. Overcoming a personal problem in ourselves makes it much easier for others to overcome the same problem in themselves.[27]

Places of hope and positive vision for the world

Centers of Light

In India they have many pilgrimage places where people have worshipped for thousands of years. But here we don't have this, there's no-where to go. We don't have a Lourdes, etc. So we need to start creating centers of Light again. We have to bring that Light to a focus, just as electricity is everywhere, but you need it in a bulb before you can see it.

—Swami Kriyananda

Benefits and Purposes of Community 57

On the deepest level, a community can serve the purpose of being a "center of Light," a place of hope and positive vision in the world. A center of Light is a place of spiritual energy, created through the blending of the powers of spirit and earth with the conscious invocation of individuals who join together for spiritual growth and service to others. Of course, not only new age communities but also traditional religious centers like churches and temples can also be centers of Light. The power of a Light center depends on the quality of Love, Light, and alignment with the evolutionary force (i.e. God's Will) which it expresses. A Light center creates the kind of environment that has a finer vibration, a more focused and pure energy that enables people to touch more deeply their own spiritual essence, their soul, and find their soul's purpose in life.

> You grow spiritually so much quicker when you're with other like-minded people. Out in the world you have to contend with the opposing forces. You sometimes are battling up against a brick wall and life can be so difficult. But in a center of Light, you haven't got that opposition from the forces of Darkness. There's a certain protection.
> —Peter Caddy

The Light illuminates the darkness, and the dark and negative places in each person can be seen more clearly and so transmuted into positive qualities. Sometimes it's very challenging to live in a center of Light, because we see our own darkness more clearly. These centers serve the plan of human evolution by their transmuting function, revealing spirit in matter and redeeming matter.

Centers of Light fulfill the function attributed to the "philosopher's stone" of the old alchemists: transmuting the "lead" of human negativity into the "gold" of the Divine self. We serve as transmuters and uplifters for others just by our "beingness" when we're in a centered and loving space.

> If you leave and come back, you realize what a haven these [communities] are. There's an atmosphere, a vibration you feel when you walk in here. The students create the atmosphere as much as the staff who teach the classes...I see people coming into this center feeling so inspired, feeling they've found a home, a place where they can have salvation. A good percentage of the people who come here are quite overwhelmed. It changes their life—it's what they're looking for, what they need, and they know they need it.
> —Swami Chandra Shekarananda
> Sivananda Yoga Vedanta Center

The land on which many communities in America today are located is land once held sacred to Native American tribes. In Australia, many are on land sacred to the Aborigines, and in England, on land sacred to the Druids. Early tribes were drawn to areas of the earth that have a powerful nature energy and an alignment with cosmic forces. Through their ceremonies, rituals, and invocations to the Great Spirit and the forces of nature, they began to create a sense of the sacred in these areas, the early centers of Light. Later, those who started spiritual communities were often guided in their meditation to these locations. There are many examples of this, including Lama in New Mexico, Koinonia in Maryland, Sevenoaks in Virginia, The Bear Tribe in Washington, The Dawn Horse in California, Sunray in Vermont, and the Center of the Light and Sirius in Massachusetts. These communities continue to act as good custodians, rather than owners of the land, and many carry on some Native American ceremonies such as sweat lodges today. At least four new age communities around the country were actually started by Native Americans: Sunray in Huntington, Vermont, started by Dhanyi Yawhoo; Mettanokit in Greenville, New Hampshire, by Medicine Story; the Bear Tribe in Spokane, Washington, by Sun Bear; and Metatantay in Carlin, Nevada, by Rolling Thunder. A number of communities were started on land that previously was used for other spiritual purposes. Kripalu in Massachusetts is an old Catholic Monastery and the Abode in New York is in an old Shaker village, for example.

Most importantly, however, a center of Light, as a *place*—as a form and structure—is not separate from the people who create it. The real center of Light begins with what is within each individual, the inner Light of Spirit.

③ Problems and Conflicts in Community

He who cannot change the very fabric of his thought will never be able to change reality and will never, therefore, make any progress. —ANWAR SADAT

The new communities are not utopias where life is always easy and joyful. Creating something new is always a struggle. As members of Central Point Community in New Zealand point out, "The idea of any community that is totally safe, absolutely certain and tranquil all the time is a myth. It does not exist except in fantasy. To have ups and downs is to be human."[1] All the big issues in personal life—money, power, sex—are also big issues in community (see chapters 5, 6, and 7), but the basic agreement of community life is to work these problems out consciously and not to avoid them. In addition, the very nature of group life itself often creates problems which are not as frequently encountered in personal life, such as issues of privacy. And people re-create the same problems in community life that they experienced in their former life in the mainstream—such as goal obsession, workaholism, etc. People may join communities to escape their problems, only to find that community life makes them come face to face with what they were trying to avoid. If we flee something and do not forgive or release it, we recreate it in each new situation, as Danaan Parry of Earth Stewards in Washington explains.

> I have seen hundreds of people come into intentional community, each thinking that they have found a place where they won't have to deal with "that" (each of us has our own unique "that"). Yet within six weeks, the entire communal preoccupation is focused on making her or him confront "that". It's uncanny; intentional community always shines a spotlight on whatever you join community to avoid.[2]

And Myrtle Glines from the Findhorn Community adds:

> Findhorn is no refuge or haven from the problems of society. To the extent that those problems are inner created through our own personal imbalances, we bring them with us wherever we go, and at Findhorn, our inner contradictions are brought to the surface with uncomfortable intensity.[3]

Carl Jung said that the search for utopia is a projection of the inner life. People who are inwardly dissatisfied often expect community to compensate for their emotional frustration. But true utopia, Jung felt, is possible only with people who are conscious of their inner needs. If needs are unconscious, they get projected on the whole community and never get fully met. Community members are learning how to recognize these inner needs and how to deal with some of the conflicts which arise in group life. In a society that conditions its citizens to be very individualistic and competitive, the very tension between individual and group needs is often the cause of much of the conflict in community. Some of the insights gained by community members in dealing with these tensions may be of interest to non-community members dealing with similar issues and may have something to offer to institutions in the larger society as well.

Problems and Conflicts in Community 61

The Group vs. the Individual:
Getting over-cooked in the "group-soup"

One of the major issues in community is that of maintaining a proper balance between the group and the individual. In some communities—especially the "cults" that have received much media attention—there is a real danger of group tyranny. The "cults" are actually an expression of what we would call "mass consciousness," where the individual is not valued, unlike true "group consciousness," where there is an emphasis on individual integrity. Most of the public has a stereotyped image of all communities as following the "mass consciousness," and there is a popular fear of communal life because of this. But fortunately this sterotype is the exception rather than the rule. Most successful, long-term communities find an appropriate balance for themselves between group needs and individual needs. This balance varies from community to community, depending on the people who live there.

The main re-orientation that has to happen for any new member of a community is a shift from a self-centered focus to an expansion of one's identity so that it includes the whole community. As Bree of Twin Oaks Community explains, "All the people at our community are trying to live as part of that whole. That's a lot of what life is all about—longing to get back to that whole."[4] Since we have all been conditioned by society to think mainly in terms of ourselves and how we can meet our own needs, it's a huge shift to have to think in terms of the whole community and the needs of everyone. It takes some careful re-education to be really considerate of others and to learn to trust that other people can also think about you and be aware of your needs. And at the same time, you have to maintain your individual integrity so that you don't get overwhelmed by an over-identification with the group or by too much dependency on it.

Community doesn't seem to work very well if it is too individualistic and creates too much of a sense of isolationism and competition, as this is no different from the rest of society. One community we visited in upstate New York had this problem and consequently lost many of its original members who had become disillusioned with it.

And yet, conversely, if there's too much emphasis on the group and on conformity to group standards, then a community can create an authoritarian situation, even though there may not be a strong leader. David Wickenden of Auroville Community points out that

In order to deal with a tremendous amount of diversity in community, you need to form some kind of coherent collectivity. Then there is the tendency to define more and more what that collectivity is, and then to subtly or not so subtly enforce that. And it may not be any literal arm twisting, but just a psychological pressure to conform or to toe the "party line." It may not even be something written down, but just something in the atmosphere. And then people who are not toeing the line, or who are voicing a different opinion, start to get outside the circle. This kind of pressure gets to be very oppressive and constrictive on individual development and initiative. Instead of the individual surrendering his or her self to the Divine, which is the ideal where everyone is totally free, the individual instead surrenders his or her self to the collective. And then it becomes a group ego, instead of a group soul...Instead of the collective being a means to the end, the collective becomes the end in itself.

Sociologist Rosabeth Kanter found that group pressure is often "more oppressive in anarchist groups that lack formal statements of rules and understandings."[5]

Another problem with too strong a group orientation, with too much conformity, is that a community seems to attract mainly martyr-personalities, who eventually burn out by giving too much to the group and not nurturing themselves, and passive participants, who have difficulty thinking for themselves and easily fall into dependency patterns, often not doing their share of the work. In addition, too strong a group orientation may also draw out the rebelliousness in people, as Freddie Ann of Twin Oaks observed:

I had to define *me, Freddie,* and what I believed in and what my place was in the whole group. People in the group scenes at Twin Oaks prove their identity, to the detriment of the group process. Also, because it's so hard to establish an identity in the group, you get lost in it.[6]

Another trap of a community that becomes too group-oriented is the feeling that members have to do *everything* together as a group.

There are people in our community who want to have more farm land. They could get together and buy more land as a small group. Instead they continually try to convince the entire community of the need for more land. For the entire co-op to buy land requires the approval of everybody and makes the task very difficult. Those who want land would be better off getting together and buying land on their own.[7]

To receive the maximum growth experience from community living, individuals often choose a situation that provides a cutting edge for them, stretching them and challenging their old patterns. For example, a person who hasn't yet learned to think for herself/himself or to actualize her/his full potential is not motivated toward growth in a strong group-oriented community. If a person doesn't feel a certain amount of confidence in being able to stand on her/his own two feet and survive in the world on her/his own, then a strong group-oriented community only reinforces a pattern of immature dependence and prolongs a basic adolescent stage, even though the person may be thirty-five years old! This is the problem with most of the "cults" that don't encourage individual development and responsibility.

On the other side of the coin, if a person is already a very independent, self-reliant type who finds it difficult to help others or to share her/his resources, then a strong group-oriented community provides her/him with new challenges in personal development. If a person has too extreme a pattern of privacy, then living with other people in a communal house is a great growth process in which one can develop flexibility and consideration of others.

In truth, the only individuality a person has to give up in community is the "right" to take advantage of others, to be dishonest, or to attempt to obtain from others or from the community more than s/he is willing to give them.

Some communities are flexible enough to adjust to the needs of their members by having alternating cycles of outbreath (where there's a strong group-orientation and everyone feels they're all in it together) and inbreath (where members have more space and time alone to pursue their own needs and interests). And within the larger cycles of the community's inbreath and outbreath, individual members may experience their own cycles and needs for more individual space or more group activity. May of the Renaissance Community, for example, found that after many years of living in large group houses, she needed to live alone for awhile. After six months of being on her own, she was ready to return to the group house and give to others what she had learned from her time alone.

Sometimes the growing edge for all the members of a community is to learn to take more of an inbreath, to learn to nurture themselves as individuals, as Mary Kate Jordan of the Center of the Light notes.

> In the past, all of us here have followed a path of total sacrifice of self to the community. One of the temptations that we know we are not to fall into this time is to totally sacrifice ourselves. But rather, we are to bring to community a group of fulfilled individuals. Total sacrifice of self is not healthy, it's not appropriate. But it's easier because we've done it a lot before—being noble and sacrificing, etc. What we feel is really important here is to learn how to receive the abundance of God, the beauty and the joy of God.

Ideally, each cycle of focus on the individual or on the group greatly enriches the personal development of a community member as well as of the community as a whole. At each change in the cycle, a higher level of development is experienced. Lessons learned in the cycle of strong group orientation are applied to the individual's growth, and those learned in the cycle of strong individual orientation can strengthen the whole group. Not only do communities go through cycles of individual focus and then group focus, but civilization as a whole does as well. Humanity evolves in a spiraling motion, and each change of focus is on a higher turn of the spiral, as lessons learned in one phase are applied to the next.

In the '60s there was a strong group orientation. Today it is the opposite. Those communities which can incorporate the best aspects of the current cycle of exaggerated individualism (self-responsibility and individual creativity and initiative) will survive and prove to be the strongest in the next cycle of exaggerated groupism.

Eva Pierrakos of the Center for the Living Force Community in New York comments that true "group consciousness," as opposed to "mass consciousness," is only experienced in a group when

> the individual has found himself and has brought his full self-realization to fruition and can thus benefit from and give to the group without losing selfhood, autonomy and self-responsibility. Neither does he lose his "privacy", his right to be different, his need to express his uniqueness—quite the contrary. In the group that has become so evolved, there is not conflict between those individual needs and the needs of the group as a whole. Group consciousness does not level off uniqueness, but furthers it. The group is no longer used as a crutch because the self cannot handle life. Nor is the group an author-

ity that one needs to rebel against. The group is truly an extended self in which one can function as a free agent. The highest organization of group consciousness is that within which each individual has found his autonomy.[8]

Private Space vs. Communal Space:
The old territorial instinct

How much space should each individual have relative to group space? How much privacy is healthy in a community? Ken Kesey, of Merry Prankster/acid-tripping fame, who lived on a communal farm in Oregon, observed,

> The real source of stress is spatial...When people are pressed together for a long time it homogenizes them, it breaks down that sense of space. Without that, we don't know what we are. We're into each other's drawers, we're stumbling over each other...and the worse thing about it is that it's with your best friends.[9]

Overcrowding is sometimes done intentionally in some communities to foster personal growth—the "pressure cooker effect." But over-crowding can also breed real pettiness. Lack of space and privacy is a major reason members leave communities. A Twin Oaks member comments:

> Living with a lot of people I experience all the fluctuations in their lives. We give up predictability in favor of being more human and alive. I am subjected to people's vagaries, to their ups and downs. It takes a lot of energy to go through that with sixty to seventy people.[10]

While some people need lots of privacy, others feel very uncomfortable if they have to be too much alone and isolated. They'd rather be in the thick of things, with lots of people and energy around. Although appreciating community life very much, Bhavani Siegal of Mt. Madonna Community, for example, sees a major difficulty there as "lack of free time, a lack of privacy—everyone eats together, and everyone helps with the retreats all the time." A member of Twin Oaks Community decried the lack of personal space in the community, but she also acknowledged, "When I want to sit alone at lunchtime or breakfast, I put up a kind of barrier and people stay away."[11]

In the initial stages of joining a community, being around

lots of people all the time is very exciting. But when you live, work, play, and eat with the same group of people day after day, it can create a sense of ''people overload.'' Community veterans usually learn the importance of creating balance in their lives. Linda Burnham of the Center of the Light in Massachusetts learned,

> It's been very important for us as healers to take personal space when we need it—to nourish ourselves—otherwise we get burned out and we're not of use to anyone.

Sociologists who studied rural California communes came to the conclusion that ''a big house approach'' and lack of privacy were typical of only the first year in the group they studied. ''As soon as a group's coherence is established, members create individual or family spaces, but share kitchens,''[12] they noted.

A third factor in this privacy issue is age. Many young people just out of college love to live in big, crowded houses with their peers; it's a variation of the college dorm or fraternity/sorority scene. Young people also tend to be more tribal and have a greater need to find their identity with their peers, as they're still involved with trying to dis-identify from their parents' values. But as community members grow older, into their late thirties and forties, they tend to individualize more and don't need an over-identification with peers by living closely with them. They usually become more involved with their own individual projects or life work and often have a family to provide for. They prefer more private space than when they were younger. Communities that are flexible with this life change and sensitive to different temperaments tend to retain members longer and don't have as rapid a turnover as those that insist solely on group living in large houses.

Most successful, long-term communities strike a balance in this private space/communal space issue, as Dolores Hayden found in her in-depth survey of the architectural designs of nineteenth-century communities.

> Most of the communities which believed that the abolition of private space would strengthen group cohesiveness, in time refined their designs to develop more of a balance between communal and private space...The Shakers increased their use of communal space in three stages of members...The first Oneida mansion...was replaced with a second mansion where most adults had private rooms...[But] groups who built private dwellings often broke up quarreling over

Problems and Conflicts in Community 67

private vs. public ownership. Some communities were skillful enough to design accommodations which combined some of the best features of both communal and private dwellings, but developing such designs usually required years of experience with communal living.[13]

Dependency vs. Autonomy: Community as welfare state

One of the major traps of community is the creation of dependency. Often people who are terrified of having too much freedom or lack of structure in their lives gravitate toward community as a way to ease their anxiety. The search for community as extended family often becomes the unconscious search for substitute mother/father figures to provide for one's material and emotional security.

Often the conflicts which arise in community stem out of either the perceived non-fulfillment of this unrecognized need for dependence or out of rebellion against perceived parental figures, in order to establish one's independence. Freddie Ann of Twin Oaks Community realized that "...some of the hardest problems of community are that people start acting worse than a little kid does, to show you that they're there."[14]

Although sometimes overt, more often this dynamic is very subtle and is usually denied when brought to one's attention. Inappropriate dependency patterns are not unique to community, of course; they crop up in the typical family situation and in all social institutions. But in communities, at least, these patterns can be examined and changed more easily as they are more obvious in a community than in society, and yet they are not as intense or as historical as in a small family situations.

The way that mature communities have dealt with this issue is through structural solutions and/or through psychological awareness and honesty on the part of both the "parent" and "child" figures. A structural solution is for members to take full responsibility for making their own income and paying for their own living expenses, and many communities do this. Or if a communal system is preferred, systems are set up to ensure a rotation of responsibilities for all aspects of communal life so that each person gets a turn at providing leadership or at managing the community's money, for example.

Regardless of the structural solutions for dealing with this dependency problem in community life, bringing it to conscious attention has been essential for maintaining a healthy emotional environment. It is here that psychological tools are most helpful in a community. Sevenoaks Community, for example, arranges "sessions" with "Pathwork helpers" or counselors to help members explore their own negative attitudes and "parental stuff" which they might be projecting on others. Donovan Thesenga of Sevenoaks reflected on how important it was for members to honestly confront their own attitudes in this area:

> Some people in our process groups expressed it very clearly when Eva [the community's charismatic founder] died and changes were necessary: "I don't want to grow up. I liked it the way it was. I thought it was terrific. All these good mommies and daddies (the training group people, the leadership) making the decisions. They seemed like good decisions, they created a happy community. Why the hell should I do it? I liked it the way it was." People who got clear about this and put it out this way are the ones, I feel, who can stay and grow. It's the ones who get freaked out and leave and aren't clear about their motives or tack it onto something else—they'll have problems.

Mandatory vs. Voluntary Activities: "What? Me Work?"

This is another of the basic polarities in community, a kind of subset of the group vs. individual issue. The issue usually is whether something is accomplished best through making it required or making it voluntary. Should work be mandatory in the community? Should spiritual practice be mandatory? One community member observes that social pressure, which tends to emerge as a replacement of coercion, often has the opposite effect from the one desired, promoting deviance rather than adherence to group norms.

> Those who worked hardest and most consistently were inclined to interpret the sporadic efforts of the others as lack of commitment—to the factory, to the community, to themselves...[Those who] do more than their share resent those who do little. The latter accuse the former of being judgmental, and dig in their heels all the more firmly. A game of stand-off develops, and the house becomes an appalling mess...
>
> The games of ego can be played with monetary or sexual counters, and also with those of labor. One person's exertion can be

interpreted as pressure on others to exert equally. Thus one can develop an ego-stake in *not* working, a resistance to being manipulated...We have gone through phases of complete paralysis. Some have stopped working because they felt pressure to work. Others have stopped because they don't want to be perceived as exerting pressure. But their very inaction is seen as only another form of pressure...Values and personal worth are threatened...Some believe that necessity warrants pressure and manipulation of others. These evoke resistance. The right to freedom of choice is perpetually tested.[15]

Most communities have learned to have at least some bottom lines, minimum requirements for membership, such as contributing so much money and/or labor or sharing in specific tasks, such as cooking or cleaning. Required minimums can either be enforced by an authority figure, a guru or leader, or by an institution like a "personnel group" or a "financial department," or they can be supported by peer pressure, feeling "bad vibes" from other members who may even confront people directly.

Communities have different ways of handling the coercion/mandatory issue. In many of the Eastern ashrams, for example, there is a more detailed code of membership requirements. In other communities, there is a wide range of acceptable behavior and belief, with some members contributing a great deal more work and/or money than others. The Findhorn Community, for example, has what it calls "rhythms" of community life, rather than "rules," as "rhythms" has a more flexible feeling to it.

Rather than 'rules,' the Findhorn Community has what it calls 'rhythms' of community life

Some communities have changed their requirements considerably over the years. For example, in the early days of Findhorn, if members didn't show up for morning group meditation, Peter Caddy, the community's leader, would later knock on their door to ask why. Today, attendance at group meditations is voluntary, as the community feels that people should freely choose their spiritual practice in order for it to be really valuable for them.

Renaissance Community used to make all community meetings (often four evenings a week) mandatory, but they learned some interesting lessons from this.

> We used to make the meetings mandatory, but in the last few months we've begun to feel that if enough people do it, and hold to it because they really want to—especially the spiritual part of it—it brings about a feeling in the others that they also have to be responsible to it. The people who really want to get together can do so and this creates a higher energy which attracts the people who aren't really into it even more, and that works better than making everyone go when they don't want to. When people go just because they have to, it creates the kind of resistance in the room where you have to be really strong just to say anything into that kind of energy. But there are certain times when everyone living here should attend a particular meeting, and it should be made clear that if a person won't attend at these special times, then they should pack their bags because they don't belong here. Because after a certain point, people will drain it if there isn't some kind of responsibility to the whole. You have to keep a balance in this.
> —Robin Paris

Also, people are clearly at different stages of growth and need different degrees of freedom at various times in their lives. While exploring Sirius and comparing it to living in a more structured community, one visitor felt that she was too new to her spiritual path and needed the support of required activities to help her establish a disciplined spiritual practice. Our more voluntary approach wouldn't work for her, she realized.

Sometimes a community's approach can be too voluntary. Most people are not self-disciplined enough to make anything work on their own without some things being required. However, there are people who immaturely rebel at rules of any kind, so choosing a community with few rules gives them nothing outside themselves to react to. They must then deal more directly with their own internal conflicts and negativities. And there are some people who have really matured beyond the need for external rules because they've internalized them and are self-disciplined, responsible, and inner-directed, able to follow their own guidance and intuition. These rarer souls also do best in a community with more freedom.

The delicate balance in any community is a sensitivity to the real needs of each member's growth so that the choice of making something mandatory or not is most productive. When a person voluntarily does something out of her/his own inner sense of free choice, then a special quality, a certain radiant power seems to infill it, unlike the drudging compliance often associated with mandatory activities. Judson Jerome comments:

> To function without [rules] each member of a commune has to develop an organic, intuitive sense of his relationship to others and to the group, to become an organ in an organism, to recognize at a subliminal level that his own fulfillment depends upon the fulfillment of other individuals and the health of the group as a whole...Gradually a new consciousness grows; we hear our own inner voices more clearly, hear them tuned to those of others and to larger purposes beyond us all.[16]

Idealism vs. Realism: "Don't 'should' on me!"

> Many communal experiments had boxed themselves in, not by structure, but by ideals: they *had* to live under the same roof, *had* to work together, *had* to get along.[17]

In any communal endeavor, there is usually a faction of idealists and an opposing one of realists. The idealists are always aiming towards perfection and towards new qualities in consciousness. They often mistake the rhetoric of their ideals for the reality. The realists are often afraid to approach a problem from the perspective of changing consciousness, and so they look for the most practical and mundane methods to solve problems.

Idealists at the Findhorn Community, for example, felt that the solution to all the community's financial problems was for everyone to meditate more frequently to strengthen their faith in God and raise their consciousness to affirm abundance. The realists, on the other hand, felt that the solution should be practical—like starting businesses, re-financing loans, etc. But the real solution, it seemed to us, was for the realists to develop more faith and meditate more, and for the idealists to get involved with bookkeeping and business. In other words, each needed to develop the strengths of the other, as both changes in consciousness *and* practical solutions were needed.

Another characteristic of idealists in communities is that they typically bite off more than they can chew. They over-extend themselves and burn out. Realists, on the other hand, tend to get stagnant and inert, stuck in the status quo, even if it's something they don't enjoy. They often don't challenge themselves to change things or create something new.

An idealist in a community we know, for example, was always expecting that the common rooms would be clean because people should clean up after themselves. So when they didn't, the idealist got very judgmental and self-righteous and then took on even more work for herself cleaning up after others. The realist, in contrast, just expected the place to be a mess, saying, "that's human nature," and so made no effort to do anything about it, but at least he had a more relaxed life!

The idealists in community are always trying to change the world and change other people to fit a perfect image they have. But the problem with idealism is that it often leads to heavy burdens of expectation of change on the part of people. When these aren't met, it creates resentment on the part of the idealist. The problem with realism is that it's often rather boring and unimaginative.

The proper function of ideals is to create *direction* and forward movement, not expectation. It's always good when idealists take their narrow blinders off and see more of the whole picture, more of the perspective of others, so that they can then bring a sense of balance to their journey towards the ideal.

Like all polarities, the real strength of a community lies in its ability to synthesize both approaches, to be "realistically idealistic," letting ideals guide yet not dominate to the exclusion of common sense. Some communities have learned to move towards ideals and goals in a step-by-step manner, being both conscious and practical, improving with each step, and consolidating and grounding that growth before taking on the next challenge.

Goal Orientation vs. Process Orientation: The "feelers" meet the "doers"

Some communities tend to be very goal-oriented, always accomplishing new and amazing tasks. Arcosanti in Arizona, for example, is building and growing at a rapid rate, aiming to complete a city for 5,000 people. Other communities seem to be very process-oriented—more interested in *how* something happens than in *what* happens. Alcyone Community in Oregon spent over a year working out their interpersonal problems with each other before trying to build anything on their land.

Most communities seem to have more of a split within the community of goal-oriented members and process-oriented members. And often there is a great deal of tension between the two approaches. Many goal-oriented types experience extreme impatience with the group process so typical of community meetings where everyone has to feel good about something before going ahead with it. And "goal types" get even more irritated with what they see as "the touchy-feely types" who always want to explore everyone's emotions around every little issue that comes up. From the traditional perspective, the process approach is a very inefficient way to achieve goals, as it takes too much time. But to a process-oriented person, it's not so important whether anything is actually accomplished in a tangible way, or whether any goals are reached. People should enjoy the process of getting there and grow a lot from the experience.

The negative aspect of process-orientation is that it can be overused as an avoidance of responsibility, indicating an inability to face reality and a tendency towards self-indulgence. The negative aspect of goal-orientation is that it's often very insensitive to people's needs.

Lisa Paulson of High Wind describes the debate within her community on the goal/process dilemma.

> We may like to think that *how* we get things done, how people learn and how projects unfold is all-important; it is the only humane, enlightened way to proceed in the new age. We all need to be allowed the leeway to express our creativity freely and in our own timing, to re-invent our own wheels, perhaps...There may be times when it's better to give up the project for the process, as there's no such thing as failure. Others see an urgency in the world situation and say there may not be time to discover slowly. If we are indeed dedicated to planetary interconnectedness, the good of the whole may have to come before or along with individual agendas. Beware of narcissism, cry some. But to others, there can be no whole without fully functioning individuals...Often we're suddenly up against nasty things like deadlines set by circumstances beyond our control. Some say we have no business getting into these situations; others argue that we'd never get off the ground if we didn't have such prods. Part of me says that the lessons of community are revealed in the way we live day to day.

Most of the new communities have a strong belief that the ends do not justify the means, but rather that *the means and the ends are identical*. In other words, any idealistic goal is actually created through the day-to-day process of being that goal; e.g., to attain a peaceful world, one must practice *being peaceful* inside. The quality of love and harmony used to build towards a goal ultimately determines its final outcome. The ideal, of course, is honoring both goal and process and working to effectively accomplish goals in a loving, harmonious way.

Planning vs. Spontaneity: "Go with the flow, man."

In the 1960s, hippie communes highly valued spontaneity and abhorred planning and structure of any kind. After leaving behind overly-structured institutions like schools and corporations, they longed for a completely free life. But unfortunately this was too idealistic; communities that had no planning also tended to not be very sustainable and usually folded in a year or so. If no one happened to feel like cooking or bringing in firewood, members starved or froze. And those members who took on more responsibility often became exhausted while providing for others.

Today it's rare to find a community based solely on spontaneity. Twin Oaks, for example, is able to be a stable community with no leaders or dogmas through an immense amount of structure and planning. Most communities have a strong leader and/or discipline and belief system. Work projects, meetings, finances and decision-making are usually fairly structured to allow efficiency and fairness. But it's likely that within any given community, there will be strong polarizations and often heated conflicts between the advocates of spontaneity and those of planning and structure.

Planning and structure help use people's time and resources efficiently. Spontaneity and "going with the flow" assure flexibility and enjoyment. But on the negative side, planning also can create rigidity and bureaucracy, and spontaneity also can create chaos. "Spontaneity types" detest meetings and often try to subvert them. "Planning types" often get carried away with control and can create a feeling of suppression and disempowerment of others.

Some communities have solved this dilemma by planning some activities and events, like meetings, very carefully and leaving other events, like celebrations, very spontaneous. In our com-

There are often heated conflicts between advocates of spontaneity and those of planning and structure

munity, a cooking schedule is planned with cooks signed up for each dinner. But clean-up is spontaneous. Whoever feels like it that day will do it, with everyone agreeing to do a minimum number of clean-ups per week. Other communities, like Findhorn, develop budgets and financial plans, but then maintain a flexible attitude towards actually following it, so that changes can always be made when it's important to listen to intuition rather than logic.

Workaholism and Meeting-itis:
Catching the contagious diseases of the mainstream

Living in the midst of a flow of people and within the demands of our goals causes tension and anxiety. There is a tremendous amount to be done. In a close group of committed people there is no escape from the immediacy of our living. There is no television, there is no sense of leaving it all behind at five o'clock, and there is no indifference. The joy and the difficulty of our communal effort is always with us. We all care a lot.[18]

Many people drawn to communities tend to be the "workaholic" types. They're never happy unless they're working all the time. Workaholism is a peculiar disease first caught in the mainstream, and it is hard to shake. In every community there's always more work to be done than there are people or time to do it. Nevertheless, you'll still see people scurrying around as if they really believed that if they only worked harder and faster, it would all get done! Not only must community members take care of their own needs and those of their family, as people everywhere do, but they're also trying to create something new, and this takes work.

What sometimes gets lost in the process is the peaceful feeling that people left the 9-to-5 rat race to find. What gets lost is the heart connection and the sense of caring between people. People in communities haven't all learned to leave their city conditioning behind. But unlike in the cities, at least there's usually someone around to remind others to "mellow out," as everyone is trying to change this old pattern. A balance is what is aimed for; outbreath (dynamic action/busy-ness) balanced with inbreath (rest/reflection). Some communities, such as Ananda, manage to be very efficient, getting a lot done, while at the same time maintaining a loving, centered consciousness and a peaceful environment.

*A widespread community
disease is called 'meeting-itis'*

For those who aren't the "workaholic" type, there is another widespread community disease called "meeting-itis,"
known to afflict especially those communities where there is a
strong emphasis on including everyone's input on every issue,
and everything is decided in lengthy group meetings. This can
exhaust members' time and energy. Lama Community in New
Mexico at one time had insisted on consensus of the whole community on every issue, large or small, as they had had such a
negative experience previously with someone trying to take over
the whole community. As a result they would have day-long
meetings every week! Finally they realized the mistake of this and
decentralized their decision-making process to smaller groups.

Not only do too-frequent meetings prevent work from getting done, but they also imply lack of trust that other people can
make a good and fair decision by themselves. And it produces a
lot of tension from having to sit patiently for hours just listening.
Tempers flare easily as patience dwindles.

One community in Maryland was started recently by people
who were so fed up with too many meetings in their previous
community in New York that they decided to have a "non-
community community" whose outstanding feature was no
meetings!

Other communities have dealt with this problem by keeping
a reasonable balance of time for meetings, enough so that real
conflicts can get aired and resolved and major decisions made,
with smaller decisions decentralized to specialized groups. Members are also encouraged to work out their conflicts on more of a
one-to-one basis before bringing them to the meeting, so that personal issues don't cloud business decisions.

Problems and Conflicts in Community 77

Transiency: **The grass is always greener on the other side of the fence**

In some communities, members come and go too frequently, so more time is needed to continually integrate new members and train them in the jobs others have left. This is a major problem often discussed at Twin Oaks Community in Virginia. Not only is this very inefficient in terms of productivity, but it often creates too much of a sense of temporariness in the community, leading to vague feelings of insecurity and sometimes fear of getting close to people, as they might leave.

Young people are most attracted to communities and are also the most transient segment of the population generally. They are often involved in a search for purpose in life, for their own identity, and for a place to live out their ideals. So a community is at first very appealing. Although no community can be ideal, these people are often easily deluded after staying a short time and believe "the grass is greener on the other side," and so they leave the community without trying to make it better. Commitment and perseverance are not strong points in most young people in this country.

But even older members find challenges in staying in communities, although these are based on a different set of needs. Joseph Blazi of the Harvard University Project for Kibbutz Studies found:

> Warmth and informality have not proven to be enough to retain members beyond certain life stages. Twin Oaks needs to respond to other individual needs which manifest themselves at other stages of life...If Twin Oaks does not include sufficient room for personal development, advancement, achievement, or hopes for greater economic resources (to allow for more personal choices), occupational diversity and challenges, how can these individuals see it as a long-term commitment?"[19]

Blazi also warns communities about making ideological purity paramount and belittling achievement.

At the Findhorn Community in Scotland, the transiency problem was improved by creating paid "staff jobs" to encourage longer-term commitment, and by providing better housing for those making longer-term commitments. Although sharing housing with others can be very stimulating for new members, longer-term members usually seem to require more space to avoid a sense of burn-out and overload with too many people. And longer-term members often begin having families, who require more space physically and psychically. Housing is a key reason for transiency problems. Communities that help provide for members' real needs and long-term considerations, with reasonable housing and balance of individual freedom, offer a more stable environment for attracting long-term members, especially families raising children.

The average American moves once every four years, according to studies, so actually transiency in communities is on a par with most of America. Even in Twin Oaks, one of the more transient communities, the average stay is four years.

Unresolved Family "Karma": "You sound like my mother!"

Communities tend to be important places for family "karma" to be worked out, as members often re-experience their previous home-life and attitudes. Regardless of a person's ideals about community, the reality is that on a subconscious level, a community recreates a family. Unfinished business with parents or siblings, relationship issues that have not been previously resolved, often come to the surface in a community. On a subtle, or sometimes even overt level, people gravitate toward archetypal roles: stern father/nurturing mother; controlling mother/ protective father; rebellious child; "Daddy's girl"; etc. There are often subconscious agreements in communities to act out these roles for each other in order to learn certain things or resolve something from the past.

It's very common, for example, as the Farm Community experienced, for feelings of rebellion against a father to get projected onto a figure of authority in the community or onto any strong male figure. Dependency issues—needing a mother figure to nurture and take care of us—can get projected onto a strong female, as happened at High Wind Community. Unresolved sibling rivalries that manifest as intense competition are also common.

Food Issues: The battle of the ages

"I've seen more people in communities ready to kill each other over food issues than anything," says Sun Bear, of the Bear Tribe in Washington. "What's important is not what you eat, but what's eating you!'' he adds. And Rick of Alpha Farm comments, ''The kitchen, dining room, and meal preparation have been a major community discussion item for the last six years!''

Food is obviously an important aspect of everyone's life, but it becomes a major issue in communities for two reasons. First, food is a symbol of nurturance, and if members are not feeling nurtured by the community in other ways, they may look unconsciously to food to provide what they feel is lacking. And secondly, diet is not just a matter of personal preference in many communities but also a matter of philosophy and belief.

In some communities a strict diet is uniformly adhered to. In other communities there's a diversity with some members having a macrobiotic diet, some a raw foods one, some a lacto-vegetarian one, and others a ''meat-and-junk-food'' attachment. So agreeing on a diet can be a political issue, a power struggle over what is the ''correct'' system. Some communities such as Sirius and Findhorn have dealt with this issue by providing communal meals based on majority preferences, and then allowing individuals to cook additional food according to their own preferences at home. Ultimately, many communities have learned that it's not what goes *into* our mouths that is important but what comes out—how loving one's words are, for example.

Cleanliness vs. Messiness: ''Your mother doesn't work here so you'll have to clean up after yourself!''

Do you really want to live in a commune? Get up early to cook for twenty people, find the kitchen littered with dirty bowls and cups half-full of cold tea...no milk, no bread (midnight munchers are always someone else of course, never me)...Another day, looking for a clean paint brush in the workshop—not one in sight...And who used the wood chisels for screwdrivers? Another day...Sewing. Eventually track down the sewing machine, but—surprise, surprise— it's messed up. Forgot to mention the cars. Have you heard what happens to cars that join communes? Too gory to tell!...Why don't I leave? You must be joking. This is only half the story![20]

There are always individual differences of tolerance of messiness, but beyond personal preferences, cleanliness is often an arena for power struggles. Sociologist Rosabeth Kanter found:

> There are more fights about cleaning than about any other single issue in urban communes...because relationships in communal households are negotiated rather than authoritative...Proponents of "clean" and "neat" are also proponents of order and collective responsibility. Those who are messy tend to resist order and deny the legitimacy of collective demands. This is a political issue and not entirely one of differing standards of cleanliness. One woman whose own room is spotless, for example, is among the messiest users of common space.[21]

Dr. Kanter also noted that community members respond to the state of the cleanliness of the house as a symbol for the state of the group, the quality of relationships among people at any given time. The cleaning issue is also discussed in terms of equity, she found. "Clean" people resent the fact that they must do more to make a comfortable environment for themselves than the "messy" people. And "clean" people who tend to get particularly fanatical about it may often have deep-seated "control" issues which may be the real cause of the problem, wanting to control their environment and/or other people.

In the 1960s hippie communes, cleanliness was seen as "bourgeois" and "anal-compulsive," so messiness was very revolutionary. This messiness repulsed middle-class visitors more than anything else in their lifestyle, and their repulsion delighted the hippies! This messy image still persists in the public's mind, although today most communities recognize the health value of cleanliness as well as the beauty that order creates, and they make a strong attempt to keep communal spaces clean. We've had quite a number of visitors to our community, for example, be very pleasantly surprised at how clean and orderly it is and comment on this to us. But since most communities have many adults and playful children using common spaces, keeping order is practically a full-time job and one that is seldom as well done as some members want it. Community living therefore also provides tremendous lessons in detachment from the physical plane!

Community property supposedly belongs to everyone. But from the way things are often treated, they seem to belong to no one! There's something about taking care of things held in common that seems to be a real challenge to many in communities. Some people have trouble taking care of their own property as well. They exhibit a lack of awareness of the physical plane in general. But for others who seem to take meticulous care of their own property, it's a real stretch for them to consider the good of the whole and take as good care of others' as they would of their own possessions. There's always the excuse that "someone else will fix it or clean it. I'm too busy and have more important things to do." There's also a tendency to continually "borrow" community property and "forget" to return it to its original place for the next person to use. A member of a British community notes:

> An aspect of ecology, which is what we're supposed to be into, is cherishing resources. Too much are we careless and abusive of what we have. There's an overall shabbiness and at times shittiness about communal areas (not so for private units). And lack of care breeds more uncaring, another discouragement to work.[22]

Somehow all our conditioning in society about private property orients us towards being very careful with our own things. If we don't fix them, who will? But look at how people treat public parks and buildings! In this context, the problem in communities is to be expected.

Often one or two very conscientious people in a community end up being the ones who clean up the communal living room after everyone else or fix all the broken tools and machinery. Sometimes these good people leave a community very disillusioned, leaving behind those who don't have much awareness of the good of the whole. And this is sometimes a reason why people who are able to take care of things, both their own and everyone's, don't join communities.

But on the other hand, community living can teach detachment from physical things as a good spiritual lesson. Not everyone takes good care of things, and you learn that people are more important, ultimately, than things. But learning how to take care of community or public property is what good stewardship of the earth is all about, and community gives plenty of hands-on training in this. Fortunately, there is a trend in some communities, such as Findhorn and Sevenoaks, towards training people in how to love and care for the physical environment, as there is consciousness in everything—mineral, vegetable and animal kingdoms as well as human. We honor all life when we care for it.

4 The Roots of Community: A Historical Overview and Comparison from the Early Monasteries to the Hippie Communes

*All things by immortal power
Near or far,
Hiddenly to each other linked are,
Thou canst not stir a flower,
Without troubling a star.* —FRANCIS THOMPSON

While the community movement certainly has its "wings," its inspiration and lofty visions of the future, it also has its "roots" in the rich experiences of the past. Historical contexts are often very helpful for understanding the evolution of present forms. Closer examination of the communal experiments of the 1960s is especially relevant in understanding the new communities of the 1980s.

The Old Monasteries and Ashrams

The roots of alternative communities actually go back to the ashrams and monasteries of ancient times, and some similarities are apparent between ancient and modern communities. For centuries, spiritual ashrams in the East have carried on the communal tradition, as students lived and worked communally and gathered around some spiritual teacher or sage. Historically, the Essenes and the early Christian communities were some of the first known intentional communities in the West. The Essenes banded together away from the world in 200 B.C. to live a spiritual life and purify themselves for the coming of Christ. They developed deep bonds with each other, shared various spiritual practices, ate a vegetarian diet, and lived a simple lifestyle. After Jesus' death, many of His followers formed similar communities to follow His teachings and learn to love one another. St. Paul started the first Christian communities all over Asia Minor.

The later Christian monasteries (Benedictine, Franciscan, Jesuit) carried on the tradition of community to support their spiritual life.

> The monasteries were by far the most imaginative, popular response to the protracted social crisis [of the Roman Empire's decline] . . . [The monks] had created a network of independent domestic economies that were the most stable, orderly, and productive in their society, with more than enough surplus to care for the needy, the aged, the indigent. . . They became the best farmers and craftsmen of their age, the inventors and disseminators of many new technologies . . . They traded goods, kept schools, distributed alms, transmitted the culture. . . Many of the most hostile wilderness areas of Europe were pioneered by the monks; many of the Western world's most basic techniques and machines were either invented or perfected in the monasteries.[1]

These early monasteries are an important monument to the

practical accomplishments of the communal lifestyle. And like many of the communities of the 1980s, they attempted to balance work with spiritual growth and to balance technology with ecology. Some modern communities seem to be a new incarnation of the old monastic tradition, on another turn of the spiral and minus the robes and celibacy.

The American Colonists

The American communal movement actually began with the Plymouth Pilgrims who set up the first community in America in 1620. Their "City on the Hill" was to serve as a model of the ideal Christian community with members pooling all their resources. Whenever there was a crisis in the community, a famine or an Indian attack, the community would declare a day of fasting and prayer to find out how they were out of harmony with God's will and so had drawn this crisis to themselves.

In 1663 Plockhoy's Commonwealth was founded in Delaware as a communal endeavor, but it was plundered by English conquerers a year later. The Ephratans founded an early community in 1673. Labadie Community was established in 1683 and lasted for forty years.[2] A community of Pietists and Rosicrucians was begun by Johann Conrad Biessel and John Peter Miller in 1694 in Philadelphia to enjoy religious freedom.[3] Benjamin Franklin attended meetings conducted by Biessel and published many of Biessel's works between 1730 and 1736.[4]

Each of the new towns established in America actually began as a small community, with new members signing a covenant to join, in many cases.[5] Each town usually had a shared ideology, and decisions were made through discussion and consensus. Town members pioneered a new way of life in the wilderness, cooperating with each other, working together on common projects, and sharing resources and skills for survival. These early towns were much like the intentional communities of today.

The Utopian Movement of the 1800s

In the 1800s in America, a wave of several hundred communities formed what is often called the "utopian movement" as its members envisioned the creation of a new and better society. The first of these communities had a religious orientation, carrying on to some extent the tradition of the Plymouth Pilgrims. Later ones, however, were founded by persecuted European Separatists and Pietists. The best known are Harmony Society (1804-

1904), The Shakers (1787-present), Oneida (1848-1881), Zoar (1817-1898), Amana (1843-1933), Brook Farm (1841-1847), and the Hutterian Brethren (1873-present).[6]

Between 1825 and the Civil War, over a hundred new communities were started, based more on a political-economic ideology than a religious one.[7] This was something new in the history of the American communal movement and was largely a response to the injustices and inhumanism of industrialization. These socialist communities were based on the ideas of Robert Owen, Charles Fourier, and Etienne Cabet in Europe, and Horace Greeley and Albert Brisbane in America. New Harmony (1825-1827), North American Phalanx (1843-1856), Modern Times (1851-1866), and Utopia (1847-1851) were the best known of these.[8]

Less well-known than these socialist communities were the spiritually-oriented Vedenta and Theosophical communities started around the turn of the century. Pt. Loma (started in 1897), Halcyon (1903), and Krotona (started in 1912 and still continuing today along with its sister community, Taormina) all were early Theosophical communities in California. Halcyon was the site of the first x-ray machine, and Pt. Loma had the first Greek theatre in America, featuring Greek mystery dramas and Shakespeare's plays. The role played by Theosophists and Vedantists in introducing ideas sacred in the East to Western culture is a historic example of the fruits of communal endeavor. The early efforts of these groups helped to make accessible the wide body of Eastern religious writings that are attracting so much interest today.[9]

Some lasting contributions to society have been made by these communities of the 1800s. For example, New Harmony (founded in 1814 in Indiana) pioneered the first kindergarten and infant school in America, the first public free school system in America, the first trade school system, the first free library, and the first geological survey. The Shaker communities produced furniture so finely crafted that it is still in demand today, over one hundred years later.

All of the utopian communities of the 1800s and early 1900s were rurally based and encouraged isolation from what they saw as the evils of society. Resources were pooled, through economic necessity as much as ideology, and the community was often organized around a single charismatic figure. This was especially true of the religious communities. Most communities encouraged sexual restraint or even celibacy (as did the Shakers) and were based on the nuclear family. The communities were often mini-societies, providing for all of their members' needs but requiring much hard work and personal sacrifice, along with renunciation of the ways of society.

The Roots of Community 87

Similarities Between Communities of the 1800s and 1980s

Communities of today are similar to those of the 1800s in that their purpose is to create a simpler way of life, living close to the earth, sharing resources with each other, and learning to be loving and giving in their relationships. The goal of communities now and then has been to create a life based on human equality, nonviolence, and cooperation. Like those of the 1800s, many communities today have arisen out of a response to the problems of society and the need to create a supportive environment in which to practice one's spiritual and/or political beliefs. In many ways, society today is experiencing a historical cycle similar to that of the mid-1800s, with an overemphasis on materialism, aggressiveness, and economic depression. Communities of both eras have usually asked certain disciplines of members, in addition to financial commitments. In the 1800s it was often celibacy or sex only for the procreation of children; today it might be vegetarianism or meditation. All of the communities in the 1800s and today have drawn committed, hard-working, pioneering people who enjoy the challenge of creating something new and dedicating their lives to a larger purpose.

Differences Between Communities of the 1800s and 1980s

The differences are very striking. Most communities today are not as communal or as restrictive as those of the last century. Oneida Community in New York required new members to transfer all property and possessions to the community, and all members' income was pooled. Even clothes were shared. Everyone lived in one large house and ate all meals together in a large dining room. Children were raised communally, and permission to have children needed to be obtained from the central committee. The entire community met every evening for prayers and discussion of community business. Mutual criticism was used to ensure conformity to group standards, and praise was mixed with fault-finding.

Most communities today do not require members to give all their possessions, pool their income, or raise their children communally, although a few do. Most contemporary communities do not eat all their meals together, and most members live in smaller group houses or even in individual houses.

Today, a great majority of communities are much smaller

than the large communities of the last century. While some, such as Spring Valley in New York and Findhorn in Scotland, have a hundred or more members and are creating their own mini-society to meet most of their members' needs (becoming "institutionally complete," in sociological terms), most groups today range in size from six to thirty, more like extended families than alternative societies.

Unlike communities of the 1800s, nearly all modern communities use some kind of psychological techniques, such as gestalt or psychosynthesis. This psychological sophistication is probably a major reason for their success. Since creating good relationships and working out interpersonal conflict is the major task of building community, this psychological orientation has been essential.

A most interesting change in modern communities from those of the previous century is the attitude toward sex. While most communities of the 1800s (with the notable exception of Oneida) encouraged celibacy or limited sexual expression, communities of the 1960s encouraged "free sex." Communities of the '80s seem to have learned from these experiences and have struck a balance between the two extremes—"responsible" use of sexual energy—neither repressing it nor over-indulging in it. The celibacy of some groups of the 1800s, like the Shakers, contributed to their non-survival: new recruits didn't replace the old members who died off, and there weren't enough potential new members being born to carry on the community. (Today's communities have the opposite problem: too many babies being born!)

A most important change from the 1800s is that a majority of today's communities govern themselves through some form of egalitarian process, such as a democratic vote of the majority or a group consensus process. Nearly all of the communities of the last century were governed by a more hierarchical and centralized leadership, usually one charismatic, authoritarian figure.

Another difference from the 1800s is that today there are many urban communities and shared households, whereas previously there were only rurally based ones like Zoar and Amana. Only a very few communities today are isolated. America has changed tremendously since the 1800s and become far more populated, so it's very difficult to maintain isolation. Increased communication, through telephones, mass media, convenient travel, and more opportunities for different kinds of relationships, lifestyles, and career choices, have prevented the insularity characteristic of communities in the last century. Most communities today encourage some interaction with society in order to build bridges with the mainstream, both to include the conveniences that society has to offer (such as electricity and medical services) and to keep in touch with the best of the intellectual and cultural developments of the city. In exchange, communities bring their spiritual and/or political values to society through educational or healing projects.

Another factor contributing to the lack of isolation today is the networking and interchanging membership among communities themselves. This is a new feature of communities, something rarely heard of in the 1800s. For example, even in our small community, four members lived at the Findhorn Community in Scotland, one at Ananda in California, one at a Zen community in Hawaii, one at Sandhill in Missouri, and two at a Rosicrucian community in Pennsylvania. In addition, everyone in our community has visited a few other communities, and this exchange is fairly typical of most communities today.

An important aspect in communities today which helps prevent isolation is the emphasis on "planetary consciousness," a concern for the well-being of the whole earth, rather than only for one's own group. Francois Dusquesne of the Findhorn Community comments:

> The communities of the nineteenth century failed because they attempted to create a separate utopia, as a negation of the advance of industrial culture, as a reaction. Community has to be on a higher turn of the spiral—identifying the planetary impulse behind community is of the utmost importance.

According to Rosabeth Kanter, communities today have a much greater chance of influencing society than did the communities of the 1800s

> partly because they are so much more numerous than in the past century, partly because the mass media and instant communication make them more visible, partly because of the stronger need for them, and partly because they exist in so many different forms and varieties, to almost all of which planners and architects of the social environment are giving serious attention.[10]

The Kibbutz

In the twentieth century, the most successful communal movement to date in terms of size, longevity, and economic stability, has been the kibbutz movement in Israel. Begun in the early 1900s by the worldwide Zionist movement, with a strong nationalist purpose in establishing and securing a nation for the Jewish people, the communalism of the kibbutz was essential for survival in the hostile desert areas of Israel.

The kibbutzim were strongly influenced by humanistic and socialist thought. There is a strong emphasis on equality and the ideal of "from each according to his/her ability, to each according to his/her need." Pooling all income and resources, collectivizing work, and communalizing child rearing all helped to build strong, self-reliant mini-societies. Originally the kibbutzim were mainly agricultural in focus, but in the last decades there has been a strong trend towards industrialization as well. With less than 4% of Israel's population, the kibbutzim produce 40% of the country's agricultural output and 7% of its industrial exports. The kibbutz provides for all food, housing, entertainment, education, and medical needs of its members. The kibbutzim are run as direct democracies with everyone having an equal say at weekly general meetings. Today there are about 250 kibbutzim in Israel, varying in size from two hundred to two thousand members, with a total of 110,000 members country-wide.[11]

The youth movement in Israel and in Jewish communities around the world has been extremely helpful in building the kibbutzim. The kibbutz has produced some of Israel's top government officials as well as artists, poets, and athletes. Unlike the American communities of both the nineteenth century and today, the kibbutzim are very involved in their state and in building a new nation. The government provides the land for new kibbutzim. Each individual kibbutz is part of one of the national kibbutz movements, unlike American communities, and there is mutual aid between the stronger and the weaker kibbutzim. Unlike American communities, which have all been pacifist in principle, the kibbutzim have always been committed to armed struggle for Israel's defense and security as a nation.[12]

Prof. Joseph Blasi at Harvard University's Project for Kibbutz Studies compares the kibbutz to an American community.

> It is more management-efficient, more family-oriented, richer, larger, less inter-personally cozy, less ecological, more technology-oriented, more involved with national defense and the realities of security and politics.[13]

The kibbutz also has a stronger sexual division of labor than most American communities, with more limited occupational choices for women.

The idealism and self-sacrifice prevalent in the founding groups of the kibbutz have been hard to maintain in the second and third generations, however, when the survival issue is not so prevalent. Some kibbutzim today have learned that total communalism may not be the ideal system to meet people's real needs on a long-term basis. There is now a blend of communalism and individualism in most of the kibbutzim. Members may now have personal bank accounts, and children sleep at home with their nuclear families rather than in communal houses.

According to sociologist Ira Cross, who teaches a course on the kibbutz at the University of Rhode Island, Israeli kibbutz members tend to seek institutional methods for solving interpersonal problems, and they could learn much from the conflict-resolution techniques used in many American communites. Today, there is beginning to be much interchange and dialogue between the kibbutzim and communities in other countries. Several international conferences on communities and kibbutzim have been held in Israel and Scotland.

The 1960s Hippie Movement

They took off in an odyssey of VW buses...and crisscrossed the country in search of parcels of unspoiled ground in between the polluted sprawl of cities. Like the immigrants of another century, they became homesteaders. Some were reborn to old gods. Some took their places among new brethren, acknowledging new teachers. They reclaimed earth as their mother, embraced strangers as sisters, and founded extended families. Easily they recognized each other in a kinship that flamed brighter than blood. And they called what was born at Woodstock—to the pulsing beat of their rock songs, what rose out of the rain and the mud—a new nation. Its name was...community.[14]

In the 1960s the largest wave of communalism up to that time spread across America. In 1970, the *New York Times* reported that there were over two thousand communes "of significant size" in thirty-four states—a conservative estimate, as the many thousands of small, urban cooperatives were not included.[15] Rejecting the rampant individualism of American culture and the greed, injustice, and violence of society, members of the counterculture—the "Woodstock Generation"—sought a return to a simpler and freer way of life, a childlike innocence in the purity of nature. Through the use of mind-expanding drugs and free sexual expression, hippies sought to free themselves from the conformity and rigidity of society.

For many hippies, the real urgency to move towards community came from a sense of total alienation, intense anger and despair about society. They felt a moral imperative to withdraw participation from the spiritual degeneracy of society which manifested as greed, violence, and war. They wanted to join with other like-minded souls for mutual support, for reinforcement of a shared identity, and for the celebration of liberation from social fetters.

Historically, the role of hippie communes in the '60s was one of de-crystallizing the rigidities of society, breaking up some of the old negative patterns. In the Hindu religion there is a triune deity: Brahma the Creator, Vishnu the Preserver, and Shiva the Destroyer. It is this last aspect of deity that was needed in the 1960s, and perhaps the role played by the radical political activists served a divine purpose in a society grown fat, complacent, and unjust. The movement was needed to crack open society so that it might receive the impulses of a new age that was dawning.

Life magazine, in a 20-year anniversary look at the '60s, recently reported:

> [These people] wanted to change the world. And in unexpected ways, they did. They helped end the Vietnam War and began the women's movement. Their love of health food, rock and roll, and drugs turned those trends into mega-businesses; their fierce outspokenness about nuclear power and the environment and the arms race made those major political issues. They altered American consciousness forever.[16]

All who experienced the tremendous exhilaration and freedom of the hippie movement have never been the same since. We ourselves were among these. We knew the power that comes from being totally unpredictable and flexible, able to change at any moment, so we could never be pinned down and trapped by society's games and security needs. We all had tremendous courage and a strong sense of moral integrity that obligated action against injustice. We felt powerful because we constantly reinforced each other by gathering in the thousands at mass political demonstrations, mass rock concerts, and "be-ins." The influence of our peers was all-pervasive; deep bonds of friendship and trust grew out of our shared political struggles, acid trips, and communal adventures.

One of us (Corinne) lived in several different kinds of hippie communes of the time—the urban crash pad, the political commune and the rural commune—and what follows are descriptions based largely on firsthand personal experiences. Exploring the hippie communes of the '60s is helpful in understanding the current trends in the new communities of the '80s.

The Urban "Crash Pad"

If you go to San Francisco
    Be sure to wear some flowers in your hair...
Summertime will be a love-in there.
    All across the nation
    There's a strange vibration
    People in motion, people in motion
    There's a whole generation
    With a new explanation...

—Scott McKenzie
If You Go to San Francisco

In 1967, the Haight-Ashbury "Summer of Love" and the flower children who wore bright beads and headbands caught the imagination of the media. Thousands of would-be hippies flocked to San Francisco. Hippie "crash pads" (communes where hippies could spend a night or two) began popping up in cities and college towns across the country. The hippies saw themselves as the children of the future, come to awaken the sleeping masses of society and free them from their chains. "Freaking people out" by crazy behavior was a total "high." The spirit of freedom was alive, and it was just what society, with its conformity and uptightness, seemed to need. To the hippie communards, life was an exciting adventure once they had freed their hearts and minds from 9-to-5 slavery. They worshipped those among them who could be the most crazy and "far-out." Their motto was "go with the flow"—go along with whatever was happening in the moment, and don't try to control things. And above all, "do your own thing."

Of course, being hippies, they weren't "into" having any house rules in their communes, so whoever felt like cooking would cook, and whoever felt like washing dishes would do so. Needless to say, it was a male chauvinist heaven, as the men would spend most of the day hanging out, trading dope stories, and the women always seemed to keep things together and feed everybody. Keeping the place clean was, of course, very "bourgeois" and "square."

The crash pad element was exciting as all kinds of "fellow freaks" would show up to crash on the floor or share a sleeping bag. Hippies believed in being as sexually free as possible. "Make love, not war," they proclaimed. Sexual hang-ups got society into the mess it was in, they claimed. Sexual frustration was subliminated into violence, war, and oppression, so it was a good idea to "sleep around."

Hippies often lived on food stamps and unemployment, drove old VW buses with paisley tapestry on the ceiling, and wore gypsy or Indian costumes to "freak out the straights." Many religiously dropped acid with fellow commune members every Saturday night, to the mind-exploding music of the Jefferson Airplane, the Moody Blues, and Grateful Dead. Many of these rock groups, like the Dead and the Airplane, who were their heroes, lived communally themselves in the Haight-Ashbury in large group houses. Hippies believed that frequent acid trips helped overcome "ego hang-ups," like power trips and status and security needs, and helped them merge into a sense of oneness with each other.

Hippie communards worked on creating a real feeling of community and neighborhood in certain parts of the country where they congregated, and many service projects were set up. Food co-ops (originally called "food conspiracies") were set up, selling healthy food at good discounts to members. Free health clinics and self-help centers were established. Free food was given out in the parks by the Diggers. Free concerts with big name rock groups were held in the parks. Neighborhood child care centers were opened. Tool exchanges that worked like libraries where tools could be checked out were created. Neighbors tore down the fences between their houses and created cooperative gardens. Empty lots became community gardens. Hippies were creating their own society to meet their needs, and the sense of euphoria and empowerment from these experiences has never left those who were part of the special magic of those days.

These co-ops, clinics, and gardens created by the hippies were the seeds of a whole new culture that is flourishing today. It was the positive, life-affirming, creative impulse that balanced the destructive impulse of the '60s. Many of these projects are still continuing today in the same form or in new ones, while others have folded.

Today the Woodstock Generation is not so visible and there are few, if any, hippie crash pads still around. But there are literally thousands of urban and suburban shared households—legacies of the '60s—where people live together to cut costs and to experience a sense of mutual support in an extended family.

Shared households of the '80s are generally more structured and organized than the earlier crash pads. Members usually share the household tasks and houses are fairly clean and tidy. Usually there are rules about visitors—how many, where they sleep, how much they contribute in work and money—in order to maintain a balance between members' needs for privacy and socializing. Some households are still using drugs; some prohibit it. Some are couples in committed relationships, others are into open relationships. Most houses are somewhere in between. Some houses have communal child rearing, but most give parents the primary responsibility, with others helping out. And most interestingly, today a large number of shared urban households are made up of middle-class professionals! The number of shared household members today who would call themselves "hippies" is probably small, but most of these members would probably identify certain aspects of their lifestyle as "alternative," since many of them are interested in personal growth, health foods, alternative energy, and radical politics.

The Political Commune

Come mothers and fathers throughout the land,
And don't criticize what you can't understand.
Your sons and your daughters are beyond your command,
Your old road is rapidly agin'.
Please get out of the new one if you can't lend
  your hand
For the times, they are a-changin'.

—Bob Dylan
The Times, They Are a-Changin

Sixties communes of the political variety were distinguished by their strong ideology and activist orientation. These had a distinctly political purpose: to organize demonstrations against the Vietnam War, against racism, against corporate imperialism abroad, against an irrelevant educational system. In those days, it was far easier to identify what they were against than to say what they supported. Political communards worked to create a new way of life, a model of a non-monagamous, cooperative, socialist lifestyle. The goal was to try to break up bourgeois or middle class individualistic, possessive, separative traits. In some of these communes, all money and possessions were pooled.

Political communards were more serious than their crash

pad counterparts. They were very idealistic and spent much of their time organizing demonstrations against what they saw as the "imperialist evils" in the world. Endless meetings were held to plan strategies. They printed posters, leafleted campuses and factories, learned karate and self-defense for possible confrontations with police, and studied books by their socialist heroes, Che Guevera and Mao Tse Tung. They usually made sure that all household tasks were shared by everyone; men as well as women cooked and cleaned up. Some of the first women's liberation groups to fight male oppression grew out of political communes.

Communards smoked a lot of dope, dropped acid with each other, and played endless rock and roll. The acid trips brought deep soul-searching about the nature of reality, about the reasons for the injustices and hypocrisy of society, and about the fear and confusion they all felt about life. Sometimes they'd feel that the situation was so desperate in the world that they'd probably lose their lives fighting in the coming revolution.

But one of the main problems in these communes was that members were not very psychologically sophisticated. Their method of trying to change themselves and each other was guilt-tripping. Everyone was expected to express qualities of the true "socialist revolutionary" overnight. When making a revolution, there was no time for organic growth and gradual change. And to focus on oneself and personal problems was considered self-centered and not "serving the people."

> [T]here was a feeling that we were just not moving fast enough in transforming our personal lives, a fear that we were just still too bourgeois...
>
> When any of us [withheld commitment] at some level of consciousness we were each painfully aware of it and of the consequences. Constantly aware of our shortcomings, we suffered from guilt and self-hatred which was often unburdened on our communal sisters and brothers. The more bourgeois someone felt, the more she or he bourgeois-baited others...We pushed one another to live up to unattainable, necessarily frustrating, abstract revolutionary ideals.[17]

Needless to say, guilt-tripping didn't work very well. It created much tension between people as a result of judgments about who was more socialist than whom. And this would often cause a terrible "vibe" or feeling in the commune. (One couldn't always change twenty years of middle-class conditioning overnight, just because one wanted to!) Many political communes broke up due to the lack of skill in resolving interpersonal conflict and in building living, supportive relationships. But their failure to survive was also partly because of the intensity of the times, the political harrassment by police, FBI and CIA agents, and the ever-present fear of arrest.

The political communes of the '60s were similar in some ways to communities of today in that they had a strong sense of purpose, of a mission to change the world and to create a more just and humane society. Many communities today have a similar purpose but differ considerably in their philosophy and in the strategy which they use to attain their goals. Some current communities, such as the Farm in Tennessee and its Plenty Network, and the Community for Non-Violent Social Action in Washington, D.C., work to provide food for hungry people, both in American ghettos and in the Third World. Other more politically-oriented communities, such as Traprock Peace Center at Woolman Hill in Massachusetts and Movement for a New Society in Philadelphia, still have a strong focus on demonstrations and confrontations with injustice, but they are more aware psychologically and work on their own personal traits of injustice or aggression.

The Rural Commune

By the time we got to Woodstock, we were half a million strong,
And everywhere was a song and a celebration.
We are stardust, we are golden,
And we got to get ourselves back to the Garden.

—Joni Mitchell
Woodstock

A third type of community that has its roots in the '60s, and still flourishes today, is the rural commune, part of the "back-to-nature" movement. Many of the Woodstock Generation felt burned out (and smogged out!) in cities. They felt there had to be a simpler way to live, a way more in touch with nature. So great hordes of hippies packed up and moved to places like Woodstock, New York, or the then-famous Wheeler's Ranch in northern California, or communal farms all over Oregon, New Mexico, and Colorado.

The communal wooden A-frame dwellings, the Indian teepees, the domes, all built in beautiful forests in the mountains, caught the imagination of the hippies and spoke to a deep longing in their hearts to return to the purity and healing power of nature. Like the pioneers of early America, the hippies left behind the conventionality and the degeneracy of the cities. As poet Gary Synder observed, their generation was the first to grow up on TV. Having seen images of all historical periods, they had the whole range to choose from. Many of them liked the pioneer/ Indian scenario on TV the best, so why not create it for themselves?

The rural communes the hippies created were survival-oriented. Their main focus was on surviving in the wilderness, building a self-sufficient community, growing all their own food, producing as much of their own energy as possible, and making much of their own clothing and tools. This kept them very busy and there wasn't much time for other pursuits. Life was simple and basic. Politics or abstract philosophical issues were not of much interest, nor was talk of the latest events in the cities. Some communards seldom played radios or read newspapers. Evenings were often spent around the fire, playing drums, singing songs, telling jokes, discussing the garden or the goats, passing around a few "joints" of marijuana.

The rural communes often seemed like paradise, at least in the summer, with the cool streams and lush gardens of rural farms. But then the inevitable snows would come, and with them came the hassle of cutting wood to stay warm, the restlessness of cabin fever, and the impassability of mountain roads. And as happened in the political communes and the crash pad scenes, the lack of psychological skills and awareness in human relationships led to tremendous unresolved tensions among members.

But many of these commune members were hardy souls, and they survived the harsh storms of winter and the harsher storms of human conflicts and went on to build new farms and even small villages. Inspired by visions of healing the earth ("caring for the Mother," as they called it) and following in many of the traditions of the Native Americans, these new pioneers armed themselves with tools and simple techniques from their bibles, the *Whole Earth Catalogue* and *Mother Earth News*. And they survived...and grew.

Today there are thousands of rural communes all over America, some started in the '60s and others more recently. The less structured ones, such as Drop City in Colorado, have long since collapsed, as did their counterparts in the transient crash pads of the cities. But those that were more organized and drew committed members, such as The Brotherhood of the Spirit (now called the Renaissance Community) in Massachusetts and the Hog Farm in California, have survived even to this day. The communes that had a clearer sense of purpose, a positive vision of the future, and took practical steps to accomplish that vision have continued. The others drew searchers and curiosity-seekers who banded together merely in rejection of society and not to create something new.

Some Comparisons: '60s Communes/'90s Communities

The following comparisons, based on our personal experiences, are generalizations (there are always exceptions, of course):

1960s	1990s
• Freedom and "doing your own thing" most important value; "laying a trip" on someone is a cardinal sin	• Cooperation with others and "the good of the whole" important; everyone needs to contribute his/her share; erratic behavior less acceptable
• Few rules, restrictions, or expectations; largely unstructured; "work only if you feel like it"; spontaneity highly valued	• Agreed-upon rules and expectations; fairly structured work and financial requirements
• Mainly alternative lifestyle and values—drugs, rock and roll, "free sex"	• Variation in lifestyle in different communities—ranging from alternative to middle-class professional
• Primarily negative orientation—reaction to a society seen as bad and harmful	• Primarily positive orientation—building a new society, new institutions and/or bridging with best in society
• Retreat or withdrawal orientation	• Service-to-others orientation
• More transient membership; communes dissolve easily; "crash pads" very prevalent	• More committed membership and long-lasting communities
• Non-exclusive; usually anyone with same lifestyle can join	• More restrictive about membership—must be harmonious with group and committed to group's purpose
• "Bad Karma" to turn any visitors away	• Open to visitors by prior arrangement only

1960s	1990s
• Visitors not always requested to contribute money or labor; no formal guest programs	• Visitors usually requested to contribute money and/or labor; more structured guest programs
• "Free sex;" emphasis on learning to lose one's inhibitions; sometimes group sex practiced	• Sexuality somewhat more restrained but looser than conventional standards; celibacy in some groups
• "Male chauvinist" attitudes; clear male/female roles	• "Women's liberation" prevalent; breakdown of traditional roles
• Mostly single members and non-exclusive couples	• Often a majority of monogamous couples and families
• Little emphasis on personal growth techniques and therapeutic tools	• More psychologically sophisticated; personal growth techniques in most communities
• Return to a romanticized rural past; rejection of technology; few communication links with society	• Closeness to nature highly valued, but appropriate technology also welcomed; more communication links with society (telephone, TV, radio, some computers)
• Return to innocence of childhood; rejection of responsibility	• Generally more mature and responsible adult attitudes; valuing some balance of playfulness, although sometimes too serious
• No formal ideology, except belief in "going with the flow"—whatever happens is meant to happen	• Well-developed belief system—usually spiritual and/or political
• Personal liberation most important	• Creating a new social and/or economic order is as important as personal liberation
• "Hanging out" very valued and "living in the now"	• More of a work-orientation, with accomplishment more highly valued and some retreat time available. Sometimes too "workaholic"
• Usually anti-intellectual; body and feelings more emphasized than mind	• Wholeness most important in most groups—integration of mind/feelings/body/spirit

1960s	1990s
• Emphasis on "dropping the ego"—transcending ego needs	• More acceptance of the role of ego in personal development; necessity for ego first to be strong before truly going beyond it
• Anti-political (except for intentionally political communes organized around a specific ideology)	• Some political involvement in most groups; "planetary consciousness" important—awareness of earth itself as a being
• "Tribal" orientation—strong emphasis on the group; togetherness emphasized; often over-crowding; privacy was "bourgeois"	• More of a balance between individual and group needs; private space more respected
• Order and cleanliness regarded as "uptight" and "bourgeois"	• Order and cleanliness valued in most groups
• Little true self-sufficiency; often food stamps and contributions from parents essential for survival	• Self-sufficiency in food and energy increasing, but emphasis on interdependence with local area (with some outside donations if non-profit)

The 1970s: The Real Story Behind the "Me Generation"

You say you want a revolution, well you know
You better change your head instead...

—John Lennon
Evolution

The media presented 1970 as the "Me Generation," people forsaking the idealism of the 1960s and "copping out" by focusing only on themselves in a selfish way and forgetting about the world. But, in fact, a tremendously powerful seed has been nurtured in the womb of the '70s in a quiet and subtle way. It is the seed of self knowledge and inner strength.

In the '60s many young people developed the courage to stand up and oppose evil and violence in the world. In the '70s many of these same people developed the courage to face an even bigger enemy: the evil and the violence within each of us. They gained the strength that comes only from facing their own shadow, beginning to battle their own negativity and inner darkness in order to create real peace in the world.

The lessons of the '70s were essential for building solid foundations for the new communities of the '90s. For many, the journey inward to change themselves came at a point of desperation. They had felt disillusioned to discover that many of the ideals they'd been taught about America as a land of truth and justice were actually lies. Many were angry and confused. The only positive ideals they found were in being together with their peers—their "brothers and sisters"—and getting high through music and drugs. They knew clearly what was wrong in the world and what they wanted to get rid of: the war in Vietnam, racism, oppressive government and schools. They tried so desperately to awaken the consciousness of Americans to the evils of its government that they nearly burned ourselves out.

By the early '70s many of the formerly inspiring political leaders were dead, in jail, or underground. And those who weren't seemed to be on a power trip of some kind. Most of the hippie communes of the '60s had folded, and heavy heroin use and violence haunted the former enclaves of "flower power" in the cities. The choices for many young people seemed to be between becoming a martyr for the cause in a doomed attempt to catalyze a revolution, or else retreating to the wilderness. In order to survive physically and psychologically, many felt they had to leave the political movement and find something more life-affirming.

An answer came from Bob Dylan, the prophet and mirror of his generation, in his "New Morning" album. A message of hope—a new beginning—was proclaimed after all the "hard rain" had fallen. People "headed for the hills," as his songs advised, to be healed by the beauty of nature. And they also journeyed inward to explore their own inner world. The images of a positive world, which beckoned in psychedelic drug experiences, held up a promise of light at the end of the tunnel. But drugs were a mirror; they showed the light within each person but also the shadows. Many came face to face with the reality that they had to change themselves *first*, not society, if they wanted to create a truly new order and not just replace one oppressive structure with another different, though equally oppressive one.

Drugs began the process of self-revelation, but they produced only temporary flashes of insight, previews of coming attractions. People always came down after a drug trip and seemed to be right back where they started. It soon became clear that only a deep commitment to truly working on their own negativity through their own efforts—without chemical crutches—would

The Roots of Community 103

create the real inner change. It was meditation and the newly discovered tools of the human potential movement that would really help the inner journey.

The biggest change experienced in this inner journey was that people no longer blamed *others* for the wrongs in the world or for the wrongs they personally experienced. Since they no longer saw themselves as victims, they could experience a greater sense of power and effectiveness in the world. Many began to take responsibility for the reality they were creating, knowing that they draw difficult situations and experiences to themselves by their own attitudes.

By resolving inner conflicts with parents, for example, people stopped projecting rebelliousness against parents onto other authority figures in society and so developed greater strength and clarity to fight against real abuses of power in the world. By first owning and then working to overcome their own power trips, people learned how to use real power for the good of others and for transforming society. By learning tolerance and respect for differences, people learned how to truly dialogue with their "opponents." By developing spiritual detachment from the success or failure of actions and projects, a great deal of emotional energy was freed up for other uses.

There was a growing realization among many on the inner journey that polarizing into positions of "us" vs. "them" and "we're right, you're wrong" actually increased the negativity in one's opponent and empowered them, thus adding to the problem. (For instance, the police in the streets of Berkeley became more violent and more like "pigs" the more people fought them and called them "pigs".) Becoming more at peace within oneself and more centered was slowly being acknowledged as a way to increase peace in the world.

The inner journey of the 1970s brought the realization of how interconnected we all are, how much we affect each other unconsciously. When one goes deeply enough into the "me," oneness, the shared ground of being, is discovered. From this experience, the more one truly understands former "enemies," the more one is able to find real solutions to problems by emphasizing one's shared humanity. As Theodore Roszak says, the needs and rights of one person are congruent with the needs and rights of the planet. As we understand ourselves more deeply, we can help the world more wisely.

In the '60s, hippies had to prove to the world that they were different from "straight" society by their wild clothes and behavior. Perhaps they had to be so demonstrative because they were trying out this new identity and weren't so sure deep down that they were really all that different. But by the '70s and '80s, with all the real inner growth and development, many knew they were profoundly different from much of society. So they no longer had to look so outwardly different. Instead, they could focus attention on building bridges to those in the mainstream who were open to more real and lasting change. Love has to build the bridge so that truth may cross.

Political activists who dropped out of the movement in the '70s to focus on their inner growth are often now bringing a greater wisdom and power to the peace movement, as evidenced by the peaceful and positive nature of the march of half a million people in New York in June of 1982, and by other recent marches. From our own research and experience, and contrary to the media image, the majority of real activists from the '60s have not "sold out" at all. Many who took the inner journey are still organizing people around nuclear issues, women's issues, ecology, etc., but they are doing so in a more loving and inclusive manner. Many are working to change the world in new and effective ways: humanizing business and government; developing alternative sources of energy to reduce dependence on nuclear energy; organizing citizen exchanges with the Soviet Union; educating young people in peaceful and cooperative values; teaching people how to become self-sufficient in food and health needs. (California State Assemblyman and activist Tom Hayden noted that many former hippies he meets now in coats and ties still have "the old fire of radicals in their eyes.") and it is these same former activists and veterans of the inner journey who are often starting and joining the more mature and stable communities of the 1990s all over the country, bringing with them the spirit of freedom and celebration that was the hallmark of the 1960s.

Once a person has begun to work on her/his own negative emotions—the "shadow," in Jungian terms—it's much easier to get along with other people and to live with them. Today's communities, where members use tools for personal growth, do not fold after a few months as they did in the '60s, before the wisdom of the human potential movement and the "Me Generation" helped people learn how to release more of their negative patterns. In the cycles of human growth, there must always be an inbreath, a turning inward to the source of one's being, before there can be a truly balanced and mature outbreath to help and heal our world.

As social researcher Daniel Yankelovitch observed:

Those engaged in their own search for self-fulfillment are at the same time doing society's necessary work, conducting experiments with their own lives that will in the long run benefit society...The search for self-fulfillment is not merely as its critics claim, an outpouring of self-centeredness and self-indulgence—the excesses of a "me generation" made decadent by too much affluence...[It] may yet prove to be a transition phase from slavish rejection of the old rules to a synthesis of old and new...It is nothing less than the search for a new American philosophy of life...the leading edge of a genuine cultural revolution.[18]

The Cults and How They Differ from True New Age Communities

At the same time that the hippie communes were attracting major attention, the so-called "cults"—manipulative, authoritarian mass movements—began growing in popularity and attracting many young people who were burned out on drugs or generally confused and lost. People often substituted dependency on the cult leader for their dependency on drugs.

Today, the cults are still recruiting large numbers of people and are still sensationalized in the media. Cults are very attractive to some types of personalities. Many people are desperate for a way to change themselves and to change the world, and they are so confused and frightened by all the rapid changes they (as well as society) have plunged into, that anyone who seems to offer the security of having all the answers (and who can tell them what to think and do) is hard to resist. Many are so lonely and alienated, having dropped out of school, family, religion, and/or friendships, that any group which looks loving and supportive is very magnetic, even if the price is one's personal freedom. Many people are so insecure that they are looking for someone who will accept responsiblity for their life. In these cases, a cult leader doesn't have to brainwash someone. As psychologist Ken Wilbur puts it, "all they have to do is show up and smile."[19] In weak personalities, the very legitimate search for truth and for spiritual values and transcendence is easily exploited by power-driven "cult" leaders. "People are starved for spirituality," says Jacob Needleman, a philosophy professor at San Francisco State College who has studied the new religions. "It's a need as basic as anything else."[20]

The problem with defining exactly what a cult is, and the point at which a group actually crosses the line between what is acceptable and what is not, depends a great deal on a person's values. As Ken Keyes of the Living Love community expressed it:

A "cult" is a term you would use to apply to that which you don't like...So I don't really have much use for that term in my life. I could tell you the groups that I feel are sincerely trying to do something good for the world, and that I like, so I don't consider them "cults." And I could tell you the groups I don't like that I would call "cults."

A recent work by two university professors explores the phenomena of "cults" and their effectiveness in changing peoples' attitudes and behavior.

Attempts to shape attitudes are part of every church, school system, military establishment and government. Ultimately there is nothing inherently wrong, in the moral sense, with the practice of shaping attitudes, even if it brings about radical change. The "wrongness" depends only on whether we approve of *who* is shaping the attitudes and for *what* purpose. This is the fundamental issue with which we as citizens must come to grips.[21]

Saul Levine, head of the Psychiatry Department at Sunnybrook Medical Center in Toronto, has been thoroughly studying the so-called cults for over fifteen years and has interviewed over one thousand cult members. He found that:

The reality of these groups did not accord with press sensationalism. I have seen "bad things," but in the hundreds of groups I know of firsthand, I have never seen excesses worthy of the pejorative label of "cult."[22]

Levine found that recruitment of members by the cults couldn't be too sinister because only one out of every five hundred young people approached by cult members actually joined. In his view, young people join these groups as desperate attempts to grow up in a society that places obstacles in the way of normal youthful yearnings. Joining a radical group is a way to begin the necessary separation from parents and the formation of an independent identity, but within the context of an "extended family" and a sense of safety and belonging. He found that more than 90% of these young people return home within two years and resume their previous middle-class lives, but few feel the experience was a mistake. Most take back with them permanent values and integrate these into their present lives.[23] *Newsweek* magazine reports:

For all the talk of cultist "mind-raping", "brainwashing", and "spiritual fascism," most members eventually simply drop out of their own free will. In the end it is often a matter of disillusionment.[24]

The most important safeguard against experiencing a cult is examining one's own motivations for joining a group. Ram Dass warns:

In truth, we are only ever entrapped by our own desires and clingings. If you want only liberation, then all teachers will be useful vehicles for you. They cannot hurt you at all. If, on the other hand, you want power, a teacher may come along who talks about liberation but subtly attracts you by your desire for power. If you get caught and become a disciple of such a teacher, you may feel angry when this teacher turns out to be on a power trip, not leading you to enlightenment. But remember: at some level inside yourself, you already knew. Your attraction to this teacher was your desire for power. Your anger is nothing more than anger toward yourself.[25]

Although it may be hard to define exactly what a cult is since it is such a subjective, emotionally-laden label, we would, however, like to warn people about groups that manifest many of the following traits:

1. Encourages the violation of personal ethics or encourages deception to prove loyalty to the group

2. Encourages the relinquishment of personal responsibility for actions

3. Restricts access to outside people or information

4. Inhibits critical thinking so that "group think" predominates, and many subjects are taboo for discussion

5. Restricts the ability to leave the group

6. Restricts privacy

7. Uses intense indoctrination

8. Demands absolute obedience

9. Applies intense pressure towards group conformity

10. Demands sterotyped behavior physically and/or psychologically—the "assembly line" effect ("cloning")

11. Encourages over-dependency

12. Manipulates feelings in a conscious way

13. Appeals to fear of not being saved or enlightened

14. Appeals to greed

15. Appeals to power

16. Appeals to the glamour of being the elect

17. Appeals to vanity and flattery of the ego

18. Uses guilt to control behavior

19. Uses humiliation to control

20. Uses intimidation or threats

21. Plays on low self-esteem or feelings of inadaquacy

22. Encourages sexual relationships with teacher

23. Uses high-pressure sales pitches and plays on loyalty of friends to attract members

24. Evidences extreme paranoia and the stockpiling of firearms for "protection"[26]

To us, the bottom line that distinguishes what might be called a cult from communities described in this book is the interference with a person's free will rather than the nurturance of its use. Free will is the most basic and inviolate spiritual principle on earth. A true spiritual teacher will respect a person's free will and encourage a follower to freely make her/his own choices, to take responsibility for any mistakes made and to learn from them.

5 The Diversity of Economic Systems in Communities

When you work you are a flute through whose heart the whispering of the hours turns to music. To love life through labor is to be intimate with life's inmost secret. All work is empty save when there is love, for work is love made visible. —KAHLIL GIBRAN,
THE PROPHET

Introduction

New age communities have developed economic systems ranging from totally communal systems (where all resources and income are pooled, businesses are communally owned, and all expenses are paid out of a common pot) to totally individual systems (with individually owned houses, land, and businesses, but shared values and activities.) Today, there's probably a community with an economic approach that is suitable for every type of person. To some people, sharing of income and resources is what community is all about; to others, it inhibits real feelings of community because it's forced. Our purpose here is to illustrate the options available. Each has its positive and negative aspects; communities choose an economic system that most closely fits their values.

The majority of communities have some mix of individuals earning their own income, with a voluntary sharing of some income to meet the expenses for shared land, housing, and other resources. More and more new groups these days are being formed as "villages" rather than as "communities." Places like Sparrow Hawk in Oklahoma and Monroe Institute in Virginia are centered around a church or educational facility. Members buy their own house lot, and often some land is held in common.

It is instructive to look at some of the positive and negative aspects possible in both communal and private systems. From our research on communities and from our own experience of living in communities for many years, we have made the following observations and recognize that there are exceptions.

• Communal models provide a vision of the potential for humanity to live in a relationship of deeper sharing. They give people the experience of the processes of compromise, tolerance, conflict resolution, synthesis and right relationships, if the community works well.

• Communal sharing seems to work most effectively with a strong authority figure or a very structured system with a planning group who have the power to enforce sharing and income-producing activities and to allocate people to work when and where they're most needed. Although more efficient economically, the trade-off here is less individual freedom.

• Communal sharing seems to attract mainly younger people and those with few resources to share. It sometimes attracts dependent-type people, rather than self-responsible types, and those who are projecting needs for parental figures to take care of them and create a sense of security.

• For communal or partial sharing systems to work well requires mature individuals who have learned how to take full financial responsibility for themselves; otherwise dependency, strong authority structures or burn-out of competent people result. Although people are often drawn to communities looking for a simpler, more relaxed lifestyle, in fact, they usually end up working harder but enjoying it more because it's for things they believe in and with people they enjoy.

• Strongly independent, individualistic people do not usually stay in communal systems for long. Either the system changes or they leave. Yet even without the economic incentives of an individual system, some of these types of people will work hard when they are inspired by high principles and ideals. Often these people "burn-out" and need to learn to nurture themselves.

• Many communities that have remained viable for longer periods of time have gradually shifted from totally communal economics to a more individual system. The needs for privacy and autonomy in people apparently run deep. (The most recent and dramatic example of this trend is The Farm community in Tennessee which almost went bankrupt with its communal system and so changed to individual incomes with some shared resources.) There are a few notable exceptions to this change, however, such as Twin Oaks and Alpha Farm.

• Patterns of individually-chosen cooperation and sharing of resources by degrees seem more in tune with American values, as most people are not willing to accept the strong central authority that usually accompanies communal systems. When the community doesn't provide employment for people, they have to grow and take more responsibility for themselves.

• Communities often face the challenge of creating systems that provide for the needs of two types of people drawn to them: young people with no resources to share, who need to learn how to take more responsibility and to develop their skills; and secondly, older people who have learned responsibility and have developed skills and financial resources to share, but are looking for a simpler and more meaningful lifestyle.

	COMMUNAL		PRIVATE	
	Positive	*Negative*	*Positive*	*Negative*
Money and Time	+requires less individual income & time & energy to live well	-difficult to attract wealthy & professional members	+easier to attract wealthy & professional members	-requires more income & time & energy to live well
Resources	+efficient use of resources +equality of resources	-possible conflicts over use of resources	+no conflicts over resources +easy to have sufficient resources if motivated and skilled	-inequality of resources -inefficient use of resources -difficult to have sufficient resources if not motivated or skilled
Sharing	+develops greater sharing, cooperation and sense of good of whole +helps provide for less able			-reinforces old patterns of selfishness -continues societal competition and alienation
Community Spirit	+develops greater sense of community because all economic decisions affect all, so feel in it together +builds close relationships & trust	-more group meetings needed to decide on finances	+less time spent in group meetings	-can be dispersing to sense of community -relationships often not as close -can be resentment over inequalities
Freedom		-less individual freedom of choice -less incentive to innovate -more uniformity	+more individual freedom of choice +greater incentive to innovate +more creativity and uniqueness	
Individual Development	+more time freed for personal growth	-creates dependence on more competent people	+develops more individual responsibility	-easier to get locked into careers and not have time for personal growth
Beauty		-standards often reflect lowest common denominator	+can reflect higher standards, depending on individual	
Society		-difficult to do; it is counter to societal conditioning	+easier to do as it is in line with societal conditioning	

• If communities get too far into debt, members are often pushed to work outside the community to produce cash income. This can be either helpful for members' growth or debilitating, depending on the type of work and work environment.

• Some communities are able to develop as a business through healing, educational, or skills training programs for the public. This helps alleviate the dichotomy of work inside/low income, work outside/high income.

• Entrepreneurship is a recent trend in many communities, as members are starting small businesses with new ideas and products in order to survive financially. Small business entrepreneurship is becoming more positively valued in communities when it creates goods and services that support cooperative and ecological values.

• Communities that have developed worker-owned and managed businesses seem to have the most success. The level of commitment, creativity, and caring put into people's work increases dramatically when they make the decisions themselves about how the business is run, what is produced, and how much they are paid.

• The economy of a community and its businesses have to be based on trust, with good relationships among members and with customers. The more love and caring present in economic transactions, the more effective an income generator an activity will be.

• Community businesses need to make a positive energy exchange with the world—that is, be financially viable—or they are not loving and serving the world. No matter how lofty the ideals, if the business doesn't pay the bills, then it's a message from the world that it's not serving peoples' needs and shouldn't be functioning. The positive aspect of community businesses is that they break down the isolation of a community as members must do more interfacing and bridging with non-new age neighbors, and they often bring in greater cash flows into the local town economy.

• Although members of most communities live on fairly low incomes and have minimal expenses, it's always surprising to outsiders how good their quality of life can be both spiritually and materially.

• Most groups go through an evolution of having fewer resources in the early years—except people's skills and some initial funding—and gradually developing and improving their standard of living over the long term. There are exceptions, of course, if community members have attitudes rejecting a comfortable lifestyle as part of their belief system. It's also common in some communities to so overemphasize the importance of reduced living expenses that they neglect the value of beauty in uplifting the human spirit.

• There is a strong work ethic in most communities today. Work is often referred to as "love made visible," in the words of Kahlil Gibran, and community members enjoy doing work that is connected to their values and sense of purpose in life. A humane and healthy work environment is also highly valued. Physical work is seen as both necessary for survival and as a healthy balance to too much "head work." Work is mentioned as one of the binding forces in community, a commonly shared value. Communal work projects, like gardening and construction, where many members join in, provide especially joyous times. But sometimes in communities, as elsewhere in society, the work ethic gets out of balance, and work is used as a way to avoid relating to people or as a way of making others feel guilty for not working as hard.

• Many jobs, such as cooking and cleaning, are rotated in communities to share the load and prevent boredom. Stereotyped sexual roles are broken down in most groups as men help with cooking and child care and women join in heavier work such as construction or auto repair. The most popular community businesses tend to be education, crafts and small cottage industries.

With the small sample populations provided by communities, economic experiments can be tried and systems changed more easily to meet members' needs. In this rich hotbed of diverse mutations, important learnings about useful types of economic structures are emerging which could prove valuable for society as a whole.

We have chosen to study the economic systems and businesses of eight communities more in depth in order to illustrate the similarities and differences among them. Most of these communities are not focused mainly on economics and business. Their main focus may be education, healing, or spiritual practice. But for our present purposes, we are considering their economic aspects. All of these different approaches are working successfully and seem to meet the needs of the members of each community. As economic systems, these eight communities span the spectrum from totally communal to almost totally individual. The range illustrated here is based on the degree of communal/private holding of income, land, houses, businesses and resources, and the degree of shared values:

Twin Oaks/Alpha/Renaissance/Sirius/Ananda/Shannon/Alvastra/Fare Thee Well

COMMUNAL   INDIVIDUAL

The first two groups on the left of the spectrum (Twin Oaks and Alpha) have shared values and a communal economy with all income, land, houses, businesses, and most resources shared; the third (Renaissance) has shared values, land, houses, and most resources and businesses shared; the fourth and fifth (Sirius and Ananda) have shared values, land and some resources, but mostly individual houses and businesses; the sixth and seventh (Shannon and Alvastra) have few shared values, but shared land with individual houses, resources and businesses; the eighth (Fare Thee Well) has shared values, but individually owned land, houses, businesses (except for its healing center), and resources. The further on the left of the spectrum, the more likely the community will share meals, work, and other activities. Even without sharing many material aspects, the community farthest on the right is still very strong as a community because its shared spiritual values are so important to members. Physical sharing in itself doesn't necessarily create a tight community, we've learned.

TWIN OAKS COMMUNITY:
Total Communal Economy and Light Industry

Twin Oaks Community in Virginia is based on a totally communal economic system. Land, labor, and resources are held in common, and the community receives the products of the mem-

bers' labor and distributes goods and services equally. Members share a belief in the importance of cooperation, equality, and non-violence. They feel that they offer people a real alternative to a competitive and consumption-oriented world. Twin Oaks sees itself developing a model social system which includes solutions to problems of land use, food production, energy conservation, industrialization, and technology. They believe that their communal economic system creates true equality among people, encourages cooperation and sharing, and reduces expenses, so that members can "live lightly on the earth." This is accomplished through a highly structured and somewhat bureaucratic system of "labor credits."

The community is located in Louisa, Virginia on four hundred acres of land, and has sixty adult members and fifteen children. Members are a diverse group of people with individual orientations varying from the utopian to the spiritual to the pragmatic. When new members join Twin Oaks, they are expected to share the resources they bring with them, except for personal items that fit into their room. Members are allowed to keep resources outside the community but are not to benefit personally from their use while in the community, for example, by using the interest on their savings. They are encouraged to loan any savings to the community and are repaid when they leave. After ten years, members must donate everything to the community. If tools or cars are brought to the community, they are shared with everyone, so as to not cause envy and to maintain a sense of equality.

Twin Oaks Community - a real alternative to a competitive and consumption-oriented world

The Diversity of Economic Systems 117

Because of Twin Oaks' communal system, members can live on an average of about $3,000 a year each, which would be below poverty level outside the community, but which is actually quite comfortable for them, with many middle-class amenities. In addition to having their food, rent, and basic necessities covered, each member is provided with a small spending allowance (currently $35/month) for travel and entertainment. Each member also gets at least 2 and 1/2 weeks of vacation a year, and the average member works overtime and actually takes about seven weeks.

Developing self-sufficiency not as an isolationist move, but to provide economic security

Twin Oaks currently produces about 60% of its own food: vegetables, dairy products, meat, fruit, and some grains. It sees itself developing self-sufficiency, not as an isolationist move, but as a further development of its economic security, a major goal of the community.

Twin Oaks supports itself mainly through hand-crafted hammocks and chairs which it produces and markets with its sister community, East Wind in Missouri, but there are also smaller industries which produce some income: editing, book indexing, publications, lecturing, and construction. Each member works an average of forty to fifty hours per week, which includes domestic and income-producing labor. A labor system has been set up so that the work can be organized and shared more equitably, and labor credits are assigned to various jobs. There is a planner/manager system of government, and managers cover all areas of community life that need supervision. There are dozens of jobs as managers and anyone who so desires can be one. Managers and planners get no special privileges for their jobs.

There is a large amount of freedom to choose the work a member would like to do. Kat Kinkade, one of the founders of Twin Oaks, comments on the advantages of group living.

> A lot of small responsibilities that fall on private householders go away naturally when one operates in a group. Car repair, for example; balancing the checkbook; laundry; plumbing. All of these things have to be done, but in a fair-sized group, there is someone who likes doing them.[1]

A strong effort has been made in the community to open work areas that might not be easily accessible outside the community to men and women, such as executive work or heavy labor for women, child care for men.

> It seems a wonder, somehow miraculous, that in this age of specialization, there is a whole little world where English majors become furniture designers, pre-med students turn into solar engineers and erstwhile hippies assume management.[2]

All members are encouraged to explain their work to any other member who desires to learn it, and there is a lot of job rotation in the community. Although not always contributing to maximum efficiency in getting the work done, this policy has been very educational for members, as Warren notes.

> Part of the attraction of being at Twin Oaks, after spending six years working in the same factory, was that we worked our own businesses...I learned a whole lot there. The few years I was there felt equal to 15 years of living outside the community. At Twin Oaks I got exposure to a variety of people and views, and an opportunity to try all different types of work; to see what management is like and what being a bureaucrat is about, and trying out all the different roles that people can play. It was a really broadening experience for me.[3]

It is important to Twin Oaks that members find challenging and desirable work. Work is not just seen as a means to an end. Members try to make it an enjoyable part of their lives.

> The hammock shop has been an ideal laboratory for the creative development of humanely oriented conditions in a worker-controlled

industry...there is an atmosphere of trust—no time clocks, no sign-in sheets, no ten-minute coffee breaks, no time limits on lunch hours. The weaver reports the actual time worked on co's labor credit sheet according to an honor system. No matter how nervous the sales people or production manager may be about filling a big order on the production date requested by the customer, none of them would dream of pushing the workers into a speed-up.[4]

"cos" is a word coined by Twin Oaks' members to avoid using a male possessive noun when the gender is ambiguous—another example of the community's commitment to overcome male chauvinism.

Twin Oaks hammock business - creating more humane work environments

The integration of work and play is a key factor in community life, and the line between the two is often hard to discern. All work is given equal value, and this has had quite an impact on members, as Ingrid Komar explains.

The knowledge that one hour of honest work, say...at picking corn...was valued as highly as solar research or teaching math to the children...was profound. To my amazement, cleaning bathrooms became an act of love. Experiencing the reality of egalitarianism is qualitatively different from merely reading economic theory or a utopian novel.[5]

But Twin Oaks is far from a perfect society. It seems that the benefits of egalitarianism accrue mainly to the workers. The community's experience clearly proves that strokes or appreciation from members are adequate substitutes for the monetary rewards and prestige given in capitalist society. But unfortunately, because members experience a lot of conflict over relying on a capitalist business with sales and marketing to support their socialist community, the managers of the business are the most short-changed in appreciation and pats-on-the-back. They are often ignored or hassled instead.

Kat Kinkade is concerned that the Twin Oaks system ''accidentally punishes management, commitment (seniority) and self-discipline.'' In order for the community's system to function more effectively, this is an area that needs attention.

Another problem is the astounding amount of bureaucracy needed at Twin Oaks to operate its labor credit system fairly. Its government is more centralized than it needs to be, according to some members. ''If you want something here,'' member Martha commented, ''there are a million committees to go through.''

The renewal of the social order must begin with ourselves

ALPHA FARM: Cooperative Corporation with Farm and Businesses

Alpha Farm was started in 1971 on 280 acres in Deadwood, Oregon, by a group of eight adults and four children. To join the community is to join a cooperative corporation, an innovative idea which has been very successful for them. Alpha's early prospectus proclaimed,

The renewal of the social order, we now see, must begin with ourselves. We seek to change our basic assumptions and patterns of daily living; to accomplish this we must alter our patterns of thought. We must live ourselves into the future we seek.

Today Alpha governs itself through consensus, in Quaker fashion, of its twenty members and seeks to listen to "that of God" within each person. Alpha members are very close and supportive of each other's growth process. Members are committed to "living lightly on the earth" by living in harmony with nature, growing most of their own food, recycling resources, and being good stewards of the land. They grow vegetables and fruit. They can much of their produce for the winter. They have an apple cider press for making juice and also raise chickens, cows, and goats to produce milk and eggs. With this lifestyle, they are able to live comfortably on about $140/month each.

Alpha Community's Hardware Store

The community has established several businesses in a nearby town: a restaurant/bookstore (started thirteen years ago), a hardware store, and a construction business. Two members also work at "outside" jobs, one for a local newspaper and one for a rural health clinic. The community holds the contract for the local star route mail delivery, and several members rotate the job.

The collectively-owned enterprises and the farm are all part of Alpha's cooperative corporation. Members accrue shares in the corporation for each year of their membership, and these shares are assigned an annual dollar worth by the membership. No initial investment is required for entry into the community. All members are economic equals and have equal decision-making power. A member can invest up to $25,000 in the corporation, and if s/he chooses to leave, the money will be paid back to her/him in full on a predetermined payment schedule with no interest. (Any resources over $25,000 that members have when they join is put in a trust until they leave.)

All income made by members is pooled, and each individual receives a monthly allowance and annual vacation stipend. The community covers each person's basic needs but not any expensive habits or desires. The community has supported, when they could, members who wanted to return to college. Each member agrees to work a minimum of forty-five hours a week at community work and businesses, and it is not uncommon for members to work more. Twenty work days of vacation a year are given to members.

Each area of the community is administered by at least one manager and two "team" members, and an overall "planner" coordinates and administers all work projects and the weekly work chart. The general notion is that if people find themselves doing what they really like to work at 50% of the time, they are doing well.

A central idea of the community is that their service to others can best be manifested through doing tasks from the most conscious and loving space they are capable of at the moment. Cognizant that the work of the world will always need doing, Alpha strives for a visionary practicality somewhat in the spirit of "head in the clouds, feet on the ground."

Getting along with neighbors has been important to Alpha from the beginning and is a natural consequence of their original vision of changing the world, not by proselytizing or politicizing, but by allowing a fullness of spirit and an openness of heart to be dominant. Creating a common ground for meeting the public was a priority, so "Alpha-Bit" was opened to offer what was hoped would be useful services: a restaurant with wholesome food, well-selected books, and quality crafts. The name "Alpha-Bit," a bit of Alpha, reflected their purpose in wanting to extend to the public an atmosphere of friendship and lightness of spirit. As member Laughing Heart explains it,

> The stores serve us well in regular community outreach, without having to politicize people. The message is more subtle this way, but it definitely comes across. You sell a pound of nails to someone, and you're right there helping them. Or you're answering their questions about plumbing or electrical things, or about their garden. And next time they come in, they say, "What's this farm you're connected with—what's it all about?" And they get this feeling of solidity that

you're not just selling them a pound of nails or a bag of manure, but that you're there to serve their needs as best you can, without giving them a lot of bull. And they'll come back again and again.

Community members are also very involved with regional networking with other new age groups, and they've helped organize several large conferences on communities. And as worker-owners of all their cooperative businesses, members feel empowered to create the kind of lifestyle that supports their values. A member of Alpha Community expresses their growth process this way.

> The daily life dramas at Alpha are the challenge—to live the life I truly believe in. To struggle through an argument, only to turn it around and find that I created the situation, and that arguing was not the best way to manifest the solution, nor the only way. To learn control over the many complexities of emotions so that a calm spirit can be present during difficult times. To listen to someone tell you something critical and not get defensive. To appreciate small gifts of love, that are more valuable to me than any diamond, gold or silver. To be able to stop during the middle of a work day to take in a rainbow, a flower in bloom, a hug, a few moments of laughter...it's an art of learning how to—how to give, how to receive, how to find that centered place.[6]

RENAISSANCE COMMUNITY: Economic "Share System" and Self-sufficiency

Renaissance Community, with sixty adults and forty-five children on eighty acres in Gill, Massachusetts, is based on a "share system" of economics, a blend of communal and private systems. The community emphasizes love and sharing as its most important values. It is working to bring spirit into the music world and to develop a self-sufficient community at its "2001 Center." Renaissance's principal text for its spiritual beliefs and practices is *The God Within* by Charles Hapgood and Elwood Babbitt (a local psychic). The community is based on what it believes are the "Seven Immutable Laws of the Universe": order, balance, harmony, growth, God-perception, spiritual love, and compassion.

Much of the membership of Renaissance has been together for fifteen years or more, having joined when they were teenagers in the 1960s, so they are an especially tight group. Nearly all

the members are in their twenties and thirties, and their lifestyle is still "counter-cultural" in appearance. A member describes the basis of the community's success.

The Renaissance Community - love and sharing are the most important values

> Friendship is the thing that makes the Renaissance Movement work. We have learned how to be real friends; it takes giving, it takes loving, it takes knowing that you're in it together for keeps. When you've got the kind of friendship we have, there is no limit to what you can do. You can even build your own world.[7]

Founded in 1967 by Michael Rapunzel and originally called "The Brotherhood of the Spirit," Renaissance pooled all its income for several years but found that this inhibited individual creativity and spontancity and also allowed one person (the financial manager) to have too much power and to "play God." Renaissance then developed its "share system," where all the expenses of the land and the resources held in common are added up, and then divided by the number of members. This

The Diversity of Economic Systems **125**

results in a "share" to be paid by each adult member, adjusted so that women pay slightly less per week than men (currently $75 as compared to $85 for men), as local jobs for women are lower-paying. Each member is then provided with food and housing in the community but pays her/his own utility bills and other personal expenses. If someone doesn't have money for something they need, there's always spontaneous sharing by some individual or by the community itself. Members' accommodations vary considerably, from very large and comfortable communal houses to teepees and small cabins, and all members now live on the land.

Everyone in the community works, either bringing in income through the community's businesses and outside jobs or by doing support jobs within the community, like gardening, bookkeeping, or child care. The community pays part of the share required by the members working at these internal jobs.

> We all have to bring in a certain amount of money to make the community work—that's the bottom line. There's not a person here who has not done a lot of different jobs in the years we've been here. Eventually you get to the point where it's not so much what you're doing, but that you're doing it with love. And if you're doing it with love, you end up at a particular place where that work energy is needed.
> —Robin Paris

Legally, Renaissance is organized as a church in order that unrelated adults could live together in one house and practice their "religion" on their land. (Massachusetts law, like that in many states, discriminates against communities by not allowing groups of more than four unrelated adults to live together.) In addition to the non-profit, tax-exempt church, Renaissance also has a for-profit aspect of the community which owns the land and several businesses: a bus company which rents buses to touring rock groups, a professional recording studio, and a construction company. Community-owned collateral, like land and buildings, is used to start new businesses, and this arrangement works very well. The business manager of Renaissance is a professional, trained at the UCLA business school, and this has been very helpful for the community.

The managers of each community business have a lot of freedom to run the business as they feel is appropriate and to pay themselves salaries commensurate with the jobs. But in practice, most managers of these businesses don't take large salaries for themselves, and they usually return to the community as much of the profit as is not needed to further expand the business. "Business managers and other department heads get together to guide the flow of profits into the various projects agreed upon by the community at large," explains Robin Paris.

Above all, it appears that a key ingredient in the success of their businesses is the joy and satisfaction felt by the workers themselves. The boundaries between work and play are blurred in any truly new age endeavor.

As in any business or group, conflicts between people do arise, but everyone just sits down and talks about how they're feeling to get everything out in the open and to work it out. The commitment to face conflict and have faith that anything can be resolved if enough love and trust have been built up is what distinguishes a new age business from the usual pattern.

Developing self-sufficiency with solar energy and electricity from windmills

Renaissance has recently been developing a great deal of self-sufficiency, producing most of its own vegetables, fruit, dairy products, and meat, and they store a lot of food in a large root cellar for the winter. Nearly all the community's buildings are heated with wood and solar energy, and one large house gets all its electricity from a windmill.

Sirius Community - everyday life as the spiritual teacher - respecting the oneness of all life

SIRIUS COMMUNITY:
Non-profit Educational Corporation
and Worker-Owned Cooperatives

Sirius, the community we founded in 1978 near Amherst, Massachusetts, is organized as a non-profit educational corporation to offer classes, retreats, and educational materials for the public and to help people with their spiritual growth. We are committed to being good custodians for our eighty-six acres of land, once held sacred to three tribes of Native Americans. We honor the oneness of all life and are learning to work in harmony with the forces of nature in our garden and forest to create a healing of the earth.

We respect the presence of God within each person and see everyday life as our spiritual teacher, mirroring back to us our own internal state, showing us where we're stuck and need to grow in love. We have a sanctuary for group meditation and emphasize contacting our own inner source of Divinity for guidance, rather than relying on outer teachers. Members are free to follow whatever spiritual disciplines are most inspirational and helpful to them.

We have an egalitarian governing process using group meditation and consensus decision-making. Weekly "personal sharing" meetings are held to share inspiration, resolve interpersonal problems, and decide business issues. Community tasks such as gardening, cooking, carpentry, and maintenance are shared by both men and women. Work is seen as "joyful productivity," an opportunity to put love in action. Work begins with a moment of silence, an "attunement," to affirm our oneness with God, each other, and the plants and tools with which we are working. We value both nature and technology in the community, as we have gardens as well as computers. We grow much of our own food organically, can and freeze goods for the winter, and heat all our houses with wood from our land. All new buildings have been built with an energy-efficient solar design to conserve the earth's resources. We use a variety of wholistic health practices for preventative health care.

Work begins with an 'attunement' a moment of silence

As a community, we've had the opportunity to experiment with designing different economic systems to find which would meet our needs most effectively. In the process of applying our ideals to real life situations, we've learned a great deal about the positive and negative aspects of these systems and their spiritual value, both for us and for society.

The Diversity of Economic Systems 129

Because we observed so much over-consumption, greed, waste, and inequality in the private enterprise system operating in this country, we assumed that a socialist system of total sharing of income and resources, more akin to the early Christian monasteries, would be a more spiritually-oriented economic system for our community. So we began our community in this way. Our income for the first couple of years came mainly from donations, our education programs, and later from a construction business. We pooled all our income and paid all expenses—mortgage, food, utilities, entertainment, clothes, doctors—out of this central pot.

This arrangement created economic equality and a feeling of mutual support among us. For several years the system supported eight adults and four children in the community. It taught us a high level of cooperation and sharing, as everything that any one of us spent money on affected everyone else, and members were very conscientious about spending the group's money. It taught us how interconnected we are, both in the community and as members of the human family in general. It also helped us see more clearly the challenges of economics on a national and planetary level.

Mutual support, cooperation and sharing

However, we also began to notice a certain lack of freedom with this system, in that everyone had to have the same lifestyle for it to work harmoniously. Or at least, everyone had to be extremely tolerant of differences, as it's difficult to work hard to provide someone else with goods or services that one does not value. In making decisions about spending community money, we had to get involved in the details of each other's personal life, which was very time-consuming and seemed unnecessary.

It was also difficult to have everyone producing an equal amount of income, as not only do people have different levels of income-producing ability on the job market, but also everyone preferred working inside the community rather than at outside jobs to bring in money. Since work in the community (in the garden, kitchen, office, or construction) was always very needed, no one was ever forced to get an outside job if s/he didn't feel "attuned to it on a soul level," didn't feel the rightness of it. But this work in the community did not always produce the cash we needed to meet our bills easily. So we worked fervently on improving our faith in God and the abundance of the Universe, praying that if we were doing the right thing, the money we needed to pay all our bills would be available. And it always was—though just barely at times, and usually with nothing left over to really expand and build the community. We seemed to only have faith in getting the bare minimum. There were perhaps

Developing faith in God and the abundance of the Universe

deep-seated feelings of unworthiness about receiving greater abundance.

From this experience we realized that a workable communal (or socialist) system depends on having very structured rules and requirements, with a system of authority to force people to work outside and bring in money when needed. We weren't willing to do this, as we felt it limited the individual freedom that is necessary for a person's growth in different ways. We also began to recognize that spiritual values are inherent in an individual or free enterprise system, as well as in a socialist system, although they are different. Freedom is important in allowing each individual to choose her/his own lifestyle and develop in her/his own way, learning the particular lessons offered by these choices. Individual responsibility and dependability is another spiritual value fostered in the private system. Often people want to skip over this value and be part of a group, but, in fact, we found that groups only work if they're composed of people who are able to be deeply individually responsible. Another problem with communal economy, we learned, is that when things aren't flowing financially as well as they should, it's difficult to know who or what is responsible. There's no clear one-to-one feedback system, as there is for an individual, about negative attitudes (lack of faith) or lack of practical work that is limiting the financial flow.

The opportunity for individual creativity and initiative was also limited in our economic system. Community members had started several independent businesses, as a form of service for bringing spiritual values into the world, and they needed the financial independence and flexibility to build the business.

So we decided to change our economic system and create a blend of private and communal systems, including what seemed to be the spiritual aspects of both. We have a communal system for the areas of our life that we mutually value and share: the land, tools, machinery, food, and community buildings. Each Full Member of Sirius contributes an equal share towards these expenses (after donations are subtracted) and works a minimum of eight hours a week on community projects. The Full Members, who are staff for the educational center, can then build their own house or shared houses on the land, and some have begun to do so. We still buy our food together in bulk as a co-op and share evening and weekend meals together. This sharing of resources is continuing to build the sense of cooperation and mutual responsibility and support that we had experienced in our communal economy. At the same time, each individual or family is providing for their own living expenses and choosing their own lifestyle. This allows greater freedom with finances, business, and personal development, and it develops personal accountability.

Sharing the garden, food co-op and evening meals together

Interestingly enough, since we created this new system we have experienced more income both as individuals and as a community, with increased donations for new projects. Two new businesses were started by members when the system was changed, so it seems to have encouraged individual initiative and creativity in our situation. Businesses started by community members include solar construction, rug-cleaning, auto parts, and sales of books and tapes.

The most successful and most innovative business started by Sirius members and friends is Rainbow Builders, a worker-owned and managed solar construction company. Started in 1980, Rainbow Builders is a separate legal and financial entity from Sirius. Half of its eleven members are women, and this helps break down old stereotypes of sexual roles.

Organized as a cooperative, Rainbow Builders has a unique structure that has been an important cause of its success. Each worker owns one share, currently worth $2,000, in Rainbow Builders, which is purchased when s/he is accepted by the group as a worker/owner (following a trial period of several weeks or longer). This share can be paid for at once or taken out of the person's salary over time.

Rainbow Builders' financial structure differs from the traditional cooperative model in that 10% of its profits at the end of the year are allocated to charity, to service organizations or non-profit groups that benefit society. Twenty per cent is saved for a capital fund, for emergencies, and 70% goes to the workers as salaries and profits. The workers then loan the profit portion back to the business for capital re-investment. They receive interest on this loan and have equity which they can then borrow on from banks, if they need to. Eighty per cent of this loan is then returned to them when they leave the business, along with their initial investment of $2,000.

Rainbow Builders' structure is based on the Mondragon Cooperatives in the Basque region of Spain, which are the number one producers of appliances and tools in Spain. They have over twenty thousand workers, who are all guaranteed jobs for life, in one hundred cooperatives. It also operates its own banks, insurance companies, and social security system.

According to Ed Pless, a worker-owner of Rainbow Builders and a member of Sirius:

> Our motivation is higher because we're working for ourselves—the workers own the business—so we're not just making someone else rich by our labor. Each of us is also involved in many different aspects of the business: estimates, design, finances, relationships with customers, hiring new people, deciding on which jobs to take, etc. We have greater flexibility in choosing the hours we work, our pay scales, the jobs we take, who we hire, because we decide all this as a group by consensus.

Rainbow Builders - a worker-owned solar construction company with both men and women

The Diversity of Economic Systems 133

Bruce Davidson, another member of Rainbow and of Sirius, explains:

> What especially appeals to me is that we each have a strong commitment to personal growth and consciousness development. We spend time working through our personal problems with each other and develop very close personal ties, which fulfills a lot of needs that traditional businesses don't.

People are more important than profits

Besides making a profit and serving the individual's need for a more humane work environment and for personal growth, cooperatives also serve society by returning a percentage of the profits to non-profit groups and service organizations. Cooperatives help stabilize a local economy because the worker-owners in the cooperative live in the town and make all the decisions themselves and so are unlikely to move the business to areas where labor or resources are cheaper. In cooperatives, people come before profits.

ANANDA COMMUNITY: Non-profit Village and Spiritual Values in Business

> One of Yogananda's disciples, Sister Gyanamata, said, "Your religion is tested in the cold light of day." This is something we really feel. If you can't manifest what you're feeling in your meditation in your day-to-day world, then to that extent it's too weak, or even unreal...So if it weren't business, which it is, to a large extent for us, then it would have to be something else, so people could learn and grow.
> —Margie Stern

Ananda members feel that the qualities of a successful business person are compatible with those of the striving seeker on a spiritual path, as Mary Kimmel, founder of their natural foods store, explains:

> Concentration, enthusiasm, and perseverance are the pathways to success in yoga and in business; and yet the spiritual seeker renounces the self-involvement and the self-interest of a business person. Instead of thinking, "Well, this business is here to help me become independent or to make money or earn a reputation," you see the purpose of your business as God's way of serving others. You

think, "What can I do to make this business more serviceful?" The business then takes on a greater identity than one person's thing. The blessings to those it serves and to those who work for it are brought through God.

Ananda Community - spiritual lessons are applied to business to see if they've really been learned

Ananda is a community of two hundred members living on seven hundred acres in Nevada City, California. Founded by Swami Kriyananda in 1967, Ananda is based on the teachings of Paramahansa Yogananda, and practices daily meditation, chanting, and yoga. Calling themselves a "village," rather than a "community," Ananda members share the land and have common spiritual beliefs and practices, but they generally own individual homes and some of the businesses.

To join the community a person must first take one of Ananda's courses in spiritual training for one to two months and then take four months of weekly classes. A single person contributes $1500 to join, a couple contributes $2500. If a member lives on the land at Ananda, s/he pays rent of $110 a month. Those living off the land pay less per month. Members provide for their own food and usually eat at home. In addition, most members tithe 10% of their income on a regular basis. Members are encouraged to build their own homes on the land or to buy one from another member who is leaving, and sometimes there are houses available for rent.

There are no minimum work requirements at Ananda, but members are encouraged to volunteer in the community at various jobs that need doing in the garden, dairy, publications, office,

The Diversity of Economic Systems 135

and guest programs. For regular jobs in these areas, members receive a small salary, which is sufficient to cover rent and basic living expenses. Community salaries are not large enough for saving money to build or buy a house at Ananda, so members often get outside jobs or start businesses on their own.

Ananda Village, the land where most of the members live, (as distinct from the retreat center and monastery land up the road), is organized as a non-profit corporation. The Village takes care of membership, planning, land use, and marketing. Some of Ananda's businesses, like its dairy, community store, health food store, and handicrafts store in town, are part of Ananda's non-profit corporation; others are privately owned. Sometimes members in these privately-owned businesses take lower wages in order to donate more money from the business to the community.

Ananda's handicraft store in town

"The real focus of the community is our spiritual life and the deep friendships and sharing between people, as well as creativity in the arts and children's education," says Purushottama, who is co-manager of Ananda Village and oversees Ananda's businesses.

Originally the community only had a few "new age" businesses—like incense and oils and health foods—but now they've expanded and run a construction company, a clothing and jewelry store, a health clinic, a bookstore, children's schools (with over sixty students), and a hot air balloon business. Purushottama explains their process with businesses this way:

What we've learned as a community is that you do have to be grounded in this world. You can't shun parts of the world because you don't want them to be. You have to accept them and bring your consciousness and attitudes to them; that's the transformation. The transformation isn't that you never use dollar bills any longer, but you use them with a higher consciousness and with a new attitude. This attitude took awhile to develop. When I first came eight years ago there was definitely a strong feeling that some business was okay, but a lot of it wasn't. Some types of business, like incense and oils, are okay because they have a new age feel to them. But ordinary house construction companies are mainstream so they're suspect. But I think now we've worked through that. I see in neophytes to the spiritual path an attitude that the spiritual path and money are separate existences. And we disillusion people rapidly who come and say, "I don't have any money; take me in." We tell them, "It doesn't work that way." You have to be able to spiritualize everything: business, music, art. Everything can have a spiritual consciousness.

Ananda's businesses have been very successful financially. Swami Kriyananda explains why.

Some people talk as if a practical, hard-headed approach is the secret of success in business. But the secret of our success is that people like us. And if they like the people in the store, they're going to come back there. That's an enormous strength that people don't usually talk about. I always say, "Be loving to people. That is what brings them in, that is our strength." So people come in droves to our bookstore, East/West, in Menlo Park.

Although he oversees the community's businesses, Purushottama tries not to interfere too much, so that the managers of the businesses have some independence. If it seemed to him that a manager were making a mistake in some business decision, Purushottama might support him anyway and let him go ahead with it, if the mistake weren't going to really harm the business.

Purushottama - Our real investment is in people

Our growth has been slower because our real investment is in people. We often put untried people instead of our business experts in charge of a business because they show so much spirit and enthusiasm.
—Purushottama

The consciousness with which Ananda members work is as important to them as getting the job done. A guest at Ananda

The Diversity of Economic Systems 137

who was working in their publications business on a "rush job" was told by a member that he should feel free to stop and do something else for awhile if the folding and collating work was getting to him. The guest asked, "Shouldn't the job have priority over how I feel about it?" He was told, "No, your *head* has priority!" Ananda members feel our heads are instruments for receiving intuition/guidance from God in each moment as to what is best to complete, so we have to take good care of ourselves. They also feel that their businesses are the place where they apply their spiritual lessons and see whether they've really learned them.

Ananda Community's World Brotherhood Center

SHANNON FARM: A Working Anarchy with Shared Land and Individual Houses

Started in 1974 by a group of thirty people as an intentional community based on participatory democracy, Shannon Farm is committed to creating an egalitarian society: non-sexist, non-racist, and non-ageist. Consensus, equality, nonviolence, and individual responsibility are the primary values shared in common; other values are left to the individual. Although some members have an ideological commitment to a kind of simple lifestyle and to the consensus process, others do not. The community seems to thrive on a diversity of values, lifestyles, and types of people. Shannon is a community of individualists who feel it's important to protect the individual in community from group domination. In the early days, some members held a study group on anarchism, the political theory advocating a society based on voluntary cooperation and free association of individuals and groups. "In many ways, Shannon comes very close to what some would call a working anarchy," claims member Peter Robinson.

Although Shannon's values are similar to Twin Oaks', the main difference is that there is no community-wide income sharing or labor credit system at Shannon, and houses are individually built and owned. The community is run by consensus of all members, with rotation of leadership positions. Shannon Farm is located on 500 acres in the beautiful Blue Ridge Mountains of Virginia, which were once the home of the Monocan Indians. Two creeks which run through the land have been named by members "Anarchy Creek" and "Establishment Creek," which seems to symbolize the community's bridging of two worlds.

Shannon has two worker-owned businesses started by members. One is a woodworking and cabinetry shop called Heartwood Design, which also sells lumber dried in a solar kiln. All eight workers receive an equal hourly wage regardless of skill level. Starburst Computer Group, the other worker-owned business, employs six members in the sale and servicing of business computers and software. Ten other Shannon members are on the land during the work day as homemakers, retirees, or income producers. The remaining seventeen members hold jobs off the land, primarily in health, education, and food services.

> Many members come here on a downwardly mobile trip. They're trying to get away from high mortgage payments, etc. and want to live a simpler lifestyle. Some people come here with certain values, and two years later, they've had a life change. This place stimulates life changes.
> —Daniel Christenberry

Member Peter Robinson adds,

> Because Shannon started with thirty members and had a common thread running through the group, they didn't need nearly as much ideology to carry them through as they would have if they were only two or five people to start.

Today only ten out of the original group of thirty are still at Shannon, but the community has grown to a total membership of about forty-two adults and sixteen children, with ages ranging from newborn to sixty-five. The membership is stable, with turnover averaging only about 10% annually. Almost half of the members have been at Shannon for eight years or more.

Seventeen houses have been built on the land, and more are on the way. These range from simple huts with no bathrooms or kitchens to very beautiful two-story houses with several bed-rooms, a bathroom, and kitchen. There is no common community kitchen or dormitory accommodation, so visitors have to contact individual members about staying overnight with them. There are three large garden plots where individuals can cultivate their own garden if they choose, but there is no common garden.

Members can build and own a lease on their own homes after the community approves building plans. The land is owned in common by all the full members of the community, and there are common agreements about the ecological care of the land. If a member leaves the community, s/he can sell the lease on the house (or rent it) to a new member, but not to a non-member.

There are three housing clusters and a commercial cluster on the land, and they share a 3 1/2-mile road system. Each cluster develops its own water and electrical systems. Cluster members must agree on any member who wishes to move into their cluster.

Early members assumed that most of the housing would be built by groups, with only a few individual and nuclear family houses. But things have worked out exactly the opposite. Only two group houses have been built, since most of the members prefer more personal autonomy in their living arrangements.

It takes a lot of initiative and resources to actually get to the point of building a house, and this process tends to be self-selective. "Anyone who thinks they need to be here can eventually convince enough others that they should be here," Peter observes, "but for people to establish themselves, it takes a lot of hard work." Dan Christenberry adds, "Many of us will support someone for membership because another member cares for them a whole lot." The membership and house-building process is very decentralized and requires a lot of individual effort. To achieve support for their membership, people must commit themselves to spending the time to personally get to know at least a portion of the current members. The best way to do this seems to be to help other members to build their homes and to join in community business meetings, work projects, potluck suppers, and celebrations.

Provisional membership, for six months or more, is extended to those who receive the support of one-third of the full members, generally by written petition. After six months, a provisional member can request full membership, which requires the support of two-thirds of the full members. Full members agree to pay 7% of their after-tax income (or a minimum of $42.50/month) in dues, and they contribute at least a day and a half's labor per month to community projects. All dues are vital to financing the mortgage and common operating and development expenses, yet the community is generally tolerant of members who fall behind in their payments. Only full members may build or lease houses or make long-term investments in the land.

Since the diversity at Shannon reflects the diversity of an average American neighborhood, the community may be developing a model that is very relevant to mainstream America. It appeals to those who want the support of good friends nearby, without the limitations of required values, beliefs, and activities. The community has functioned surprisingly well for over ten years with no common belief system or charismatic leader or guru. In some ways, Shannon may be viewed as a blend of intentional community and traditional rural village with shared land.

Alvastra Land Trust - an innovative way to avoid the high cost and exploitation of real estate

ALVASTRA: Community Land Trust with Individually Owned Houses

Land trusts are an innovative way to avoid the high cost and exploitation of real estate in modern society and, at the same time, create more of a sense of community than buying individual plots of land. A very different type of community emerges from a community land trust arrangement than from a community where members share values and resources and have a strong group orientation. Land trusts place a higher value on individual freedom, and cooperation is based purely on choice. Finances are kept separate, with the exception of land-related items.

Alvastra member Bob Swann explains how it works.

A land trust is self-selecting. We don't require people to have certain values or certain ideas. But when they join the land trust, they give up their right to profit on the land. And that builds a common bond between people, because they've already given up something—something that's as American as apple pie—speculation.

We want to preserve the land and at the same time provide a better economic basis for living on the land. It's a kind of land reform, in one sense of the word, in that it provides access to the land for more people in a practical way, for farming, for housing, for industry, etc. The land trust reduces the cost for people who couldn't afford land in the usual way. But it also has a broader social philosophy in that it slows down or prevents speculation and also ensures ecological use of the land. Just as today we recognize that no one has a moral right to own human beings and exploit them, the same is true for land. No one really has a right to own and exploit land. So instead of ownership rights, we change it to "usership rights."

Alvastra Community Association members lease land for ninety-nine years for a monthly fee of $60.00 from the Community Land Trust of the Southern Berkshires (in Massachusetts). This lease is both renewable and inheritable. The fee covers the mortgage and taxes on the land and eventually will be used to buy more property in the area so that more people can have access to land cheaply. Members become owners of any houses or improvements they make on the land and can sell their houses and transfer the lease. But they cannot sell or sublease the land itself. This type of lease agreement discourages the tying up of productive land purely for making a profit on skyrocketing property values.

Alvastra has ten acres of land, with a small section developed for housing for the four families on the land, and the rest is an apple orchard. Like many land trusts, part of the land is used for agricultural purposes to increase food self-reliance in the region, prevent soil erosion, and protect the land for future generations. Improvements made by the members, such as planting trees or developing irrigation systems, remain their equity and can be sold if members decide to move.

Alvastra members share common management of the ten acres. In order to manage their common driveway, for example, they've bought tools in common: a rototiller, lawnmower, etc. Member Susan Witt describes how the experience of community works for them.

The social forms begin to build here not by force, but by choice. For instance, people join our local food buying club, the co-op, because it's convenient, not because they have to. There's a lot of sharing between one of the families and ourselves in particular. I do a lot of babysitting for them, use their tools.

And Bob Swann adds:

In a land trust each individual family is quite free and independent; there's no built-in connection between any of the families. So whatever develops by way of cooperation and mutual interest is purely on a voluntary basis; there's no requirement.

In addition to those people actually living on the land at Alvastra, the Community Land Trust of the Southern Berkshires includes local people who share a common land ethic, non-exploitation of the earth and maintaining ecological balance. This then creates more of a broad-based organization, as Bob Swann notes.

A community land trust, as opposed to an intentional community, has more of a sense of out-going. Instead of looking upon yourselves and the outside world—a "we" and "they" kind of thinking—"we" *are* "they" because they are part of us. "They" can belong; all of our neighbors are welcome to join the land trust. They can help support the land ethic by joining us and learning more about it. It's an educational process. And then more people might want to give or sell their land to the land trust.

Bob recommends that when membership in a land trust gets too large for everyone to be involved in decision-making, then a board can be elected composed of one-third people living on the land, one-third the broader public, and one-third (appointed by the first two groups) of people with specific skills like land use planners, landscape architects, etc.

Without the Community Land Trust, most Alvastra members couldn't have afforded the down payment for the land. Instead, they were given access to the land with just the lease fee, and their houses were built with sweat equity. As Susan Witt comments.

I'm so grateful for the experience the Land Trust provided. It gives me tremendous energy to help make it happen for other people, too. This is the first time I've been in a house that I built, that I have an

The Diversity of Economic Systems   143

ownership in, that I have equity in. I've made a commitment to stay here for a long time, and that's what has changed my relationship to working with people, not just the neighbors, but with the whole area (as local people are members of the land trust, not just residents of the land). You're building long-term commitments.

Alvastra members are also experimenting with new forms of energy to help reduce their expenses. One family has a solar greenhouse attached to their living room in order to produce year-round food and to help heat the house. Another house has a windmill to provide electricity. Other members have started the SHARE credit fund in cooperation with a local bank to make loans to local individuals or businesses that are developing local self-reliance, conserving energy, using environmentally sound production methods, or increasing local employment and community services.

Fare-Thee-Well - helping people connect with their own inner healing process

FARE-THEE-WELL COMMUNITY:
Individually Owned Homes and Land with Shared Values

Fare-Thee-Well began originally in 1974 as a non-profit Healing Center in Huntington, Massachusetts. Started by an ex-Congregational minister, Floyd McAuslan, and his wife Priscilla, Fare-Thee-Well offers Sunday services, spiritual counseling, healing services, and educational programs ''to introduce a broader concept of healing" to people of all walks of life and all denominations. Both traditional and alternative wholistic approaches to health are used, with the main focus on helping people connect spiritually with their own inner healing process through the use of thought, concentration, and alignment with the Divine Mind, the One Source. "Thought creates the energized form to bring what's needed," Floyd notes. "We ask for the highest good to be done, not what we think should be done." Members are encouraged to seek their own guidance for their lives from the Divine Mind.

Herbs which are grown on the land are regularly used for healing purposes, and nutritional counseling is also offered. An herb and whole foods store was operated at Fare-Thee-Well for awhile, but when members observed that people became too dependent on herbs and nutrition for healing, instead of first working on their own inner spiritual process, they closed the store. As a result, members feel they are now more aligned spiritually and more healthy, and they are doing better financially even without the store. They felt it was a case of putting first things first. The spiritual life had to come first.

After some years of working together at the Healing Center, Floyd explained that, "We wanted to form a residential community because we were concerned about the future and possible earth changes. We wanted to be prepared and be together if something happens." So for several years, members tried to make the land at the Healing Center communal so they could build houses and live there. "But it didn't work," explains member James Molyneux, "because we weren't doing what we were supposed to do, what God wanted us to do, and there was too much conflict."

Interestingly enough, four families came to a similar conclusion totally independently in the same week, and each separately inquired about moving onto another piece of land which was owned by Floyd and Priscilla in nearby Worthington. Each family proposed to buy an individual lot and build their own home. Once this was agreed upon, everything flowed smoothly and rapidly, and a residential community developed on the land in Worthington.

Today there are seven families who have each built their own homes on acre lots, with two acres of gardens shared by all the families. The remainder of the eighty-five acres is left as forest, as there is a limit on the number of lots that can be used for houses until more roads are created. There are also plans to build a community meditation building on the land, and later a community center.

For some reason, a communal sharing of the original land where the Healing Center is located was not appropriate, and so it never worked out. But privately-owned land and houses were meant to be. The thirteen adults and thirteen children who live on the community land at Worthington are creating a model of a community that is very similar to the way many middle-class Americans live. But although community members experience the same economic independence and freedom of lifestyle as the average American, there is an important difference. Each family's neighbor at Fare-Thee-Well Community shares the same spiritual path, and they all support each other in their spiritual growth. All the members have known each other for many years before moving onto the land, and so they've had time to build trust and close friendships and work out any conflicts.

Many spiritual practices are shared. The community gathers at 6:00 a.m. each day for a meditation service, and each takes a turn leading it. There is a regular healing service every Sunday morning as well as weekday evening meetings for prayer, music, spiritual reading, and members' sharing. When there aren't regular meetings, members "get together in thought" at an agreed-upon time. They stop wherever they are and whatever they're doing to have a short meditation, focusing on themselves as a community and sometimes on their own spiritual growth or on healing for someone.

In addition, Fare-Thee-Well Community members grow much of their own food in their community garden and have plans to jointly raise asparagus for income. And unlike most people today who may not even know their next-door neighbors, Fare-Thee-Well members are practicing old-fashioned good neighborliness: helping each other with barn raisings and sharing child care, weekly pot luck meals, tools and heavy equipment, and harvesting wild herbs on the land together.

Lessons of Community Economics Applied on a Planetary Level

From our own experiments with manifestation, faith, and with different types of economic systems and businesses in our community, as well as from interviewing members of other communities, we've learned some important spiritual principles that might be useful when applied to our current problems on a planetary level:

Economics as 'earth household' - giving is an act of faith in the abundance of the Universe that will circulate and return

• **The Earth Household**—Economics literally means "earth household," a key image for understanding what right economics requires. If we care for the planetary economy as we would our own household or our own community, we can then see that it must work for all members of the earth household, or it really won't work for any part of the human family in the long term. Just as we wouldn't tear our house apart to make a fire to keep warm, or dump garbage in our living room, so we must learn to see the larger household of the earth as we do our own. And we must be concerned about the effect of our actions on future generations who will inhabit the earth.

• **Circulation**—The body of our earth, just like the body of a community, is a living organism. All economic interactions from the individual to the larger whole take place within this body of moving energies. If circulation through the system is blocked through manipulation, hoarding, etc., then all parts of the organism suffer. When there is free circulation of goods, resources, and services throughout the body, nourishing all parts of the system, then the system as a whole flourishes. Equally, when the whole is cared for, all the parts within it are nurtured.

• **A Creator/Producer First, A Consumer Second**—As individuals and communities develop their creative abilities connected to their spiritual Source, the need to consume from an inner sense of lack transforms into the ability and

The Diversity of Economic Systems 147

urge to create and give to the world. We then find our true vocation and trust that what we put forth from our inner Self will be of value to others and that we will receive what we need to live in exchange.

• **Abundance and Sharing**—When we realize the great abundance-producing creative energy and potential within us, we overcome the fear of lack, "scarcity consciousness." And when we see with the eyes of unity, the polarity of giver and receiver dissolves as we realize that to receive is also to create the opportunity for others to give.

• **Faith**—As we have faith or trust in the abundance of the Life of the Universe, we find greater abundance flowing to us. Faith allows us to act "as if" there is abundance and to do what we know is spiritually right for ourselves and others, trusting that it will work out economically for everyone, despite how it may appear to the rational mind. Faith eventually grows into knowing that God's law works as we experience it in our lives.

• **As We Give, So Shall We Receive**—We "prime the pump" of the universe by creating a vacuum in our lives in giving to others our time, money, energy, and love. Giving is an act of faith that the abundance of the Universe will circulate and return. The ancient law of tithing 10% of all income to spiritual purposes honors the Source from which all abundance emerges.

• **Custodianship/Stewardship**—From a higher perspective, we can ultimately possess nothing on the material level, although it may possess us (because we are too attached to it and worried about it). We can be good custodians of what God has given us. The Great Economist is highly resource- and energy-efficient, and we harmonize with universal laws when we keep our resource channels clear and flowing. When we care for and improve what has been entrusted to us and release to others things we don't use, we see a new inflow of abundance.

• **Decentralization of Control**—Wealth-producing resources are the "common heritage of all mankind," as recognized by the UN in the Law of the Sea Treaty. The benefits of developing productive capacity through ideas, technology, labor, or capital need to be shared between those who create the innovation and the social-planetary web that makes the production and wealth possible.

• **Love/Good Will**—Love is the state of being which creates a positive sense of connectedness and allows harmonious economic interaction to take place. In legal terms, it is called a "meeting of minds" that forms the basis for all contracts. In business it is called the "good will" a business has generated with customers, and it is assigned a dollar value in the worth of the business. It is the deeper ground of being which gives rise to the values of trust, honesty, and fairness.

• **Interdependence**—The attempt to achieve total self-sufficiency through self-centered independence emerges from the dominance of the illusory separativeness of the ego consciousness. As we participate in the economic life of our community and our local town, we learn that we are part of an interdependent web of complex interactions. Changes in one part of the web affect all the participants. Establishing just, harmonious, and honest relationships is the key to economic well-being for all.

• **A Fair Profit**—When an individual, business, or community through their labor transforms material substance or provides a service which truly benefits others, without creating harm anywhere, then a fair and equitable profit for the work done is in order. Profit thus allows the service or "good" to continue to be provided to others. Profit must include considerations of being good for the whole, on all levels, both short- and long-term, or distortions are created.

• **Money as Concretized Energy Flow**—Money is a symbolic medium of exchange among humanity and represents accumulated human and planetary creative energy. It is essentially neutral and its value depends on the uses to which it is put. The highest view of money is to see it as a sacred trust to be used for the good of the whole community and of all humanity.

6 New Patterns of Governance and Leadership

Leadership is a way for a group to focus its service to itself. It is a channel for the group's empowerment. Leadership is a gift that a group gives itself—to try out aspects of being which would not be called forth in other situations...Leadership is sacrificial in a certain sense: a leader says, "Let's go in a certain direction," and the group says, "Give us the energy to do it."

—DAVID SPANGLER

Decision-making is of primary importance to the new communities, as the major portion of the time community members spend together is involved with it, according to sociologist Benjamin Zablocki, who studied hundreds of communities.[1] But relative to businesses and villages of the same size, communities—even the larger ones like the Israeli kibbutz and the Hutterite colonies—have far less complex governance structures.

Communities are pioneering important new approaches to governance that could be helpful to both business and government. Corporate executives are already integrating techniques pioneered by communities and other alternative groups into their leadership style: non-linear, non-rational problem solving and conflict resolution, with fuller participation and feedback from workers.

An important part of the pioneering work in communities concerns the role of leadership, an area of both successes and difficulties for many communities. Of the communities he studied, Zablocki found that 25% of those that disbanded offered reasons relating to the exercise of power and authority: the power of leaders over followers, of males over females, of founders over newcomers, or of the less committed over the most committed.[2] Members of new age communities feel the importance of creating right relationships in the area of power and authority. Although there is much experimentation and diversity in style, there is also much commitment to live up to certain ideals in this area.

In research on communities for her book, *Earth Community*, Susan Campbell found that communities which had a more centralized authority structure minimized intra-group power struggles and role confusion. These groups generally were able to direct most of their energy outward into service projects in the world and had a more visible impact on the mainstream culture. In communities with less centralized authority, more energy was required to deal with interpersonal differences and identity issues, and more time was spent in community meetings on decision-making. Individual learning and responsibility was thus fostered, but there was less energy available for directing out into the world. Fewer tasks got done, but they were done with a greater sense of team spirit and ownership by all the members.[3]

Centralized leadership, on the other hand, can offer important spiritual growth lessons in obedience and surrender of the ego that are definitely useful to people at a certain stage of spiritual growth. But when that stage should be outgrown and centralized leadership is carried to an extreme, it can create childlike dependence on leaders and thus hinder self-development, leading in extreme cases to the excesses of the "cults."

A contrast in the responses of leadership was shown in the handling of scandals at both the San Francisco Zen Center and the Siddha Yoga Dham ashram of Swami Muktananda in New York state as reported in *Co-Evolution Quarterly Magazine*.[4] In both cases, the spiritual leaders of their communities allegedly became involved in sexual scandals with the students, while denying it and isolating themselves from feedback about it. In Muktananda's case, authority in the ashram was centralized and almost deified, with unquestioned obedience to the leader regarded as a virtue. Therefore, the issue was simply ignored in public by the leadership, while there were allegedly some threats privately to individuals who threatened to reveal information.

At the San Francisco Zen Center, on the other hand, the Board of Directors and senior priests confronted their teacher directly and asked him not to lead services or give lectures, as he was not practicing what he preached and was not being a good model to emulate. The Zen Center has not folded as a result of this crisis in leadership, but the senior members of the community have carried on, having learned some essential lessons, as Zen student Katy Butler, explains.

> I believe that as our communities mature, we will learn to treat these talented teachers with a realistic American kind of respect they need. We have been driving them crazy by accepting everything they do as an expression of religious teaching. Living without feedback in a community of emotionally dependent people is something like living in a sensory deprivation tank. It distorts the perceptions and isolates the leader.[5]

Jack Kornfield, a teacher in the Theravada Buddhist tradition at the Insight Meditation Society in Massachusetts, comments on this situation.

> Our Western culture stresses individuality and participation, which makes it very different from the hierarchical ways of the East. Certainly a great deal of surrender and trust, and working with a good teacher, is necessary to go deep in practice. But for Americans there won't be so much the "yes, boss, yes guruji," authoritarian quality without questioning. There is already a greater sense of openness, a questioning of forms and authority and a desire to participate in decision making by all members of the community. This is part of our heritage.[6]

In our opinion, one of the highest functions of leaders, spiritual or otherwise, is to facilitate the development of responsibility and leadership in others, with no thought of self-aggrandizement. One of the essential qualities of good leadership is integrity: living by example the values that s/he feels the whole community should follow. There are examples of communities with strong spiritual leaders who do listen to feedback from followers and who work to empower them, delegating more authority as members demonstrate ability to take on more responsibility. Swami Kriyananda of Ananda Community in California is one example, working with a pattern of responsive leadership within a traditional Eastern path. Swami Kriyananda calls his approach "creative leadership."

> Good leadership means giving service, not receiving it. It means accepting responsibility for successes as well as for failures...A good leader is not concerned with praise or blame nor with his personal reactions, but with *action*—with getting the job done...To win loyalty, love and support from others, he first gives them loyalty, love and support...A good leader works with people as they are, not as he would like them to be. He is willing to allow others to make mistakes so they can learn from them. He never assigns any job to someone else that he is not willing to do himself...A good leader only accepts as much authority as people are willing to give him...His work is best done by inspiring people and inviting them, never by bossing them.[7]

In recent years, there has been much change and transition in the whole area of leadership in communities, with many groups learning similar lessons and coming to the same conclusions about the use of power. There has been a kind of gentle revolution afoot in many of the originally more centralized communities. Those that have made changes gracefully and wisely—for example, Findhorn, Stelle, The Pathwork, and The Farm—have been gifted with a greater strength to face a new cycle of growth. The original charismatic leaders of these communities stepped down, and after some period of confusion and upheaval, a new pattern emerged with a more decentralized and shared focus of leadership.

Many communities have worked on creating a balance between centralized and decentralized leadership by having a rotating system of leadership, with different people taking turns at leadership at different times, or through having leaders for different functions or tasks (e.g., administrative, social, spiritual, educational). Some communities, such as Findhorn, encourage leadership in people by selecting quieter, non-dynamic types to "focalize" or direct various work departments.

Sociologist Rosabeth Kanter, in her study of hundreds of urban communities, found that

> Negotiation rather than authority is the basis of relationships...even when some people have more influence than others, that influence has to be negotiated, and it may not even be overtly acknowledged by others.[8]

Group consensus is one of the most popular modes of decision-making in communities. Historically, consensus has been used most extensively by the Native Americans and the Quakers. Consensus means agreement by the whole group with the general direction of a decision, with no serious objections. Consensus is experienced intuitively as a sensed unity within the group on a specific issue. The advantage of consensus decision-making over traditional majority/minority voting is that each person feels the decision is her/his and feels a responsibility to carry it out. There is no losing minority to feel resentment. The best thinking of all members is included in the decision. As Lama Community members put it,

> Consensus is based on a recognition of human limitations: that no one being or group can at all times make decisions in the best interest of the whole community. We trust that we may hear the Spirit of Guidance moving within our midst. If everyone can say "yes" from the heart to a proposal, we know that in our decision we move forward as one body.[9]

Not only have communities which began with highly centralized authority shifted towards more decentralization as members take on more personal responsibility, but also communities which began with a decentralized and organic structure have moved in the opposite direction. These have begun developing clearer lines of authority as they learn from experience to be realistic about what works and what doesn't.

Sun Bear of the Bear Tribe comments:

> I've tried for a long time to make people equal, to empower people, and they wouldn't respond. They won't move beyond a certain level. I'll come up with a flashy idea...and they're not interested. So I take care of this person and let them do what they're capable of doing—

chop the wood, take care of the garden. But as long as they're functional and they take care of their part of it, that's all that matters. Some people are institutionalized in community: they can function in community, but not outside of it. They couldn't survive outside the sheltered atmosphere of community, and those are the people you have to look after. And what they return to you for helping them is that they carry part of the weight. For example, not everyone is capable of running our Medicine Wheel Gatherings, but you've got a lot of people who can park cars. The important part of the game is learning how to utilize the energy of all these different kinds of people.

The Bear Tribe, like many communities, learned that although you might create *political* equality, where everyone has equal rights and equal voting power, you can't create total equality. People are at different levels of ability to take responsibility, and so authority and power should reflect that. You can't have one without the other. Some members of a community seem naturally to feel a greater commitment to make the community work and to identify more with it than others. Not everyone in a community may be concerned that a bill is late in being paid, for example, as they don't feel it reflects on them personally. But for others, it's just the same as if their personal bill is late in being paid.

Although everyone is equal in potential, not everyone is at the same level of actually manifesting their full potential. Pir Vilayat, founder of the Abode Community, speaks of "the democracy of the ego and the aristocracy of the soul." On an inward, spiritual level there is hierarchy, but, outwardly, in dealing with human rights, equality is essential. Even though there may be equal rights among members of a community, the founder still has a responsibility on an inner level to maintain the spiritual vision and essence of the community.

Too strong an emphasis on a belief that "everyone is equal" in all things often creates an unrealistic idealism and puts a tremendous burden of expectation on people. And it usually leads to resentment when people don't live up to that expectation. Demanding that everyone *should* be equal is also a way that people avoid taking full responsibility for themselves, for fully recognizing, accepting, and developing their own abilities. And being overly concerned about finding equals or peers often comes from a fear of accepting one's own leadership responsibilities. Sometimes an overemphasis on equality can reflect a feeling of lack of self-worth, as it is subtly a demand for reassurance that one is just as good as everyone else.

A distorted sense of equality can also cause the community to express the lowest common denominator, with some members being threatened by the achievements of other members, so that a true excellence cannot exist. Sometimes it's very difficult for the more developed and self-actualized members of a community, as they feel the jealousy of others. Sometimes structures are created which make it difficult for any individual in the community to have access to very much power. And at other times, it's the very lack of structure that creates the problem: "The tyranny of the structureless group," as it's often called today. No one is empowered to act on behalf of the group. Betty Didcoct of Linnaea Community in British Columbia reports, for example: "We had such a devotion to non-leadership, that leadership wasn't allowed to evolve when it was necessary." An avoidance of clear lines of power and authority can often be the result of a lack of trust, covered up by lip service to "equality."

Even if there are clear lines of authority, as for example with the planners at Twin Oaks Community, there still can be difficulties, as Bjorn observed that: "Twin Oakers are uncomfortable with power. They refused to expel someone who refused to do any work and flagrantly violated the community's agreements."[10]

"Most leadership issues in a community are really ego issues," observes Betty Didcoct. "When we put our egos aside, leadership problems don't arise." Power issues are difficult to avoid in community, even when there are no "leaders" or current leadership issues. The biggest power struggles are often over seemingly mundane issues like house-cleaning—how to make order and whose standards prevail—and over food. Power issues always have to have some arena.

From our own experience of many years of community living and from experiencing firsthand both sides of the leadership/ equality issue, it seems that a great deal of what goes on in community is in reality just people dealing with their own issues of power and slowly learning to empower themselves. We've recognized three essential steps or tests of power in community:

1. **Individual clarity and insight**—Before you can really challenge someone else's authority, it's important that you get clear within yourself (seek your own guidance) about what is right, what is the real truth of the situation, regardless of other opinions.

2. **Courage**—Speak up and confront those in authority with what your own inner sense of truth is, even if it's very unpopular.

3. Love and non-polarization—Don't be attached to the results of your position when those in authority don't agree, and remain able to keep your heart open to your opponent without reacting negatively.

Usually it's difficult for community members to maintain integrity in all these areas, so conflicts arise. But power struggles are usually resolved when there is willingness on the part of both sides to really *listen* to each other, to hear an opposing perspective; when the person in authority becomes more identified with the membership, more sensitive to their needs, and shows a real willingness to yield; or when the membership becomes more aligned with the community's purpose and goals as represented by the person(s) in authority.[11]

Where there is rebellion against authority in a community (even if it's justifiable), it's important to recognize whether it is really a manifestation of the need of a person to claim his or her own authority. Often the cause is an inner conflict in the person about being a leader himself, which then gets projected outward onto an authority figure. Community leaders who are psychologically aware are able to help members deal with this internal conflict, rather than getting caught in the position of having to put down rebellion and assert external authority.

Ultimately, power is not something that can be given to someone. Someone is powerful because of their personal qualities: vision, confidence, creativity, good judgment, enthusiasm, consistency, strength, etc.

The whole concept of power is being redefined in communities. Rather than the traditional "power over others," the goal is "power with others." If a community is responsive to the innovative spirit seeking to express itself everywhere, then its main goal will be to *empower* individuals, to draw forth leadership in everyone, rather than to create dependence on leaders, no matter how enlightened they are.

Community governance is based on one of two assumptions. The old assumption was that people are basically unable to direct themselves or take responsibility, so leaders have to take care of them. The new assumption is that people already have the potential wisdom and creativity within them, so the task of leadership is mainly to educate and encourage. How you set up a situation has a lot to do with how people respond. It can be structured so that people are encouraged and inspired to do things for themselves, to make their own decisions, and to take on more responsibility. They are helped to develop self-confidence and a sense of self-worth. An expectation of responsibility helps to draw that out. People have tremendous creative power to affect each other. This is not to say that there is no leadership function per se, but rather that leadership is educative, rather than directive. As the ancient Chinese sage Lao Tsu said, "Leadership is best when the people say, 'We have done this ourselves.' "

All of the communities discussed in this chapter have this orientation—leadership as educative, rather than directive—and all are very innovative in their styles and techniques of governance. Like Ananda Community's concept of "dharmacracy," these communities are "trying to do what is right" in a given situation for both the individual and the group. This involves listening with the heart, as well as the head, to tune into what is trying to manifest in a situation.

The innovative approaches to governance developed by the communities in this chapter span the spectrum from political to emotional to spiritual techniques. Emotional clearing and meditation are used at The Pathwork communities; a political emphasis on equality and consensus at the Philadelphia Life Center; a Buddhist approach of release and detachment at the Ojai Foundation; a non-structured attempt at "Divine anarchy" at Auroville; and the use of meditation and group attunement to receive guidance at Findhorn. Each community is pioneering in a very conscious way, hoping to discover new and useful tools for age-old problems of humans living together and governing themselves.

THE PATHWORK COMMUNITIES (SEVENOAKS AND PHOENICIA): Core-energetics and Inspiraling

Susan and Donovan Thesenga, co-founders of Sevenoaks

The Pathwork communities in New York, Center for the Living Force, and in Virginia, Sevenoaks, have effectively used the spiritual growth techniques developed by their charismatic founders, Eva and John Pierrakos, to work through a dramatic change in leadership and to establish self-governance. Beginning in 1957, Eva "channeled" spiritual teachings which are now studied as the Pathwork lectures. John later developed "core-energetics," deep breathing and cathartic therapeutic techniques to release body blocks, character defenses, and negative emotions. These techniques added an experiential dimension to the concepts of the Pathwork lectures and attracted many people, including professionals. Those who joined the Pathwork met regularly with trained counselors who helped them work out personal problems and integrate their "lower self" with their "higher" or spiritual self.

The Pathwork Community at Sevenoaks - turning inside to find one's own authority and guidance

In 1971, John and Eva Pierrakos started a community in Phoenicia, New York, on three hundred acres to provide a center where Pathwork members in the city could come for weekend therapeutic programs. The community now has about forty residents and has built many homes and community buildings. A second Pathwork community was started two years later on 130 acres near Madison, Virginia, by Susan and Donovan Thesenga and now has about ten residents.

Eva Pierrakos' death several years ago created a lot of pain and turmoil in both communities. But something very positive came out of all the ensuing changes, as Donovan Thesenga explains.

There was a feeling in the group that "we've got to get our act together and understand what we're about as a community," especially with fewer people coming up from the city to take the programs here. That was how the economics was structured, so when the attendance started falling off, people in the community said, "We have to look at who we are, at our strengths and weaknesses, and if we want this community to continue, we have to find our own way to pay the bills." So that led to a lot of changes and more self-sufficiency as a group.

New Patterns of Governance/Leadership 159

And Susan Thesenga adds:

> The whole structure needed to topple. We each had to go back to the
> beginning, to the source in each of us of the wisdom and love we
> sought from Eva, or anyone else outside ourselves. We needed to
> look at everything anew.

John Saly, a founding member of the Phoenicia community,
learned some important lessons from the upheaval that followed
Eva's death. To other communities who might face similar difficulties following the death of a strong leader, John advises:

> Don't try to prop up the old structure. Don't put new authorities in
> place of the old ones and continue to expect direction to come from
> those new authorities. It fails. Instead of looking to authority outside
> themselves, people must turn inside to find their own authority and
> guidance.

After Eva's death, the community formed a self-government committee that was open to any member who felt the call
and volunteered for it. The committee met for a year and put out
position papers. They asked for feedback and suggestions and
then came up with a rough draft interim constitution. A spiritual
leader was elected for the Washington/Virginia branch of the
Pathwork and one for the New York branch, and each has an
elected council which handles most of the government of the
community.

The Pathwork communities at Sevenoaks and Phoenicia
have developed some very effective and innovative methods of
conflict resolution and decision-making in their groups. They
work on a conflict in three stages: intellectually, emotionally, and
spiritually. When someone has a conflict with someone else in the
group, they try to first understand from an intellectual perspective what the issues are factually. Then they work on understanding the conflict emotionally. Members are encouraged to express
their negative feelings more fully, not to just talk about them. A
person who's angry works on feeling the nature of her/his anger
and expressing it to the other person if s/he is willing to hear it. If
not, the anger is expressed to a pillow, or whatever.

Pathwork members are well trained in facilitating and understanding this kind of emotional expression, and so the person
usually experiences a greater depth with it. S/he may realize, for
example, that "It's not just *this* which is making me angry, it's

The Pathwork Community at Phoenicia (Center for the Living Force)
- trying to understand an issue intellectually and emotionally and discharge negative feelings

something in addition. It's not the issue at hand, but something you said to me a week ago that I repressed and am now sticking onto this issue.'' Sometimes the two people in conflict can work through their interpersonal problem in the moment, but if the issue is deeper and more substantial, they are asked to make a commitment to meet together sometime before the next meeting to resolve it, with the help of a counselor, if necessary.

After working on an issue intellectually and emotionally, the next step is to go to the intuitive level, to seek guidance from their higher selves. Donovan Thesenga explains.

We feel that you have to get clear on the intellectual and the emotional levels before you can truly get guidance. Once the blocks are removed, the guidance ought to be there. You don't have to do a lot of special stuff to get there; it's a natural function the same as your eyes seeing. You don't have to strain to make your eyes take in the data. But if you have a lot of fuzz in front of your eyes, you're not going to see very well. That's the way we view clearing the obstructions out—first you clear the fuzz out, then your intuitive channel will work clearer, we presume. For a lot of smaller decisions, we might just talk about it and see if everyone agrees, but if it's something bigger, we might formally seek guidance. And if it's a really big deal, we might devote the whole meeting to it and spend the first two hours dealing with people's opinions and feelings. And then we might pass out pencils and paper and meditate together for five minutes, and then every person there seeks written guidance—they write the question on the page and then write down what they get in the meditation. If we're discussing an issue, and there's no emotional

New Patterns of Governance/Leadership 161

blocks in people, but just different points of view intellectually, then we'd just go directly to guidance.

When we go to get guidance, out of a group of twelve or thirteen, maybe half the group will say, "Boy, something really came through and I want to share it." At least nine times out of ten using this process there's a sense of what we should do and which direction we should go in. Sometimes three or four people would read their guidance and would be similar and what you would expect, and then the fifth person would read his, and it would be a whole fresh slant on it. And the whole group would say, "Right on! We think essentially that the clearest truth came through you this time."

Although Donovan was elected the "spiritual leader" of his community, he or any other member might sometimes feel very fuzzy on an issue or have many unresolved feelings about it, and so he'd just say, "Well, I yield. I hope someone else is clear."

In their council meetings at Sevenoaks, members aim for consensus on decisions. If there is no consensus, however, they'll table the decision until the next meeting (even if the vote is as close as eight to one). But if there still is not consensus at the second meeting, they'll vote, with two-thirds of the group needed to carry the decision.

At Phoenicia, members have developed a unique method of decision-making which they call "inspiraling." Member Judith Saly describes the process.

> We go around the circle and each member has a chance in turn to say what he/she feels about the issue being discussed. It relieves anxiety because when it's your turn, you know everyone will listen to you. (Some people would speak two or three times, when someone else might have trouble expressing himself in the usual kind of discussion, so this "in-spiraling" process is fairer.) We keep going around the circle, with each person taking a turn, until what needs to be emerges. We don't vote. We may stop, and go inside ourselves, having a moment of silence, and then people will speak from this place [of inner guidance]. And usually a solution comes from this.

THE PHILADELPHIA LIFE CENTER (MOVEMENT FOR A NEW SOCIETY): Consensus Decision-Making

The Philadelphia Life Center is an urban community of about eighteen cooperative houses whose residents are members of the Movement for a New Society (MNS). Started in 1971, MNS is a network of autonomous small groups around the country who actively work for nonviolent social change. MNS believes its goals must be incorporated in the way it is organized, so it has an egalitarian, decentralized structure and uses consensus in its decision-making process. Members have developed a very clearly-defined process for reaching consensus that they explain in several books they've published and in training sessions given for the public.

Inspiraling in decision-making

The cooperative houses of the Philadelphia Life Center were formed as support groups for activists working on various causes: disarmament, racism, ageism, women's liberation, gay liberation, American interference in Latin America, and anti-nuclear issues. Members share house expenses, meals, clean-up chores, and personal growth techniques like co-counseling. Casey Capitolo, an MNS activist and trainer from The Philadelphia Life Center, explains:

> People who are doing a lot of serious work, social change work, get burned out and need a lot of support. They can't deal with that level of energy and spiritual drain and then go home to people who don't understand or agree with them. These people started a politically-oriented, live-in community, so that their politics would not be separate from their lifestyle. They wanted an egalitarian community of mutual support and trust and felt it was essential for doing a lot of creative and innovative work.

MNS feels that the political issues they actively work on in the world, such as racism and sexism, also have to be worked on

New Patterns of Governance/Leadership 163

within themselves and within their group dynamics. MNS has developed "Macro-Analysis Seminars" which offer analysis, vision, and strategy to help people "raise their consciousness" about these issues within themselves and within the world. They also give trainings in nonviolent direct action and in skills for more effective decision-making, conflict resolution, and unity building in group living and working situations.

MNS members see leadership as a key issue in creating social change, as they feel that in our society leadership is often confused with authoritarianism and the wielding of undemocratic economic and political power. In contrast, MNS members feel that

> ...Leadership can best be understood as a set of functions rather than as a personal trait. Dominating leadership is fulfillment by one person of many group functions and roles of leadership at the expense of, and *with the cooperation* of, other members. In group-centered leadership, all members take on responsibilities that often would fall to one person:
>
> > —stating all sides of a controversy fairly and objectively;
> > —sensing the development of tension in the group;
> > —aiding the group's insight into its feelings and attitudes;
> > —summarizing group discussion;
> > —bringing a group to the point of decision-making without threat;
> > —coordinating the questions and steps a group needs to consider in order to reach a decision;
> > —encouraging others to gain experience in and learn skills of leadership.[12]

In order to maintain group-centered leadership, MNS members at the Philadelphia Life Center use consensus decision-making. Consensus is the cornerstone of all trainings in MNS and all meetings of political groups as well as households. MNS has strong roots in the Quaker tradition, which has a long history of decision-making by consensus. The MNS training manual describes consensus in this way.

> Consensus is a process for making group decisions without voting. Agreement is reached through a process of gathering information and viewpoints, discussion, persuasion, a combination of synthesis of proposals and/or the development of totally new ones...Consensus does not necessarily mean unanimity. A group can proceed with an

action without having total agreement. In the event that an individual or small group cannot agree with a given proposal and is blocking consensus, the facilitator may ask if the individual(s) are willing to "stand aside" and allow the group to act, or if they feel so strongly about the issue that they are unwilling for the group to act. If the individual(s) are not willing to stand aside, action is blocked unless a compromise or substitute agreement can be found.[13]

MNS members feel that the consensus process in itself is a powerful tool for consciousness raising. They see consensus as a concrete example of the real healing work that is needed in the world, the elimination of power relationships between people and the celebration of our mutual humanity. It teaches people to open up on a more spiritual level, on an interactive and intuitive level with others. Each person in the consensus process has to take a lot more responsibility for himself in the meeting. The facilitator is not there to take care of people and make everything happen. It is each person's responsibility. Philadelphia Life Center members admit that consensus sometimes means having three times as many meetings that run three times as long, as Casey notes:

> You must have a tremendous commitment to each other and to the work you are doing to use it. I've watched people using this process grow tremendously from slumber, from spiritual slumber, personal slumber, disconnectedness from other human beings, to being excited about working together, about being fully equal participants in a group.
>
> The usual things that are done to keep women and blacks and others out of decision-making cannot be done with a consensus process, where everyone has equal opportunity to participate. Groups of people can't be voted out, shouted down, excluded.
>
> Consensus is a strong breaking away from the old cultural values of a dominating, aggressive society that is very patriarchical and closed off to spiritual values and to human interaction. Consensus is like learning how to walk for the first time, or like being on another planet—it's that kind of difference. People come into a consensus workshop or group thinking it's just another decision-making process, before they become aware that it means changing your life. It means reaching out, opening up to others. You can't lie, and you can't hide. You can't be a power mogul. Consensus is based on openness and trust.

MNS training workshops have developed a specific process to help people use consensus. A facilitator, whose job it is to make sure that everyone has the same level of information to make the decision, is chosen for the meeting. People with pertinent information are asked to share it, and charts and other papers with specific information are put up on the walls for all to see. The facilitator is the focus for the group energy and has to be intuitive and responsive to group needs. A facilitator never directs the group without its consent. He takes responsibility for reminding the group of its task, tests for consensus, and initiates process suggestions which the group may accept or reject. A good facilitator helps participants be aware that *they* are in charge, that it is *their* business that is being conducted, and that each person has contributions to make to the group.[14]

In addition to a facilitator, a note taker is chosen, and there is also a "vibes watcher," whose job it is to monitor the feeling level of the meeting, to point it out if the emotional level needs to be addressed because people are angry, restless, fearful, etc.

Casey explains the step-by-step process they use to reach consensus:

A. Information and proposals are presented.

B. Clarifying questions are asked.

C. The group breaks down into smaller groups to discuss the issues.

D. Everyone returns to the large group, bringing reports from their small groups.

E. Any new clarifying questions are asked.

F. (Return to small groups if necessary for further discussion.)

G. The question is then called, and there is a progression of objections that are given priority:
1. Major blocking objections—someone not only doesn't agree on the issue personally but doesn't want the group to take action on it either.
2. Major non-blocking objections—someone doesn't agree with the issue but says they will stand aside and let others act on it if they want.
3. Minor objections.
4. Amendments, compromises, further clarifying questions, additions.
5. Check for consensus—facilitator asks if there is now consensus on the issue.

6. If no consensus, then several techniques can be used:

   a. Mediation sessions can be held for people holding opposing views. The specific problems are identified, and the people are asked where they are willing to compromise.

   b. "Fish-bowling" is used. People with similar views sit in the center of the group and discuss the issue more fully, without being questioned or interrupted by the rest of the group. This allows for freer discussion, as the rest of the group just observes without comment. Each opposing group gets a chance to do this, with the rest of the group just listening. Fish-bowling helps to identify camps and create support groups.

   c. If there are personal, emotional issues between two people, conflict resolution is used on the spot with them, to help resolve their problem. Parent Effectiveness Training techniques are used, such as:

      (1). Using "I" messages rather than "You" messages: "*You* never get here on time, *you're* really inconsiderate," should be changed to "When you're not here on time, I get irritated, because it makes me late for my next meeting." In other words, people take responsibility for their own feelings, rather than blaming someone else.

      (2). Active listening: one person explains her/his feelings about an issue, while a second person just listens, and then restates or summarizes what the first person said in her/his own words. The first person then corrects or clarifies what s/he said, and the second person again tries to restate it to the satisfaction of the first. This continues until the first person agrees with the second person's restatement. Then the situation is reversed, and the other person explains her/his feelings and has it restated back to her/him. This process helps both parties really listen and understand each other and then see clearly the points of agreement or disagreement, without the emotional charge.

           (3). Role reversals: each person alternatively argues for the other person's position and listens without comment.

     d. Brainstorming alternative solutions is used to come up with creative new ideas and approaches which can then be presented for consensus.

  7. If there is still no consensus even after the personal emotional issues are worked on and after alternative solutions are brainstormed, then the issue will be tabled for a later meeting, when new factors may alter things.

H. Evaluations: at the end of each meeting, time is set aside for criticism of the session and self-criticism, as well as positive comments and appreciations.

I. The meeting ends with a feeling of togetherness, a song, shaking hands, a moment of silence, a group hug, etc.

During the meeting, if the energy breaks down—people are tired, restless, etc.—some "light and livelies" are used: a stretch, group game, a shout, song, a moment of silence, etc. To draw out the quieter types in a meeting, several techniques are used:

• A "go-around"—each person in the circle gets equal time to speak to the issue. A conch shell or any object can be passed around and held as each person speaks to remind them that they have the group's attention and can't be interrupted.

• "Fish-bowling"—quieter types are asked to sit together in the center of the group and have a discussion among themselves, with the rest of the group just listening and not commenting.

• "Three matchsticks"—everyone is given three matchsticks at the beginning of the meeting, and each time a person talks, s/he must throw a matchstick into the center of the circle. No one can use the second matchstick until everyone has used the first. No one can use the third until everyone has used the second.

The Ojai Foundation meditation yurt - becoming the guardian of the empty center

THE OJAI FOUNDATION: Becoming the "Guardian of the Empty Center"

The Ojai Foundation was started in 1980 by Dr. Joan Halifax on land in the beautiful Ojai Valley of Southern California that was originally obtained in 1927 by Annie Besant of the Theosophical Society. The community now has about twenty members who serve as staff for their year-round educational programs. Teachers from many diverse spiritual traditions, East and West, offer courses at Ojai. Members meditate together in Buddhist fashion each morning in a large "yurt," a tent-like round structure, and hold regular celebrations in Native American fashion, honoring the cycles of nature. Reflecting its de-emphasis on form and its embrace of Spirit, the community has avoided building any permanent structures on the land until they first experience enough seasons to listen to the land itself and know what it needs and what forms are appropriate.

Ojai is pioneering a new style of leadership based on Joan Halifax's years of experience with Tibetan and Zen Buddhism. As "director" of the community, Joan knows that she is responsible to the outside world. But in reality, she feels there is no one at the "center" of the community. It is an "empty center," and as Joan remarks, "Whoever is running this center is not in a body." God is ultimately responsible for the community, she feels, so her true role is to be "the guardian of the empty center." Here is how she describes the function of that empty center:

> The empty center is the intelligence of the greater whole that you are part of. And all you have to do is to die [release] every moment, and you're brought into the next step...that empty space provides a tremendous amount of room for whatever is becoming. And whatever is becoming, we can't define, because there is no training which we can receive which has any relevance for what is happening right now and tomorrow. The only thing which you can do is to become a Zen Master, which is to cut off all thinking, and realize everything is right here, right now—complete connection moment to moment...
>
> The responsibility for the organism is at its center. And if that center is empty, then someone has to be the guardian of that center. And that person is usually perceived as the director of the community or the president or whatever. But it's very difficult not to be perceived as the full center . . . I would call this center the caldron or the crucible—the sense of fullness in the empty space. The crucible is where the transformation takes place in alchemy.

The structure of the community is very flexible and responsive, in an attempt to operate from "inner authority," not external authority—from sacred law, not secular law. Ojai members feel that when an individual is in touch with her/his inner authority, then that authority is divine, and the individual will think from the point of view of the greater whole, not just from the individual point s/he represents. An over-determined bureaucratic structure takes power away from the inner authority, they feel, because it doesn't trust individuals to behave in a coherent, sane manner, and so it needs to control everyone's actions.

The actual governing structure of the community has evolved into a "Four Winds Council" with four people: the office manager; the programs, publicity, and faculty manager; the land projects manager; and the community manager. This council meets weekly to make major decisions, with input and feedback from a larger community meeting which everyone attends.

Leadership at its best is by example, not force

At its best, leadership at Ojai has been by example, not by force. The person with the highest standards works the hardest. Values are embodied in a person's actions and spirit, but when only one or two people have these values, the community has had difficulties. When a critical mass of members has embodied the values, it has inspired the whole community.

The structure of the community is growing from the fabric of the situation, and not from a mental concept, as Joan explains:

It's very humbling. You can see how it will be, but you're not patient enough. It's like innoculating a culture. You create the template, the key, the pattern for the organism's development. Now frequently, when you innoculate, the organism appears to die. However, the pattern for its life field is there. And actually what happens a little while later—it comes back to life in that pattern. So if you're a visionary, then basically you have a sense of the appropriateness of a particular situation for the future. You innoculate your culture with your vision, and it will take a week or a month or six months, and then it will fizzle

New Patterns of Governance/Leadership **171**

out. It's like an engram. You've created a track in the field, and pretty soon stuff starts to collect around that template, and there you've got it...the new vision gets integrated into the community by a process of continually dying, and then popping up again better, and getting refined. It keeps getting stronger, clearer, and simpler, usually. In a small system every ebb looks like a death, and every flow looks like a victory. After awhile, its just ebb and flow.

Joan Halifax (left)
director of Ojai Foundation

As director of the community, Joan has also learned that she has to be very adept at delegating responsibility and authority in order to let people make their mistakes so they can learn from them. "Flexibility and integrity are the two most important qualities in a director," Joan feels. "If you can't be flexible, you better not be around community."

Like many communities, Ojai seems to have the kind of atmosphere that provides its own screening process for people, so few actual rules are needed, as Joan notes.

If you can't move toward virtue, this place just kind of rejects you, it just doesn't work out. It's been a great dance in patience for me because some people that I thought were awful have come to live here, but I've just kept my mouth shut, and something starts moving and changing, and I think, how wonderful. That's pretty much been our experience, that movement toward the good. I loathe the idea of a super-ego controlling the whole thing. In a way, I'm so strong that if I start giving orders, everyone cringes in the corners...so the less I say, the more that gets done.

*Auroville Community -
building the Matrimandir, a
large spherical temple*

AUROVILLE COMMUNITY:
"Divine Anarchy"

> The more the outer law is replaced by an inner law, the nearer man
> will draw to his true and natural perfection. And the perfect social
> state must be one in which governmental compulsion is abolished
> and man is able to live with his fellow men by free agreement and
> cooperation.
> —Sri Aurobindo

"Auroville comes as close to a functional anarchy as any
place I know of," says David Wickenden, a long-time resident.
"Anarchy in the true sense, when you take it to its root, means
'no leader'," he explains. Auroville is attempting to evolve beyond a traditional hierarchical structure or pyramid where there
is an individual or a group of individuals at the top who delegate
authority to those below. The idea is to have a more circular structure which breaks down the pyramid and spreads power and responsibility out horizontally, instead of vertically.

Auroville is an experimental, international community
started in 1968 and located in Tamil Nadu, South India. Originally
envisioned as becoming a "planetary city" holding fifty thousand
people, Auroville received the active support of both the Indian

New Patterns of Governance/Leadership 173

government and UNESCO. Auroville today is spread over eleven thousand acres and includes over forty settlements with a present population of five hundred people from twenty-four countries. Residents are building a huge spherical temple called the "Matrimandir" as symbolic of the soul of Auroville.

Auroville is founded on the work of India's modern visionary and saint, Sri Aurobindo, and his co-worker, a French woman known as the Mother. The community is engaged in a variety of developmental activities ranging from land reclamation and afforestation to handicraft production and the construction of small-scale renewable energy systems. The purpose of Auroville is to create a spiritual and material environment that will hasten humanity's evolutionary development. Closely connected with Auroville is a smaller community in upstate New York called Matagari, which helps promote Auroville's work in the U.S.

Auroville's vision is "to spiritualize human institutions without institutionalizing the spirit." The Mother envisioned Auroville's becoming an expression of "Divine Anarchy," but she knew it would take a long time, or a great evolution of consciousness, before that ideal would be reached. In the meantime, she felt there were steps along the path that could be taken. One step would be to consciously work on avoiding crystallization of structure. People were always asking her, "What should we do about this or that?" And she would reply, "I know nothing about it. Rather than form a this or a that, you work it out as the consciousness develops." She also commented,

> It is the experience of life itself that should slowly elaborate rules, which are as flexible and wide as possible—always progressive. Nothing should be fixed.[15]

This approach is very difficult, and there are a lot of problems that arise, given human nature. People at Auroville understand this difficulty, and they're not destroyed year after year by this kind of trouble. They believe they're moving towards something new that's very important.

Auroville is attempting to create in miniature a whole new society. David Wickenden feels:

> If there are enough people and enough services (education, economics, politics, land use, etc.), then we should be able to work out in microcosm, in miniature, many of the patterns that exist in the larger society...If a society, *small or large*, has enough people who are con-

Land reclamation and afforestation projects - causing the desert to bloom

scious, who are working on their own inner development and working with other people in the same way, then theoretically there should be no need for the imposition of an external structure, whether it's a police force, or a government, or a legal system.

The ideal, he says, is that no one needs to cede authority to someone else in an artificial way, because everyone is taking responsibility for his own behavior.

Creating a new relationship to the concept of power by keeping it decentralized

How well is this ideal working in practice at the present time in Auroville? Members are working on creating a new relationship to the concept of power by keeping it decentralized as much as possible. There are fifteen cooperatives in Auroville (the food co-op, handicraft co-op, etc.), and each has a certain degree of autonomy. Decisions are made in that area by the people who are involved in it. If there are larger issues that directly affect the whole community, these get taken up in a weekly general meeting called "Pour Tous" ("For All"). There are usually at least sixty to eighty community representatives at this, and all members are welcome to attend if they wish. According to long-time member Sally Walton,

There is no official voting in this group, but issues are discussed until there comes a point where there is no one strongly against whatever is being decided; there might be some people who don't totally approve, but if they say, "go ahead," then that is all that is needed. There really is an attempt here to try to listen to each other, and the

New Patterns of Governance/Leadership 175

success of our process depends a lot on the success of how well we do that. As long as there are a few individuals who haven't learned it, it hurts the whole...Sometimes there is a spontaneous silence that comes about in the group, or occasionally someone will say, "let's just have a few moments of silence," if there's something outrageous happening. But it's not an official thing. We have a big thing about not having any forms. But sometimes everyone will just be quiet for awhile and usually after that things go much better.

Financial policy, often a very "hot" issue in the community, is usually decided upon in one general meeting. Auroville's most interesting system is the "Envelopes Group," a representative body of thirty to forty community members which meets weekly to assess the community's priorities and allocate available funds. Each area of the community that has expenses has its own "envelope." When money is allocated, those areas that provide basic necessities for the community have the highest priority, and their "envelopes" are filled first. If there's any money left over, the other envelopes are filled.

People wishing to contribute financially to an aspect of the work in Auroville put the money in the envelope under which that activity is funded. Once the money is put in an envelope, it cannot be transferred to another. So funds in the food envelope, for instance, can be spent only on food. And if there's a low amount in the envelope, the community eats only what money in the envelope will buy. Michael Tait, a former financial manager of Auroville, explains why they use this arrangement.

We adopted this system to avoid going into debt and borrowing money, as we did before, when there was a general fund...Now what happens if an envelope is only half full is that the people or activities funded from that envelope have to adjust accordingly or find the rest of the money themselves.[16]

This system of envelopes was also developed as an attempt to decentralize the management of money and to involve as much of the community as possible. David Wickenden explains,

When Aurovillians were not involved in the process, nobody except the managers of the general fund knew exactly where the money was going and what our needs and priorities were...The managers tended to get targeted as the people with the power, which wasn't healthy for them or for the community.

Each working group in the community, like the agricultural co-op, for example, has a representative in the Envelopes Group, and its meetings are open to any community member who wishes to attend.

The Auroville Cooperative is a group of five to ten members who represent the community in official matters and monitor its organizational policy and procedure. This body represents the community to the Indian government but is not a decision-making body. (Auroville has had to ask the Indian government to intervene to protect it from the Sri Aurobindo Society in Pondicherry, which had been mismanaging funds intended for Auroville and claiming proprietorship of the community's funds and assets).[17]

Auroville members sometimes see its philosophy of government as one of "perpetual revolution," where structures are always changing, always falling apart and re-forming, in an attempt to find a living organization truly responsive to the community as a whole. Five cooperatives have been dissolved by the whole community at various times, because they'd lost track of what they were supposed to be doing. For several months there would be nothing in that area, and then gradually a new cooperative would re-form. When members are themselves continually changing and evolving, and are not attached to any particular form or structure, something can be changed if it is no longer useful.

But there are some problems with Auroville's anarchistic approach which are intrinsic to the nature of the place. Because Auroville started as a desert, with absolutely nothing, it required very strong people who could survive under extremely difficult conditions on their own, with no support systems. And because it is still very basic, it draws very tough individuals, much like the American West, which was wild and lawless, did. The spirit of having no forms or structures can sometimes create more of a problem than a help, as David Wickenden points out.

> We were recently trying to draw up a list of minimum guidelines about living at Auroville, like minimum number of hours to work per day, etc., and the meetings we had about this were very heated and went on for weeks and weeks, until a list was finally drawn up. But then a lot of Aurovillians wouldn't sign it because it was something on paper, it was some kind of structure. So this begins to be a problem.

Although the Mother had envisioned a "Divine anarchy" at Auroville, she had also talked about the idea of a "spiritual hierarchy," a council of the wise, who could see and know exactly what to do. But curently at Auroville, no one is ready to acknowledge anyone else as being spiritually superior. This is the problem with the heavy emphasis on the group, David feels.

> Group governance is designed in part to mitigate against abuse of power by one or two charismatic individuals; "group wisdom," however, too often becomes simply the rule of the herd. The pressure for conformity in a collective situation, and the tendency to level all to fit a collective mold, is often unbearable for exceptional people, especially artists and intellectuals. This is a very serious drawback to collective life, and I don't know of any intentional community that has been entirely free of this tendency.
>
> The only way something like the experiment at Auroville can work is if there is a very profound commitment to the spiritual path, to individual spiritual growth and the manifestation of the group *soul*, not the group *ego*.

The Findhorn Community - government is a reflection of people's idea of who we as humans are and how we should behave towards each other

THE FINDHORN COMMUNITY:
Inner Guidance, Group Attunement and Focalization

I'm coming to understand that what we call "government" grows out of a set of beliefs about human identity. The government of a people can only be a reflection of that people's idea of who we humans are, what our purpose is and how we should behave towards each other. At Findhorn, we are saying that our identity is Divinity, our purpose is service, and our power is co-creation through love.[18]
—Rue Wallace

Findhorn has experienced a very remarkable evolution of its governance process over the years. Beginning with a clearly defined hierarchy, Findhorn slowly evolved into group governance by "attunement," a process of meditation and consensus. It is a process that many see as a step beyond democracy, a higher turn of the spiral in human attempts at self-governance.

Findhorn was started by Peter and Eileen Caddy and Dorothy Maclean in 1962 in a remote area of northern Scotland, in a trailer park near a windswept beach. From a small handful of members the community has grown to two hundred residents of all ages from many different countries and backgrounds. For the first ten years or so, the community was run solely on the guidance which Eileen received in her daily meditations, along with Peter's strong administrative leadership. Community members experienced Eileen's guidance as having a divine source, so obedience to it was unquestioned. As Peter explains,

> At Findhorn, we had Eileen's guidance and my leadership and the combination was unbeatable, because I had the absolute certainty, with Eileen's guidance confirming my intuition, or with her guidance directly and I would take action. And if anyone didn't agree with it, they knew what they could do—leave—found their own community. But this was how it was. No argument, no discussion. That was it. Then as we grew, I would delegate more responsibility to others. But I still held the reins.

Then in 1971, Eileen was told by her inner voice in meditation to stop sharing her guidance with the community. Each person was to seek his or her own transcendent source of guidance and help to take responsibility for the whole. This was called by some "the democratization of guidance." The purpose of Findhorn was not to develop "good-willed, obedient servants" but rather to empower individuals to be self-initiating and responsible. Findhorn was still to be guided by the God within, but now that voice was no longer to speak with the accent of one or two individuals whose alignment with the Divine was unquestioned. Rather, it sought expression through a broader source, encouraging the whole community to turn within for guidance.[19]

The first step in this transition from hierarchical to group leadership was the establishment of "focalizers" or facilitators for community work departments. Sarah James describes the process of focalization.

> I always felt that being a leader meant that you were responsible for keeping an organization running. At Findhorn a focalizer is not this

Eileen Caddy, co-founder of Findhorn - each person is to seek her/his own guidance and take responsibility for the whole

kind of leader. For me, focalizing the maintenance department is like being a funnel through which one pours water into a bottle. A funnel directs the water into the bottle, but the energy for the action is not in the funnel, it is in the water. It's a service you are providing, a particular input into a circle of people.[20]

Rather than being a leader in a traditional sense, focalizers hold the focus for a work department. Stephen Clark adds:

Leadership at Findhorn is based on a hierarchical pattern, not of power, but of responsibility. If my responsibility, as focalizer of the publications department, is to ensure that deadlines are met, the way that's carried out is not to insist that someone meet a deadline, but rather to share, in the most open and clear way possible, the reasons for it to happen. Being a focalizer, holding a broader awareness of the way a whole system operates, I try to share that awareness and allow each person to contribute his or her part.[21]

Peter Caddy, co-founder of Findhorn - handed over focalization of the community to Francois Duquesne

As Peter and Eileen began traveling a great deal, accepting invitations to talk about Findhorn to groups around the world, it became necessary to establish a Core Group to make overall policy decisions and to maintain the vision of the community. Membership in the Core Group is by invitation of other Core Group members and by self-selection. Later, additional groups were formed to help decentralize decision-making in specific areas: personnel, for membership and work allocation; the College group, for educational programs; the Administration group, for finances; the Guest Department, for visitors' programs.

Finally, when the Core Group was able to stand totally on its own two feet as the major policy-making body, and the community as a whole was strong enough, Peter Caddy was able to leave the community and hand the overall focalization to Francois Dusquesne (and later to Jay Jerman). The community began decentralizing even further with each work department and large living unit moving towards taking more responsibility for its own internal membership and financial decisions. For a time, Findhorn also had a Village Council, with representatives from all the large living units and work departments. But today there are monthly meetings of the whole community where major decisions that affect everyone are discussed, as for example, buying the caravan park where the original part of the community is located.

This decentralized model of community governance has been very popular and has worked very well at Findhorn as long as there has been trust and good communication among the various groups, which has generally been the case. Francois Dusquesne explains the growth in people that has made its system of governance effective.

> People at Findhorn are more responsible and mature than they were. It's their community. They're not just living at Findhorn in a welfare state, but they're saying, "I have something to give, I have something to create here. It needs my total energy for it to work."
>
> When people shift from that consciousness of being in a place that cares for you to one where it's your creative expression, this raises the energy considerably. As more community members step forward and take responsibility, it makes it more exciting. More members now focalize community meetings.

Leadership at Findhorn works to draw out the natural leadership and awareness in others

Leadership at Findhorn is neither aggressive nor dictatorial but rather works to "draw out" the natural leadership and awareness in others.

In decentralizing governance functions at Findhorn, the principle of leadership has not been eliminated. Rather, a balance between hierarchy and democracy is being created, according to Francois.

> Dough doesn't rise without yeast. There always are a few people carrying the initiative in a community. There are always natural leaders, initiators, pathfinders. What is needed, though, is to find creative, harmonious ways of relating that dynamic, initiating energy with the

sustaining, maintaining energy, which is just as important. Clear transactions between the initiators and the maintainers need to be found. If there's too much initiative, leadership runs off and is cut off from the grass roots. So disease sets in both ways. To negate the need for yeast or leadership, though, is to ask for trouble. But the leaders must build a bridge of communications with the rest of the community.

Findhorn is based on a threefold social order, an ancient principle of organization. There is a political sphere, a socio-cultural sphere, and an economic sphere. Members work on respecting the independence and unique qualities of each area. Applying the values of one sphere to another—like that of the political sphere (a hierarchy of functions and responsibilities) to the economic or socio-cultural sphere—ends up in conflict because the values in each of these are quite different. Cooperative association is needed in the economic sphere, but inner freedom is more valued in the socio-cultural sphere.[22]

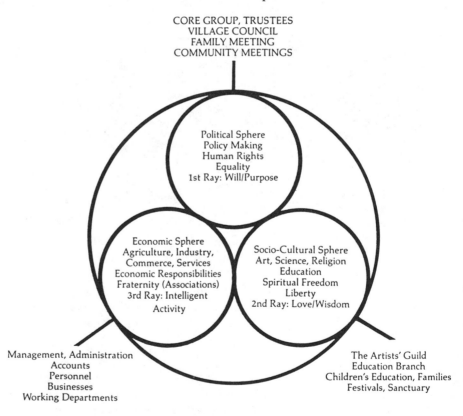

CORE GROUP, TRUSTEES
VILLAGE COUNCIL
FAMILY MEETING
COMMUNITY MEETINGS

Political Sphere
Policy Making
Human Rights
Equality
1st Ray: Will/Purpose

Economic Sphere
Agriculture, Industry,
Commerce, Services
Economic Responsibilities
Fraternity (Associations)
3rd Ray: Intelligent
Activity

Socio-Cultural Sphere
Art, Science, Religion
Education
Spiritual Freedom
Liberty
2nd Ray: Love/Wisdom

Management, Administration
Accounts
Personnel
Businesses
Working Departments

The Artists' Guild
Education Branch
Children's Education, Families
Festivals, Sanctuary

*Governance by group
attunement or meditation*

The most unique and important feature of group governance at Findhorn is its process of "attunement," basing decisions
on inner guidance. Everyone is recognized as having the ability to
tune into the Universal Mind and offer her/his unique perspective
and contribution to the governance of the whole. The ideal that
Findhorn is working towards is a governance through synergy,
where individuals know their own authority and power and are
not threatened by each other but work together to create a whole
greater than the sum of its parts.

Former Core Group member Helen Rubin adds:

> I feel that guidance comes through a group like pieces of a puzzle
> being added. When we have a group meditation, different people
> bring different aspects. Intuition is influenced by one's background,
> environment, training and education. What I see happening in all the
> groups in the community is people trying to work together from a
> space of clarity.[23]

The form the attunement process usually takes is for group
members to begin discussing the facts surrounding an issue and
then to express their own feelings about it. This lays the ground-
work for the group meditation. It's like laying all your cards out
on the table, so to speak. Then each person works on releasing
personal opinions and asks for guidance from the Divine Mind on
what is the right decision for the good of the whole.

New Patterns of Governance/Leadership 183

A short meditation is held, often with members holding hands and sitting in a circle. Afterwards, each person has a turn to share what s/he experienced in the meditation. Generally, a clear consensus emerges from this—all the divergent views fit together like puzzle pieces and create a whole picture. If not, it may not be the right time to make the decision, as other factors need to come into the picture first. Or perhaps one or more people in the group haven't really released their personal opinions and don't feel very clear about the issue from a higher level. As long-time member Michael Lindfield explains:

> If there's a minority who don't agree on an issue, the majority usually doesn't just steamroll over them and go ahead. In most groups my experience at Findhorn has been that where any major decision is being made, if two or three people haven't felt comfortable about something, then we've persisted until all present have been able to reach a point where they can support the decision even though they don't necessarily agree with it. It's important that we take care, on the whole, to have group consensus, even though it may take a long time to reach it.[24]

And Leona Aroha adds:

> Fusion comes though the development of trust within a group. If anyone goes into the meditation mistrusting any one person or the situation, it doesn't work.[25]

The word "attunement" is used at Findhorn to mean a technique for getting guidance on decisions as well as for creating a sense of "at-one-ment" with God, with other people, with the tools one will be working with, with the plants in the garden, etc. This can be done through the form of holding hands together in a circle before working or meeting together and having a short meditation. But ultimately, "attunement" is a way of *being*, not a technique, as Francois suggests. "The definition of "attunement" I like most is living, breathing, working every moment in the presence of Spirit."

As a community, Findhorn has had to learn about, and grow a great deal around, the whole issue of guidance and leadership. At first, Peter and Eileen and the Core Group would decide where the community should be going and would ask the community to come along. Later they developed more of a tendency to try to figure out what direction the community was already headed in and then stay two steps ahead, ready with policies when they were needed. It was a case of trying to tune into the community's vision rather than get a vision for the community. As Jeff Dienst sees it:

> The organism has natural instincts to grow in the right direction; it's attuned to it. If the organism listens to itself, it will grow true. It will be hard not to. It will be more painful not to. Also, on a practical level, to the extent that people feel that something is laid on them, they won't go along with it as well. But if the community feels like they're all participating in the decision, you'll get much more support for it— that's the idea of consensus—to get complete support for the decision, rather than little groups that aren't in agreement.

And Eileen Caddy offers her changing experience with the use of guidance.

> I would never use guidance to hit people over the head now, but the guidance that I had was sometimes used like that in the past. Instead, I see it as planting seeds. Instead of calling it "guidance," I just make suggestions. Then it's up to the person. If the ground is fertile, it will grow. But if the ground is barren, you build a bridge of love between yourself and the situation, and then walk across the bridge and sow some more seeds. And if the seeds I sow fall on fertile ground, it's amazing the things that happen. They've received their own inner direction—that's the wonderful thing.

Another issue in the use of guidance is that different people are more or less skilled at receiving clear guidance from a higher level from the inner Divinity. To use the analogy of a radio set, some instruments are more finely tuned and so receive less distortion in picking up a signal. And some receivers may not really be tuning into the Divine signals at all, as Nick Rose suggests.

> It's taken us up to now to accept the fact that guidance can come from many places, including our own subconscious or collective thought-forms in the community. And I feel that only now are we really prepared to start examining the sources of guidance with some discrimination.[26]

A good way to tell if guidance is coming from a higher level or not is to examine whether the action suggested would be for the good of the whole or would just serve the desires of the individual who received it. Guidance from a higher source always reflects "Divine economy"—it will serve the needs of the individual and the group at the same time. And the words used will be brief, inspirational, and to the point, not flowery language that just serves to build up the ego of the receiver. "Guidance coming from a higher level stretches people," Jeff Dienst adds. "It makes them do things they would never want to do on their own."

The effectiveness of the new system of governance that Findhorn has pioneered may offer some important new insights for evolving a more humane and viable government. It is an attempt to synthesize hierarchy and democracy, centralization and individual responsibility, the spiritual and the practical. As historian William Irwin Thompson observes,

> At Findhorn, more than in India, I found the balance between American politics and Eastern mysticism. And looking at the spiritually unbalanced politics of the older Americans, and the politically unbalanced mysticism of the younger ones, I knew that was as important as anything I had found around the world.[27]

7 Innovative Approaches to Relationships, Sex, and Child Raising

If I speak in the tongues of men and of angels, but have not love, I am a noisy gong or a clanging cymbal. And if I have prophetic powers, and understand all mysteries and all knowledge...but have not love, I am nothing.

—CORINTHIANS 1:13

Relationships, Sex, and Child Raising 187

Although once the most exciting aspect of the communal scene from the media's perspective, sexuality in communities today is a much quieter, more personal issue. With a few exceptions on each end of the spectrum (such as Kerista Village's group marriage, Camelot's celibacy, feminist communities such as Hardscrabble Hill, and a few gay men's communities), most communities today don't have a strict philosophical stance about sexual behavior. Although sexual patterns vary considerably from community to community, most of the groups mentioned in the text of this book have a mixed collection of monogamous couples, a few non-monogamous couples, a good number of single people, and sometimes a few gays.

Most group marriages or triangles attempted in communes of the '60s or early '70s (such as at The Farm in Tennessee) didn't work well. The human proclivity for at least serial monogamy, if not lifelong monogamy, seems to run deep in people. Robert Hourriet, in his book *Getting Back Together*, notes that the famous group marriage experiment in the '60s by the Harrad West commune in Berkeley failed because "They had nothing *but* sex to hold them together—no common culture, no non-sexual forms of communicating and expressing love."[1] And sociologist James Ramey points out, "Free love groups [were] very short-lived; probably a group that is uncommitted sexually is uncommitted in general and thus unable to sustain the level of cooperation necessary to the survival of a commune."[2]

In the early days of Shannon Farm in Virginia, for example, there was more trading of partners and more bi-sexuals and gays, but today there are mainly monogamous couples. Four years ago a new couple was told, "You won't survive here as a monogamous couple." Now they're told, "You won't survive here unless you're in a monogamous relationship." This trend toward monogamy is not unique to communities. Time magazine ran a front page story recently called "Sex in the 80's: The Revolution Is Over."[3]

Dr. Susan Campbell, in her research on communities, found that, contrary to common beliefs in the '60s, "Pairing, when it occurs in the context of a committed community, seems to enhance, rather than diminish community involvement." When men and women find their life partners, they feel empowered to focus more energy on the group's goals. Dr. Campbell also noted that communities with a monotheistic spiritual orientation seem to have more of an emphasis on monogamy and nuclear families, while those with a socio-political or ecological-scientific orientation tend to emphasize the group itself as family.[4]

Most long-term, stable communities attract a larger number

of couples than singles today, but this seems to stem from practical considerations rather than philosophical ones. Couples, especially those with families, are more interested in stability, in putting down roots in one place, and in developing community for the long run. Singles are often younger, with more of a need to travel and explore different options. They are often either looking for a long-term mate or at least interested in the availability of enough short-term relationships. Unless a community is itself large enough to provide appropriate sexual partners when needed, singles are likely to move on. Communities that are not only large enough but which also emphasize sexual equality and social experimentation, with economic structures that make it easy to come and go, such as Twin Oaks Community, attract singles more easily. And if the community has communal child raising or does not allow individual houses, families who prefer to retain some aspects of nuclear family living may be deterred from joining.

Today there is a definite openness and yet also a new maturity about sex in most communities. Sex isn't seen as an end in itself, but rather as an integral part of the wholeness of life. Lessons have been learned from the freedom and experimentation of the communes of the '60s when it was necessary to break up the suffocating, crystallized attitudes about sex in order to live life more fully and to ensure a real equality of the sexes. As one commune member noted:

> There is no way we could live together comfortably in such close quarters without overcoming embarrassment and squeamishness—and most importantly, lustfulness and possessiveness in regard to sex.[5]

The sexual experimentation of the communal movement of the '60s made a real contribution to society, according to sociologist Rosabeth Kanter, by reducing the primacy of blood ties, age and sex differentiations, and authoritarian relationships in favor of negotiated, egalitarian, intentional relationships.[6]

Sexual mores have changed considerably in the mainstream since hippie communes first shocked the public with open sex among non-marrieds. Today over half the population feels it's not immoral for unmarried couples to live together, and 63% of parents of college-age youths feel pre-marital sex is okay if two people love each other.[7]

Now that all these changes have been adopted by the mainstream, the pioneering work of communities has moved from the sexual frontier to the emotional frontier, experimenting with new ways of working out conflicts and getting along together, not just in sexual relationships, but in all areas. In order to make a community sustainable over the long run, the age-old issues of how to achieve social harmony are still very important. While very useful for overcoming fears and hang-ups and freeing up blocked energy, sexual experimentation, per se, doesn't always create a deepening of human bonds over time unless there is a corresponding commitment on a heart level. So today's communities are more directly addressing the issue of emotional sustainability. Instead of emphasizing specific forms of sexual expression, they are working on developing certain values in relationships, such as honesty, open communication, respect for differences, and personal responsibility for actions.

To have sex or not to have sex is no longer the question. Of concern is whether sexual expression is in harmony with one's emotions, mind, and spirit, so that one is acting in wholeness. Rather than having sex in order to meet one's own unfulfilled emotional needs, the emphasis now is more on developing wholeness in oneself. Ideally, if two people come together it should be as whole beings, not as incomplete parts looking for what they're missing. Instead of approaching relationships out of a need for romance or for security, the motivation in most communities today is personal growth. Relationships are used as a learning process, and differences are used to catalyze personal growth. Unlike traditional relationships, where problems result in either a break-up or in a passive, "victim"-type attitude, many community relationships today are based on a commitment to work out problems and to release attitudes of possessiveness or jealousy.

The community context provides caring friends who can act as mediators and counselors and who have often faced the same problems themselves. The movements for women's and men's liberation have provided additional support for community members. The community context also adds the potential of deep but non-sexual friendships. And living with many members of the opposite sex in community provides excellent training for future relationships and/or marriages through learning to get along together and respect differences.

Another new relationship in communities is the "co-creative couple" which comes together out of a need to create together as partners, rather than out of a need for romance or security.[8] There are a number of male/female pairs in key leadership roles in communities like High Wind, Sevenoaks, and Chinook, and the energy and creativity expressed is very powerful. However, a problem often faced by these couples is having too much energy going into their shared work and not enough into nurturing themselves or the relationship.

An interesting development in communities over the last few years, which also emphasized personal growth, is the shift towards working on the masculine and feminine energies *within* each person. Eileen Caddy, co-founder of the Findhorn Community, says she has worked on developing the dynamic, masculine side of herself—strength, mind, and will—to balance her feminine side. Her former partner, Peter Caddy, has worked on developing his feminine, receptive side—love and nurturance—in order to create wholeness within himself. Where there is more of a balance of both masculine and feminine qualities within each person, there needn't be such a desperate search for the perfect complement in another person. Two people can relate to each other from a place of wholeness within themselves. Barbara Rhodes of the Providence Zen Center has been working on creating this balance within herself, and she says she finds it essential in her life. Men at the Twin Oaks Community have been working on developing their feminine, nurturing qualities, and women, their strength and dynamic qualities.

The co-creative couple - going beyond needs for romance or security to serve society in some creative way

While most communities today are returning to stable monogamous relationships after a period of sexual experimentation, the communities where sex is still a major issue are the ones which emphasize celibacy and/or strong emulation of a central guru figure. A member of Esalen Institute wryly commented that couples in their community seem very stable compared to the situation in many spiritual communities, perhaps because sex is open and not repressed at Esalen, as it often is in spiritual communities. A lack of honesty about sexual behavior on the part of the teacher/guru, along with isolation from feedback on behavior, can be devastating for devotees who believe they are emulating a perfect master.[8]

A number of spiritual communities have been experiencing a change in sexual attitudes. Swami Kriyananda of Ananda Community, after years of celibacy, became involved in a relationship that nearly led to marriage. This opened things up in the community and modernized the traditional Eastern approach to spiritual life, so that now a number of the community's celibates are getting married. The Providence Zen Center is also now allowing more couples and families to live at the Center, instead of requiring the traditional monastic arrangement. To provide for those wanting a supportive environment for a celibate life, a new monastery is being built on the Center's grounds.

Relationships, Sex, and Child Raising 191

Today there is much less communal child rearing than was attempted in the '60s. However, most children in communities today are still raised quite differently than in the average American family. Children are treated more as people who are able to make their own decisions, speak for themselves, and do their share of chores. There is an egalitarian ethos, with children given fewer directions. The main emphasis is on self-discovery and learning to trust.[9]

The opportunity to relate to many different kinds of adults and children, like having many aunts, uncles, and cousins, seems a positive benefit for most children in communities today. These children are often far less shy than other children are around adults, since they meet many visitors in the community. But there is a problem for these children in living in an adult-dominated world. When all the adults in the community are together, they tend to focus on each other too much and ignore the children. A child's world holds a special magic that is more accessible to adults when there are fewer distractions in the environment. Communities which work best set aside special times of play or celebration when all the adults focus on the children (as does Mettanokit Community in New Hampshire), and they have other times when only adults are present. In this way, the children are not constantly competing for the adults' attention when the whole community is together. This can help avoid negative "acting out" on the children's part as a means of getting attention.

Not surprisingly, child raising in communities tends to be one of the most controversial issues, as different philosophies are often in competition. Much is learned by community members in observing the various approaches used by different parents and noting the results. Interestingly enough, when children in communities become teenagers and begin longing to fit in with their peers, they often reject the community and want a more traditional nuclear family life, just as youth in the '60s rejected their nuclear families and wanted to live in community. On the other hand, as some teenagers in communities mature, they decide to choose this lifestyle for themselves.

Each of the communities in this chapter is exploring a new approach to creating better interpersonal relationships or to sexual roles or child raising. Twin Oaks has a major focus on developing equality between men and women and raising children communally. The Farm has developed an extensive midwife program for natural childbirth. The University of the Trees is developing a non-sexual "group marriage" through the use of a personal growth technique called "creative conflict." The Living Love Community helps people "de-program addictions" and find win/win solutions to interpersonal conflicts. Esalen Institute has applied the insights of the human potential movement to male/female relationships in order to create more freedom and at the same time, more responsibility.

Twin Oaks Community - communal child raising for freeing up parents' time and providing parenting for childless adults

TWIN OAKS: Sexual Role Equality and Communal Child Raising

Twin Oaks Community is based on a nonviolent, non-sexist, egalitarian philosophy with communal income sharing. For over fifteen years it has been one of many groups pioneering a new approach to relationships, going beyond traditional sexual roles, and allowing people more freedom to be themselves. Women can do construction work and executive work; men can do cooking, cleaning, and caring for the children. At Twin Oaks, even language has been changed to reflect a non-sexist attitude. Instead of using the masculine pronoun "he" or "his" to describe ambiguous or general situations, a new word, "co," is used—as in "whatever co chooses" or "co's job." Community members have a strong commitment to overcoming sexism and sex-defined roles. Linda, a Twin Oaks member, expressed her experience this way.

The community supports women taking on work that is not tradition-ally women's work, and a lot of the stuff I did was like that: forestry, E.C. [furniture-making], supervision work. I never would have at-

Relationships, Sex, and Child Raising 193

tempted something like that on the outside—doing heavy physical labor, or fine working with my hands. I was always conditioned to think I was clumsy, to think that I should work at a desk and use my brains more...The men here encouraged me and shared their skills with me, at the type of work that a man is supposed to be "good" at and a woman isn't, like fixing the big machines at E.C....People were gentle and caring in their teaching, and I was taught with a lot of respect...I feel people encourage and expect women to take on managerial jobs and work that could be considered "executive work," like economic planning, managing the business, getting involved in the government.[10]

There is also a strong emphasis placed on developing greater honesty and openness with people.

> Probably the biggest thing that's special about Twin Oaks is that it's more comfortable interpersonally. My relationships are not strained by trying to make impressions. I feel I can be myself. I don't feel pressured to live up to expectations. On the outside there was a lot of gameplaying and roles—men chasing women, women playing hard to get—those bullshit games. Here it's a lot more friendly. We live together and know each other. It sort of demystifies relating to someone of the opposite sex.[11]

Sexual role equality and greater honesty and openness between people

The greater honesty and openness at Twin Oaks also helps improve relationships among members of the same sex. Corb continues:

> There's a lot less antagonism and competition here between me and other men. I can go and have a walk with any number of men here and talk about some really deep emotional things and spend intimate time with a man. It's really exciting...it's not something you have to be ashamed about. I don't mean just homosexual relationships. I mean support/friend relationships—having the support of other people you live and work with, instead of their scorn.[12]

To overcome sexual hang-ups, there is an encouragement of nudity in certain places like the swimming hole, and there is an open-door policy in the bathrooms. Doors are never shut, and at any given time there are usually several members of opposite sexes sharing the bathroom.

There are a few monogamous couples at Twin Oaks, but the majority of members are single people. A few are homosexual and a few are celibate. But one of the big attractions of Twin Oaks is all the available singles, according to Kat Kinkade, one of the original founders.

> Twin Oaks is a first-class mating society. You can move from one relationship to another, and there's the sheer availability of all those unmarried people, including a lot of visitors.[13]

The sense of openness and freedom to explore other relationships also has it drawbacks, as Kat's daughter (now thirty years old) admits, "Jealousy is one of the hardest problems we have to deal with."[14] But this also provides a great opportunity for personal growth through working on jealousy issues. And another member, Will, adds:

> When we came, the sentiment was that monogamy wasn't cool, it wasn't communal. Twin Oaks is an extremely hard place to carry on any monogamous relationship because there's such an incredible freedom to get involved with other people. When we first broke up, I was like a kid in a candy store. But when I decided I wanted a child, I knew that would require more of a commitment.[15]

Today monogamy is more acceptable in the community, and there are more monogamous couples.

Personal support groups

Co-counseling is regularly used by members in order to help discharge negative emotions. "Clearness" meetings, developed by the Movement for a New Society, are used to help individuals make difficult decisions. "Group feedbacks" are used to help

Relationships, Sex, and Child Raising 195

new members overcome certain behaviors, such as sexist attitudes. There are also women's support groups and men's support groups. Over the years there have been various personal growth groups working with dreams, yoga, aikido, and meditation.

Androgyny is an important concept in the community. Twin Oaks rejects the idea that there are right or wrong, natural or unnatural forms of male and female behavior. Some members even have androgynous names like "Wane" and "Soto." On a typical day at Twin Oaks, a visitor might find a man sewing a skirt to wear or hanging out diapers to dry, or a woman working on a big machine in the industrial building.[16]

An unusual aspect of Twin Oaks, compared to most communities in America, is that of communal child raising. Children live together in a children's house and are cared for by a rotating team of "metas" (from the term "metapelet" used in the Israeli kibbutz). The original child philosophy of the community emphasized collective care and decision-making, using a behavioral approach. In negating the nuclear family approach, members hope to minimize the mistakes that they felt occurred in their own upbringing and to teach communal values at an early age. "The goal has been to dilute the possibly neurotic patterns which exposure to only two parental figures might impose," as one member expressed it. Over the past two years, Twin Oaks has evolved towards more a kibbutz-like situation, where biological parents and other adults called "primaries," who want a deeper relationship with a child, can spend several hours in the evening with the children. This sort of one-to-one interaction is now valued and encouraged to a greater degree than before.

The children's building is a quarter of a mile from the "courtyard" where most of the adult members live. An adult residence, also housing the older children, was built nearby. The building contains rooms for nursing mothers, where women live for the first year of their child's life, with a nursery at hand and the children's building and metas close by.

Twin Oak's communal child-raising system works especially well for mothers, as Linda describes it.

> What's special and good about it is that I can have my baby and my work, too. I don't have to hold down three jobs to have enough money to support her, like I would on the outside, and then not have time to be with her. I can leave my child with them whenever I want to. Some of my work quota is child care. When you first have a baby, that's your work. Then gradually, as the baby gets older, you take on

more and more of other kinds of work. So that when the baby is a year old, other work becomes full-time and you spend just your free time with her. After Leah starts sleeping through the night and gets a little older, she'll probably start sleeping at the children's house. That will mean that I'll have my nights free too, to go to parties and stuff, something which I do not do much of now.[17]

And the child's father, Corb, adds:

There's a real difference in being a father here. Leah has a lot broader support system. She has a lot more people in her day-to-day life who have energy for her, who are caring what's going on in her life. In a way, you might say that's watering down my importance, but it helps our relationship. All her support doesn't have to come from two people. I can take all the time with her I need. When I am with her I have much better attention for her. I can spend as little time as a few hours a week with her or as much as a bunch of hours a day. I feel really good about the child care. I think it shows—our kids in general are really healthy emotionally, and that says a lot for the program they have been brought up in.[18]

Gerri, who is one of Twin Oaks' longest term members (thirteen years), loves the child care system, as she finds constant exposure to her children draining and difficult. She comments:

One reason I'm still here is that I like the way my children are being raised. Their ability to work things out with the other kids is phenomenal. Sometimes instead of punching each other, they'll say, "Hey, I think we should talk about this."[19]

Being a meta is a very popular job at Twin Oaks, and quite a number of men are "metas" as well. Metas work an average of only fifteen hours a week with the children and really look forward to their time with them. Eleven to twelve per cent of the community's income goes to children. (There are currently about sixty adults and fifteen children in the community.) Metas are careful not to lay "power trips" on the kids, not to use their adult status to coerce actions or behavior unless absolutely necessary. The children's building was designed to be safe for children; it's a place where children needn't hear, "No, don't touch."

The advantages of this communal system are many. It frees children from exclusive dependency on two adults for love and guidance, and it frees those adults from that heavy responsibility. It affords people who are childless the opportunity of interacting with children. It protects children from violent upheavals in their lives when their parents divorce. It frees mothers to develop their talents in other areas. It allows fathers and other men a more active role in bringing up their children.[20]

As wonderful as some aspects of this communal system for children are, Kat Kinkade observes, ''This program is expensive—it can't be offered to outsiders with ready-made families. We have all we can do to keep up this standard for the children who are born here.''[21] Another problem is that the community has a lot of control over children, as Tomo observes.

> There is a controversy at Twin Oaks now about how many children the community can handle—how much resources it takes, as the budget is growing all the time. Members have to apply to the board about having babies. There is currently a restriction on having visitors with children who are interested in joining Twin Oaks. The community also requires that no child can join who is older than the oldest child in the community, if that child hasn't lived in community before.

Another problem is that there is turnover among the metas who care for the children, as they leave to do other work at Twin Oaks or leave the community entirely. So this does not provide the long-term stability that parents can offer their children. And although there is agreement on some basic issues in child raising, there is still quite a disparity among different metas.

Decisions involving children at Twin Oaks are among the most emotionally charged, as Josie observes.

> Basically we let all the people who want to have kids fight it out. The Planners decide if there's enough money for us to have children, and the Child Board decides who gets to do it.[22]

Unapproved pregnancies in the community are rare, but members try to make the best of them when they occur.

Young children at Twin Oaks, aged three and one-half to five, have a Montessori classroom that includes work with visual perception, phonics, movement, manual skills, and vocal exercises. Older children attend classes using a more eclectic approach that reflects the community's basic diversity of values, and some children attend local schools.

*The Farm Community -
Spiritual midwifery and the
sacredness of childbirth*

THE FARM: Spiritual Midwifery

Started in 1971 by Stephen Gaskin and 250 of his followers, The Farm is probably one of the best known communities in this country and was, until recently, one of the largest. Farm members run a medical clinic, a midwifery program, an ambulance service, a book publishing company, a soyfoods business, and children's schools. One of The Farm's most important contributions has been its natural childbirth program. For many years, unwed mothers could deliver their babies free of charge at The Farm and leave the child, if they chose. If they ever wanted the child later, they could come and get him/her.

Relationships and child rearing have always been an important focus in the community. Married couples are in the majority, and there have always been as many children as adults. High ethical standards are applied to relationships. Members are encouraged to let go of their vanity, ego, and the sexual games learned in society in order to become more honest and real human beings. There is a very high value put on the sacredness of life and the spiritual role of motherhood. Midwives are especially highly respected and childbirth is a special honor. Ina May Gaskin, Stephen's wife, wrote in The Farm's book on *Spiritual Midwifery:*

The knowledge that each and every childbirth is a spiritual experience has been forgotten by too many people in the world today, especially

Relationships, Sex, and Child Raising 199

in countries with high levels of technology. We feel that returning the major responsibility for normal childbirth to trained midwives rather than have it rest with the predominantly male and profit-oriented medical establishment is a major advance in self determination for women.[23]

Spiritual Midwifery is a very popular book and contains complete instructions on how to deliver a baby naturally at home, with diagrams of the mother's and child's anatomy, advice on pre-natal and post-natal care, what to do about complications in labor, etc. The Farm's approach is very down-home and common sensical yet at the same time, very intuitive and conscious of the subtleties of energy flow in the mother. The support of the father during the birthing process is especially encouraged. The mother is taught how to relax, as this allows the birth to be much quicker and easier.

Farm mothers speak of childbirth as a deeply moving religious experience, becoming One with all mothers. Strong bonds of love and compassion are forged when a couple has a spiritual experience at the birth of their child.

Farm midwives emphasize the importance of energy and learning to flow with it during childbirth. Contractions are called "rushes," since this indicates the way to relate to the energy they represent.

> Every birth is Holy. I think that a midwife must be religious because the energy she is dealing with is Holy. To one who understands the true body of "Shakti," or the female principle, it is obvious that [a woman] is very well designed by God to be self-regulating. We are the perfect flower of eons of experiment—every single person alive has a perfectly unbroken line of ancestors who were able to have babies naturally, back for several millions of years.[24]

Ina May Gaskin and twelve Farm midwives have delivered over one thousand babies by natural childbirth at The Farm. The techniques they use have been shown to be far superior to those used in hospitals, they believe, especially in the area of caesarean sections. They've only had to have nine caesareans out of 750 births, while hospital caesareans range from 10% to 50% of all births. In forceps deliveries, they've only had one in 750, as opposed to a national average of 25%.[25] A typical home birth at The Farm costs only about $15.00 for materials, so they've saved the mothers they've delivered a total of nearly a million dollars in hospital costs.

By 1984, 269 women had come to The Farm specifically to have their babies, instead of going through with abortions. Only twelve of these women actually left their babies at The Farm in foster homes. Most chose to stay at The Farm, although they were free to go and leave their baby, if they chose. Until 1983, Farm members paid all costs of the mother's care before and after delivery, and this contributed to their financial difficulties. Now The Farm has a more realistic approach with a fundraising program, and they ask those who can afford to pay towards the cost to do so. They are also establishing a school for midwives and making videotapes of home births available.

The Farm has a premature and intensive care nursery with incubators, bilirubin lights, oxygen therapy, and round-the-clock nursing personnel.

Farm women have developed a "cooperative method" of birth control, determining fertile periods with temperature and mucous tests, and they have published a book with instructions for this method.

The mother is the central figure in The Farm health care system. From the moment her child is born, she is given information and instruction about how to give her child adequate care, good nutrition, and basic sanitation. Mothers are considered the natural nurturers of the newborn, so most women spend most of their time at home with their children. This contributes to a strong sexual division of labor at The Farm. Mothers share child care with each other, so young children can always be left with someone nearby if a mother wants to work. Farm fathers are more supportive and involved in their children's upbringing than the average father elsewhere. They frequently feed, bathe, dress, and play with their children, and this helps them develop their nurturing side.[26]

Much attention is given at The Farm to providing the right environment for the children. They are not allowed to "rip off energy" from adults by clamoring for attention, but they are given firm, loving feedback about what's acceptable. Visitors are often very inspired by the loving relationships between parents and their children. The Farm's schools emphasize participation and feedback, and conventional subjects are taught along with topics like environmental awareness. Farm children become apprentices on community jobs and work crews, and thus they learn specific practical skills like building, farming, health care, and cooking.

Although relationships and child raising have remained very much the same over the years at The Farm, the community's recent political and economic evolution has been very tumultuous. For most of its history, The Farm had a membership of over eight hundred adults and seven hundred children, with seventeen other Farm-connected communities around the country.

In the last two years, however, membership dropped dramatically to only 150 adults and 150 children, as the community was going bankrupt. The "simple lifestyle" advocated by The Farm for spiritual and political reasons had gone to an extreme. Many long-term members left because they felt their children weren't even getting an adequate diet.

> We used to pay too much attention to the spiritual dimension, ignoring the physical. We'd say, "We'll just have good karma and it will all work out," but it didn't work because it was too unbalanced. We were living the communal myth, saying, "Give us your huddled masses, and we'll feed them, clothe them, pay their bills."

Fortunately, in recent months, things have begun to change. The remaining members have totally reorganized the community politically and economically and put it back on its feet. The failing communal economic system was changed to a cooperative so that members can keep private property, earn their own income, and then contribute for monthly rent and taxes. The land is still owned by the non-profit corporation but may soon become a land trust. Some Farm businesses are now separate corporations, operating as worker cooperatives, charging for their services and paying employees from the proceeds. Visitors are now asked to pay for their stay, unlike in the old days, when thousands were supported by The Farm in exchange for their labor. Community midwives can no longer take any outside unwed mother and deliver her baby free of charge.

Although Stephen Gaskin was the major spiritual teacher for members for many years, there is an openness to other spiritual teachings now. Stephen still lives at The Farm, though he travels frequently around the country to give lectures. Leadership in the community is more decentralized, with a return to participatory democracy and an elected governing board. The Farm is actually beginning to resemble a small town now.

Today The Farm is paying more attention to the material side of things to keep the community financially together. Many members have cut their hair and shaved their beards (every man had long hair and a beard until recently) in order to get jobs in town. They're still pacifists and vegetarians, dedicated to the same spiritual ideals, but in a more practical way. Members still volunteer to work with Plenty, the very effective international relief organization working in many Third World countries, which Farm members started several years ago.

*University of the Trees -
'Creative Conflict' is the glue
that holds the community
together*

UNIVERSITY OF THE TREES:
"Creative Conflict" Technique and
Spiritual "Group Marriage"

The University of the Trees was started in 1973 in Santa
Cruz, California, by Dr. Christopher Hills, who had previously
directed Centre House in London. The community has grown
now to about forty members living together in several houses in
town. The University offers courses in Dr. Hills' Theory of Consciousness, Nuclear Evolution, Meditation, Yoga, Wholistic Healing, Solar Energy, and Self-Government. The Bachelor of Arts
and advanced degrees are offered and are state-authorized but
not accredited. Correspondence courses are taken by hundreds of
students around the world.

The community started several businesses over the years as
a way of putting their spiritual beliefs into practice. Business is
seen as a "tool for evolving consciousness." Members feel that
the measure of a person's spirituality is how s/he applies it practically. Businesses are commonly owned by members. University
of the Trees Press publishes thirty titles; Ion Research Center produces air and water filters; and Tree of Light markets spirulina, an
edible algae rich in protein. The community also runs Evergreen
School for children.

Long-term members of the community who are committed
to its vision can become part of the community's lifelong "group
marriage." A union of heart and mind on the spiritual level rather

Relationships, Sex, and Child Raising 203

than a marriage on a physical, sexual level, this group marriage is described as "a profound experience of oneness" by its members. They feel that through this experience, "group consciousness manifests most intensely and [they] sense the incredible evolutionary potential for mankind." The intensity results from the deep commitment members have made to each other, to their spiritual values, and to working out any conflicts with each other. This group marriage is referred to as the "Nucleus" of the community, the "pacesetter and heartbeat of community life."

Members of the Nucleus are elected each year to leadership positions in the community. The method of selection used is very unusual: throwing the *I Ching*, an ancient Chinese system of divining. The people who receive hexagrams with the strongest "yang" lines on top are chosen as leaders. This method is very effective, according to member Wendy Rickert, because "the normal leadership types are not always chosen; it's often someone for whom it's time to draw out leadership potentials, for his/her own growth process."

The foundation of community life at University of the Trees is a process called Creative Conflict. It's taught in classes to new students and used regularly by all members. According to Rod Glasgow,

> Creative Conflict is obviously the glue for the community. It's not used to just smooth over differences, but to penetrate to the cause of the differences...the ego and the separative faculty of the human mind. The spiritual principle behind it is: "You are whatever disturbs you." In other words, the problem we're facing is never "out there"—it's within us. We have to own our disturbance and get to its cause.

Members feel that Creative Conflict can teach each of us how to free up the creative energy locked in a conflict by showing us that the "other" with whom we are in conflict is in reality a part of our larger self. The "other" represents something in us that we need to deal with for our strength. We can get inside and understand the "other" only if we can get past our egotistical identification with our personal perspective.

Christopher Hills believes that conflict is inevitable in humans, and so therefore its energy must be used creatively.

> Conflict is built into nature to evolve the creation, to push it along the path of evolution. Conflict is so very important because it is the major

propelling evolutionary force, although it is not the evolutionary goal. When together we can discover the creative keys to mastering conflict, we will be on the threshold of a new society.[27]

Creative conflict works by challenging each person to confront her/his ego, the part of the self that is prideful and that experiences separation from others on all levels. The first step in dissolving the separating self-sense of ego is to get out of our little self and into the inner world of others. Working on conflict in a loving, committed group using this process allows the group to mirror back to each person exactly what s/he needs to work on. The group becomes a soul mirror for each person's ego position so s/he can see her/himself more clearly. Christopher Hills describes the process.[28]

Centering: Using meditation as a way to relax the body, feelings, and thoughts, we get in touch with our inner being and listen to ourself. We can't really listen to anyone else fully until we can listen to ourself. Regular meditation practice helps us to gradually become more clear and open.

Receptivity: We clear our mind of what is going through it so we can open our mind and our heart to focus on the "other," to let them in, to merge the consciousness of each other, to meditate on the other while he communicates. In India, this technique is called "samyama"—inner listening.

Active Listening: We repeat back what the other has said to us as clearly as we can, using our own words. This helps the other to feel we understand.

Mirroring: We use our intuition to reflect the feelings behind the words used. We mirror back the vibration, experiencing the other as he inwardly experiences himself, and we become one. As soon as the other feels heard, the mirroring touches him, and a heart contact results—being-to-being communication. But if the person's block lies very deep, mirroring may not penetrate the heart. It may take some time before it's reached, because the person isn't ready to see the block yet. So we don't push it but rather back up and give the person space.

Confirmation: The other confirms the mirroring by saying, "Yes, that's how I feel." If he doesn't confirm it, then he will communicate again, and again we try to mirror both the words and the feelings behind them and wait for confirmation.

Response: When the other person confirms our mirroring

or asks us to explain further, then we may respond to the communication, but not before. We then ask the other person to mirror our response, to be sure the communication is deep on both sides.

"I" Messages: These are used throughout the communications to keep the finger of blame from pointing too much towards the other person, instead of taking responsibility ourselves by saying our own feelings. The moment we accuse someone with a comment like "*You* make me mad," we have left the level of sharing and the possibility of touching the other person's heart. The four parts of an "I" message are:

A. We begin by stating our own feelings in the situation: "I feel..."

B. We then indicate what emotion has been triggered in us: "...angry..."

C. We state what action or words triggered the feeling: "...when you don't believe me..."

D. We become more honest and vulnerable by sharing our motivations and the fears behind the feeling: "...because I am afraid I will lose you."

This last part is the most important step, as it leads to a deeper self-probing and to the nitty-gritty questions of life, where tremendous energy is locked up that can be released for maximum spiritual growth. It takes us closer to total honesty with ourselves, to the domain of the heart.

Member Sybil Green comments:

With Creative Conflict the idea is not just to lay down your ego so you become passive, benign, powerless, with no individuality. It's rather to empower people more fully and to get past the ego blocks that bring harm to others.

And Rod Glasgow adds:

The idea is to do enough work in meditation and yoga that we become steeped in the experience of our cosmic self and so are able to face penetrating our ego.

The Living Love Community - everyone you meet is your mirror

LIVING LOVE COMMUNITY (THE KEN KEYES CENTER): "Reprogramming the Human Bio-computer"

A loving person lives in a loving world.
A hostile person lives in a hostile world.
Everyone you meet is your mirror.[29]

The Ken Keyes Center and Living Love Church in Coos Bay, Oregon, is focused around a series of workshops called Clear-Mind Trainings, which help people open their hearts and find a win/win solution to conflicts. Ken Keyes, the community's founder, has developed techniques based on a kind of Westernized Buddhism to help release desires and negative "programming." Ken has written half a dozen books on these techniques. The most popular of these is *The Handbook to Higher Consciousness*, which has sold over 600,000 copies.

Those wanting to join the community must take a series of trainings, and the techniques learned are used daily in the community to improve interpersonal relationships. Tim Brunn, a former Luthern clergyman and one of the community's trainers, comments:

We're a demonstration project to show how these tools work in our community and business—keeping the building and meals together. We're a very diverse group of people, but because of using these techniques we can enjoy living together.

Relationships, Sex, and Child Raising **207**

Ken Keyes feels that these techniques have been essential in helping the community run smoothly.

You have to have a way that helps people harmonize their differences. You've seen and I've seen countless communities that were formed with the greatest of idealism, goodwill, and self-sacrifice, and two years later they split up and explode apart. The great thing about [being] here is we have a method to work on our conflicts that helps us go beyond our stuff, to create unity where before there was separateness. It helps us to go beyond our righteous demands and get back to the love between us so we can work things out. It's structured in as the foremost aspect of our community.

Small experientially-oriented study groups, called "Vision Centers," have been set up all over the country for people to apply these techniques in their daily lives. The techniques used in these groups and in the community are based on what Ken calls "The 12 Pathways to Higher Consciousness."

These pathways can show you the way to find the beauty and happiness that is hidden within you. You were erroneously taught that happiness lies in getting people and things outside of you lined up exactly to suit your desires. But our desires multiply so much faster than our capacity to satisfy them! In the Living Love System, an "addiction" is any desire that makes you upset or unhappy if it is not satisfied. Life is warning you to get rid of an addiction every time you are emotionally uncomfortable in any way.[30]

The 12 Pathways are a series of affirmations that are repeated often to help an individual release addictions and "re-program" his/her human bio-computer:

1. I am freeing myself from security, sensation, and power addictions that make me try to forcefully control situations in my life...and keep me from loving.

2. I am discovering how my consciousness-dominating addictions create my illusory version of the changing world.

3. I welcome the opportunity...to become aware of the addictions I must re-program to be liberated from my robot-like emotional patterns.

4. I always remember that I have everything I need to enjoy my here and now.

5. I take full responsibility here and now for everything I experience, for it is my own programming that creates my actions and also influences the reactions of people around me.

6. I accept myself completely here and now and consciously experience everything I feel, think, say, and do...as a necessary part of my growth into higher consciousness.

7. I open myself genuinely to all people by being willing to fully communicate my deepest feelings.

8. I feel with loving compassion the problems of others without getting caught up emotionally in their predicaments.

9. I act freely when I am tuned in, centered, and loving, but if possible I avoid acting when I am emotionally upset.

10. I am continually calming the restless scanning of my rational mind in order to perceive the finer energies.

11. I am constantly aware of which of The Seven Centers of Consciousness I am using.

12. I am perceiving everyone, including myself, as an awakened being who is here to claim his or her birthright to the higher consciousness planes.[31]

Students at the Center are given step-by-step training in how to transform "addictive demands" on people into "preferences." Through the "Exploration Insight Process" (EIP), students are taught to take responsibility and avoid blaming other people and situations around them for their suffering. Whenever a separating (fear-based) emotion is felt, students are encouraged to 1) identify the emotion as concretely as possible (e.g., fear, anger, jealousy); and 2) pinpoint the addictive demand which is at the root of this emotion. The demand is something their internal "programming" is telling them they need to have in order to be happy. The "Sharing of Space" (SOS) technique is then used to communicate the insight to the other person in this form: "I choose to create the experience of _____ (anger, fear, etc.) because I choose to addictively demand that _____."[32] This form helps people take responsibility for their own emotions and stop blaming other people and situations.

Ken describes how these techniques work in a typical community situation.

> For instance, if someone's on the list to do dishes and s/he forgets, we point out that it's important for us each to be real and to do our share, and to call the games of other people when they are not being responsible for their share. But we don't use this as a way of throwing people out of our heart. We realize everybody forgets sometimes that it's their turn to wash dishes—no one is perfect. We realize that the main thing is to keep our hearts open always and at the same time, if we have to, kick someone in the ass. We can literally love someone while saying, "This is not acceptable" and be very definite about it. What we help people understand is that when a person doesn't wash the dishes, if you feel angry, it's not his/her failure to wash dishes that is making you angry. It's your addictive demand that s/he wash dishes because s/he is on the list. Whatever s/he did was just a trigger for addictive programming in your head—something your parents taught you, or a school teacher, or friends, or society.

The techniques taught in one community have been very effective for people even in extreme situations. For example, a doctor who had done the training received much national publicity when he was kidnapped and his life threatened by "right-to-life" people because he gave abortions. He was able to remain calm and centered during the ordeal by using the techniques. He said, "It really worked. They held a gun at my head, saying they were going to kill us, and I was using these methods to love them." His wife hadn't learned the techniques and still today bears deep emotional scars from the ordeal.

The approach to interpersonal conflict taken by community members is for each person to work on her/his own negativity first. They feel that if everyone "works on her/his head enough to overcome the boundaries of separateness," then there's enough breakthrough that they can get along pretty well. Chances are that if one person works on her/his stuff and keeps an open heart, the other person will work on her/his stuff.

Many of the people who come for the trainings at the Center are in a relationship or have just left one, and they want to look at what's going on in the relationship from a more conscious perspective. But when new members join the community, they are asked to not become involved in a "primary" relationship (a serious relationship with one person) for the first year and a half, although they are not necessarily required to be celibate. The purpose of this, they feel, is to not get distracted from the task of deprogramming negative patterns by putting too much emotional energy into building a new relationship. After the first year and a half, however, primary relationships are okay. Currently, there are several families among the forty staff members who all live together in one large building. But this seems to work out fine, according to Tim Brunn, as parenting is often shared.

> It's nice having families in this one building here. Three of us just had babies within the last six months, and we co-parent the other children that are here. It's very nice for me. I don't know if I'll have a biological daughter, but I have three daughters whose lives I'm very much a part of. It's a nice experience.

Esalen Institute - an incarnation of the ancient and a gateway for the yet unsung...a Kingdom of Death and Rebirth

ESALEN INSTITUTE: Pioneering the Human Potential Movement

Esalen is a state of consciousness as much as it is a physical place. It is a pagan monastery where seekers of every description come to find light. Breaking out of the crumbling structures of their past, they come to find themselves. They come to discover again their bodies, their feelings, their pain, their knowledge, their happiness at being alive.

But Esalen is Hell as much as Paradise. It is a climate only for those who are both rigorous and capable of total defeat. For here your nightmares must come true in order to fulfill your dreams. Here you are forced to fall flat on your face before you can drink the cool, sweet waters of joy. Many do not enjoy too long a stay, for here is where the mirror is ruthlessly turned around to face inward: the demons, flushed to the surface, are no longer "out there." The pace of karma quickens and comes home...

Relationships, Sex, and Child Raising 211

A threshold for change, Esalen is both an incarnation of the ancient and a gateway for the yet unsung...somehow the magnificence of its beauty draws out the full power of the human spirit. Esalen is a Kingdom of Death and Rebirth. It is a place inside each of us.
        —Rick Tarnas

Esalen Institute in Big Sur, California, for over twenty years the mecca of the human potential movement, is a legend in its own time. Here the great innovators of the human growth movement gathered to explore the furthest reaches of the mind, body, and emotions. Their pioneering work spread around the country, until today nearly every town in America has its growth center.

Begun by Dick Price and Michael Murphy amidst the social and political transformation movements of the 1960s, Esalen instead focused on *personal* transformation. Thousands flocked to Esalen to learn from Alan Watts, Willis Harman, Gregory Bateson, Abraham Maslow, and later, Fritz Perls, Will Schutz, and Ida Rolf. Over the years, Esalen hosted nearly every well-known personality in the alternative movement from Timothy Leary to Carlos Castenada, from Carl Rogers to Buckminster Fuller, and it also hosted every new consciousness training from Arica to Rolfing. Many of the alternative therapies of the 1960s and 1970s got their start at Esalen. Gestalt Therapy, encounter groups, sensory awareness, hot tubs, and nude massages were immensely popular, as visitors learned to loosen up and let go of their hang-ups. "There was a lot of freedom to explore, to do outrageous things, out here on the edge of the continent with no one paying much attention," staff member Brian Lyke observes. And Walt Anderson, in his history of Esalen, writes:

> Many marriages, new careers, and religious awakenings have been inspired by Esalen experiences...and so have a lot of divorces and dropouts, and a few deaths.[33]

"Esalen is an accident—it was never meant to be a community, but something magic happened," Brian claims. "We do have a community here, like it or not, intentional or not." To take care of all the thousands of visitors each year, a permanent staff of about thirty-five members live and work at Esalen. The membership is very stable and committed, compared to some communities. Although Esalen is basically a business, a service organization, there is a symbiotic relationship with the community of staff people who run it. "The community invests the business with a quality of something special—that wouldn't happen if people were just doing a job," Brian comments. "But people come here in order to work on themselves, not to join the community," member Craig Carr notes. And Kathy Thormod adds:

> Community is strongest during crisis. People are there for each other in very personal, loving ways, and in social ways, but the rest of the time people are so busy working and taking classes for self-development that there is little juice for community needs. And because so many staff have families, after work they just want to nestle with their family and not go anywhere.

The sense of community seems strongest in the work departments. Some departments begin their day with a group meditation. Some enjoy the garden with group singing and others like a group hug. "Process groups," held each week or every other week in each department, have an outside facilitator (a Gestalt or Reichian therapist) who comes in, and the whole crew comes together to work on anything that's not resolved between people. There are a few rules in these sessions.

1. Always speak from an "I" space rather than a "you" space, which is a blaming space. For example, "I feel angry," not "You make me angry."

2. Maintain eye contact when communicating feelings.

3. Don't use the word "but" when appreciating someone else, or when accepting appreciation, as it negates everything that just was said before it.[34]

By allowing structured time every other week to express resentments, small things don't get blown up into larger issues by being repressed. Sharing positive appreciations with each other allows good feelings to develop among members, since everyone needs to be appreciated for what s/he is doing and just for who s/he is.

Kathy Thormod comments:

> The emphasis here is on taking care of yourself and on clearing relationship "stuff" between people. People tend to be themselves here much more fully than elsewhere—they aren't so caught up in being "nice." So that can be a challenge and it can also be an opportunity. I can't get too complacent here. Every time I think things are fine, someone will suddenly come up with something they're having trouble with me about. You can't push conflict under the carpet here. The

level of honesty and being true to yourself is strong. People will say, "I need to express myself and be who I am and—you!" There's not as strong a sense of service, of putting aside personal differences to move ahead with a group of people or a project. People are more independent and competitive than [in] some communities.

The positive side of Esalen is that there's an exceptional magic to the place. Personal growth happens very rapidly, and there are many classes in body work and emotional therapies. But the negative side, according to Brian Lyke, is that sometimes members seem rather "self-indulgent, spoiled, and selfish" compared to other groups. "People shouldn't stay here very long," Brian says. "They should get trained in Gestalt or body work and then go out and serve in the larger culture. We need to get spread around, not all be in one place."

How does personal growth happen at Esalen? Brian explains that

Esalen has a way of chewing up people's egos. You come here and see something that you feel needs to be changed, and you seem to bang your head up against the wall trying to make it change. But then finally you get it...you have to change yourself first, instead of projecting outside yourself onto the whole the changes you'd like. You have to surrender your desire to change things, and then you see that there's a wisdom that's made things the way they are.

One of the things that makes Esalen work so well is that there is a real climate of openness to new things that pervades the place. There is a deep honoring of a person's own process and the way that person gets to his/her own truth. Over the course of living at Esalen, one sees so many different paths work for different people, and this creates a very tolerant climate. Esalen was founded on a philosophy of openness and synthesis of many paths. There is no proselytizing and no coercion to join any particular teacher, and this is one of its greatest strengths.

Esalen has always been known for its open sexuality, yet surprisingly, couples and families seem very solid. Kathy observed:

There aren't as many break-ups here among members as in other communities. People don't tend to fall in love with their "soul-mate" down the road.

Perhaps it is because of the very lack of sexual repression, allowing all the options to be available, that sexuality per se no longer holds such a fascinating allure as when it was forbidden. And at Esalen there is less judgment about how you express yourself sexually. Brian Lyke observes:

> There's a real hope that people will work on their relationship and be responsible about their use of sexual energy. People who like to play around sexually and not be responsible wouldn't be very comfortable here on the staff. There's a stability here because we've grown up— we've each gone through the gamut of being real explorers on the sexual frontier to being stable family people with children. Now people are involved in more of an inward search, instead of trying to find outward thrills in sexual explorations or in having lots of relationships. We are going more deeply into one relationship and seeking a deeper fulfillment with real commitment.

Esalen's reputation for free sexual expression seems to come more from visitors who view it's nonchalance about sexuality as a golden opportunity for having a sexual fling. Walt Anderson in his history of Esalen reports:

> If you come driving into Esalen on a sunny afternoon, you may pass a section of lawn where people—staff employees, usually—are playing volleyball in the nude. You may well have come prepared for nude sunbathing and massage and hot-tub soaking, but all those jiggling appendages and tanned bodies, before you even get to the registration desk, serve notice that you have come to quite a liberated place. Yet overall Esalen managed to avoid being as wildly naked and free as some of its leaders, notably Fritz [Perls], thought it should be. . . its programming never ran heavily into sex therapy or the advocacy of sexual freedom. Once you get past the volleyball game you can probably manage to have a quite unerotic time, if that is what you came for.[35]

A new interest at Esalen is in family therapy, pioneered by Virginia Satir and Carl Whittaker, who have given seminars there recently. Family therapy studies the whole gestalt of the family; it's not just the mother and father working out an issue but the children and the family dog, too. This therapy deals with the whole system—how everything relates—and not just with isolated parts. Esalen families have found this approach very effective.

Ten years ago at Esalen there were no children allowed, but today all that has changed and probably half of the staff have children. There's a lot of opportunity for growth as a family in an environment like Esalen. Brian Lyke commented:

> One of the things that has most helped me grow and change has been my family scene here. I met my wife at Esalen and we had a baby here. It was not an easy time for us; we went through a lot of changes. Esalen is very hard on couples, the way many communities are. If you can live together here and make it as a couple, than you can probably do it anywhere. Being here with the opportunity to go through my changes, learn about myself, and have a support system around me is something I couldn't pay for anywhere.

Several years ago, in order to educate staff children as well as local children, Esalen established the Gazebo School which offers an experiential approach to learning. Under the direction of Janet Lederman, the Gazebo is a learning environment that utilizes its natural surroundings and the inherent curiosity of children as motivators for acquiring knowledge. "Every situation is seen as a teaching/learning situation," notes Joyce Lyke, one of the school's teachers. Children are allowed to learn at their own pace, primarily by an apprenticeship or learning-by-doing method. The Gazebo involves members of the community in sharing their knowledge in special areas with the children. There is a strong emphasis on what they call "life cyles" teaching, like learning how to grow food. Students are taught how to plant seeds, harvest vegetables, prepare food, and make compost with leftovers, weeds, manure, etc. They also raise goats, chickens, and ponies. "If a dog eats a chicken, we use this as a learning situation about death," Joyce adds. "Teachers don't always create the teaching situation; they let the children lead the way."

Children start going to the Gazebo at eight months, and the school has students up to eight years of age. There are now about twenty children in the school with four credentialed teachers. The school ground is a very exciting place for children. Babies are taught in a teepee; two- to four-year-olds in a boat; five- to eight-year-olds in a large converted bus equipped with computers. There's even a hot tub for the children to play in.

Esalen itself has been going through some changes and expansions in the kind of programs offered. Now that personal growth centers have sprung up in every town in America, co-founder Michael Murphy is exploring new frontiers to keep Esalen on the "cutting edge" of consciousness. Courses such as "The Politics of the Solar Age" are offered, and there are extensive programs in Soviet Studies and Soviet-American citizen exchanges.

⑧ New and Timeless Approaches to Self-Reliance and Self-Healing

...A path toward consciously learning the skills that enable us to touch the world ever more lightly and gently...allowing us more time and energy to develop the heartfelt aspects of our lives.[1]

Amidst all the news reports of polluted food and water supplies, rising costs of fuel and medical care, threats of nuclear war, economic upheaval and possible earth changes, it's easy to feel powerless and at a loss as to what to do. Today's communities are meeting this challenge and providing what they see as the Community Solution to these problems. They have been quietly pioneering new approaches and relearning old skills that were nearly lost, in the belief that human survival in the future may well depend on these skills.

The workability of alternative sources of energy (such as wind and solar), wholistic health techniques, ecologically-balanced architecture, and organically grown food is being researched and demonstrated today in hundreds of communities around the country. Unlike corporate research into some of these areas, community experiments are open to the public, and "hands-on" classes are usually offered to teach people how to do it themselves. A hallmark of these innovative technologies is their sustainability. Renewable sources of energy are used so as not to deplete the earth's resources. And these new technologies are usually relatively inexpensive and easy to learn.

Preserving ageless practical skills and teaching them to city dwellers

Communities have also become the preservers of many ageless practical skills known by our grandparents which, until recently, were almost lost to most of our population. Community members are now teaching some city dwellers how to grow their own food, build and heat their own homes, care for their own health, and recycle usable resources often wasted by society. One of the first communities in recent times to teach these self-sufficiency skills was The School of Living in Pennsylvania.

Community members also practice what they call "voluntary simplicity," generally reducing their level of needs and simplifying their lifestyles. This allows them to have more time for what they see as important pursuits—self-development, time with family, friends, and with nature—and it makes an important moral statement about the level of over-consumption, waste, and resulting pollution in society.

Although the number of communities established primarily for the purpose of developing total *self-sufficiency* and *independence* is small, most communities recognize the value of *self-reliance* and *interdependence* with others. Self-reliance develops a satisfying sense of well-being and of control over one's own sustenance. Interdependence, through bartering and exchange of goods and services, develops a sense of caring and connectedness. Perhaps it is the lack of connection to the earth and lack of ability to produce one's own sustenance that adds to the sense of alienation and restlessness often felt by city dwellers.

Working with wholistic techniques and the healing power of nature's herbs

Self-reliance skills are being developed in communities not because members fear a great natural catastrophe on earth, but because it's empowering to be self-reliant rather than dependent. Community members grow their own food not only to avoid dependence on supermarkets, but because it's healthier, cheaper, and more personally satisfying. The increasing use of pesticides and other chemicals in store-bought food provides impetus enough to grow your own, along with the satisfaction of working directly with the earth and the healing powers of nature. Likewise, community buildings are heated with solar energy and

Self-Reliance and Self-Healing 219

wood because they are renewable sources of energy and are cheaper and more pleasant than gas or electricity. Preventative and wholistic health techniques often save lives as well as pocketbooks. The whole system—mind/body/emotions/spirit—is treated, not just isolated parts. Ecologically-sound architecture often combines comfort and beauty with concern for nature and for the planet as a whole.

Significantly, all of these self-help techniques embody a deeper ecological awareness of the planet as a living system whose balance must be maintained. Often called "Gaia" by the ancients, this term for the earth as a living system is being used again today by community members who feel both an awareness of the inter-connectedness of all life and a deep reverence for nature. Living close to the earth, in harmony with the cycles of nature, provides a greater sense of the wholeness of life. Often the land itself provides a strong sense of bonding among members. Love of the land and the richness of the experience of working the land together creates a strong sense of unity among people. "Living lightly on the earth" (as poet Gary Synder once called it) is highly valued in communities in order to conserve the earth's resources and to restore the ecological balance lost through pollution, de-forestation, over-grazing, mono-cropping, and pesticides. Many communities such as Findhorn, for example, have massive tree-planting projects to renew the earth for future generations. Auroville community has planted thousands of trees and raised the water table, thereby causing the desert to bloom.

The majority of communities mentioned in this book have incorporated some innovations in health, agriculture, energy and/or architecture in their work. Most use some form of wholistic health care such as herbs, homeopathy, or reflexology, for example. Most have built new buildings with a passive solar design, and they grow their own food organically.

In this chapter we highlight several communities that are pioneering new approaches in these areas. Center of The Light and Kripalu teach people how to heal themselves through the power of the mind and spirit and by using techniques such as homeopathy. Spring Valley grows abundant gardens using bio-dynamic principles, and Findhorn uses a process of attunement to the "devas." Stelle and High Wind have developed various forms of alternative energy, and Arcosanti has built ecologically balanced "arcologies."

The Center of the Light -
helping people to take
responsibility for their own
health care

THE CENTER OF THE LIGHT:
Wholistic Health through Self-Help

The Center of the Light is an educational center founded in 1979 by Gene and Eva Graf and a group of dedicated healers. A small group of healers and teachers of wholistic health created the nucleus of the community, and they maintain the energy of healing that is generated on their eighty-three acres in western Massachusetts. Other teaching staff live nearby.

The community grew out of the Church of Christ Consciousness, established by Gene and Eva several years earlier. There is a strong reliance on prayer and meditation in the healing process they use. Weekly "healing services" are held with praying, singing, and "laying on of hands" to help those in physical or emotional pain.

The staff of the Center of the Light teach people ways to take responsibility for their own health care, believing that each person has within her/himself the ability to discern what is true or healthy for her/him. The staff works to sharpen the individual's own knowledge and intuition and to help people establish a personal connection with the moving spiritual force behind all experience. Students begin learning techniques to use with simple ailments like colds, stomach aches, and bruises. As their confidence and training progress, they learn to work emotionally, mentally, and spiritually to create health and wholeness. Staff member Linda Burnham explains:

Self-Reliance and Self-Healing 221

By giving people something that they can do for themselves, such as knowing what to eat, what herb tea to drink, what affirmation to say, or what technique they can use to help them forgive themselves or others for past or present problems, then they can get a handle on their problems and can get stronger. As they get stronger, they can connect more with their own Divinity, their own self-worth. Then they are truly on their way to self-healing.

Staff member Mary Kate Jordan explains their philosophy of health.

Any physical dysfunction or disability is a reflection of an emotional or mental dysfunction. In perfect health there is a total alignment between the spiritual, the mental, the emotional, and the physical. We're given constant spiritual messages, but when the mind or emotions don't go along with them, there's a misalignment. With enough of these misalignments, it begins to reflect in the physical body as disease or pain. Fortunately, aligning the mental and emotional with the spiritual aligns the physical body and healing results.

Much of the Center's unique approach to healing and their work with herbs, nutrition, and various alternative techniques comes from spiritual guidance received in meditation by staff members, especially by Gene and Eva Graf. Graf Body Systems®, a spiritually channeled method of healing that considers the totality of a person's being, teaches anatomy and physiology from both a physical and a spiritual standpoint, and it offers contact point and energy-release techniques and a practical introduction to herbistry and nutrition. Although it appears to be Oriental in some ways, Graf Body Systems relates to a Western system of physiology. This material is taught in the community's Training for Healers program. This two-year program offers massage and bodywork, spiritual counseling, and a grounding in the spiritual use of psychic tools. Mary Kate explains:

Many people have psychic talents that they use all the time, but they don't think of them as anything special. Feeling energy is something most of us do all the time and it's familiar, so we don't even call it psychic. What we teach is how to expand this native ability. We teach people how to listen to their bodies. Everyone has a truth signal inside them—it may even be as tangible as a chest getting tight.

Eva Graf first learned the Body Systems material in a dream/vision right after she made a decision to learn the use of herbal remedies rather than have an operation. A being of light appeared to her in the dream and showed her places on the body that she could touch that would bring energy to the different systems that needed healing. There are a different set of points for the digestive system, the nervous system, the circulatory system, etc. Herbs, nutrition, and affirmations are also used for each system.

The two-year Training Program at Center of the Light is primarily for people who want to act as healing channels for others. "Although there is a tremendous volume of practical information and guidelines on healing in the course, there is a very strong focus on your own process of self-healing," observes member Linda Burnham. "As you begin to clean up your own act, you have a lot more strength and integrity to help others." Some of the people who take the training are already professionally based psychologists, nurses, and sociologists who want to augment what they are already doing. Some people take the training to get involved in a wholly new field of service, and others take it to experience community and a sense of loving support as they grow spiritually. "It works in many ways," Linda notes. "You get training in the healing arts, and you do a lot of insightful work on yourself at the same time."

None of the staff of the Center gets a regular salary. They do both the teaching and the physical maintenance and building of the Center on a volunteer basis, receiving only room and board in exchange. Their tremendous dedication to their work and their quiet faith in God (though they come from many diverse religious backgrounds) has helped to create a very healing environment for those who come to the Center to learn their self-help approach. They see their work as augmenting, rather than competing with, traditional medical approaches. In certain situations, for example, they might recommend that someone go to a surgeon, if that's what is needed.

Most of the staff are trained herbalists who teach others about the cultivation and use of herbs for nourishing the body and spirit. Herbs are an integral part of their lifestyle and healing philosophy and are seen as one of nature's most important gifts to humanity. Much of the detail about the specific combinations of herbs into formulas and tinctures has been given to staff members in meditation. Herbs such as yarrow, red clover, burdock, and valerian are grown wild in their meadows; garlic, sage, and chamomile are cultivated in their garden. They use these herbs for such imbalances as strep throat, ulcers, open wounds, arthritis, and nervous disorders.

Over two hundred varieties of herbs are used for various

ailments. Some herbs that are commonly thought of as weeds, like dandelion, chickweed, and "live forever," are eaten in salads for their nutritional value. Dandelion is a tonic and a stimulant, and tradition has found that it acts to remove poisons from the body. Yarrow is used for stomach cramps and to stop bleeding. Eucalyptus has been found to be useful for colds, sore throats, and lung diseases. They use blackberry leaves and roots for treating diarrhea and bleeding gums, and horehound for sore throats and to heal the entire respiratory tract.[2] Cayenne (raw) is used for internal and external bleeding and ulcers.

Staff members teach people how to use whole foods to take care of vitamin and mineral needs, instead of relying solely on vitamin supplements. Brown rice, bee pollen, and yogurt are recommended as strong sources of B vitamins, for example. Dulse and other seaweeds are strong in iron, calcium, and manganese; greens such as parsley, comfrey, and spinach are rich in iron and chlorophyll which build and cleanse the blood. Cayenne pepper, rosehips, and kelp are great sources of Vitamin C, needed to prevent colds.[3]

Community members don't recommend the use of sugar because they've found that herbs don't function effectively with it. It also inhibits the absorption of water into the body, and therefore prevents the proper absorption of food and nutrients. "It also seems to make pancreatic-type people act very crazy," Mary Kate notes. "Although honey is the same as sugar chemically, it is a whole food, a complete enzymatic package, pre-digested by the bees, so it's not stressful for the body to absorb it."

How well do the Center's herbal and nutritional remedies work? Alice Hunt testified to what she called "a miracle of natural healing" in a letter she wrote to thank the Center's staff.

> Four years ago I was hospitalized with an attack of angina. The doctor put me on medication. . .and I found myself taking nitroglycerin just to walk a block and a half to the office. I could not face cold, wind, or exertion of any kind without experiencing pain in my chest all the way up to my ears. Last May. . .I followed a natural vegetarian diet. . .and was introduced to herbs and the benefits of cayenne. Within two weeks I was. . .digging out tree roots. . .moving large stones and doing really strenuous work. I had given up all medication, so freedom from pain had to be the result of my new diet, cayenne and other herbs and vitamins I was using. . .I feel so good about myself, I would like to shout from the rooftops the difference in my life physically, emotionally and most of all spiritually.

In addition to the work with herbs and nutrition, Center of

the Light members have also been pioneering more unusual alternative healing practices and teaching them to their students. Gemstones are used in healing, as the very focused and orderly geometric pattern of their electromagnetic field has a specific stabilizing effect on a person's electromagnetic field and etheric body.[4] For example, emeralds have been used in many cultures to alleviate back ailments, diamonds to help certain eye ailments and rose quartz to straighten out the ascending colon.[5]

Mary Kate Jordan - teaching people Shiatsu, herbs, nutrition, homeopathy, flower essences

The Center offers other alternative approaches to healing such as:

Flower essences: essences distilled from a wide variety of flowers to balance the emotional/spiritual levels, where disease first originates;

Guided Imagery in Music: use of music for allowing an individual's own internal symbols and imagery to arise from the inner self to release locked-in feelings, develop creativity, and provide spiritual insight and understanding;

Reiki: a unique type of "laying on of hands" treatment, a specific "ray" of healing energy which can gently and profoundly balance the body's energies as it restores harmony;

Foot reflexology: a tool for opening capillaries and for releasing lymphatic flow, energy blocks, pain, and disturbance in the organs and systems of the body by massaging the feet, where there are connection points to these organs;

Self-Reliance and Self-Healing 225

Shiatsu: an ancient oriental system of applying stimulation to points in the body for healing;

Homeopathy: remedies based on applying minute amounts of the elements which cause the disease or problem, so as to activate the body's healing systems; for use in first aid and common everyday ailments like colds, hay fever, nausea, and constipation;

Visualization: a tool for helping the mind to create images that enhance health and well-being, as the mind controls the body and is aware of the body down to each individual cell where emotional blocks, disease, and traumas are held.[6]

In addition to the classes taught at the Center and the training programs for healers, members of the community also operate an herb-related business and prepare herbal products themselves. Weeds of Worth, Ltd. provides herbal remedies such as burdock healing salve, a natural insect repellant, cough syrup, mullein oil often used for ear distress, goldenrod oil for the skin and to aid in weight problems.

Kripalu Center - a supportive environment to help people make lifestyle changes needed for improved health

KRIPALU CENTER: Applied Yoga and the Body/Mind Connection in Health

Kripalu is a wholistic health center and yoga community of two hundred members started by Yogi Amrit Desai in 1971. Kripalu has two main centers and forty affiliate groups around the country. The original center in Pennsylvania is developing into a community for families and others who want more flexibility in their lifestyle along with more financial independence. The main facility on three hundred acres in Lenox, Massachusetts offers a more traditional ashram experience (with celibacy among singles, and shared income) as well as health programs for the public. Two medical doctors, a clinical psychologist, and fourteen therapists provide health services for members and guests. Kripalu's doctors work to bridge traditional medicine with alternative approaches such as homeopathy.

Founder Yogi Desai - teaching an application of the ancient Hindu system of Raja Yoga

Kripalu was originally a center for yoga training under the guidance of Yogi Desai. His guru, Swami Shri Kripalvanandji, for whom Kripalu was named, observed that the ashram lifestyle appealed to only a few people, and that a new and less exclusive approach was needed to reach out to many other people who could benefit from yoga. "Humanity is one," the Swami said, "so if you are happy, it is your duty and your pleasure to extend the love, peace, and health that you're experiencing to others. Health programs are a major way to reach people." Kripalu now offers classes in nutrition, physical fitness, and wholistic health techniques such as polarity therapy, reflexology, Touch for Health, massage, shiatsu, and acupressure. It trains health professionals as well as lay people. Morning running and yoga are offered for members and guests, as well as saunas, hot tubs, and evening "satsangs"—meditation, chanting, and free form dance to "mantras" (sacred words).

But Kripalu staff don't believe in just teaching techniques for better health. They provide a supportive environment to help people make the lifestyle changes needed for improved health—a lifestyle that they themselves have tried, tested, and lived. And like any true center for health, the very atmosphere of Kripalu exudes healing and nurturance as soon as you walk through the door. In addition to learning techniques and lifestyle changes, students learn how to improve their work, their relationships, and their level of self-fulfillment. Kripalu staff are all actively working on their own self-discovery, so they teach from their own experience. Malti Karpsen, a long-time member of Kripalu and a bodywork therapist, comments:

> Someone becomes a therapist here, not because they had the skill before they came, but because they integrated the lifestyle and developed the spiritual consciousness while they're here. Yogi Desai says, "Self-love, self-acceptance is the mother of all healing energies." Before we begin to work with someone else, we have to love ourselves.

Self-Reliance and Self-Healing   227

Besides supporting a healthy lifestyle, a community setting has other advantages, according to Dr. Jeffrey Migdow, one of the resident doctors who sees patients at Kripalu.

> When people first come into this building, into the energy field of the community, they go through a shift. So they're already more open by the time they get to my office. They already trust me and are open to trying out new things, so it makes my job easier...The community setting is helpful because I treat members here also...brothers and sisters whom I know really well. They're very honest with me about what works for them, so I get daily feedback and this causes some real breakthroughs...Also, people come through the community as patients who often have things they teach me.

In addition to classes, Kripalu offers a Rest and Relaxation Program of individual care. A staff person does a lifestyle assessment and helps an individual pinpoint where the imbalances in her/his life are. As important as the actual program content that's taught is the lifestyle that's offered: a vegetarian diet, exercise, yoga, meditation. "In the context of this healthier lifestyle, people feel their energy change and their attitudes change; they feel more positive, more energetic," Malti observes. The staff can then reflect back to people that it's not what the staff is doing, but what the person himself is doing. The keystone of the Kripalu approach is people taking responsibility and feeling empowered when they leave Kripalu to continue the healthy feelings they have while they're there. The lifestyle counselor helps people fit the changes into their lifestyle when they leave. Dr. Migdow comments:

> We always talk to people about diet and nutrition and exercise. Most people are afraid of their own power, afraid of what they might have to do if they were healthy. So we talk about that—the real reasons why they're not becoming healthier. And once we get to the real reasons, we laugh about them, and say, "You really do want to feel healthier so you'll do these lifestyle changes."

An important reason for Kripalu's success with health is that the staff help people understand the body/mind connection—how their thoughts and feelings affect their bodies and vice versa—as Malti Karpsen explains.

> An example was a woman last week who has a problem with her cervical vertebrae. It was manifesting as numbness in her fingers. She has restricted mobility—they were either locked open or frozen shut,

so the motor communication was not happening. She booked a body-work session here and the therapist didn't want to work directly on it, so he went to the foot reflexes for the cervical region, and worked them. The woman experienced that her hands could work—she felt like she had her hands in hot oil, she had mobility again. And in the process of dialoguing about the experience, she talked about her children and difficulty she had relating to them, and as she talked her hands began closing up again. So it was a perfect learning situation there about the body/mind interaction.

Dr. Migdow uses guided imagery with his patients to help them understand the mind/body connection. He has the patient visualize the inside of his body, and then he guides the patient to a place where there is pain or injury or illness. The patient visualizes healing this area with light or color—or whatever works—visualizing washing it away, burning it, melting it, etc. Dr. Migdow has found that everyone can do this imagery process if he has someone leading him through it correctly and if there is an openness to and trust of the guide. First he has the patient focus on his body, and then he has the patient focus on the emotions that were experienced at the time of the injury or illness. The emotions are re-experienced, and the patient uses the breath to release them. This really teaches people how their mind and their body are connected, and they learn that they can control their feelings. It's not that they caused the disease, Dr. Migdow feels, but that they are responsible because of certain decisions they made at certain times which had a lasting effect on their body.

Although many people feel that this visualization and affirmation process is something new, it's actually something very ancient—one application of the ancient Hindu system of Raja Yoga—according to member Malti Karpson.

Kripalu's doctors use homeopathic medicine to treat illnesses and injuries. This approach believes that disease is caused by weaknesses in a person's whole system. A homeopathic remedy accelerates the person's innate healing ability by stimulating their vital force or healing energy. By discussing with the patient the physical, emotional, and mental symptoms which s/he experiences, the doctor chooses a correct remedy from among the eight hundred or more natural substances that comprise homeopathic medicine. Homeopathy follows a rule of nature which is called the Law of Similars. This means that substances which create disease in a healthy person will, in minute amounts, cure disease in an ill person. For example, a homeopath uses a minute quantity of poison ivy to cure poison ivy. Dr. Migdow describes his experience with homeopathy:

Self-Reliance and Self-Healing 229

Homeopathic medicine uses natural substances on a very small energy level so it helps shift healing on all levels, mental, emotional, physical, spiritual. I see it as a bridge for people who aren't interested in yoga, in energy, etc., but at the same time they like taking regular medicine, so they can take homeopathic remedies instead. They're natural, so people like that, and they're very subtle, so it makes it mystical and magical. And it definitely works, so it gives them more faith in their healing process, even though they can't figure out how it works rationally. If you find the right homeopathic remedy, changes occur very quickly on all levels. It works on an energy level and goes through the acupuncture points. Even if people don't believe in energy, they believe in acupuncture. For example, I gave Apis (made from honey bees) to a woman who had swelling and stinging pain from a bee sting on her hand for twelve hours. One hour later the pain and swelling had disappeared.

Body/mind therapeutics - learning how thoughts and feelings affect the body and vice-versa

A major focus of Kripalu's health programs are the physical exercise classes that Yogi Desai refers to as "body/mind therapeutics": yoga, Hara Kinetics and DansKinetics. Classical yoga is taught as a therapy which stimulates specific areas in the body—the neck region, solar plexus, lower back—where tension blocks the flow of inner energy or "prana." According to member Rajendra, "The yoga postures not only stimulate the endocrine system and massage the inner organs, they conform the body to mental and emotional attitudes which are impressed into the subconscious to become part of one's daily posture in facing the world."[7]

Kripalu Hara Kinetics, developed by Yogi Desai, is a system of body/mind exercises for breaking through the barriers between ourselves and the power within us. "Hara" is the Japanese word for the seat of life force within us, located in the area of the body just below the navel. "Kinetics" means movement. Hara Kinetics are thus "movements from the hara." The exercises draw on the energy of the hara and activate its movement within the body to free physical and emotional restrictions. This mobilizing of the hara energy results in naturally-occurring muscular, skeletal, and psychological adjustments. Feelings that have been locked in the muscles and joints are discharged, and memories and insights associated with the feelings often emerge. Simple movements, breathing techniques, and meditation are used. Each exercise works on a key joint in the body. "Micromovements," tiny circular motions, expose the constricted muscles surrounding the joint. Once the movements are completed, the constricted area is isolated and held open to the activated hara energy. The physical and emotional clearing thus effected makes more energy available for expanded awareness and conscious living.[8]

DansKinetics is a synthesis of dance exercise and Kripalu yoga developed by dancer and gymnast Ken Scott with Yogi Desai. The emphasis is not just on doing the exercises but on the meditative attitude with which the exercises are done. The movements become a way to cultivate self-awareness. It's a way not only to improve physical fitness but also to go deep inside and see how one's attitudes affect fitness potential. DansKinetics, like all of Kripalu's programs, helps people understand more deeply how our minds affect our bodies, and vice versa, through applying ancient yogic science to modern health needs.

Spring Valley Community - reflecting Rudolf Steiner's teachings and relating the ecology of the earth to that of the entire cosmos

SPRING VALLEY COMMUNITY: Bio-Dynamic Agriculture

Spring Valley is a thriving community of three hundred members on one hundred acres of land northwest of New York

Self-Reliance and Self-Healing 231

City. It uses a synthesis of practical and spiritual approaches to organic gardening. Started in 1926, Spring Valley is one of hundreds of centers world-wide which are based on the teachings of the brilliant Austrian philosopher, Rudolf Steiner. In thousands of lectures and over one hundred books, Steiner presented innovative approaches to everything from agriculture to medicine and architecture.

Green Meadow Waldorf School at Spring Valley, based on the philosophy of Rudolf Steiner

Today Spring Valley is the home of a community called The Threefold Educational Foundation, with Green Meadow Waldorf School for three hundred children from preschool to high school; a Eurythmy school for expressive movement; a nursing home for the elderly called The Fellowship Community (with pottery, print shop, weavery, candle studios, and medical clinic); and three businesses—the Anthroposophic Press, the Pfeiffer Foundation (compost preparations), and Weleda natural body care products (made largely from plants grown in the community).

Most residents are members of the Anthroposophical Society, which holds several study groups and occasional lectures, conferences, or festival celebrations. Many Spring Valley residents are scientifically or artistically oriented. There are quite a few Europeans in the community and a wide range of ages. Spring Valley is more of a village than a tightly-knit community.

All of the activities at Spring Valley carefully reflect Rudolf Steiner's teachings, which encourages thoughtfulness, careful experimentation, and observation of results. Bio-Dynamics is the name given to Steiner's unique approach to agriculture, which is practiced at Spring Valley, as well as at 1500 Bio-Dynamic farms world-wide. It is a unified approach that relates the ecology of the earth-organism to that of the entire cosmos. Like ordinary organic gardening, Bio-Dynamic gardening avoids chemical fertilizers and insecticides. But unlike other methods, one of the primary goals of Bio-Dynamics is to promote the gardener's spiritual relationship to the land. The soil is seen not just as a mixture of chemicals, minerals, or organic materials, but as a living system, according to Dr. Ehrenfried Pfeiffer, who helped pioneer Bio-Dynamic farming in the United States. The gardener learns to cultivate the cosmic, formative energies which stream down to the earth from the sun and other heavenly bodies, and which affect the quality of the food grown as well as the health of the people who eat it. Spring Valley gardeners learn to study in an almost meditative fashion the relationships betwen the plants, the animals, and the humans on the land. Owen Holder, a resident of Spring Valley who is on the Board of the Bio-Dynamic Association in America, illustrates this type of studious approach.

> The farm is not complete without the cattle. The cattle walk over the land and take an interest in the particular plants. They have a certain routine and a certain rhythm of eating and laying in the woods. They decide where they will go to eat. These choices come through a specific kind of being, who experiences the field, the time of day, the sunlight, the environment, etc. in a special way. But the plant that's eaten can't make any choices...It feels the consciousness of the cow as it goes into the cow's body and sacrifices itself to the cow. It enhances and completes the cow's life, as it drops out of the cow and becomes manure on the land.

Peter Escher, another Bio-Dynamic gardener, stressed the importance of developing an intensive reverence for the land. He said, "If a farmer is devout, if he realizes there's something in the soil that's greater than he is, he'll get a touch for the land, and go on to learn what to do and when."[9]

The Spring Valley approach is not just to let things run their natural course but to intensify certain natural processes. Bio-Dynamic gardeners work to support the good rather than fight the bad. In other words, rather than focusing on eliminating insects, they work to build up the soil and their relationship to it as the way to treat the problem. Bio-Dynamics is seen as an essential remedy for a dying earth—aiding Nature where she is weak after so many centuries of abuse, as Wolf Storl, author of *Culture and Horticulture*, puts it.

The practical side of the Bio-Dynamic approach used by Spring Valley gardeners begins with building a compost pile. Rather than just randomly heaping together a bunch of organic leftovers, they use a more scientific method of producing humus,

Bio-Dynamic farming - building up the soil as a remedy for a dying earth

having researched the ideal settings, sizes, shapes, moisture content, and ingredient combinations that yield the most beneficial microorganisms and the highest concentration of usable nutrients.[10] Everything which is apt to decompose is used—leaves, grass cuttings, weeds, hay, corn stalks, garbage, pond cleanings, animal refuse, bone, hoof and horn meal, wool—and these materials are piled up in alternate layers, interlayered with earth and a thin coating of lime, and treated with Bio-Dynamic preparations.[11] After several months the compost is spread on the soil.

In his agricultural lectures, Rudolf Steiner spoke of compost as "a means of kindling the life within the earth itself...the compost heap really contains ethereal and living elements and also astral."[12] Gardener Owen Holder describes the compost-making process used at Spring Valley.

> The piling up of organic material is a human activity—only human beings do this, no other entity in nature does. A compost pile generates heat and goes through metamorphic and metabolic change. Each compost pile is a living being, an individual being, having a skin and its own form, changing as it develops. Into this organism, a Bio-Dynamic gardener places an enhancing atmosphere (not a material, but rather an atmosphere). Homeopathic medicines are used which are like radiations, rather than something material, as they are very diluted and used in small quantities (one ounce to five tons of compost). The medicine is made of the flowers of camomile, yarrow, dandelion, with oak bark, whole nettle plants, and the flowers of valerian pressed into juice. Each one is processed in a special way in animal coverings, placed either in the earth or in the sunlight, and processed in nature, within the seasons. The medicine is formed in what you'd call an alchemical way, using both biology and chemistry. It is the creation of a material which carries certain forces into the compost pile and so affects its living being, not so much its material content. The compost is then spread on a field as a specific being which has been incarnated for a particular time and place.

These medicines used on the compost pile improve the intake of light and the maturing of aromas and root formation. They allow the dew to penetrate deeply into the soil, and encourage flowering.[13] They also enhance the utilization of potassium, calcium, iron, nitrogen and phosphorous by the plant.[14]

In addition to the medicines, cow horn manure and cow horn silica are sprayed on the land or on the plants to increase the effects of sunlight and the "cosmos." Other products of nature also are used when needed—finely ground lime from corals to neutralize over-acid soils, and basalt dust from volcanic rock to "warm" cold soils consisting of loam.[15]

The homeopathic medicines added to the compost are produced and packaged in a "compost starter kit," together with some fifty different bacteria, and offered for sale by the Pfeiffer Foundation, one of the businesses at Spring Valley.

During the growing season, the fields at Spring Valley are never left exposed to the elements. They are planted with ground cover to preserve the rich and varied soil life. Quick-growing yellow mustard and Persian clover are grown to suppress the weeds that normally appear on cultivated ground. Clover is especially indispensable for building up a healthy topsoil because it "fixes" nitrogen from the air needed for bringing life into the earth.[16] Owen Holder comments on the role of nitrogen in agriculture.

> Nitrogen is not just a molecule that can be disassociated from the atmosphere and combined with oxygen to become a plant nutrient. Nitrogen is an interactive factor in nature—it is a living being...The five components of amino acids—oxygen, hydrogen, carbon, nitrogen, sulfur—are the tools of the "elementary beings." They carry forces and wield spiritual power and have functions as tools within the world of nature.

Steiner said of nitrogen that it is "the bearer of the astral spirit...the bearer of sensation...It guides the life into the form...Its task is to mediate between the life and the spirit essence...Nitrogen is so essential to the life of the soul."[17]

Another method used by the Bio-Dynamic gardeners at Spring Valley is crop rotation. Plants fall into three main categories: heavy feeders, soil enrichers, and light feeders. They are rotated on a three-year cycle. First in rotation are the heavy feeders, which includes all members of the cabbage family, leafy vegetables, celery, squash, corn, cucumbers, corn, etc. Second are the legumes, the soil enrichers which help restore the areas depleted by the heavy feeders by forming special nodules on their roots which capture and store nitrogen from the atmosphere and other nutrients from the soil. The legumes are the peas, beans, clover, and alfalfa. The last in rotation are the light feeders, which thrive in soil recovered by the legumes. These are the root vegetables like potatoes, carrots, and beets, as well as onions and herbs.[18]

Raised beds are used at Spring Valley to aerate the soil and allow for more plants to grow closer together, as the soil is looser and roots can spread more easily.

Mulch made of hay, nettle, grass, or straw is often used to

protect the soil during the hot season and to prevent moisture from evaporating. Mulching eliminates weeds and keeps crops clean, adding nutrients to the soil when it breaks down.[19]

Companion planting—putting plants that aid each other's growth next to each other—is used at Spring Valley. Beets react favorably when placed next to cabbages, celery and leeks do well near pole beans, and lettuce thrives near cabbage. Most herbs of strong aroma are effective pest repellents—oregano is used to keep the cabbage butterfly away, for example.[20] Insects in the garden are held in check this way, as well as by the encouragement of their natural predators such as certain beetles, wasps, toads, snakes, and birds. A single mole can clear an acre of beetle grubs, and ladybird larva consumes up to five hundred aphids in twenty-four hours.[21] A garden free of chemicals and poisons is more likely to preserve this natural balance of predators and also to enable the plants to get a well-balanced supply of nutrients so they won't be susceptible to insects and disease. Weeds are sometimes suppressed by burning their seeds and scattering them on the field, according to another "homeopathic" technique initiated by Steiner.

One of the most unusual techniques of Bio-Dynamic agriculture used at Spring Valley is planting according to the cosmic cycles of the planets. Bio-Dynamic researchers Maria Thun and Eugene and Lily Kolisko have done more than thirty years of detailed experiments to study the relationships of celestial bodies to plants, and their conclusions are published in an annual Kimberton Hills Agricultural Calendar. (Kimberton Hills is another Steiner-based community.) For example, the waxing period of the moon (the two weeks when the moon goes from dark to full) is the best time to plant, in general. The time to transplant, prune, or weed is during the waning moon, when the growth forces are less active. Steiner taught that the moon works on the earth primarily through moisture, influencing not only ocean tides but also the sap in plants.

> With the moon's rays the whole reflected cosmos comes onto the earth...It is indeed a strong and powerfully organizing cosmic force which the moon rays down into the plant, so that the seeding process of the plant may also be assisted, and so that the force of growth may be enhanced into the force of reproduction.[22]

There are two main community gardens at Spring Valley— one at the ThreeFold Community and one at the Fellowship Community. According to Owen Holder, the Fellowship Community in particular is growing better crops with fewer insects than ever before, even though it has poor soil. This is because it makes great use of the Bio-Dynamic methods. They grow most of the vegetables needed for their eighty members, and both the food and the work itself is seen as curative for the elderly who live there. Providing foodstuffs is part of their medical program, through carrying the life-enhancing forces from the compost, according to Owen. He adds:

> Fellowship Community members develop special ways of making the beds in their garden that relate to making the beds they sleep in inside the house, and this relationship helps both the people and the plants. When people prepare themselves for death in a special way, a new relationship with plants shows up. The compost pile is also a death process.

The Findhorn Community - respecting the consciousness in all life - plants, animals, rocks, as well as humans

THE FINDHORN COMMUNITY:
Co-creation with the Forces of Nature

At the Findhorn Community in Scotland a very special experiment has been taking place. It has had a profound impact on thousands of people who have visited the community over its twenty-three year history, as well as on gardeners, ecologists, and lovers of nature around the world. The community has pioneered a new co-creative effort between humanity and the forces of nature and has demonstrated what is possible when a group of people establish an intuitive rapport with these forces through their love and caring. This rapport has created a magical feeling that seems to pervade the entire community of Findhorn. The work harkens back to the attunement of native peoples to nature and in more recent times, to the work of Luther Burbank.

In the early days of Findhorn, unusually large vegetables were grown in sandy soil in a harsh northern climate. Unlikely varieties of flowers (including tropical ones) flourished in the garden and roses bloomed in the snow. Prof. Lindsay Robb, a soil expert and consultant to the Soil Association of Britain, visited Findhorn and commented:

> The vigor, health and bloom of the plants in this garden at mid-winter on land which is almost barren powdery sand cannot be explained by the moderate dressings of compost, nor indeed by the application of any known cultural methods of organic husbandry. There are other factors and these are vital ones.[23]

What are the other factors that are responsible for this amazing growth? Findhorn members say it is a process of attunement or at-one-ment with the "devas" of the plants. "Devas" is an ancient Sanskrit word which means "shining ones" or simply "angels." (The Hopi Indians called them "kachinas.") The devas are the architects, or guiding forces, which give structure and energy to the plant world. They carry within them the patterns of life, the blueprints, for each species of plant. Devas work in what are called "mantras"—movements which produce a sound and make a pattern, working up to a certain pitch. By these moves, they put a certain quality of life force into the garden. Devas work in the formless worlds, and are not bound or rigid in form as humans are.[24]

Communication with the devas was first established at Findhorn by Dorothy Maclean, one of the three founders of the community. As she became in touch with the love she felt for the plants in the garden and focused on their essence or inner spirit, she received messages from the devas giving specific guidance about the practical care of the plants as well as guidance on how to work with the devas. One of the early messages that Dorothy received from the devas said,

> Everything manifest is in our care and we know its state, for under God we make plain His creation...How can we tell you how we dance with joy, that the sun dances and the moon dances and we dance around them? The earth itself dances at heart...We are in line of consciousness from the one great whole to the smallest unit of life and therefore we perform the miracles which you see in the growth of the seed.[25]

By following the advice she received daily from the deva messages, Dorothy produced a very healthy and vibrant garden, and people came from all over to marvel at it. But how could others follow the Findhorn experience and communicate with the devas? Dorothy comments, "The devas, who at first seemed to be far-off beings, through a joyous communion grew into my close companions, until eventually they made me realize that they, like the kingdom of heaven, are *within* us."[26] True communication with the devas arises out of our own being and out of the wholeness of our lives, she feels. To communicate with the forces of nature, words are not needed. The devas say, "Just tune into nature until you feel the love flow. That is your arrow into the deva world...Always it is your state that the nature world responds to; not what you say, not what you do, but what you are."[27]

To communicate with the 'devas,' words are not needed - just tune into nature until you feel the love flow . . . the 'devas,' like the kingdom of heaven, are within us

The devas might be considered the architects of plant forms, but the nature spirits or elementals—gnomes or fairies—act as the craftsmen, using the blueprint and energy channeled to them by the devas to build up the plant form. R. Ogilvie Crombie, a scientist from Edinburgh, was the first to communicate with these beings at Findhorn. Devas and nature spirits have no form, but humans often tend to see them in forms which are intelligible to them, like fairies.

Paul Hice, a gardener at Findhorn, comments:

Self-Reliance and Self-Healing 239

I've learned that it's not necessary actually to see the devas or elemental beings that work in the garden. When I acknowledge the presence of all forms of life and really align myself with Spirit, I'm somehow in touch with those energies and I can feel that I'm part of the garden.[28]

Each gardener at Findhorn is responsible for nurturing the spirit and the form of the plants in her/his garden by finding the knowledge of the devas deep within her/himself and blending this in action with practical gardening techniques. Each workday in the garden begins with an attunement, joining hands silently in a circle. Each gardener blesses the day, his or her fellow gardeners, the nature kingdoms, and the day's work ahead. Each person harmonizes himself with the group, the forces of nature, and God. Findhorn gardeners work on developing an intuitive sense of how to care for the plants, through their openness to the devic realms, and their sense of the oneness of all life. To help the plants, the devas suggested to Dorothy:

> Think in terms of light, and so add light to that already existing. Hence, you speed up growth and enhance beauty; you see truth and link up with God's perfection...When anyone contributes attention or feeling to a plant, a bit of that person's being mingles with a bit of our being and the one world is fostered.[29]

This attitude of love and caring is expressed in many practical ways in the garden. Weeds are warned ahead of time that they will be pulled up and recycled back on the compost pile, where they can give of themselves to the garden as a whole in the next cycle. They are always pulled with an attitude of love and appreciation. Some weeds are nutritious in salads, and others are used as herbs for healing purposes. The devas have said that weeds have a part to play and that they come up where they are needed, to supply something the soil needs or to indicate an imbalance in the new strains of plants humanity has created. Findhorn gardeners always leave a wild garden, a place humans will not disturb, next to a cultivated garden, so that weeds and other plants can grow wild and provide a special place for the nature spirits.

Insects are also appreciated for the part they play in the oneness of life. It is normal for plants to live with a balanced population of insects around them, Findhorn members feel. Healthy plants are not harmed by the insects they attract, just as healthy bodies are not infected by the germs with which they come in contact. An overabundance of insects indicates an imbalance in the garden. One part of nature cannot be isolated from another, so action taken against any part sets up a chain of events that affects the whole. Adam, a Findhorn gardener, explains how they dealt with a number of insects and other pests in the garden.

> We saw it as an opportunity to communicate with other life forms. The gardeners attuned as a group to each organism, and always had positive results. We acknowledged that they had a place but affirmed that the vision for the garden was to grow food for humans to eat. They were welcome if they could be in harmony with that vision. They stayed, and so did the vegetables. We had beautiful, healthy, vigorous vegetables. We communicated to the rabbits that they were welcome in the garden if they stayed on the grass banks and ate the clover and wildflowers there. We asked the moles to leave the garden completely because their presence was too disruptive, but we did suggest an alternative place for them to go. Clubroot (a fungal disease) was on all the brassicas [cabbages], and yet the plants grew anyways. The prevailing belief is that brassicas with clubroot can't grow into healthy specimens, but our cabbages disproved that.[30]

Findhorn gardeners use organic compost to fertilize the soil. Compost-making is seen as an alchemical process where balance, precision, and timing are necessary. The love and the consciousness of the gardeners who are making the compost is important, they feel, as the body of a living being is being built. The gardeners attune to the compost heap to use both their intuition and practical know-how to mix the right combination of ingredients: weeds, grass cuttings, seaweed, green vegetable waste from the kitchen, chicken manure, leaf mold, and wood chips.

Everything has consciousness of one kind or another, Findhorn members believe, so it is important to show love and respect for tools and machines as well as for plants and animals. Findhorn gardeners clean and oil their tools after use and keep the gardening shed clean and orderly.

The important thing to remember is that your garden reflects you. So the difference that cooperation will make there depends upon the change in your consciousness as it expands to recognize and accept the devic realms.

In addition to providing us with food, Findhorn believes nature also provides us with healing energy, not only physically through herbs but also mentally and emotionally. Evergreen trees in particular bring mental stability, the devas have said, and so there would be a great benefit from forests being planted beside large cities. Large trees are essential for the well-being of the land, not merely because they control rainfall but also because they draw forth inner radiances which are as necessary to the land as rain. To the devas, the presence of trees and wilderness on the planet is of vital importance—not just a luxury, but a necessity. For this reason, Findhorn has begun a tree nursery at Cullerne with hundreds of baby trees and has hosted a World Wilderness Conference, as well as publishing books on the importance of trees and wilderness.

Today, twenty-three years after the beginnings of the Findhorn gardens and the first deva messages, there are still roses blooming in the snow at Findhorn and unusual varieties of plants thriving in its sandy soil, although you no longer find giant sizes. The original garden in the caravan site has been joined by larger gardens at Cluny Hill, Cullerne, Drumduan and Newbold as Findhorn has expanded into a village with many large houses. Herb gardens in circular mandala patterns, vegetable gardens in spirals, domed greenhouses, wind tunnel and solar tunnel greenhouses are all part of the continuing experiments of the community.

Findhorn's Cullern Garden School - a ten-acre classroom where students grow food, flowers and themselves

Findhorn's Cullerne Garden School has become a "ten-acre classroom," a "school within a garden," where more than twenty-four varieties of vegetables are grown in attunement with the nature forces. Cullerne is a learning environment where staff and students grow food, flowers, and *themselves*. The garden is the classroom *and* the teacher, yielding food for soul and body. The courses are intensely practical: garden design, food preservation, seed selection, cold-frame construction, composting, greenhouse and solar-dome cultivation.

Findhorn members have also developed Erraid, a small island off the west coast of Scotland, into a self-sufficient community with a dozen residents. Members grow their own food, get milk and eggs from goats and chickens, and fish from the sea.

In working towards greater self-sufficiency, as well as interdependency with other life systems, Findhorn members are learning how to be responsible for the well-being of a piece of the planet. They experience themselves as part of the living system that is the earth, and they feel the urgency of helping to restore ecological balance and to clean up the pollution of the air, the waters, the soil, and the food supply. Findhorn's pioneering work has shown what is possible when humanity works lovingly and consciously with the forces of nature. The deserts can bloom and the tide of ecological disaster can be reversed. As the devas told the members of Findhorn,

> Humanity does not need to exercise brute force on the forms of nature to make them obey its designs. You must provide us free scope to work with you in love, respect and cooperation...for in understanding us and cooperating with us, humanity will learn valuable lessons about itself, which is one of the objects of the exercise. Your consciousness must expand to new insights and into deeper communion with and dominion over your own nature. Out of this can come a communion with us, a mating, if you will, that will embody a divine power to transform our planet.[31]

Self-Reliance and Self-Healing   243

Stelle Community - solar energy and seminars on UFO's and reincarnation disguised in a typical American suburb

STELLE COMMUNITY: Solar Greenhouses and Ethanol Fuel from Corn

The first impression of Stelle Community is of a typical American suburban development with nicely-mowed lawns and neat sidewalks and curbs. Along its streets, men in business suits hurry off to work, and conservatively dressed women take their freckled children to school. Surrounded by miles of corn fields and small towns in the middle of Illinois, Stelle, with its own plastics factory, hardly seems to fit the typical image of a new age community. But a deeper look reveals a most extraordinary place—a sort of cross between a survivalist camp and an esoteric school. Here there are homes with state-of-the-art designs in solar energy, a wholistic health center, research into extracting energy directly from the ethers, and seminars on reincarnation and UFO's.

Started in 1973 by Richard Kieninger with a philosophy based on his book *The Ultimate Frontier* (written under the pen name Eklal Kueshana), Stelle has now grown to a community of 125 members with forty-two homes, two schools, a factory, and a health clinic. Aiming to be a community of philosophers and scientists, Stelle's original vision was to develop a self-sufficient community to be a haven during a major disaster they believe will come in the year 2000. Stelle was to be a base where the needed technological contingency could be developed and alternative socio-cultural systems can be pilot-tested and refined. Stelle members saw themselves as a kind of new Peace Corps for the world after the cataclysms are over. They publish a newsletter called "Personal Preparedness," offering to help people be ready to survive any contingency.

In the last few years, however, Stelle seems to have shifted its attention from the coming disaster in order to focus more on educating its children and developing self-sufficiency with a comfortable lifestyle. Stelle recently opened up to include people who are in basic agreement with the values of the community but who may not follow Stelle's philosophy, choosing another spiritual path instead.

Stelle has an Office of Technology which researches various ways to produce the community's own food and energy. According to Director Tim Wilhelm, they are "exploring better and more effective ways to meet peoples' needs in a manner appropriate to community, so that people can have more free time for their spiritual growth." Tim feels the community is interested in developing self-sufficiency technologies that are "locally ownable, locally controllable, locally operated, locally maintained, and locally replicable." They look for economic viability, multiple-use potential, ease of maintenance, and simple elegance in design and craftsmanship. They are redefining appropriate technology as "eco-tech"—technology that is so advanced that it is both cost-effective and ecologically sound.

Developing a self-sufficient community of philosophers and scientists

Stelle has been prototyping various methods of energy conservation including passive solar homes with solar mass in the flooring to absorb heat, active solar heating systems, and solar air heaters. They've experimented with an earth-bermed home (with one side of the house dug into the side of the earth for heat conservation) and with a thermal envelope design home (where a space is left in between an inner and outer shell for circulation of warm air). Stelle has built its own water treatment plant that removes iron and chlorinates the water, producing 7,000 to 10,000 gallons of water a day. A sewage treatment plant is also operated by the community. Stelle developed its own telephone company, a cooperative video center, a food co-op store that operates on an honor system, and a State-chartered credit union.

Self-Reliance and Self-Healing 245

The community received a $50,000 grant from the U.S. Department of Energy to compile a design package for a 1,000-gallon per day fuel-alcohol production facility. The plan, according to Tim Wilhelm, was to use indigenous materials and have some level of interchange and service to the surrounding area. The design was to be on a community scale so that a small farm or farmers' co-op could produce enough energy to meet its needs and thus reduce dependence on outside gasoline and oil. It needed to be locally appropriate, taking into account the terrain, resources, types of people in the area, and their needs. Being surrounded by corn fields, corn was the obvious choice, as one-fifth of the corn harvested could then be turned into alcohol to run the machinery for harvesting all the corn. The corn fuel Stelle produced is 190 proof alcohol, an industrial grade alcohol capable of running engines of various sizes and purposes. It's technical name is "ethanol."

The process used to make the ethanol is quite similar to that used in the liquor industry. A measured amount of corn is run through a grain mill that cracks the corn, and these kernels are then cooked with water and enzymes to burst the starch cells open. The enzymes convert the corn starch into fermentable sugars after forty-eight hours, and this is then pumped into a distillation column, where it is heated by direct steam injection to boil off the alcohol and drive it up into the column to be condensed.[32]

Stelle has also been experimenting with various types of solar greenhouses. What makes a greenhouse solar is that it's oriented with its longest face to the south. A current greenhouse experiment is a 1200-square-foot building which maintains overnight temperatures of fifty degrees or more when outside temperatures are below zero. Bedding plants are produced for sale in the Spring, and organic vegetables are grown for sale to members through Stelle's Cooperative Market.

A new 30' x 100' commercial greenhouse is now under construction by Stelle, funded by a $52,000 grant from the Illinois Department of Energy. The goal is to cut energy costs so as to compete more favorably with produce grown in California and Florida. The frame for the greenhouse, which has already been completed, uses what is called a tetrahedral space truss in barrel-arch configuration. The frame members are one-inch steel tubing, webbed together in perfect triangulation. The frame was computer analyzed to guarantee it could hold a load of snow up to thirty pounds per square foot and up to a 300-mile-per-hour wind. The greenhouse has fiber-glass insulation one foot thick, and two layers of polyethylene film are stretched out and inflated with a small air blower, making it like an air pillow. This lets light

New commercial greenhouse (under construction) funded by a grant from the Illinois Department of Energy

in during the day and insulates it as well. At night it becomes a "foam home"—additional insulation is provided by a foam generator that fills up the cavity between the two layers of film with soap suds. This has the same insulating factor as fiber-glass. It works well because of storage: one cubic foot of liquid soap through the foam generator becomes one thousand cubic feet of foam insulation. In warm weather the foam blocks out the heat, and at night during cold weather, it traps the heat inside. The heat storage system will use both phase-changed salts for storing high temperature heat and water heat storage for storing low temperature heat.[33]

Another area of research at Stelle is new sources of motive and electrical power. Community physicists are tracking the development of electrical energy, not only intellectually but also through actual physical experimentation, to discover how to fuel machinery with the energy that permeates space, rather than by converting mass into energy via nuclear fission or combustion of fossil fuels. This energy permeating space is a sub-quantum medium which the ancients called "ether."

Stelle also has its own wholistic health center, called The Continuum Center, staffed by an M.D., a psychologist, and an alternative health practicioner. "Radix," a neo-Reichian therapeutic approach which releases negative emotions and body "armoring" (energy blocks), is used by the Continuum staff, along with a nutritional approach. Chemical and food tests are used to diagnose "ecological illnesses" from chemicals in foods, pollution

Self-Reliance and Self-Healing 247

in the air, or chemicals used in cleaning or building materials in the home that the patient may be allergic to. Kinesiology or "muscle testing" is also used to diagnose illness and determine appropriate remedies.

Treatments considered unusual by Western medical standards are sometimes recommended by the Center's staff. For example, when X-rays are found to be upsetting the carbon balance in a patient's body, they recommend hugging a tree for ten minutes to restore the proper carbon balance. They've also been researching what they call the "Vivaxis Beam"—the life energy. If a patient is feeling depleted of energy, they might recommend facing the direction in which s/he was born (as that is the area where her/his "Vivaxis" or energy field is connectd to the earth) and breathing deeply ten times with both hands and feet together.

High Wind Community - to walk gently on the earth and build the future now

HIGH WIND: The Bioshelter— A Non-Consuming Micro-Farm

> to walk gently on the earth,
> to know the spirit within,
> to hear our fellow beings
> to invoke the light of wisdom, and
> to build the future now.
> —High Wind Motto

This credo expresses a vison that has inspired some three hundred people from around the country and abroad to join the High Wind Association and to take an active part in supporting its experimental work. Most of this work takes place in an educational center/community located on a forty-six-acre farm bordering the Kettle Moraine State Forest, fifty miles north of Milwaukee, Wisconsin.

High Wind evolved out of a small group that had been meeting and dialoguing for several years, especially in classes and conferences organized by Belden Paulson, a co-founder of the Association and a professor at the University of Wisconsin. High Wind's physical expression began not as a community but rather as a task group coalescing around an experimental project that combined education with interests in ecology, shelter-building, and renewable energy—all seen in the context of an over-arching sacred intent.

The group took on this specific focus when in 1980 it received a $25,000 grant from the U.S. Department of Energy to start building a "bioshelter." A bioshelter is a passive solar residence with an attached research greenhouse, which can also be thought of as a non-consuming micro-farm, producing vegetables and fish.

A community of about a dozen full- and part-time residents live at the High Wind farm, and several families are now in the process of building their own homes on the land, using renewable energy and related ideas being currently tested in the bioshelter and several smaller innovative buildings. Members are exploring a time-sharing plan, where people who are interested in being involved with the community on a long-term basis, but who cannot afford to build a house or be there full-time, could jointly build a house with others and spend a designated amount of time in it. Like vacation home time-sharing plans, this would allow access to community to a wider range of people.

With the University of Wisconsin and new age groups like the Lorian Association, High Wind regularly offers educational programs on themes like "Planetary Survival and the Role of Alternative Communities." A recent course gave students from different parts of the U.S. and Canada a full semester of University graduate and undergraduate credit for working and studying at High Wind and at the Sirius and Findhorn communities.

High Wind operates the major alternative bookstore in Milwaukee, specializing in appropriate technology, ecology, futures studies, spirituality, peace, and holistic health. The store also serves as an urban connection and networking center for the Association.

The bioshelter was High Wind's first major project, stimulated by close contact with the New Alchemy Institute which pioneered the bioshelter concept on Cape Cod, Massachusetts and

The bioshelter - a non-consuming micro-farm for raising a family's own vegetables and protein

on Prince Edward Island in Canada. The Department of Energy grantors recognized the research aspect of designing such a building for the harsh climate of the Upper Midwest and the demonstration potential of the High Wind/University education apparatus. "If you build a bioshelter only for your own family," said David Lagerman, High Wind technical director, "it has little impact on the world. We wanted this to belong to everyone." The broad participation has come about naturally, partly because the bioshelter has been built almost entirely with volunteer labor. Belden Paulson observed, "This is a community development project. The whole effort, from initial designing to all phases of construction, has involved a lot of people, most of them working in their spare time but sharing common concerns. People have a stake in it because it belongs to them."

The building itself is divided between a 1,950-square-foot passive solar residence and a 1,750-square-foot research greenhouse and classroom. The greenhouse side will be the site for a line of research on a fully integrated fish-raising, greenhouse horticultural scheme, involving the rearing of tilapia fish in large translucent tanks which double as mass storage for the solar gain. Fish wastes will be utilized hydroponically and otherwise to fertilize the plants. The whole is designed to imitate natural systems and, like them, to be solar powered. The research will concentrate on furthering knowledge of such systems, anticipating the day when a family could raise a good deal of its own protein and vegetables at home, cost-effectively and gracefully enough to make the idea feasible in the city as well as in the country. Pat Kiernan comments, "With enough research and practice, it can be workable and affordable for a lot of people. Appropriate technology strikes a very sustainable path, rooted in sensitivity to natural processes." Pat, a former engineer, joined High Wind because he felt it was helping to make technology more humane by integrating it into a community setting. "There is a good balance here between technology, relationships, and spirituality," he says.

The original farmhouse at High Wind also has an attached solar greenhouse, and this grows vegetables for the community all winter. Gardening at High Wind is organic, with companion planting used to manage pests and promote the growth of plants friendly to each other. An outdoor solar hot water shower has been built for the use of summer visitors, and an old chicken coop on the land has been retrofitted with a passive solar design for use as accommodation. Two domes, the first twelve feet in diameter, and another, twenty-four feet across, have been built for use as guest accommodation and as a sanctuary. These are made from styrofoam, one cut in triangles and pieced together for a geodesic shape, the other in blocks for an igloo shape. Cement with fiberglass in it is then troweled over the outside, and an inside layer of mortar or joint cement is added. This creates a well-insulted, simple space. "The Native Americans said that rectangular structures have no power," designer David Lagerman noted, "but there is power in circles and domes."

Lisa Paulson, editor of the Association's quarterly newsletter, *Windwatch*, concludes:

Outdoor solar hot water shower for summer visitors

> Essentially, High Wind stands for an ecological ethic that embraces cooperation and stewardship on all levels, connecting people, buildings, land, spirit. At the farm our gardeners are sensitive to the interdependence and beauty of plants, soil, insects, and wildlife. The forms and energies in the natural surroundings become creative partners and inspiration for our artists. High Wind builders learn that aesthetics and technical efficiency are equally important. And visitors or students, who may come initially to see the bio-shelter, find that this effort to balance physical projects with the energies of people and of the land into a harmonious whole, is what makes High Wind a truly valid experiment.

ARCOSANTI: Urban "Arcology" —Ecologically Sound Architecture

Well-insulated geodesic domes for accommodations

For those who argue that small-scale rural communities can't possibly provide solutions to all the crises in the modern urban world, Arcosanti offers a model of a *city* for the future. Like the Socrates of Plato's *Republic*, Arcosanti members believe the city is a necessary instrument for the evolution of the human spirit. And Arcosanti is probably the most visually impressive and futuristic looking of all the communities. A visitor might feel as if s/he has come upon a set for a science fiction film. And yet Arcosanti also reminds one of something from the distant past—like the cities of ancient Aztecs, or perhaps even the old cathedrals of the Middle Ages, monuments that were never completed in their builders' lifetimes.

Arcosanti - building an urban 'arcology' for a city of 5,000 people

Arcosanti has been called "a minor wonder of the world...probably the most important [urban architectural] experiment undertaken in our lifetime, by Douglas Davis of *Newsweek*."[34] Both Arizona Senators Goldwater and DeConcini have recommended Arcosanti for federal funding, and Governor Babbitt declared a week in October as "Arcosanti Festival Week."

Arcosanti was designed by Paulo Soleri, an Italian laureate in architecture who studied with Frank Lloyd Wright. He calls his design for a city of five thousand people an "arcology"—the application of ecological principles to architecture. The word "arcology" points at the interdependence of the words "architecture" and "ecology"—the human abode within the planetary abode. Arcology is a positive response to the planetary problems of population, pollution, energy and natural resource depletion, food scarcity, and quality of life. It is estimated that Arcosanti will need 10% as much water as traditional development, due to greenhouses and recycling. Cars will be unnecessary in the city itself, thus eliminating roads, traffic jams, gasoline lines, and pollution, but they can be available for use outside the city. Residents can walk to work, to friends' apartments, and to cultural events and entertainment. Arcosanti offers an alternative to current urban dilemmas and, at the same time, seek to re-establish contact between people and an undisturbed landscape. Although Arcosanti will be a city for five thousand, only fourteen of its 860 acres will be used for the city structures, with the rest left as a nature preserve or for farming and recreation.

Arcosanti is located seventy miles north of Phoenix in the Arizona desert. Construction on the new city began in 1970 and is only about 2% complete today. There are currently about forty permanent residents. Although they often argue that they are a "construction site," not a "community," in fact a feeling of community is developing there through their shared work and common purpose. Up to 150 students come to Arcosanti for three-week workshops to learn this type of architecture. Over the years, more than three thousand people have participated in the building program, and sometimes a hundred people a day visit Arcosanti for a tour. Cement is used as the basic building material, as wood is not found in the ecology of the Arizona desert. Students learn formwork, silt-casting, concrete pouring, excavation, carpentry, metal work, welding, plumbing, and electrical work. Arcosanti appeals to people with a strong pioneering spirit, as its foundations have to be dug out of solid rock, often in the 110-degree heat of the Arizona desert. Donations, as well as income from workshops, Paulo Soleri's lectures, and the sale of bronze bells made in their foundry, support Arcosanti's building projects.

Arcosanti's "two suns arcology" (designed for the physical sun as well as the human sun) is an extraordinary energy-efficient design, integrating the effects of apse, greenhouse, chimney, and heat sink. The two apses (an apse is a quarter sphere) face south, providing shade during the hot summer when the sun is higher in the sky and letting in the warm rays of the sun during the winter when the sun is lower in the sky. The main housing structure, which has not been built yet, will be twenty-five stories high and resemble a modern skyscraper turned on its side, bent like a boomerang. Referred to as a double-bladed structure, it will face south for sun-warming in the winter and shade in the summer, like the smaller apses already built. Units in the structure are designed so that on one side they view the breathtaking wonder of the desert's mesas, and on the other side they view the pulsating inner-city life.

Below the main housing structure, a four and one-half acre terraced greenhouse is planned for growing food and trapping solar heat. The hot air will rise through giant chimneys to heat the housing structure in the winter. The top three levels of the greenhouse will use evaporation to cool the air, which will then sink through the chimneys to cool the lower parts of the housing structure during the summer. The concrete used in construction will act as a heat sink, collecting and storing solar heat, and then discharging it when the surrounding air is cooler. These elements will make it a passive solar heating and cooling system.

Work on the greenhouse began last year with horizontal semi-cylindrical retaining walls that define the terracing of the sloping greenhouse. The columns support the greenhouse membrane and are designed as large "tree pots" containing deciduous trees or vines that will shade the membrane in the summer months. In addition, Arcosanti has built two experimental greenhouses and cultivates more than forty acres of hay and green manure crops and five acres of organic vegetables and herbs. They've also been experimenting with vineyards and orchards, beekeeping, biological pest control strategies, and food processing-preservation techniques. Completed building projects include simple residences for forty members and workshop participants, a pottery apse, a foundry apse for making bells that are sold, a visitors' center with cafe, bakery, and gallery, a music center, a swimming pool, and two "vault" buildings for general usage. A new structure to be built, called the West Lab or Veleda Springs, will be a combination of residences, greenhouses, and a garment manufacturing business.

Many critics believe that clustering people so densely at Arcosanti into one huge structure will have disastrous effects. The dehumanizing high-rise apartments of our major cities make people feel like sardines, they claim. But to Arcosanti members, these were not designed from wholistic or ecological principles. They feel that contemporary cities are architecturally, economically, and socially fragmented, and are not whole.

"Arcosanti plans to prove that large-scale human development need not be inhuman," comments member Patrick Colvin. He also says they have plans to build more arcologies like Arcosanti and network them, so that people can move around and live at several of them during the year, thus creating "habitats for a mobile society."

Unlike most communities that concern themselves with trying to create the perfect system of governance, economics, relationships, etc., Arcosanti has a different approach. As member Russell Ferguson expresses it, "We need only concern ourselves with building, trusting that the urban effect will take over and the forms shape the inhabitants." It is an interesting experiment.

Arcology aims at creating a whole integrated environment, allowing its residents to identify with the whole city. "Arcosanti is an art object and is lovable," says designer Paulo Soleri. He believes that this will create a much better community spirit and alleviate the social alienation so common in our major cities. And he feels that the increasing complexity of cities enhances the evolution of the human spirit, unlike the standardized and sprawling suburbs, which appear counter to the nature of evolution, possibly lowering social intelligence. Life seems to cluster because people are social, Soleri feels. "The richness of crowding lies in its being the intrinsic facilitator of connectedness, i.e., coherence and sensitization."[35]

Arcosanti members feel that the city structure must contract and miniaturize in order to support complex economic, social, and cultural activities and to give people a new perspective and renewed trust in society and in the future. "One direct pay-off of complexity-miniaturization is direct and instantaneous access to all the institutions of the town (living, learning, working, etc.) as well as to the open countryside at 'the foot' of the town," Soleri observes. "The democratic nature of such accessibility should be evident as it is critical."[36]

Arcosanti proposes an economy of frugality as a more effective and equitable path into the future for a planet limited in resources. It is located on marginal land, not only to demonstrate the viability of a community on such land but also because of the beauty and inspiration that the land engenders. It intends to make use of its limited agricultural potential to partially satisfy the needs of its residents and keep them in touch with one fact of life: the food chain. Fruits and vegetables growing "at the foot of the town" are a tangible and educational fact, giving the town a greater resilience.[37]

> If the sacred is where life is, then the whole habitat is sacred...The city is the producer and the market place, but the city is also the temple, the city is the palace, and the citizen is the sacred carrier of well-being and of grace to be. To build Arcosanti should be to build the church and the palace in one. This is why I hope...that the physical structure of Arcosanti is not just an instrument but also music."[38]

Soleri says that the buildings at Arcosanti can glow with the light of matter transforming into spirit. When a visitor asked if anyone had seen them glow, she was met with a sudden, hushed reverence, as if entering sacred ground—a remarkable silence among such swaggering, brusque people. "No, no one has actually seen them glow...yet."[39]

⑨ Ageless Spiritual Traditions in New Age Settings

Affairs are now soul size.
The enterprise is exploration into God.

—CHRISTOPHER FRY

There is a powerful renewal of Spirit occuring across the world today, and one of the places it expresses most strongly is in the new communities, where the essence of ageless spiritual traditions has been adapted to a modern context. How do the spiritual beliefs and practices of the new communities differ from traditional religious communities? Generally, there are several distinguishing characteristics.

There is a non-dogmatic, ecumenical approach.

Although they may follow a Christian, Hindu, or Buddhist path, the new communities tend to have a more universal approach, respecting the truth in other religions and recognizing that there are many paths to God. Communities that speak about their path as the *only* way are part of an age-old approach to spirituality, more appropriate in past times. Many of the new communities, for example, The Abode in New York, Light of the Mountains in North Carolina, Lama in New Mexico, and Yogaville in Virginia, offer regular services honoring all the religions. Sevenoaks in Virginia celebrates both Christian and Jewish holidays, even adding a touch of Buddhism as well. Shantivanam in India is a synthesis of Hinduism and Christianity—a "Benedictine ashram." Chinook Community in Washington brings together clergymen from different religions for discussions and conferences. Many communities, like Ojai Foundation and Mt. Madonna in California, invite speakers from diverse spiritual traditions to speak to their members. The spiritual beliefs of some communities, for example, Findhorn in Scotland, are a synthesis of many paths—Christian, Buddhist, Hindu, Native American, Theosophist, etc. The Bear Tribe in Washington brings together ceremonies and teachings from many different Native American traditions. Although focusing on a particular spiritual path, many groups, for instance, Stelle in Illinois, welcome sincere spiritual searchers on any path to join their community. And finally, a good amount of tolerance is generally shown by these new communities when members choose to leave their group to follow a different spiritual path.

Ancient teachings are expanded for modern needs.

While the essence of the spiritual teaching is always preserved, appropriate changes are made when necessary, demonstrating the teaching's adaptability. For example, modern wholistic health practices such as reflexology, Bach Flowers, and guided imagery complement Kripalu's yogic approach to physical and spiritual growth. Healing is elevated once again to the province of Spirit, and many communities, like Center of the Light and Fare-Thee-Well, feature healing as part of their weekly spiritual services. Ananda Community adds new age businesses to traditional ashram life so that members may learn how to apply their spiritual values in the marketplace. Married couples and children are now allowed in the Providence Zen Center. Yasodhara ashram in British Columbia was started by a woman, Swami Radha, who was named successor to a line of traditionally male Indian gurus. At Chinook, the Christian Eucharist service is held in a community house or even out of doors to celebrate the Spirit in nature. Renaissance Community holds Sunday services with rock music.

Although many of the new communities believe in karma (the spiritual law that "as you sow, so shall you reap") and reincarnation (that a soul lives many lives on earth to learn lessons and achieve perfection), this ancient belief is viewed in a more positive context. Rather than being seen as a system of punishment for wrong-doing, there is a new emphasis on karma as a law of harmony and balance, and grace is possible through forgiving oneself and others.

Spiritual leadership does not have absolute authority and infallibility.

While many of the new communities have an easily identifiable spiritual teacher or guide, the "Inner Teacher" within each person is highly respected as the final authority. Members are encouraged to seek and trust this inner wisdom. At the Findhorn Community, an individual member's own inner guidance is consulted in determining work and living situations, for example. The Insight Meditation Center in Massachusetts encourages members to stand on their own two feet spiritually rather than rely on external teachers. With the passing of The Mother, the spiritual guide of Auroville Community in India, the tradition of guide or guru appointing a successor was changed to encourage each member to follow her/his Inner Guide. Rather than rely on ordained priests, many communities have created a new democratic priesthood, and each member may take turns leading ceremonies and services. Both men *and* women serve as celebrants in most new age services, as religion is no longer a patriarchical domain.

Spiritual beliefs and practices are on a voluntary basis, without coercion.

Spirituality is instilled through personal example and inspiration. There is no threat of burning in hell if someone doesn't attend a service, as it's felt that members can benefit spiritually from practices only if they choose to participate of their own free will. The Abode Community has regular prayer and meditation times, but members are not required to attend, as such a rule would go against the essential spirit of Sufism. Study groups on the teachings of Rudolph Steiner are held weekly at Spring Valley Community, but members attend only if they feel inspired to. Most members of the Findhorn Community believe in angels, nature spirits, karma and reincarnation, but not everyone does, and it's not a requirement for membership.

There is respect for the earth and an awareness of Spirit in nature.

Unlike the traditional religions, which usually separate spirit and matter, heaven and earth, and view the physical life as something to be transcended, the spirituality of the new communities celebrates Spirit made manifest in the beauty of the natural world. Everyday life is the spiritual teacher, and practical "groundedness" (taking care of mundane responsibilities in a loving, centered way) is highly respected as a spiritual quality. Ceremonies celebrating the nature festivals, the equinoxes, solstices, and full moons are held at many communities, Temenos in Massachusetts and Spring Valley in New York, for example. Meditations in the garden, affirming a commitment to work in cooperation with the forces of nature, are held at Findhorn and Sirius communities. Chinook Community held a large conference on "Christianity and the Emerging Spirituality of the Earth" featuring the "Missa Gaia"—mass of the earth—by The Paul Winter Consort.

Some communities that have a strong focus on honoring the earth call this the new paganism, harkening back to the best aspects of the pre-Christian earth religions, while including Christian elements as well. In some communities there are ceremonies honoring the Goddess, the feminine aspect of the Divine Force immanent within all Life.

For most of the communities in this book, spiritual beliefs and practices form the real binding force to keep members together as a group, willing to work out conflicts which arise. Their spiritual life is the main reason many of these communities are together. For others that don't have a common spiritual path, like Twin Oaks Community for example, there is a clearly-defined set of shared values (nonviolence and human equality) that function much like a spiritual path in that they create a strong binding force. And within all these communities, there are always some who follow a specific spiritual path, even if the community as a whole doesn't have a spiritual focus.

Interestingly enough, many of the values that we in this country call "spiritual"—love, peace, sharing, respect for the earth—are called "political" values by communities in Denmark, and most communities there call themselves "political," not "spiritual," communities. Community members in Denmark define politics as "the way we live our lives"—in other words, everything they are and everything they do. Similarly, the communities in this book might also say, spirituality is "the way we live our lives."

In this chapter, we have highlighted several communities which have transformed the essence of traditional religions into a new age approach. These include Chinook with Christianity, Yogaville with the yogic traditions of Hinduism, The Bear Tribe with Native American religion, The Abode with the Sufism of Islam, The Providence Zen Center with Zen Buddhism, and Lama with a synthesis of many religions.

Chinook Community - bridging the separation between spirituality and nature

CHINOOK COMMUNITY: Restoring the Link between Christianity and Nature

The name Chinook is a translation of a Northwest Indian word for "warm wind blowing," foretelling the coming of Spring. To Chinook members, it is a metaphor for the Spirit heralding a new season and bearing the seeds of new life. The vision of Chinook Community was born on the island of Iona, off the west coast of Scotland, where St. Columba and a group of monks in the sixth century lived a vision of a new order of life and faith as an inspiration for the society that was disintegrating all around them. This is a guiding image for Chinook members, as they see their central purpose as "assisting the transformative work of Spirit to enable a new future to be born, with the sacredness of life more fully known and celebrated."

Started on fifteen acres in Washington State in 1972 by Fritz Hull, an ex-Presbyterian minister, and his wife Vivienne, Chinook sees itself as an order of men and women not unlike the religious orders of the past, but in a form more appropriate to the interdependent global era of today. "Our spiritual devotion, if you will, is planetary transformation," member Tim Clark explains. "We use the tool of Chinook Community to help change our culture." One of the community's tasks is helping people create new forms of spiritual service or ministry in their various professions and life patterns, as a response to the call of Spirit in an emerging global age.

A particular interest of Chinook's is exploring the meaning of contemporary spiritual discipleship and the relationship between historic Christianity and the emerging issues of our time. As a former minister himself, co-founder Fritz Hull has brought together clergymen and lay people from many different Christian churches. Chinook works closely with other educational centers, universities, and churches and each year co-sponsors programs with the Cathedral of St. John the Divine in New York City and Dean James Parks Morton.

Chinook members have a perspective on life that affirms the presence of the sacred in everyday life. "Instead of compartmentalizing it and saying *this is spiritual* and *this is the rest of life*, we are working to integrate religion and life," Tim Clark explains. Meetings and community work begin with a moment of silent attunement with God and with each other. Sunday morning Eucharist services are held each week, drawing on Christian and Celtic traditions. "We link up universally with other communities and people at this time, and different people share whatever they'd like to," adds member Janet Day. Group meditations are held each Friday at Chinook, and community decisions are made by meditation. Tim Clark explains:

> When we come to an apparent choice point in our community life, we first reframe the question from "What will we do?" to "What is God's spirit asking of us?" With this attitude in mind we "attune" to the situation...We silence our feelings and thoughts and identify with a sense of what God wants this situation to become...After the

Ageless Spiritual Traditions 261

silence we share our thoughts and images. Very often someone will voice a thought that "rings true." The course of action is then clear. Other times, a common understanding is pieced together from many divergent points of view.[1]

Chinook holds four central commitments:

The first is spiritual consciousness...because through personal transformation comes the wisdom to reshape our lives and our world...The second is vision—creating a new and positive image of the future...and of a new world so that we will be empowered to bring that vision into reality. Thirdly, Chinook seeks to be a center of demonstration...giving our vision form and expression in all parts of life. And finally, service. Chinook exists not for itself, nor solely for its individual members, but to reach out in loving service to all life by helping pioneer new patterns of faith, work, economics, and community life.[2]

A renewed dedication to earth stewardship and the sacramentality of life

From the beginning, Chinook members have felt deeply inspired by the land and have experienced its mystic sense of power and beauty. A major concern has been the recovery of relationship with the natural order, learning to value all life forms and work cooperatively with the kingdoms of nature. Effective action on behalf of an emerging global future, they feel, must now include the healing of the earth and a renewed dedication to "earth stewardship." They see earth as a living entity and feel that "earth's story" has for too long been omitted from the agenda of conventional spirituality and theology. Chinook affirms the interconnectedness and sacramentality of life. Members Autumn Preble and Marilyn Strong view their work as "bridging the separation between spirituality and nature." Vivienne Hull adds that historically, "Christianity has been a part of the problem which caused people to disregard matter and the natural order by teaching a terrible dualism between God and nature."[3] Chinook members work in attunement with nature in their gardens and forest and seek to maintain ecological balance on their land. Fritz Hull sees a "genesis of a new environmental action...where the lovers of the earth become the caretakers of the earth...and demonstrate a new stewardship of the earth...A new partnership with the earth means relating to all life with the power of love."

The genesis of a new environmental action where the lovers of the earth become the caretakers of the earth

Chinook is an educational center and its twenty-five covenant members are committed to serve the vision of a new order of life through this center. In addition, three hundred associate members contribute skills, financial support, and prayer, and about fifty associated members of Chinook have moved nearby to form a support network of friends who help with work and special projects at Chinook. Chinook presently stewards about fifty acres of land, and members and associates have bought an additional 150 acres around the center, creating a land covenant and an "ecological village."

The educational programs offered at Chinook include "Core Studies", a nine-month course of study on spiritual attunement; the new cultural paradigm in theology, history, and the arts; nature and spirituality, land stewardship, permaculture; new models of community and the planetary village; creating strategies for social change. Chinook offers summer intensives on "The Call to

Ageless Spiritual Traditions   263

Service in an Emerging Global Age" that explore "the new priesthood, new culture, new earth." Weekend workshops are also offered on themes such as personal centering, world peace, creating a new economy, and Christianity and the emerging spirituality of the earth. To further their educational work in the local area, Chinook members recently opened a music and book store called Warm Wind.

Yogaville Community - LOTUS temple with altars to ten major religions and to others, known and unknown

YOGAVILLE COMMUNITY: The Path of Yoga and a Temple to All Religions

Yogaville is a spiritual community started by disciples of Swami Satchidananda in 1978 on 650 acres in Virginia. It is the world headquarters for Integral Yoga Institute, based on Satchidananda's teachings, and is the home of a temple honoring all the religions of the world. Yogaville is envisioned as a model community that will demonstrate to the world how people can live in unity and harmony while enjoying individual differences. The goal is to realize permanent peace and joy by leading a selfless, dedicated life.

Under the direct guidance of Swami Satchidananda, the one hundred or so members of Yogaville—including monks, single people, and families—live a life of purity and simplicity, based on a commitment to truth, nonviolence, and universal brotherhood. Daily life in the ashram consists of yogic practices, meditation, vegetarian meals, family gatherings, study, and "selfless service" (karma yoga). A health food store offering natural foods is operated in town by members. Classes in all branches of yoga—hatha, raja, japa, jnana, bhakti—are offered for all sides of the person: physical, intellectual, emotional, and spiritual. The yoga taught in the community includes not only the various postures, meditation, and breathing exercises, but also emphasizes the importance of living an ethical life and serving others. The yoga postures and deep breathing help to rid the body of tensions and toxins that build up, and meditation helps to calm the mind. As the Swami explains it, "Keep the mind clean, the body clean, the life well-disciplined, the heart dedicated. This is Yoga. The only requirement to see that peace and joy, or God. . .is a clean, peaceful mind."

Meditation is taught, beginning with concentration—trying to focus one's attention on a single point. The single point chosen can vary according to the faith and temperament of the individual, according to Swami Satchidanada. It can be a sacred name, a mantra (such as OM or Amen), or it can be a form. When trying to concentrate on one point, a word or a form, the mind will often run here and there. But the idea is just to become aware of this and to bring the mind gently back to the single concentration, Satchidananda says. This takes much practice, but when concentration becomes perfect, it is called meditation. It is through discipline and meditation that a person is cleared and opened up to realize that true essence that is within. Swami Satchidananda believes that we don't need to do anything to experience our attunement with God's grace except to remove the "interference" and "static" of the senses and ego thoughts, and this is what meditation helps with.

Swami Satchidananda (left) of Yogaville and Sir George Trevelyan (right) of Findhorn

Ageless Spiritual Traditions 265

Daily life in the community is fairly disciplined. Members do not use alcohol or drugs, and the diet is free of meat, caffeine, and sugar. Celibacy is practiced by monastics and single people. Members dress simply and have few material possessions. According to Swami Karunananda, a woman who was the ashram manager, the basic teachings of Yogaville are

—Service to a higher cause is most beneficial to personal growth. We strive to lead a selfless, dedicated life by having a healthy body and peaceful mind.
—There is one family of humanity. We all come from one source and we'll all be returning to that one source. So we must respect and appreciate diversity, but see the unity.

People ask Yogaville members, "How can you do all these things for your own peace when the world is so full of suffering?" Swami Satchidananda answers:

Normally we think of the world first. But Yoga believes in transforming the individual before transforming the world. Whatever change we want to happen outside, should happen within. And if you walk in peace and express that peace in your very life, others will see you and learn something.

Greed is the source of the world's problems, he feels. There is enough food grown to feed twelve billion people, and there are only four and one-half billion people in the world. The problem is not lack of food but lack of love. It is selfishness and the divisions we build between one another that create poverty, hunger, war, and calamity. Swami Karunananda adds:

There are different levels of charity: we can give someone food directly, which is an immediate solution. We can give someone money to buy food for a week. We can educate someone as to how to grow food or earn money to buy it. Or we can awaken the person to their own divine nature and help them to see it in others, and this will solve the problem of hunger for a lifetime.

Yogaville members are building a temple called the Light of Truth Universal Shrine or LOTUS that will have an altar for each of the ten major religions as well as an altar to all other known religions and one for all unknown religions. A beam of light will rise from a central altar and then be refracted so that individual beams of light shine on each of the other altars. This will symbolize that the source of spiritual light for all religions comes from one source. Swami Satchidananda has long dreamed of a place where people of all faiths can silently worship in their own traditions under the same roof, experiencing the one essence which is the source of all faiths. The shrine will also house an ecumenical religious library. The finished shrine will resemble a giant lotus blossom. Pope John Paul II has given his blessings and become an honorary patron of the shrine, as have other religious leaders.

For many years Swami Satchidananda has hosted ecumenical services with representatives from different religions around a common altar, so the shrine will be a permanent site for these services. Building the shrine and a new community as well takes a lot of hard physical work, but the Swami says, "Work is worship"—an opportunity to express one's spiritual values in action.

The foremost Indian cultural organization, the Bharatiya Vidya Bhavan, is building a residential high school for five hundred students at Yogaville. The curriculum of the school will serve to re-integrate the fundamental values of Indian culture, in light of modern knowledge, to suit present needs. Already, there is a pre-school, a grade school, and a junior high at Yogaville, all based on the community's spiritual values.

THE BEAR TRIBE: A Native American Approach to Spirit

You can be happy doing your OMs, but when it gets down to the time to eat and you can't feed the kids or yourself, the game is over. The only philosophy I want to hear about is one that will grow corn. In other words, something that will provide on an everyday basis right now for my people. We don't have to wait until we get to heaven for it to help us...Having the expertise to try and create something to keep people eating regularly is more spiritual than sitting and crying about it all.

—Sun Bear

Sun Bear, founder of the Bear Tribe Community - teaching people about their responsibilities to the earth

The Bear Tribe has a very down-to-earth, practical approach to spirituality, teaching a Native American approach to life and basic survival skills. The Bear Tribe Medicine Society was founded on fifty-four acres in 1970 by Sun Bear, a Native American medicine man of the Chippewa Tribe. It is organized as a non-profit educational corporation and owns the land the Tribe lives on. The community sees its main purpose as bringing Native American spiritual values and practical survival skills to modern society.

> The Tribe has a strong spiritual center. We believe in the sacredness of the earth. We believe we have a purpose in teaching and sharing with people how to come into harmony with the Great Spirit. We have a very strong commitment to a vision of teaching people how to come into harmony with the earth.

Bear Tribe members see everything as part of the circle of life. "Everything is part of the song of the Great Spirit," they say—unlike the typical white man's way of putting everything into little boxes where some things are holy and some are not. Bear Tribe member Wabun, a former writer from New York City, explains,

> Much of what the Bear Tribe teaches combines spirituality with good practical skills: farming, herbology, foraging, hunting, building, preserving, etc. Students don't, however, just learn how to raise and then kill a chicken. They learn how to raise it with respect, and take its life with the proper prayers and ceremonies. They don't just learn how to identify herbs; they learn how to speak to the spirit of the herb. As well as learning how to find water, keep a spring or well flowing and clean, they also learn how to pray to the water spirits every time they wash their hands, dishes or clothes.[4]

The Bear Tribe teaches people about their responsibility to the earth and all the living beings upon it. They feel, as Native people traditionally have, that there is an energy that only humans can give to these beings, and in turn, they do not take the gifts of the elements, the plants, and the animals for granted. For example, if they find a rock that they want to have because of the energy contained in it, they first ask the rock if it wants to be with them, and, if so, an offering would be left and a prayer made before taking the rock. They would never pick wild plants without leaving an offering of kinnickinnik and telling them why they need them and how they will use them, and they would never pick all of the plants in one area. Sun Bear says:

> I call the wind my brother, because we all are brothers and sisters to all creation, all living things. They're a part of us, and when we acknowledge them, we become part of them...and they respond to us...that's why some of us can speak with the animals and have

them come to us when we call them. We can speak to the trees, to the Earth, to the Creator, and ask for what we need at a particular time ...We've been doing it for thousands of years. It's not supernatural. It's perfectly natural...The Earth speaks to us all of the time; unfortunately, most folks are simply deaf to what she's saying. People are often amazed when I predict the weather for them yet that's a very simple thing to do.[5]

Bear Tribe members "make medicine" together several times a day to strengthen their love as a community. Before each meal, they join hands and give thanks for the nourishment they are receiving. In the evening they form a circle to make prayers and affirm their togetherness. They come together in a circle frequently because "it reminds us that all life is continuous, that there is no beginning or end, that all flows together in perfect harmony."[6]

The Bear Tribe calls itself a "Medicine Society," and members use the term "medicine" to mean "the power to heal with herbs, to heal using spirit forces, to work with the sweatlodge and other ceremonies, to make prayers for rain, to bless the crops, to share power and teachings with people, and much more."[7] The Tribe does many ceremonies not only to give energy to other kingdoms of life but also to release negativity from people and create feelings of love, joy, and unity.

Smudging ceremony for clearing away negative energies and attracting positive ones

One of the first ceremonies members learn is that of "smudging," using smoke to clear away negative energies and attract positive ones. Generally they mix sage and sweetgrass (or a fine-grade tobacco if these aren't available) in a bowl and then light the mixture and let it smolder, drawing the smoke towards their heart and over their heads to receive its blessing. After a person smudges her/himself, s/he then offers the smoke prayerfully to the four directions and then smudges the other people present. Smudging helps to clear rooms of negativity.

Pipe ceremonies are also shared at the Bear Tribe, and these are very sacred events. To Native peoples, the pipe represents the universe; it is a sacred altar. All of the kingdoms of life are represented in it: the bowl of stone represents the elemental kingdom; the stem of wood, the plant kingdom; and the decoration of fur and feathers, the animal kingdom. It is used by the "two-leggeds," the human kingdom, thus bringing all of the kingdoms into the ceremony. The pipe is lit and a puff of smoke is offered to each of the four directions, to the Great Spirit, and to Mother Earth. The breath of smoke taken in is the breath of the Great Spirit, they believe. And the smoke that rises from the bowl sends their prayers to the Creator, as they see smoke as an ethereal substance which can penetrate between the realms of the spiritual and material. The pipe is used for healing the earth and her people.[8] Sun Bear adds:

> If you are open and honest, and learn to work with your pipe in a proper and sacred manner, you may contact all the forces that have been on this continent for thousands of years. You can call the spirit forces; you can raise the wind or make rain...Many times, wherever we go, we of the Bear Tribe bring rain with us...Frequently, when we are in an area that's been dry for a long time, people say to me, "Sun Bear, we need some rain very badly here. Will you bring it to us?", and usually I do. Sometimes these folks get more rain than they asked for.[9]

Another ceremony used frequently by the Bear Tribe is the sweatlodge. It is a powerful healing experience that cleanses physical and emotional toxins. The sweatlodge is a dome-shaped structure made from saplings, with blankets and canvas placed over it to keep in the heat. In the center of the lodge, a hole is dug into the earth where rocks are placed that have been heated in a fire outside. After participants enter the lodge's door, which faces East, and all are seated in a circle around the hot rocks, sage is sprinkled on the rocks to remove negativity from those present. Sweetgrass is then put on the rocks to bring out positive energies. Water is then poured over the stones to produce steam, and participants begin sweating. The Great Spirit, the Grandfather and

Preparing for the sweatlodge ceremony

Grandmother Spirits, and then the powers of the four directions, are invited into the lodge. Songs are sung and healing prayers offered together or individually. When someone has had enough heat, s/he will leave the lodge, saying, "Thank you, all my relations."

Another ceremony members use individually to release their negativity is to dig a hole in a secluded spot in nature and to lie down on the earth with their stomach covering the hole. They pray that Mother Earth will transform their emotional sickness into good compost that will allow positive things to grow in the earth and in themselves. If they need to, they will cry, scream, or vomit into the hole, to get out all of their pain. "They feel the good power of the Earth surge into them—it's a strong process of self-realization," says Sun Bear.[10] Then they cover the hole with earth again and make another prayer and offering to the earth, thanking her for transforming their negativity.

The vision quest is another powerful ceremony used by Bear Tribe members and their students to find what they call their "path of power" as an individual. They go out into a wilderness area alone, with no food or water, and they cry out to the Creator asking Him to send a sign, a vision that will direct them and tell them their purpose in life. "During this time, people come closest to the spirit realm," Sun Bear says. "If a vision comes to a person and he follows that vision, then that becomes his medicine, his path of power."[11]

In the late 1970s, Sun Bear had a vision of the Medicine Wheel—an ancient stone circle used for thousands of years by

Ageless Spiritual Traditions 271

Native People for prayer, ceremony, and self-understanding. At one time there were some twenty thousand Medicine Wheels on this continent alone. Sun Bear feels that it is important to bring this ancient system back today for the healing of people and the earth. The Medicine Wheel is based on a person's relationship to the earth and all kingdoms of life: mineral, plant, animal, human. A person enters the Wheel at the point of the moon (or month) in which he was born and inherits the powers, gifts, and responsibilities of that particular moon. Then the person keeps moving around the Wheel, learning life's lessons from the various animals, plants, and minerals on the Wheel. In the ceremony of the Medicine Wheel, as in everyday life, true spiritual growth comes from moving around the Wheel, not staying stagnant. Sun Bear explains:

> The Medicine Wheel is a magic circle which encompasses all of our relations with the natural world. It is a sacred tool that can teach us how to eat well; how to heal ourselves and others; how to hear the songs and stories that the wind and water bring to us. It can teach us, too, the most important lesson, which is that we are each a small, unique part of the universe, and that we are here to learn harmony with the rest of Creation. When people feel that something is missing in their lives, they often find part of it by working with the Wheel.[12]

The Bear Tribe has a Medicine Wheel on top of a sacred hill on their land, and they teach others how to work with this process in Medicine Wheel Gatherings they organize around the country, featuring many well-known Native teachers and medicine people. They also give seminars on "Earth Awareness," "Vision Quest," and "Self-Reliance" at their community and around the country.

The Medicine Wheel ceremony - a magic circle, encompassing all our relations with the natural world, which is a teaching and healing tool

The Abode Community - the Sufi message honoring all the religions of the world

THE ABODE: Sufi Dance and Study with Universal Worship Services

May the heavens be reflected in the earth, Lord,
That the earth may be turned into heaven.

—Sufi Prayer

The Abode of the Message was founded in 1974 by Pir Vilayat Khan, head of the Sufi Order in the West, on 430 acres in upstate New York that had previously been an old Shaker village.

The Shakers were a spiritual community of the 1800s that has some interesting parallels with modern communities. Interestingly enough, there was an old Shaker prophecy that after the Shakers left the village, a new group would arise to take over. The newcomers would also see dance and song as very important, as did the Shakers, but in a different way. It turned out that the Sufis had been singing and dancing a Shaker song, "Tis a Gift to Be Simple," before ever coming to The Abode. So Pir Vilayat looked for a Shaker village to establish his community. Soon he was contacted by a family who owned two of them, and arrangements were made to purchase the one in New Lebanon. The Abode thus became a tangible link with the best of the tradition of the utopian communities of the 1800s.

Pir Vilayat originally established the Abode to be egalitarian and ecumenical. There was no requirement to be a Sufi to join, though the original one hundred or so members were Sufis from around the country who had been following Pir Vilayat as their teacher for some time. An early brochure of the Abode stated:

> We are moving towards the unity of matter and spirit. People are looking for a way to bring their highest ideals into everyday life, a way to bring heaven to earth. The creation of New Age communities is a response to this force. Communal life, centered around the ideal of bringing the divine spirit into manifestation in life, presents a way for people to live in harmony with each other, with nature, and with the evolution of the planet.[13]

Sufism, as an esoteric tradition coming out of Islam in the Middle East, uses the stuff of ordinary life—family, work, worship—as the material of spiritual development and spiritual service. Some members work within the community as staff, but most work outside in the local town in a variety of professions from carpenter to college instructor. Most members live in the original Shaker buildings, but some have built their own homes on the land. Members contribute a monthly fee to cover rent and food, and most meals are shared in a common dining room.

The Sufis are not given the promise that they are chosen to be saved but rather that, if they align with the spiritual values lived by the Sufis, they can contribute to the real progress of humanity. There is a strong service orientation among the Sufis.

The Sufi message honors all the religions of the world:

> Those who, with excuse of their great faith in their own religion, hurt the feelings of another and divide humanity, which has the same source and goal, abuse religion, whatever be their faith. The message, at whatever period it came to the world, did not come just to a certain section of humanity, it did not come to raise only some few people who perhaps accepted the faith, the message, or a particular organized Church. No, all these things came afterwards. The rain does not fall in a certain land only; the sun does not shine only upon a particular country. All that comes from God is for all souls. If they are worthy, they deserve it; it is their reward. If they are unworthy, they are all the more entitled to it. Verily, blessing is for every soul; for every soul, whatever be his faith or belief, belongs to God.[14]

At the Abode today, each of the sixty or so adult members follows his own special spiritual path. "It is not up to any one person or text to tell someone where [that path] is," comments

Akbar Scott, the community's administrator. "It is up to each of us to find our own."[15] In keeping with this tradition, ideals are used as guidance rather than as rules, according to Vakil Kuner.

Today, Pir Vilayat doesn't lead in the way he did previously, according to Gawri, a long-time member who works in the herb garden. Instead, he "acts as a mirror, reflecting ourselves to us," she observes.

Living at the Abode means sharing ideals and sometimes forsaking individual ideals when they become obstacles to harmony. Tolerance is an important value to Abode members.

Let the heavens be reflected in the earth

> It is the application of this ideal that has been the bridge over the many stormy waters that we as a community have had to cross. It is always easier to lay blame on someone else than to try to see a conflict from the eyes of the other person. Yet if we give ourselves enough space and time to reflect on each situation and view the problem from a higher vantage point, not only do problems resolve themselves, but we also are given a glimpse of the consciousness of the realized being...it is a tremendously freeing action to incorporate more and more outlooks into one's heart, rather than shut the doors in order to preserve just one point of view.[16]

The Abode has a common meditation with prayers and chanting that is held three times a day. In a rhythm recommended by Pir Vilayat, each day in the week is dedicated to a different religion. Scriptures are read from that religion, with appropriate practices, prayers, and chants. Prayer isn't required at the Abode, as Sufism is non-dogmatic. Requiring anything goes against its grain. It's the message that's important in Sufism. But it also seems that members who don't come to regular prayers usually find themselves moving out of the central energy of the community, and generally they soon leave the community of their own accord.

Attunements—singing grace before each meal—are also a part of daily life at the Abode. Universal Worship Services, honoring the major religions of the world, are held every Sunday at the Abode, and they constitute the heart of the Sufi practice. For example, there might be a reading from the Upanishads (Hindu), the Gospel of Buddha, the Songs of Zarathustra (Zoroastrian), Deuteronomy (Hebrew), the Gospel of St. John (Christian), and the Quran (Islam). Following each scripture reading, there is a prayer or offering made from that tradition. Dances of Universal Peace (referred to as "Sufi dances") often follow the Universal Worship Service. These are drawn from the religious traditions of the world and were originally gathered together and brought to the Sufis by Samuel Lewis.

The School of Universal Worship, based at the Abode, offers correspondence courses and seminars focusing on the study of the world's religions and the unity of religious ideals.

Every Thursday evening there are classes on Sufi teachings, especially on the works of Hazrat Inayat Khan (Pir Vilayat's father), who founded the Sufi Order in the West. Most members attend these classes, which begin with a half hour meditation and then break into three groups: for newcomers, recent initiates, and long-term initiates.

Retreat programs, led by Pir Vilayat and other spiritual guides at the Abode, are three-, five- or ten-day intensives. Retreat participants take a vow of silence and do breathing exercises, visualizations, and chanting for up to ten hours a day. The schedule was designed by Pir Vilayat to follow the six-stage formula of alchemy. Members and guests also do individual retreats for several days, staying alone in one of the small huts on the land, with retreat guides visiting regularly.

When a member is initiated into the Sufi Order, someone becomes their "guide," and they meet together every other week. "Some guides function more like a spiritual friend," Yaqin Aubert, Secretary of The Abode, observes, "focusing on your spiritual life and helping that awareness permeate the rest of your life. Other guides function like spiritual teachers and give you meditation practices and insights to help you unfold."

Some Abode members have spiritual names—Hindu, Buddhist, Jewish, Christian, Islamic—given to them by Pir Vilayat or their spiritual guide. These names are to help the members develop a new quality in themselves or to bring out something that's already in them that needs more attention. Not all members have spiritual names, however. Ted Johnson, for example, who functions as head of the community when Pir Vilayat is absent, is one of several who have kept their original names.

Yaqin Aubert feels that community life helps support people in their spiritual practice. "At the Abode we learn to see difficulties in life as opportunities," he says. "We ask ourselves, 'What could I develop or learn from this experience? What qualities do I need to develop?'" Julia Herman comments:

> I grew spiritually through pain and difficulties. Sometimes I felt I couldn't endure another moment, and then I would experience a flash of illumination from a friend or a spiritual teacher that would lift me completely out of my pain and give me a fresh insight and new energy to go on.

Much of the spiritual growth of the Abode happens simply through "karma yoga," selfless service, voluntary work done for the whole community. Learning to work lovingly and cooperatively with others is quite a discipline in itself.

Faith is one of the most important ideals that guides the Abode.

> Through faith in the purpose of our work, we have been able to accept the difficulties that we have met as tests to awaken certain qualities in each of us personally and as a community. In times when we had no money, when projects were not progressing, when people were not trying to get along, or when winter seemed as though it would never leave, we have always relied on our faith that no matter what happens, everything is as it should be.[17]

The Providence Zen Center - everything can be our teacher if we choose to use it that way; or we can wish we were somewhere else and not get the message

THE PROVIDENCE ZEN CENTER:
Developing the "Clear Mind" and "Koan" Training

Students of Zen at the Providence Zen Center have a strong practice based on a 2500-year-old tradition to help them develop a clear mind to deal with life. Located on fifty-five acres in Cumberland, Rhode Island, the Zen Center now has forty residents who practice daily meditation, chanting, bowing, and weekly interviews called "koan" training, to help their personal growth. For Zen students, to develop a clear mind is to see the world as it really is. Korean Zen Master Seung Sahn, founder of the Zen Center, says,

Ageless Spiritual Traditions **277**

A clear mind is like a mirror: red comes and the mirror is red; yellow comes and the mirror is yellow; a mountain comes and the mirror is a mountain.[18]

We were all born with clear minds, Zen students believe, and we once had a fresh vision of this world. But as we grew, our vision became clouded with layers of opinion and preconception. Zen is the practice of stripping away these layers and returning to clear mind. Zen students live by certain guidelines, not rules. They believe that when the mind is clear, it need not be bound by rules. All beings are kind at heart, they believe, so the clear mind will be compassionate and act correctly.

The emphasis of Zen is always on doing it, not talking about it. Meditation and experience, not reading, are encouraged. Living together in community is a path to rapid growth in developing the clear mind, according to member Shana Klinger.

Many communities work on developing a new model for what they believe could be an ideal society, with a new culture and new forms. In contrast, the Zen Center consciously uses an ancient form, one that is imported from another culture (Korean), not because it's superior, but because it's so defined. The Center is very structured and hierarchical, and it is precisely the structure and rules that provide the teaching, because the individual holds ultimate responsibility for how s/he relates to it, according to David Klinger.

We need the backdrop of a formal practice in order to see our minds clearly. Instead of being concerned with "I", "mine", "me"—"my opinion", "my condition", "my situation"—you try doing something that you have no control over for awhile. And you'll watch your mind appear. You're in the dharma room and your mind says, "I'm hungry," and you can't do anything about it. But if you're sitting in your living room and your mind says, "I'm hungry," then you go and get something to eat, and you don't see what's going on. So you can use the form to see what's going on. And we have a very clear agreement about what the form is...

And Shana Klinger adds:

In Zen training, good or bad doesn't matter. It's being able to let go of your attachment that's important. The idea is "together action"— doing everything together. Everything that is out of harmony with that one rule will appear. Even if it is a bad rule, then if you're clear, you just break the rule. If you're not clear, then many conflicts appear. The universe is the teacher. Anything that is out of harmony with the universe appears.

Master Dharma Teacher Lincoln Rhodes observes:

Community life is more of a teaching than even meditation is. You may have a great meditation, but if you walk out of the room after your meditation and you're nasty to someone, then what good was the meditation? So in community life, you get very quick and clear feedback, if the place works as it should.

At the Zen Center, there is a strong delineation between what's public and what's private, although it's not written down anywhere. What's private, you don't touch, you don't judge. What's public is very clear to residents: when you show up in the dharma room, whether you do your house jobs, pay your rent, and meet the community agreements that everyone shares. Everything else you do is private. "The positive side of this approach is that we don't 'check'—we don't judge each other. The negative side is not caring—people often feel isolated," Shana Klinger observes. And Sam Rose adds:

Life at the Zen Center is more honest than on the outside—people know where each other stands, and if it isn't pretty, at least there is less cover-up. People are more honest about their suffering at the Center and a little less likely to self-indulge it...In our approach—in "dharma relationships"—the primary relationship is between each person and his/her practice [the "dharma"], and we relate to each other secondarily, almost peripherally, on the personal level—which has its advantages and disadvantages.

Lincoln Rhodes, Master Dharma Teacher at the Center, helps students to allow everyday life to be their teacher.

The way out [of suffering] is to appreciate every moment. It's not just the beautiful version of the "trees are green and the sky is blue," but "the dishwater's too hot and the bathroom smells." All of these things. It's everything that comes our way.[19]

Members of the Zen Center feel it's important to see our true nature, to see the whole thing in all its glory—the bad, the angry, the ugly, the joyful—the *whole* thing. Our task is finding out what a human being is. As Rhodes says,

> It's *the* step to having compassion for other human beings, because then you know what you're *both* like. We're all in the same boat. The problem is we don't have compassion for other people, because we think *they're* jerks and *we're* not.[20]

According to Zen teaching, we only learn from something if we do it 100%—otherwise we create "karma." "Every single thing can be our teacher if we choose to use it that way, or we can choose to wish we were somewhere else and not get the message,"[21] Rhodes notes.

Zen students have an unusual approach to conflict and anger. No one else can make you angry, they feel; it's always something in you. So every time you get angry, there's some wonderful thing to be learned about your karma—even though this may be hard to see at first. Anger shows you where you're attached to something. At the Zen Center, the expression used for getting angry is "having your energy up." The energy rises to the head, they feel, because of some attachment, some ego involvement. So students work on their own attachment first, before trying to resolve a conflict with the other person. Meditation is used to see the experience with a clear mind.

The Zen approach to dealing with negative emotions has been very instructive to member Ruth Klein, who feels that the really important questions were never asked when she studied psychology in college. She says, "Sitting and meditating for seven days taught me more than I learned getting my Ph.D."

An important part of Zen training is weekly interviews in which the Zen Master and Master Dharma Teachers confront students with "koans" to guide them towards a clear mind. Koans are little parables or riddles to show how our minds get stuck—stuck in words, stuck in forms. One famous koan asks, "What is the sound of one hand clapping?" Lincoln Rhodes explains how the koan sessions work.

> The job of the person giving the interview is to just mirror your situation. You get asked these questions and it just tells you where you're at—if you're nervous, that appears; if you're confused, that appears; if you're being stupid, that appears. You can't just answer the questions from your ideas, from your mind. The interviewer then helps you believe in yourself and not depend on whether the interviewer agrees with you or not.

The answers you give to the questions are not as important as the space you're given to make your own mistakes. Everything that appears is your teacher, they believe.

What is the sound of one hand clapping? -Zen Koan

Zen Center members include both monks and lay people. There are five traditional monks at the Center who are celibate and seven "Boddhisatva monks" who can marry and have children. The Boddhisatva monks vow to deepen and clarify their commitment to understanding themselves and helping others.

The Zen Center will be building a traditional monastery to provide group support for a monastic lifestyle. The six families at the Center live in two large houses next to the main building. This works out well for everyone, as many silent retreats are held in the main building, so they aren't disturbed by the noise of children playing.

When couples marry at the Zen Center, they have a "dharma marriage"—taking vows to help each other attain enlightenment and help all beings avoid suffering. Zen Master Seung Sahn says to his students, "Either become a monk or get married." "It's a really good teaching," Shana Klinger comments, "because marriages between students are based on more than just attraction. They are used to help students deepen their Zen practice of developing a clear mind."

Ageless Spiritual Traditions 281

Ruth Klein comments:

> Some people here feel very strongly that sex is only for marriage. And some people feel very strongly that it isn't. So there's no general agreement about it or pressure to conform to one standard. Everyone is here with a very conscious sense of what they're doing. I haven't really experienced people here running rampant with desires. If that's what you wanted, you wouldn't be here to begin with.

To support their development, some women at the Zen Center formed a women's group last year, to share more deeply with each other and to help restore the imbalance they felt in the community in warmth and communication. Ruth explains:

> We go around the circle, and each person has a turn. We gave ourselves permission to not repress our feelings. It's been wonderful for all of us—both to share things and to get to know each other, as we don't have time as a community to get to know each other individually.

While Zen training is offered at the Zen Center, residents also believe that there may be people out in the world who never heard of the word "Zen" but who are nonetheless doing it. "They see someone who's hungry, and they give them something to eat. They don't think about it; they don't need a form, they just do it. Zen is everyday life," observes Shana Klinger.

THE LAMA FOUNDATION:
A Synthesis of Different Religions

Lama's purpose, as expressed in its bylaws, is

> To serve as an instrument for the awakening and evolution of consciousness, individual and collective, thereby aiding its membership and all sentient beings in achieving a more complete awareness of their position in the universal structure through integration of the threefold nature of man into one harmonious being.

People join Lama for the experience of "sangha"—the supportive human environment conducive to daily practice and remembrance. Located on sacred Indian land high in the Sangre de

Cristo mountains of New Mexico, Lama is one of the most peaceful and beautiful settings of all the communities. One of the unique features of Lama is that many different spiritual traditions and paths exist side by side—Sufi, Buddhist, Hindu, Christian, Jewish, Islamic, Native American. Not only is there spiritual diversity at Lama, but there are also many diverse perspectives on the nature of the community itself.

> There are as many viewpoints of Lama as there are people who have experienced it. It is seen as a way-station where pilgrims are given shelter from outer-world distractions, and as a greenhouse where early spiritual awakening is protected and nurtured. It is seen as a pressure cooker. It is seen as a blending of East and West, and a spot of hope for peace on earth. It is seen as a spiritual community, a New Age community, a place of opportunity to work on oneself, an attempt by fools to create an escapist reality. It is seen as a synthesis of paths in the realization that all paths lead to one reality. It is seen as no path at all, allowing those who seek a path the space to find one.[22]

Lama Community - to serve as an instrument for the evolution of consciousness

Lama members must see the unity beyond form, or they couldn't have survived as a stable community for eighteen years. Not only is there no resident guru or charismatic leader at Lama, but all decisions are made by consensus of its twenty-five or so members, and leadership rotates among them. (In fact, an attempt by one of the original founders to take over the community a few years ago and make it solely Islamic was successfully resisted by members.)

Ageless Spiritual Traditions 283

Lama became well known to spiritual seekers after producing the book *Be Here Now* with Ram Dass, who returns frequently to the community to offer retreats and workshops. Spiritual leaders from many different traditions have offered summer workshops for the public at Lama: Joshu Sasaki Roshi, Brother David Steindl-Rast, Zalmon Schachter, Baba Hari Dass, and Grandfather David Monongye. Individual retreats in private hermitages are also offered at Lama.

The observance of particular spiritual practices depends on who is at Lama at any given time. Currently, for example, there are daily meditations at 6:00 a.m. for practioners of Zen, Vipassana, and Theravedan Buddhism. At the same time, Christians meet for contemplation, centering prayers, chanting, or scripture reading, and there is also an Islamic "salat," the dawn ritual prayer. At 6:30 a.m., the whole community joins together for silent meditation. "This daily silent meditation really helps," comments member Mary Ann Matheson, "because the community experiences itself in practice together."

Following breakfast there is a daily "tuning meeting" with a brief spiritual reading or practice, followed by a work schedule and business discussion, and ending with a prayer, practice, or chanting.

On Thursdays there is a silent workday, from 6:00 a.m. through lunch, to help members work more consciously and make a prayer of their work. In the winter, all the women work together on one project and all the men on another during these silent work days. This is a very rich experience for the members, bringing them closer together, as some people normally work alone during the week.

Prayers from different traditions are said before each meal, and everyone joins in. If for any reason someone is not comfortable with a prayer, they just keep silent but still stay part of the circle holding hands during the prayers. Before lunch members gather for noon prayers in the dome, and there is a silent meditation each evening before dinner.

In addition to this daily schedule, there are also regularly-held practices from different traditions during the week that any member or visitor of Lama can join: "zikr" (chanting in the Sufi tradition); the Islamic call to prayer five times a day; Christian scripture reading and tapes; Eucharist service on Sundays; Buddhist "sitting" (meditation) intensives; Sufi Dances of Universal Peace; Jewish Shabbat services on Friday evenings; Islamic Ramadan fasts; Buddhist dharma study with reading, sitting, and walking meditation. Most members also spend time in hermitage each year.

*Creating 'Sangha' - a
supporting human
environment conducive to
daily spiritual practice*

Summer at Lama is a time of outbreath, of service to the many guests who visit the community for retreats and workshops. Winter is a time of inbreath, a time to deepen study and practice and to nourish the interior life, the contemplative life. Mary Ann Matheson notes:

> Chopping wood and carrying water is real—the physical life is very strenuous summer and winter at Lama. Visitors may imagine that in joining in the Lama schedule they'll be sitting on a zafu (meditation cushion) six hours a day. No so! More likely they'll be toiling in adobe pits making bricks, servicing the outhouses, trimming kerosene wicks or carrying compost to the garden. Only two hours of meditation are scheduled per day.[23]

Lama members employ intention and commitment very consciously as tools for spiritual growth. Intentions are put out in advance; making a commitment to a particular spiritual practice is used as a growth process. There is no leader or teacher to enforce this commitment, just a member's own conscience.

Although members may come from a personal background of one religious tradition, they may decide at Lama to follow another. A spirit of tolerance and respect for each other's spiritual traditions pervades the community. It's understood that each tradition provides something special needed by the individual. Some members spend time studying one tradition during their stay and then move to another. Most members regularly attend the practices of more than one tradition and feel enriched by this diversity.

Lama is demonstrating a true synthesis of spiritual traditions and providing an inspirational model of how unity in diversity could work in our world, especially in religious matters, where it's so needed today.

10 Guidelines for Building Communities

You see things as they are and ask "Why?" I dream things that never were and ask "Why not?"

—GEORGE BERNARD SHAW

286   BUILDERS OF THE DAWN

What is it like to start a community? It's exhilarating, fulfilling, creative, and intensely rewarding. But it's also profoundly challenging and frustrating, stretching one to one's limits and beyond, on all levels: physical, emotional, mental, spiritual. Starting a community is

> —staying up until 2:00 a.m. to work out a personal problem with a new member.

> —learning to tolerate people who don't necessarily like things as neat and clean as you do.

> —learning to cook for more people than you ever imagined you could.

> —letting other people take more responsibility and make their own mistakes if necessary.

> —learning how to be loving and kind, while you say "no" gently to someone who wants to join but who isn't ready or right for it.

> —learning humility and diplomacy while fundraising.

> —practicing extreme patience, filling out endless pages of details to get a tax-exempt status for your educational corporation.

> —negotiating properly with the local zoning board and/or health department, so you don't get the whole town breathing down your neck!

> —learning how to install wiring and plumbing for the first time when you build your first building.

> —being open to hundreds of strangers wandering through your living room and kitchen, and learning to welcome them with an open heart.

> —struggling endlessly not to identify too much with your community, by taking its successes and failures very personally and putting every waking hour of energy into it until you burn out.

Starting a community is *hard work*! But fortunately, the other side of the story compensates for all this. (Otherwise, who would bother?) Starting a community is also

> —the pleasure of being surrounded by loving, supportive friends.

> —living a healthy life, with fresh air and home-grown vegetables.

> —the security of being self-sufficient in food, water, and/or energy.

> —reduced living expenses, so extra money and time is available for self-development, or other interests.

Guidelines for Building Communities 287

—the freedom of living on your own terms, away from society's pressures.

—a deep sense of personal fulfillment in helping other people.

—the joy of creating something totally new and being a pioneer.

—a feeling of "coming home."

You may not find any communities in this book or elsewhere that appeal to you, although you'd still like to live in one. So perhaps you might consider starting one yourself. But before getting too carried away with idealistic visions, you may want to explore more deeply both the spiritual and the practical aspects of building a community. If you are spiritually oriented, then as Peter Caddy of Findhorn advises, "The real question is to ask if it's really God's will for you to start a community. If so, everything else will work out." Even if you're not intending to start a spiritual community, you may want to really look deeply at your reasons for starting a community to see if they are for the highest good of all concerned—or to see if it is just a personal fantasy, which will not be enough to get you through the inevitable hard times. Starting a community is not a decision to undertake lightly. Also, it's very important to face the practical realities of what starting a community will mean, such as how it will support itself economically or how buildings will get built.

If taking on the commitment of building an intentional community, quitting your job, buying land, and moving to the country seems too big a jump, perhaps it's best to start more simply. A good place to begin is to live in an urban shared household. It's excellent practice for taking on a larger community commitment. And it gives you a good idea of what communal living is like. It may be as simple as just advertising in the local new age paper for housemates (if you have an extra room or two) or finding a communal household that is already going that you can join. The main thing to look for in housemates is compatibility and responsibility.

Living with other people in a shared household offers tremendous growth in learning to be more considerate of others, more cooperative and tolerant of differences. And it gives good feedback on what areas of our personality we are stuck in—where we are inflexible and find it difficult to compromise or to get along with others and also where we have strong principles that shouldn't be compromised. A shared household can offer the companionship and support needed to take a further step towards starting an intentional community.

We learned a great deal about building communities from our years living at the Findhorn Community and from Peter and Eileen Caddy especially. Findhorn feels that one of its functions is to help others start new age communities of all kinds. As co-founder Peter Caddy expressed it,

> We were told in the early days of Findhorn [in our meditation] that there is no blueprint for a new age community. We were to live in the moment and be guided by God. And then looking back we could see the steps and the signposts that would be of help to other communities when they were forming, so they wouldn't have to make all the mistakes that we had to make to learn those lessons. The whole process of starting a community can now be speeded up.

The following guidelines are offered in the hope that they may be of help in learning from the experience of other communities. But these are not absolute, fixed laws by any means. Each situation is unique and may present an exception to these general statements, so it is very important to use your own intuition and common sense in evaluating what is appropriate in your situation.

Establish a clear vision and purpose and "sound the right note."

> When the tree grows, there will be plenty of those willing to find protection under its shade. But very few can note the significance and power of the seed.[1]

Without vision, the people perish

"Where there is no vision, the people perish," the Bible says. A strong foundation for the community is built by beginning with a clear purpose. For example, if the community is a spiritual one, then the cornerstone must be reliance on God. If it is a political community, then the cornerstone must be the highest political ideals of the group. If the community is a therapeutic one, then the highest goal of human potential must be the cornerstone, and so on. It's a question of putting first things first.

> A community needs to be clear about its own identity with its vision. If people come and they don't identify with that vision, then it should be made clear that it's the wrong place for them. They should go to another group that is more in harmony with their vision of a new age center. So it is important that you keep a clear vision of what the role, function and purpose are for each particular center.[2]

The important thing is that those who initiate the community, who plant the "seed" energy, have a clear agreed-upon purpose so that they sound a clear note on the inner levels. This clear note will attract people who respond to that note, to that purpose, through what is sometimes called the Law of Resonance. Having confusion about the community's purpose will sound an unclear note on an inner level and attract confused people who don't know why they're there. The conflicting motivations disperse the energy of the community, and nothing solid can be built. If there is not a clear purpose in the beginning, it's very difficult to establish one later, as people will bring their conflicting purposes to it and arguments may ensue.

It's far better to start with a very small group, even two or three people who have a strong agreement about the purpose of the community, and allow it to unfold organically from that strong and firm nucleus or seed, than it is to start with twenty people who have no clear agreement on purpose, and then to try to discover one.

Francois Dusquesne of the Findhorn Community comments:

> Maintaining clarity of vision as the overriding purpose of the community is the glue which holds the community together. All the other problems—political, economic, etc.—derive from a clouding of that essential vision. If at some point along the line other motivations come in, other worries, the vision gets clouded, and the sense of connectedness to the larger picture is lost, then the community functions

less by grace and more by "karma." The lessons come thick and fast—the earth-bound lessons.

Having a clear purpose helps draw a circle or a boundary around a community saying, "We will do this and this but not this." This boundary then creates a kind of container for energy, as in an alchemical or magical process. Within this circle a certain power can be generated and a transformative process can occur.

Peter Caddy notes that a strong initial vision isn't the same as a blueprint.

> Supposing we had been told in guidance right at the beginning what Findhorn was going to develop into? We wouldn't have believed it. So we were just given a little bit at a time, and that led us to the importance of living in the moment, in the "now," concentrating on one step at a time and finishing off to perfection one job at a time. You can only do that if you are willing to be led intuitively from one stage of growth to the next.[3]

There are many good purposes for a community; it's just a question of creating a focus in the beginning by choosing one, not several. Later, as a stable foundation is created for the community, the purpose can expand, if appropriate.

Each community has a seed design, an inner pattern, which the community grows into, day by day expressing more of its wholeness, unfolding organically from within. Each new member who is attuned on a deeper level to the essence of the group will then help to manifest more aspects of its wholeness and purpose. Chris Roberts of Sunbow adds:

> The "larger" vision...seems to have a life of its own—it draws us to it...It's hard to let go of the traditional "handles" of security and learn to trust what we can't yet see and touch. Repeatedly we have been shown that if we just "trust the process" and keep moving ahead in faith, Sunbow will unfold in ways far better than we could have imagined.[4]

As an example, Sirius began with only the two of us, but we held a clear vision and purpose firmly in our consciousness: to create a spiritual and educational community, with meditation as the foundation and daily life as our spiritual teacher. Individuals would be encouraged to receive guidance from their own inner Divinity for their lives and would work in attunement with each other and with the forces of nature. The community would be a center of demonstration of new age values, open to the public for visits and educational programs. Sounding a clear note about our purpose, both on an inner and an outer level, in terms of what we communicated to people verbally and in our literature, drew to us some very dedicated members who have formed a solid core group and have helped us express this vision. New members have added to and expanded this purpose (for example, focusing on cooperative businesses and Native American traditions), but the essential purpose and vision are still very clear today.

The Center of the Light Community in Massachusetts started with a very clear purpose to be a healing center and to teach people wholistic health practices for self-healing. They have successfully attracted members whose interests and backgrounds are in alignment with that purpose, and the community is flourishing and serving many people, with new techniques of healing being added. Member Linda Burnham comments:

> The most important thing in starting a community is to be moved by a mutual goal from within—not from the outside, like feeling, "Oh, this is a nice place for a community" or "Gee, I really need a place to live." And the next thing is to periodically take the time, as a group, to talk about the goals—not just abstractly, but also practically. Each person needs to be aware of what everyone else is working on manifesting, each needs to be aware of the larger picture and appreciate each person's contribution to it. Verbalizing our visions helps to manifest them.

A quantum multiplication of each person's energy and ability results when everyone in the group is attuned to the group purpose and is fully and freely giving to manifest that purpose. The group as a whole then becomes magnetic and radiatory, functioning as a powerful center of light and energy, fulfilling its destiny in giving to those who can benefit from its service.

But the group purpose, the larger vision, has to be liveable now, not just an impossible ideal, as Joan Halifax of the Ojai Foundation cautions,

> It's important to *live* the vision, not *live up to it*. The vision has to represent the "heart-est," not the "hardest" of realities. If the vision is too inflated, it's too hard for people to live up to it. There must be a balance between vision and the existential orientation.

Use both intuition and common sense to find the right location and decide on type of legal ownership.

Finding the right location is most successful when it proceeds through an intuitive rather than a rational method. The idea is to act as if the property you are looking for is also looking for you! The particular characteristics of the earth at various locations are most helpful to certain types of communities. The task is to find the right match.

For example, Peter Caddy emphasizes the importance of finding a place of spiritual energy if the community is to be spiritually based.

> It is as if there are nodules or acupuncture points or chakras in the Earth, and it is at these places that spiritual centers of Light should be started. Different centers will start in various places for different purposes. Just as there are different acupuncture points or chakras in the body and each one has a particular function, so it is with centers.[5]

In other times, the Chinese, the Aborigines in Australia, the Druids in Britain, and the early Christians knew of these power points and used them consciously. This ancient knowledge is now being rediscovered. Many successful spiritual communities in this country have been started on land that was sacred to Native American tribes, their founders having been guided to that particular place (as we were when we started Sirius Community).

But not all communities have to be started on places of spiritual power or on sacred Indian land—it depends on the purpose of the community. If no specific guidance or vision is received with regard to where to locate your community, then it is wise to proceed with common sense. Look for land with adequate water and good soil for growing food, for example, and check out how the land feels to you when you spend time on it.

At the early stages of the development of a new way of life, a certain degree of isolation from dependence on old patterns of living facilitates the creation of new ones. Urban settings tend to disperse the shared focus of a group as members get pulled in many directions by all the options available, and old patterns get reinforced. A rural location helps to overcome this, but it's not absolutely essential. It's also wise to not pick too isolated a location, as there's little opportunity to produce income.

A defect in certain communal experiments has been a tendency to isolationism. A group of people that seek to cut off all ties with the outside world will find themselves forced to work tirelessly simply to produce the bare necessities.[6]

Most communities need to produce some income in order to pay off their land and taxes and to build new buildings, even if they are able to grow all their own food (which is rare) and make their own clothing. Producing income within the community itself necessitates either a market of people nearby to buy the product or service (such as vegetables or educational programs), or some kind of mail order business. And new community businesses usually take some time to develop, so it's best to be realistic and explore the outside job opportunities before picking too isolated a location.

Also, if land is too isolated, you have to be prepared for many months (or years) of hard work just to make it liveable with roads, wells, telephone and electrical lines, septic systems, etc. Generally, in the first few years of a community, all the energy has to go into survival issues of the physical plane: income production, buildings, gardens. Later, more energy can go into things like culture and art.

When you have found the right location, there are several legal options for land ownership:

- **Sole Proprietorship or a Partnership**
    One or more people may buy the land in their own names and maintain control over it. Even if controlling it isn't their intention, others members joining the community will never feel as committed to it or as responsible for it as the owners are. So be realistic about your expectation of others if you choose to remain owner of the land. People don't feel identified with something if someone else owns it; it's not an empowering situation for them. But it still can work if the control is up-front and honestly discussed and new members accept that limitation as the rules of the game.

- **Corporation**
    For-profit corporation: People buy shares in the corporation and receive one vote per share in decision making. People who put in more money have more votes and more power. A for-profit corporation can pay dividends on its profits and sell shares of stock. It is a good route to go if the community wants to set up businesses on the

land for self-support, such as running a farm as a for-profit business, etc.

Non-profit corporation: Each member of the community can receive one vote in decision making, regardless of how much money has been donated by any one person, so more of a sense of equality is created. Non-profit corporations cannot sell shares or pay dividends. The land must be used primarily for religious, educational, or scientific purposes, so donations are usually received from the public for support. Non-profits can also apply for tax-exempt status so donations can be tax-deductible.

Limited partnership corporation: General partners own and control the corporation, but a limited partner (or partners) puts up capital and has limited rights. This form is often used to allow wealthy individuals to receive a tax break from their financial contribution.

Cooperative corporation: (Sometimes called a "membership corporation.") Members collectively own the land and invest in the corporation. Each person has one voting share in the corporation, regardless of how much money s/he invests. Usually a minimum investment is required as a demonstration of commitment, and this can be paid over time. Any investment over the minimum is treated as a loan and is repaid, usually with interest. The land and improvements are used as security for the loan. Unlike a non-profit corporation, a cooperative does not have to use the land for any specific purposes—educational, scientific, or religious.

Land trust: This is a specific form of corporation (for-profit, non-profit, or cooperative) or a legal trust that specifies that the land be taken off the market and not be sold or bought again. This keeps the price from inflating each time it's on the market and prevents banks from receiving huge interest payments with each new owner. The purpose of a land trust is to prevent speculation on land. Those wanting to buy land for a land trust community would set up a corporation as a land trust, either with members contributing what they can afford or with an amount fixed for membership. The land trust then buys the land and rents it to the community. It's generally recommended that the board of the land trust be controlled by those actually living on the land, with perhaps a minority of board members being outside representatives, in order to have their input about issues affecting the local

Guidelines for Building Communities 295

area. The land trust board then oversees the land to make sure that it is used only in alignment with its established values. Even if the community itself folds or decides to leave, the land won't be sold again or possibly fall into the hands of developers. The land trust could only rent the land to another group that would agree to use it according to the stated values of the land trust.[7]

Establish a common practice.

It is very helpful for groups to have some kind of regular practice that unites them on a higher level. If there are no common spiritual beliefs, then group singing, dancing, or celebrating the solstices or holidays with some kind of group ritual can be very helpful. Sharing practices or rituals of this kind creates the positive, inspirational energy necessary to carry a community through the more difficult times. Living together with different types of people often causes a lot of tensions and interpersonal conflicts that can pull a group apart. Activities of an inspirational nature are important for harmonizing the group and creating unity. Kathy Thormod explains:

> At Esalen, some work departments start work with group singing and hugging, providing a chance for people to connect with each other before starting their day. The garden group sings around the statue of the Buddha in the morning, the farm group sings together, and the office group hugs each other.

Sharing a common spiritual path is correlated very highly with community stability, according to sociologist Benjamin Zablocki, who systematically studied hundreds of communities over a ten-year period.[8] (Those notable examples of successful communities which do not share common spiritual beliefs, like Movement for a New Society in Philadelphia and Twin Oaks in Virginia, have common political beliefs that create the same unifying effects.) Most of the communities we visited had been stable, on-going groups for a number of years and shared some kind of practice together: yoga at Ananda, chanting at The Abode, healing services at Center of the Light, and Indian sweat lodge ceremonies at Mettanokit.

Group meditation, even if it's just a few minutes of silence together each day without any particular structure to it, is an extremely powerful tool for receiving inspiration and for creating a sense of unity in the group. Pendle Hill, for example, a successful Quaker community for over fifty-four years, makes use of a type of silent meditation called "worship" on a daily basis, and this has been the real core of the community.

Members of Lama Community in New Mexico advise:

> Create the center—the meditation room or alcove—first, before you get the kitchen and bedrooms in order...Keep that area very special...Try to build a natural ritual into your lives so that you use the space to share a daily moment when you transcend your ego games. Perhaps early morning meditation, or evening chanting, or reading from holy books aloud.[9]

Meditation helps to fuse the energies of the group on an inner level so outer conflicts can be minimized

Meditation helps to fuse the energies of the group on an inner level, so that outer conflicts are minimized. It can also be a source of nurturance and help for individuals in their own growth process. One community that we know of had daily group meditations for many years and was doing very well. But when attendance at the meditations started falling off, the community experienced a lot of internal conflicts and financial difficulty, and visitors felt a lessening of the spiritual vibration of the community.

Group meditation is a potent form of service. It can generate healing energies for individuals in need and for planetary peace and transformation. Group purpose and direction can also be clarified through meditation. Both Findhorn and Sirius communities have made effective use of meditation in decision making.

People need not be in the same physical space to share a meditation, however. Members of Fare-Thee-Well Community in Massachusetts use a regular time several nights a week to "get together in thought" wherever they are. They take time to stop and meditate for a few minutes and focus on themselves as a community or to send healing to someone in need. This creates a feeling of unity, as each member knows all the other members are doing this at the same time, each in their own home or workplace.

Joan Halifax of Ojai Foundation notes, however:

> There's a great virtue in all of us practicing the same form of dharma, the same spiritual practice. But the planet will never do that—all of humanity. And that makes for great cultural strength—diversity, heterogeneity. So diversity of worship, of practice, is a great strength. But it's very important that each individual have some form of daily practice—something that puts the body, mind and spirit into that state of equilibrium, of harmony.

Build solid relationships among members.

Build a solid framework to hold the community as it grows by cementing solid and committed relationships among the members *first*. We know of so many groups of good people who came together and built wonderful buildings—solar designs, domes, etc.—before they did anything else. But then they discovered that they couldn't get along together and so moved out and left behind their beautiful, empty buildings. David Spangler notes:

> Community takes mutuality—the willingness to be connected, to take on another's well-being, to recognize oneself in the other...communities are woven from personal social contracts of accountability and commitment.[10]

The hard work in a community is not the *physical* building but the *emotional* and *spiritual* building—the work with people in building trust, friendship, and a good group spirit, in improving communication skills, and in resolving conflicts. It's amazing how difficult it sometimes can be to live with your best friends, let alone those who may have different values or lifestyles. And it's often the smallest, most mundane affairs—like washing dishes—that cause the biggest interpersonal problems.

Community takes mutuality and is woven from personal social contracts of accountability and commitment

The most important decisions a community can make are the ones about who should join, because this will affect everything else in the community. As Greg Heuston of Stardance Community in San Francisco observes from his long experience, "Unless there's a natural affinity between members, all the processes and techniques won't create a harmonious community." From his experience of recent upheavals in his community, Stephen Gaskin, founder of The Farm in Tennessee, comments:

> What it comes right down to is that those who really want to live together...will be willing to go through a few changes to protect it. It's important that folks be *friends*—drawn to both the idea of community and to each other. You shouldn't force anyone to be part of the community who aren't friends.

The consciousness of a potential member is far more important than the particular skills he brings. One person who is inharmonious on a regular basis will cause the more attuned people in the group to use much of their energy just to maintain the balance, and less energy will be left for creativity and growth. Each group needs to determine what percentage of less harmonious or less responsible people it can handle at a given time without harming the group.

Guidelines for Building Communities **299**

Jeff Dienst of the Findhorn Community cautions people when they're trying to form a group about being too idealistic.

> Although the person coming in may seem to be the highest spiritual being and have great skills—be very conscious about whether they fit in with the personality level of your community. If you can't have a good time with them, if it isn't easy, then be prepared to spend a lot of time working on that. It can be very hard and painful. You may have a great carpenter you're bringing in...but you'll pay for it— especially in a small group. A large group can handle it. If a person looks like they're going to take more energy than they can give, you can't afford it.

Virginia Satir, a well-known family therapist who's observed many communities, emphasizes the importance of attracting members who have a strong sense of their own self-worth. Without this, she notes, members will be constantly needing the approval and support of the community and will drain energy instead of helping to build the community.

If the community makes decisions by consensus or by some kind of democratic vote, new members are even more important, as they will help determine the future direction and policies of the community.

Whoever you have in your community at the beginning sounds a note and will attract people of that same note. In the beginning, the quality and consciousness of the people who are there is very important. Kat Kinkade of Twin Oaks Community suggests there are unconscious "selectors" in a community, which select for certain types of people. "Everything we are, everything we do, everyone we live with operates as a 'selector' for other members,"[11] she observes. For example, serving vegetarian food will attract other vegetarians. Leaving the place messy will attract people who don't care about cleanliness. Although a community may not consciously want to attract only vegetarians or messy people, like attracts like. So it's important that a community realize what unconscious messages it is communicating to potential new members.

It's also very important to have a clear, agreed-upon process for accepting new members and integrating them into the community. The stringency of admissions standards is directly correlated with community stability, according to the findings of sociologists Zablocki (1980) and Kanter (1972).[12]

Joan Halifax of the Ojai Foundation shares the process they use for membership.

Three questions are asked of people who ask to join the community: "How will being here serve you?", "How will you serve the community, the land, and the vision?", "How does your being here serve God?" These questions are asked of the person with a tremendous amount of power as we sit around the fire. And if the person can't answer the questions, then s/he is not ready to be here. And if his/her answers are funny, the person will know it first, and it's a great divider. People who are out of integrity generally get ejected out of here by natural means. Only one person had to be asked to leave.

It's also essential that the number of old members in a community be in balance with the number of new members and/or visitors. Otherwise, the older members will feel too stretched or will burn out quickly, as there will be too few people who understand the vision of the community and its purpose. Older members are needed to teach the lessons already learned in the community so that new members are not continually having to "re-invent the wheel."

Careful attention should be given to each new member, helping her/him understand the purpose of the community and to develop responsibility for the whole, while at the same time being aware of her/his needs. Regular times for new members to share their process with the community, with the personnel group if the community is large, or with a special "buddy" (an older member and friend), is very helpful.

But Ralph Durphy of Fare-Thee-Well community warns:

It's not always best to rush in to help someone in need, unless the person asks for it. The depth of help given should depend on the person's openness and how ready s/he is to receive help. When a person is in need, there is usually a lot of growth going on, and when that need is finally expressed and shared, then the person can move on.

Develop a good process for resolving conflicts.

Having the "right" philosophy or belief system isn't enough to make a community work. Good communications and relationship-building skills are essential. As Brajesh of Mt. Madonna Community pointed out, it's especially important to develop good communications between those in authority in the center of the community and those who are more on the fringes.

Leaders need to learn to listen to feedback, but good listening is really essential among all members of a community. Eileen Caddy of Findhorn explains:

> In loving people, caring for them, you can draw out what's going on within them...what they're feeling, and you can transmute the negative things—just by sitting, asking questions...and listening. People can do their own work as they discuss something. You don't have to do it for them. In talking about it, they find that they have the answers themselves.

It's wise to have an agreed-upon process for resolving the inevitable conflicts that arise

It is wise to have a clear process for handling differences that arise between individuals. These conflicts should neither be dwelled upon nor suppressed. It is important to assume that the underlying right relationship between people is love and unity and to work to bring all relationships to that state.

> We learned how essential it is to start a new venture in a consciousness of love and peace. If any of us were in disharmony or upset or feeling negative, we would stop working and find that inner center so that the right vibrations could be put into what we were doing. Those vibrations are what set up a magnetic force field which draws people to you.[13]

To deal consciously with conflict in a group, a regular time for "personal sharing" can be very helpful, as the spiritual energy, support, and clarity of the whole group is available to individuals to work through problems within themselves or with others. Chris Roberts of Sunbow Community notes:

We stuffed, ignored and suppressed personal differences for the sake of an ideal and finally had to lift up the rug and clean house! Lo and behold, we are still so human—it's kind of a relief to be able to be more real in our relationships! We are beginning to share these parts of ourselves more openly and freely, and have found the trust level of the entire group has deepened considerably as a result...I had great reluctance to share some of my more "grungy" feelings on some issues, but found that until I cleared them, I couldn't get past them. I highly recommend that groups create some way for personal clearing. What goes underground will come up in some other form— usually in meetings—and create blocks in the flow.[14]

And Katherine Collis of the Lorian Association and formerly of Findhorn adds:

Unspoken criticism is the most destructive force in a community. Most of our communication with each other is non-verbal, so people sense criticism. It's essential to bring things up and work it out. When the relationships among people in a community are working, everything else works—economics, decision making, etc. When there's unresolved conflicts, nothing works well.

Although conflicts need to be brought up and resolved, it's also important not to dwell on problems continually through endless emotional processing. Too much attention on problems, without the balance of positive, unity-building activity, can be used negatively to divide and conquer the group.

Mt. Madonna community in California has members who serve as ombudsmen or impartial mediators in conflicts that can't be resolved on a one-to-one basis. "The yoga system that members work with provides a framework for people to look at themselves first, instead of blaming others when a conflict arises," says Program Director Brajesh. But if they are unable to work it out within themselves, then an ombudsman can be available. Twin Oaks Community provides a similar service which they call "facilitated meetings," and The Farm in Tennessee also uses third parties frequently as mediators.

Center of the Light community makes use of third parties or what they call "grounders" in a conflict situation, but they are not always arbitrators in the usual sense. Their role is more as participant observers. They repeat what the two people say in their own words, such as "What I hear you saying is..." or "What I hear you need is...Is that accurate?" This third person helps create clarity for people who are in emotional turmoil. The two people in conflict are like electrical wires that will spark if they touch. And as in the electrical analogy, what's needed is a ground. So a third person can act as a ground, simply by her/his presence. At Center of the Light, the main function of the "ground" is to pray and to ask for clarity for the conflict. "I've been on both sides of this situation," member Mary Kate Jordan comments, "both as the ground and as a person needing a ground, and it's an amazing tool to help the energy flow continue in a whole way and not get short-circuited."

Center of the Light members have learned how unaddressed emotional needs can block a group from effectively dealing with business issues. Mary Kate notes:

> In the beginning we would combine emotional issues and business items. But now we acknowledge our emotional needs first by going around the circle and each person sharing how he or she is feeling. We then ask for a prayer of healing, and then do our business. It's surprising how little business there is after doing the emotional and prayer work first!

Like many groups, they've found that many so-called business items that people want to discuss are really just personal needs for attention or appreciation. When these can be dealt with directly, and when any emotional conflicts can be resolved in an open way, then business discussions can be clearer and briefer.

Mettanokit Community in New Hampshire uses a lot of co-counseling techniques on a one-to-one basis and in their meetings, as Medicine Story explains.

> We usually start out with having little mini-sessions of five minutes each way in couples before the meeting, so that whatever feelings are there on top we get to express to each other quickly. This clarifies your thinking a whole lot and takes a lot of the steam off, so you can go into a meeting much clearer and more relaxed. We've also formalized our appreciation of each other by going around in a circle with each person appreciating him/herself for something s/he has done

recently or some really good thing s/he's working on or is successful with. And then we'll usually end the meeting by going around the circle again and appreciating the person on either side of us. We also have times of "tune-up" where we renew our agreements with each other.

Movement for a New Society members have regular "hypes and gripes" sessions to begin each community house meeting.[15] For the first five minutes, the hypes part, people are encouraged to say only things that they appreciated about the community in the last week—things that have pleased them. Members have found that most people need encouragement to look for positive things and to express appreciation, so this exercise is very helpful. The second five minutes, the gripes part, is for members to express things that have irritated or bothered them about the community in the last week. People are encouraged to express their gripes without qualifying or explaining them away, and no response is allowed until after the five minutes is up. Members have found that this is a reasonably low-key way to deal with small problems before they grow into big ones. They feel it's important not to sweep conflicts under the carpet and not to be afraid of offending or hurting someone by stating one's own dislikes.

To avoid breakdown of communication between members and to aid mutual understanding, Birchwood Hall community in England (which produces the *Communes Network Newsletter*) uses a technique which they call "the ten-minute meeting system." During every two-week period, every adult in the community must meet alone in a room with each other adult for at least ten minutes (and sometimes for an hour if necessary). They meet to discuss

    —negative feelings they may have towards one another,
    —their relationship in general,
    —other things important to one or both of them.

At the end of the two weeks, they have a general group meeting as well. Sometimes two people will agree that a spontaneous conversation that is particularly meaningful for them will count as the ten-minute meeting for that fortnight. Liz Singh comments:

> The ten-minute meeting system seems very tortuous but we believe that in couple relationships it happens anyway. Couples like to talk about who they are getting on and what they don't like about each other. This is preventative. [The ten-minute meetings] have been go-

ing on for five years, and the community is ten years old. During the first five years we had many conflicts and many rifts between people—unbridgeable gaps. In the last five years [since using this method] we have had none, so we feel it is worthwhile.[16]

Joan Halifax of the Ojai Foundation describes their unusual way of giving each other feedback.

We do all-night chanting circles and we generally start out with songs everyone knows. But pretty soon you run out of those, and what happens is the chant becomes a medium through which truth can truly be expressed, much more than through a verbal expression in the usual way. We give each other reflection or feedback in this way, and it's very effective.

The Bear Tribe in Washington uses an ancient Native tradition called a "talking stick" when meeting together, in order to encourage conciseness. A stick is passed around the circle, each person holding it as s/he talks. This reminds each person that the speaker has the group's attention and energy.

To help speed up slow meetings or to give feedback to overly-verbose members, The Findhorn Community has developed the "ting" technique. A member can shout "ting"— meaning "wrap it up." A lot of "tings" will end any long discussion quickly.

Build centripetal force by focusing on the good of the whole and synthesis.

This might be called: "Ask not what your community can do for you, but what you can do for your community." As David Spangler explains,

To have a community...that demonstrates a new consciousness, steps must be taken, right from the conceptual outset, to insure that the seeds of wholeness and synthesis are planted and can be nourished to outgrow and to replace any growth of separation and divisiveness that so marks present human enterprises. This is especially true when the enterprise that is contemplated involves several activities and more than a dozen or so people. Synthesis, like liberty, cannot be taken for granted, especially not when present mass habit patterns move in the opposite direction. For every activity that might tend to separate, there needs to be an activity of synthesis.[17]

In the initial stages of a community, there needs to be a strong emphasis on attitudes and activites that focus on group goals, that build group identity, that help members learn to serve the good of the whole. Individuals do not lose their identity, but rather the individual becomes the "figure" against the "ground" of the group. This might be seen as building centripetal social force, which moves energy to the center, as opposed to centrifugal social force that pulls energy to the periphery. Centrifugal force is that which builds individualism and is a predominant force in our capitalist, competitive society. Most people join communities because of what they need personally. Since they already come from a very individualized lifestyle, they need to learn to focus more on the group, on its central goals, and on thinking in terms of the needs of others.

And as Tom Olinger of Twin Oaks in Virginia puts it,

I've learned to regard my actions in the light of how they affect everyone else who lives there. So when I do something, I'm very aware of being part of a group rather than just an individual, going ahead and doing whatever I want.

For example, communities that begin with people buying a piece of land together and then building their own houses first, before there is any community building that will serve everyone's needs (like a dining room, or a meeting room, or meditation building), usually have a very hard time succeeding. Everyone's energy is focused on their own needs and building their own house, and it's very difficult to create a group focus. If this is the path chosen by the community, then care must be taken so that the individualistic patterns of society are not reinforced in the beginning, as it's difficult to make a change later when members have developed the habit of investing so much time and energy in their own house and their own needs.

Beginning the community with activities that promote service to others, to the whole community—for instance, cooking a meal for the whole community, planting a community garden, building a dining hall—promotes a sense of oneness, of all being in it together. This builds centripetal force, as do "communion building" activities, like meditating or singing together.

The good of an individual is intrinsically tied up with the

good of the whole. Serving the good of the whole serves all the individuals within it, meeting their real needs and helping their growth process as well. The group's power to give to everyone is thus enhanced. The illusion of separateness disappears.

> The pillar for building [community] is the unselfish dedication of its members to the [community]. Its response must be its unselfish dedication to its members...Communities are a society, a living entity with a life, identity and evolution of their own. It is the responsibility of the individuals creating the society to allow it to be happy, fulfilled and able to grow. As individuals allow the society to be fulfilled, the individuals within it are more likely to reach their own personal goals. The society will feed back to them what they feed to the society. To establish a society which will provide maximum support for its individual members requires that the individual members be willing to provide maximum support to their society.[18]

Vivienne Hull of Chinook Community comments that in her experience, "Often the people who demanded more of a feeling of 'community' here were the ones who were least able to give to make it happen." And Rick of Alpha Farm sums up his experience of community by saying, "Those who give, stay; those who take, leave."

An effective process of synthesis allows each individual in a group to contribute his perspective, and the group as a whole then synthesizes them all into a higher awareness that enhances everyone. Synthesis is not just some of everything but a completely new way of seeing and understanding. It requires learning how to feel, think, and intuit as a group. It is also the capacity to hold different perspectives in consciousness simultaneously, seeing what is positive and useful in each of them and finding the transcendent perspective where they all fuse and unite.

When the rhythm of a strong group focus is firmly established in a community, usually after several years, then it is much easier to focus on specific individual needs—for instance, building a house or taking a self-improvement class. But it is important not to swing back too far towards an individual focus as a reaction to an earlier strong group focus.

> Living intentionally in community requires a considerable commitment to people and a willingness to embrace a "we" consciousness over the familiar "I" consciousness. This does not mean losing personal freedom in deference to group will. In fact, many of the groups

I visited were comprised of strong individualists. "We" consciousness means that each person considers what is best for the whole rather than just the isolated part. Living successfully in community greatly depends upon willingness to make this shift in consciousness.

—Greg Heuston
Stardance Community

There also must be an awareness not to succumb to the *distortion* of service to the group. This only creates resentment and burn-out on the part of the martyr and ultimately helps no one.

If you're self-sacrificing, this is not the place for you to be either. What you need and what the greater whole needs has to be copasetic, has to be harmonious, one with the other.

—Joan Halifax

And as Eberhard Arnold, a member of the Bruderhof Community in Germany, advises,

Community is impossible for the person who thinks he is only giving. The opposite is also true: the person who tries to convince himself that he only receives and has nothing to give renders himself unfit for community. The secret that makes us all brothers and sisters is that we both give and receive brotherly service. We not only live *with* one another but also *from* one another...No one can do without the other. Each one lives for the others, and all live together for the one united body. That is the secret of life in community.[19]

Make clear agreements about authority, responsibility, and finances.

The ability to make clear agreements is a sign of maturity, mutual respect, and spiritual integrity. It's essential that all aspects of community life get discussed fully with new members, and where necessary, agreements should be written down. The unspoken assumptions in a group can often cause real problems later when members discover they had different expectations from the beginning. Some of the areas that can get the stickiest, which need to be discussed in the beginning, are authority, responsibility, and finances.

Authority: Who makes the decisions in the group, which decisions, and by what process? Who has the power? Does the person(s) who bought the land and/or buildings or the person who is spiritual leader have the final authority, or is there a democratic process? Are individuals free to make smaller decisions in their own work areas? What things should be brought to the whole group for a decision? Do people have to be members for a certain period of time before they can make decisions? We found the consensus process generally works best in decision making for most groups.

The consensus process generally works best for most communities

Here is a summary of the advantages, requirements and techniques for consensus building.

Definition:
—agreement with the general direction of a decision by the whole group, with no serious objections.
—group thinks as a whole, accumulating views and synthesizing them.
—unity in the group is intuitively felt.

Advantages:
—each person feels it's his decision and feels a responsibility to carry it out, unlike majority/minority voting where resentments often result, and the minority may not carry out decision.
—discourages adversarial positions—many opinions are encouraged and each one is added to the previous ones so that a larger picture can be seen.
—promotes more intelligent and creative decisions since the best thinking of everyone is included.

—discourages back-room politics and "deals," and encourages honesty.
—creates win/win situations rather than win/lose.

Requirements:
—background of shared values and shared purpose.
—belief that the integrity of the group is more important than any single issue.
—commitment to the whole group, not just to one's personal views, and a willingness to release personal opinions if they are not for the good of the whole.
—an assumption that there is a right decision that is good for everyone and that it is possible to discover it.
—belief that each person is intelligent and has something valuable to add.
—willingness to listen to others.
—willingness to listen to one's own inner wisdom or intuition, not just to one's rational mind.
—ability to state differences clearly, not to hide them or feel a pressure to conform.
—commitment to deal with conflict and know that a resolution can be found.
—willingness to point out power trips and manipulations and deal with them as a group.
—honesty about one's own personal clarity at any given time, and ability to maintain "positive neutrality" if one is not clear, rather than hold resentments.
—manageable group size, or breaking down into smaller groups to build consensus and then reporting back to larger group to build on small-group consensus.
—sufficient time to complete the process.

Techniques:
—take time to get to know each other personally first.
—create a feeling of trust, openness, positivity, respect.
—allow each person time to speak and share concerns.
—build on previous ideas and keep focus of discussion; don't go off on tangents.
—deal directly with personal emotional issues.
—develop positive attitudes by taking time for people to appreciate each other in a structured way.
—confront a person directly and lovingly when there is a difference; don't gossip behind his back.
—switch roles and role play opponent's position to develop understanding.

—seek synthesis of opposing points of view from a higher unitive perspective—nothing can be solved on its own level.

—stop and have a time of silence (attunement) if stuck or if there's too much tension, and ask for help from higher levels of consciousness.

—break down into smaller task groups when necessary.

—appoint a process facilitator, and also a content facilitator if necessary, and rotate facilitators so each person can experience this role.

—be sensitive to the possibility of its not being the correct time to make a decision.

Responsibility: This should be the same as authority but often it isn't. If a person is responsible for something, like a certain task, then he must have authority in that area. And likewise, the opposite is true; if a person wants decision-making power, authority, he must take full responsibility. We've seen many groups where everyone wants equal power, but then if things fall apart or bills are not paid, no one wants to deal with it. You can always tell who has shouldered *real* responsibility when you see who deals with the problems in a community, who takes the initiative to fix something, or who calls the creditors if a bill can't be paid, etc.

As Peter Caddy comments,

> It's one thing making decisions, but quite another thing being responsible for all those decisions and suffering from wrong decisions. I had to suffer from decisions made by people who were never there long enough to reap the results of those decisions, because they didn't have responsibility. Authority and responsibility go together.

To avoid resentments, it's essential that responsibilities be spelled out very clearly. Most people have a very difficult time learning to be individually responsible in a group context—everyone likes to pretend someone else will do it.

Members of The Bear Tribe comment:

> What we are striving for is to get free of leader-follower relationships. To do this, we must learn to take responsibility. Individuals must become clear-minded enough to be able to see what needs to be done, and to act on it in a positive way. We are each responsible for our own survival and well-being. If an individual cannot handle responsibility, he or she makes it necessary for someone or something else to lead them...Without responsibility, one cannot attain medicine power.[20]

If you insist on self-responsibility in community, you will probably find that you will have a smaller community than if you are open to those who need parental figures and who like to be taken care of. The idea of community attracts many kinds of people—some of whom can't get it together on their own. As Carol Bridges of Earth Nation remarks,

> Sometimes calling yourself a community rather than a business is like putting the sign "Hospital" on your front door—or even "Emergency room." Unlike businesses who only accept the most qualified people for the job, communities often accept those who most need help.[21]

Some of the people who are drawn to community are not those in true need but rather people who could take care of themselves but are physically or psychologically lazy. It can be a very compassionate act to take in people like this and consciously help them learn how to help themselves. By taking them in, you'll be experiencing in microcosm the problems facing our society today in dealing with social welfare issues. It can be a real service to create new approaches to this age-old problem. You will undoubtedly need to create a strong structure in your community to assure any kind of fairness and true sharing of work and financial responsibility, and to begin to re-educate people into the attitudes and skills they need to help themselves. A community that welcomes all kinds of people will probably experience a high rate of turnover as those members who carry more than their share of the load will burn out and leave. (This was the situation in many of the '60s communes.)

Finances: All financial agreements should be written down, even if (and especially if!) they are among best friends. Memory is such a subjective thing—when feelings between people are strained, it's amazing how different people remember the same situation! It's good to write down whether everyone is to contribute equally to expenses and which expenses are considered community ones; whether everyone is to pool all income and past resources; if money is borrowed, how and when it is to be paid back; if someone leaves the community, is anything given back, etc. It's far better to get clear agreements in the beginning and work out any arguments, than to try and work it out six months or six years down the road.

There are many kinds of economic systems that work well for different communities (see chapter 5 for specifics). Find the one that's right for your group. And be sure you don't choose an ideal system that you aren't really ready for or committed to live up to, or there will be a lot of friction in the group.

On the other hand, everything can be a tremendous lesson in growth. So if you're open to learn and to grow and are ready to be flexible and change if something is not working for you—then plunge right in as we did!

Focus on service to society.

A frightful emptiness appears, it seems, when there is no application of one's forces for Common Good...Without great service, life itself, like a wilting blossom, loses its meaning.[22]

Most successful communities are not just turned in on themselves, meeting their own needs, but have a larger purpose in serving society in some way. These communities attract more dedicated poeple who are willing to give, and this builds a stronger group. "Service is the self-transcending gesture," say the members of The Dawn Horse Community in California (The Mountain of Attention). Service projects can be anything from healing (The Himalayan Institute in Pennsylvania) to working with the retarded (Camphill in Pennsylvania), to education (Harbin Hot Springs in California), to research on alternative energy (Farallones in California), to political organizing (Movement for a New Society in Philadelphia).

As Jim Frid who lived at Sunrise Ranch in Colorado and started The Washington, D.C. Emissaries of Divine Light Community says,

The greatest reason why [the Emissary community's] Sunrise Ranch in Colorado and 100-Mile House in Vancouver, Canada, have lasted over thirty years is that the people there are not just drawn together on the basis of horizontal relationships. They're not merely drawn to each other. They're individually drawn to something higher than themselves, and then they naturally find themselves together, seeking to express that higher purpose. They found that they wanted to serve the larger world in various ways in that expression, and community is a natural and organic expression of that desire.

Have faith in the abundance of the Universe and create practical income-producing sources.

Most groups make the mistake of focusing primarily on only one or the other end of this polarity, instead of including both spirit *and* matter. Spirit is revealed in matter by bringing spiritual values to business, where the real test comes.

The foundation stone in the process must be *faith* (or put in a more secular context, positive thinking). If we are doing what is in alignment with our true purpose, our service in the world, then all our needs will be perfectly met by the abundance of God's universe. It begins with our intentions. If our motivation is truly to be of service for the highest good of all, then we will be guided to where we can be most helpful to others. There's no point in worrying about whether we're doing the right thing or not. We need only be sure that our motivation is sincere and then go about taking our next step—just doing what is right in front of us to be done and releasing everything else. And the results are amazing. When we "put first things first" (God, the Highest Good), all else is added to us. With practice, *faith* grows into *knowing*. As we experience it working in our lives in small ways, it's easier to trust the next time and the next.

Linda Burnham of the Center of the Light community shares some stories about their experience with this.

> Peter (our accountant) came in one Tuesday and said, "We need $1500 by Thursday," as some bill—electrician or plumber—was long overdue. And we had nothing then. So we sat down, as we usually do in these situations, and we prayed to manifest the money, saying this is what we need by Thursday. Thursday morning, Peter came in to tell us that exactly $1500 had come in the mail, between all our income accounts.
>
> Last week we wrote up a funding request and included the need for a copier machine. Just two days after writing it, a woman in one of our healing workshops sent us a check for $1,000 especially earmarked for a copy machine. Then someone else gave us $1,000 and promised to send another $1,000 next month—so we'll have our $3,000 copy machine.

To manifest the financial resources we needed at Sirius, we learned to focus on our consciousness and align it in this way:

• **Right Identity:** affirming that we are one with a loving and beneficent Universe that finds expression through us.

• **Right Visualization:** affirming that life is abundant, that there is not lack, and that all our true needs are always perfectly met. We see ourselves as openly giving and receiving.

• **Thankfulness:** feeling blessed by life and all that is given to us and affirming all that we have and all that we can give.

• **Right Custodianship:** creating relationships that allow energy to express through our group and consciously working on resolving interpersonal conflicts to facilitate group unity.

• **Right Service:** discovering what we can do to help others, to help the world.

• **Right Action:** listening to our intuition to determine the most appropriate course of action for God to be fulfilled through us and then following through on the action to co-create with God.

In our community, we learned some very important lessons about manifesting the money we needed. A united group consciousness is crucial. One time during our first year when our mortgage was due and we had no money to pay for it, we called a group meeting to work on creating unity and resolving disharmonies among us on a personal level. We then together affirmed our faith that all our needs would be met by God—although we had no idea how, and time was getting very short. But sure enough, the very next day a woman called up and asked if she could visit, and she said she had a donation for us which she had been meaning to send but hadn't gotten around to it. It turned out to be just a little over the exact amount we needed to pay the mortgage. The interesting thing was that although she had the money and was intending to give it to us two weeks earlier, she didn't actually bring it to us until we had had our meeting and had worked on our end of it—resolving our conflicts and affirming our faith. Then she could be the agent of fulfilling our faith.

We also learned that there are other important attitudes in addition to faith that help the manifestation of money and resources needed:

• A feeling of worthiness to receive it

• Trust in ourselves that we would not misuse it

• A positive attitude toward money

• Release of feelings of "poverty consciousness" and affirmation of "abundance consciousness"

• Lack of jealousy or resentment towards people who have money and release of expectations that they should give it to us.

This last one is especially subtle. It's so easy and flattering to our ego to sit self-righteously in our non-profit community or good cause and expect the world to drop money into our laps because we're such self-sacrificing people. The heavy "shoulds" towards other people and the guilt-tripping of others never seem to attract funding.

Many of the communities and good causes we know of are lacking in sufficient funds to do their good work. Rather than just waiting for money to come in, it is far better to create practical sources of income, products and services that truly express spiritual values *and* that meet a real need of people in the area. It's better to go ahead and do what we know is right, what we feel on a deep inner level is our true service in the world, and trust that as we give, so we receive.

For some groups, it is very difficult to develop faith in learning to trust the universe, so this would be their next step in growth. Other groups may need to emphasize just the opposite—learning how to be practical and grounded about money, how to work in the business world, and how to see business as a field for spiritual expression. Even though they may have plenty of faith, the flow of money may be blocked for them because they are avoiding taking their next step in growth—being practical and dealing with business.

Develop the qualities of dedication, commitment, and positive thinking.

Only if you have been involved in the founding of a community do you fully understand what is needed to start one. It takes a different energy than one that is fully established. To start a community, great strength, dedication, ability to take action, thick skin (but balanced by sensitivity) is what is needed.
—Peter Caddy

There's definitely a difference in energy between those who pioneer a community and those who later settle in one. Starting a community is *hard work* on all levels: physical (building houses, gardens, etc.); emotional (working through interpersonal problems); mental (creating visions and strategies and also dealing with finances and bureaucracies); and spiritual (learning faith, releasing negative patterns, developing positive qualities.) Great strength and dedication are needed to get through the inevitable rough times. Great perseverence is needed to surmount obstacles. Starting a community is not for the weak-hearted or for those who change their minds frequently. Lincoln Rhodes of the Providence Zen Center comments,

All it takes is one person who's really committed to doing it—money, buildings, etc., are not as important or as difficult to get as one committed person who's willing to do it no matter what. All these other things are technical matters that you can work out eventually. There's all kinds of places that have beautiful buildings and a lot of money, but it doesn't work because they don't have someone with the commitment.

Many worthy new communities have folded from a lack of perseverence and commitment. People today are often too transient, never staying in one place long enough to see a project through. Many community founders told us that one of their main problems was in finding long-term, committed members.

Tremendous focus is needed to anchor a new impulse, a new community. It is literally a process of carving out a new space in the collective psyche—a new thought form. It is birthing a new culture. Communities are built on the frontiers of consciousness—especially those that are unusually bold or unique. They must go against the accepted norms of society and build new realities that don't fit into the bureaucratic categories of regulations and building codes, or into human behavior codes. In some locations, communities must even be willing to face fear or hostility from neighbors.

Successful founders of communities are doers, people of action.

The ability to take action, rather than just talk about it, is essential. I find that those who talk about what should be done are those who don't do it. They talk, rather than act, and they dissipate the energy on the mental realm. You must act straight from the spirit. The way I work is getting an intuition and then acting.

—Peter Caddy

Also, as members of Alcyone Community in Oregon suggest from their personal experience, it's best not to spend too much time in meetings endlessly processing conflicts, etc. Some things can only be resolved through actually working together, not through talking it out.

Another important thing to realize about building community, David Spangler advises, is that

Community doesn't exist in a vacuum. It has to be earned—through relationships, through working together, etc. You get what you pay for, so to speak. You must invest yourself, give of yourself, surrender to the situation, then you will be repaid—you'll get something out of it.

Positive thinking is another essential quality in starting and maintaining a community. It's always easy to see the many ways in which the community fails, to criticize the many faults of the community and of other people. What is needed is a great sense of optimism and the ability to focus on the best, on the highest potential in oneself and in others in the community. As we think, so we are. Our thoughts create. The reality we experience daily is what we ourselves are creating through our positive and negative thoughts. We draw to ourselves situations that reflect our own inner state. We've experienced this happening over and over again in our community. Whenever we worry about something, it seems to happen. Whenever we affirm a positive outcome, that's what we experience. Whenever we keep holding a negative image of someone in the community, that person keeps fulfilling that negative image. When we think positive thoughts about people, we seem to experience their being more positive around us. Holding people in negative images of their old patterns makes it much harder for them to grow and change.

Maintain a balance of love/light/will.

Love nurtures people and creates unity and a sense of connectedness and cooperation. It is love that holds a community together.

Light, or truth, is the energy of discrimination. It is the wisdom which determines the right place and time for everything. With light, we see clearly who is ready to join the community or where someone is stuck in their process. We see clearly the truth of a given situation and can give honest feedback. But the "sword of light," as it's sometimes called, can be used successfully only with great detachment and compassion.

Will helps a group focus on its purpose and goals and overcome all obstacles. Will provides motivating energy and gives direction to activity. Will is a fiery kind of strength which is much needed in pioneering efforts like communities.

But too much of any one of these qualities—love, light, or will—without the balance of the other two, creates problems in a group. Too much love, without a sense of purpose and vision, without direction, becomes self-absorbed, sentimental, lacking a connection with the realities of the world. Without the dynamic energy of will, a community soon becomes stagnant and inertia sets in. There is no energy to motivate people to change, to grow, to innovate, to challenge themselves. This is the situation that sometimes occurs when a group of good friends who love each other try to form a community together. Without any clear purpose for being together other than liking to "hang out" with each other, community life soon becomes unstimulating and people leave. Or members feel they're being "smothered" with too much love.

An overabundance of love in a community without the balance of light, without discrimination, allows anyone to join the community or stay in the community, whether or not they are ready for group work or are in harmony with the group's purpose.

Too much love and inclusiveness may disperse the energy of the group and pull it in many diverse directions, instead of just one. A lot of time and attention must then go towards trying to integrate different needs within the community and to process disharmonies. Too much love can also lead to a group's good will being taken advantage of by someone who isn't ready to carry his share of responsibility. For example, if a community is based on sharing and cooperation, and people are allowed to join or to stay who are very self-centered and selfish, much of the energy of the other more unselfish members may have to be used to constantly try to accommodate them. Or if the community's resources are primarily committed to a specific purpose, such as wholistic health services, and people want to start an art studio and offer workshops, then the community's limited resources may be spread too thin. Then nothing will be accomplished successfully.

Too much light or truth in a community, without the balance of love, creates a lack of a sense of nurturance and support and makes an environment too harsh and alienating for people to want to stay. It is often said that love must first build the bridge for truth to cross. There must be love in a group before people can hear the truth about themselves, before they will be open to any difficult feedback. Otherwise, they won't hear it and will only become defensive. When members lack love for each other and are too critical of each other or of potential new members, the atmosphere is poisoned and the energy dimmed.

An excess of will and purpose in a group without love burns people out or isolates them. Always focusing on goals and neglecting interpersonal process often leaves behind the very people who are needed to fulfill the purpose, to make it a reality. And in the end, it does not serve the people for whom the great purpose was intended in the first place. Will without love, without the balance of the heart, easily becomes the manipulation of others and does not serve a higher vision.

The balancing of love, light, and will in a careful dance will create a strong, healthy community. In addition, a community needs to maintain a balance of other types of energy: dynamic/receptive; serious/playful; active/reflective; intellectual/intuitive; courageous/cautious. In a healthy group, different individuals will take on these qualities at different times when needed to balance opposite tendencies in the group. Different people may play different roles (leader, rebel, warrior, joker, priestess, mother, father) as needed by the interplay of group energies. There are interesting and subtle correspondences between the archetypal roles acted out in magical and alchemical processes and the roles played by members of a successful community whose goal is transformation.

Create and maintain an orderly, beautiful environment.

One thing we can observe quite obviously when watching the workings of nature is that she is orderly. Everything has a place and a purpose. There is no waste, nothing is ever lost...This principle can be practically applied within the community. The land, animals, buildings, equipment, tools, etc. have been placed here under our care and for our benefit...Things should be kept in order out of respect for the spirits of the things themselves. The kitchen should be bright and happy, not cluttered with messes and gloom. No self-respecting hammer wants to lie outside in the rain. If we truly care for it, we will place it in its proper resting place with a word of thanks...When someone fails to pick up after him/herself or do his/her share of the chores, it's a drain on someone else. Someone who is sloppy in appearance and actions detracts from the good feelings of others.[23]

Da Free John of the Dawn Horse Communion (The Mountain of Attention) writes:

The quality of your living environments is always an expression of your own state—and, conversely, the quality of your environments directly affects you *bodily*, not just physically, but emotionally, psychologically, psychically.[24]

When a place is not kept orderly and beautiful, it's very hard for people to feel inspired inside it. Thoughts and feelings seem to get messier as a result. Cleaning a building with love puts good vibrations into the very material substance of the place, and people can feel it almost tangibly. From our experience, group meetings held in a beautiful and clean environment seem to be more harmonious and more effective than those held in a disorderly environment.

Steven Leto of the Dawn Horse Communion adds:

A conscious environment can hold energy...it is a healing and supportive environment in which to live. If an environment is not orderly, if we have not had the time or attention to keep it clean and served, then it "leaks" energy. Once we become sensitive to this, we may feel very clearly how our attention is drawn out, how energy "seeps out"...There should be no areas left unserved—no "catch-all" closets, no dusty corners, no dirty windows. Everything should be completely clean all the time in appearance, in smell, and in feeling...Everything, without exception, has a place where it belongs all the time...A structured environment allows free attention. Unnecessary or unused objects should be eliminated as well.[25]

People often talk about the magic feeling at Findhorn, and our experience in living there was that tremendous love and caring went into the physical plane—creating beauty, cleanliness, and order in even the simplest of buildings. Even trailers looked transformed and inviting at Findhorn. The power of creating perfection in the mundane aspects of life was one of the most profound lessons we learned there.

It's so important to start a community with a standard and quality of excellence. When you start a center of Light, you attract the attention of the opposing forces, the forces of Darkness, and they can get a foothold where there is dirt and squalor and untidiness. So in starting a center of Light, the first thing is to thoroughly clean and paint and scrub every inch of the buildings used. The worse the condition of the buildings when you take them over, the better, because it means that a lot of energy has to be put in to anchor the Light and the Love. And that's why the monks of old built their own monasteries, because they then grounded the energy and put every stone in place with love. And that's what builds up the vibration, the vortex of energy, that attracts people to a spiritual center. Beauty, cleanliness, and order create the positive atmosphere.

—Peter Caddy

The more love and caring that goes into a place, the more it lifts the consciousness of all the people who spend time in it.

Spiritual energy flows most clearly when the mental, emotional, and physical channels are clear. Flowers, candles, artwork, meditation, singing, and laughing lift the vibration of a room.

Bear Tribe members add:

> The energy invested in establishing and keeping order is well worthwhile, as it makes for happier people and more efficient work of better quality. When we make a chair, cook a meal, or write an article, we are creating order from disorder. This can be more easily done in an organized environment, as it takes more energy to overcome the vibrations of chaotic surroundings.[26]

In visiting many communities, we noticed how often groups had built their own buildings or had completely remodeled an old building, cleaning, repairing, and painting it. The feeling in these buildings was always notably better than in old ones that had not been re-done with love. In fact, members of one community told us that the old buildings they had moved into on the land had always felt very depressing because they had never been repaired or painted with a sense of love and caring. There's even a notable lack of good feeling in new buildings that are constructed very hastily by construction crews who are not happy in their work and don't put positive vibrations into it.

Often so-called spiritual people believe the physical plane is not important, and they avoid taking care of material things. This is the old religious idea of matter as "maya" or illusion, in the Hindu system, or of the material world as the realm of Satan and the things of the flesh, as in Christian theology. But a new age spiritual perspective sees the material plane as an opportunity to reveal, or draw forth, spirit from matter—"bringing heaven down to earth." Taking good care of material things can be a spiritual task: creating beauty and perfection on the physical plane.

> If we can't learn to take care of things that are right in front of us, like taking care of a wrench and not leaving it in the rain, when we don't have to pay for it getting ruined, how on earth are we going to learn to take care of things that we don't have control of—the trees, the water, the air we use?
>
> —Caroline Estes
> Alpha Farm Co-founder

Many communities believe that not only physical cleaning but also psychic cleaning of the community—clearing out nega-

Meditation and the burning of candles or sage is used for purification of people and buildings

tive emotional and mental energies—is important. Environments can accumulate negative energies if the people using them are not happy. Unless transmuted with energies of joy, expressed by singing or dancing, these environments need to be consciously cleared on a regular basis. This can be done by meditation; for example, by visualizing white light clearing and cleansing the buildings or people. Some communities use ceremonies of purification involving the elements by sprinkling water or by burning candles or incense. Another very effective method, taken from Native American traditions, is "smudging," burning sage and fanning the smoke into areas to be cleansed. The Bear Tribe, Center of the Light, and Sirius each use these methods of cleansing. People often comment on how good a room feels after it's been cleansed this way.

Develop good custodianship of land and resources.

The Native American tradition holds that we are all custodians rather than owners of the things of this earth, and this perspective has been important to many communities. In addition to taking good care of all that we are given, we as good custodians also need to use everything wisely and efficiently. Custodianship is a very important attitude that can lead to a real economic and political transformation of our world. If we behave as custodians, rather than as owners, we need not hoard things—resources can be shared when they are not being used. Planetary economics work best when the circulatory flow of resources is moving well throughout the whole system and there are no blocks or hoarding. If any resources are not currently being used—tools, clothing, furniture, books, etc.—they need to be released and given or sold to those who can use them. This then creates a clear channel for us in turn to receive what we need from others—an inflow of abundance. This attitude of sharing what we are not using is especially important for communities that seek to establish themselves as models of a better way of life that can transform the world.

Good custodians always complete a project before undertaking a new one; otherwise, energy gets dispersed. And most importantly, an "attitude of gratitude brings plentitude." Good custodians are grateful for all that they been given, so the abundance of the universe keeps flowing to them to meet all their needs.

Develop attunement to all kingdoms of life.

Sometimes we humans have a tendency to behave as if we're the only life form on earth. When we start a new community, it's essential to recognize the other kingdoms of life that share our land with us: the plants and animals, as well as the mineral kingdom from which our tools, machinery, and building supplies are made. It's good to harmonize ourselves with all these other forces of life, to acknowledge and bless them. Through an intuitive receptivity and careful listening to their needs, we can work in cooperation and co-creation with the forces of nature and so grow a more abundant garden. The other kingdoms of nature, unlike the human kingdom, are naturally in harmony with each other and with God, so our contact with them is a source of joy, refreshment, and strength for us when we spend time in the garden or forest.

In our community, we acknowledge the presence of these other kingdoms of life by having a moment of silence to attune to them before beginning work in the garden or before working with any tools or machines—even a typewriter or a car. There is a consciousness in everything, not just in humans, plants, and animals. This process seems to help the cooperative spirit between us. We've even noticed fewer machine dysfunctions when we remember to attune first.

There is a consciousness in everything—not just in humans,

or even just in plants and animals. Tools and machinery have a consciousness as well. The Findhorn Community feels there is a "deva" or an angelic being that ensouls everything, so all their tools and machines are given names to make the relationship with them more personal. The community's bus is called "Daphne," and signs on the drawers of the cooking utensils in the Findhorn kitchen say, "Metal Beings live here" and "Wooden Beings live here."

Ceremony with Native Medicine Man to acknowledge humanity's oneness with the Kingdoms of Nature

Many communities that are founded on Native American traditions, such as Meta Tantay in Nevada and Sunray in Vermont, include various rituals and ceremonies to acknowledge their oneness with the kingdoms of nature. For example, the sweat lodge ceremony of the Bear Tribe in Washington attunes one to the earth, the fire, the water, and the rocks, which all aid in the purification process in the sweat lodge.

Another method of attuning to nature is described by Swami Kriyananda of Ananda Community.

> Here at Ananda, we have groups which specialize in bringing that Divine energy back into the plants and the rivers, as this energy is slipping away from the planet from having been ignored. We try to enliven various aspects of nature, like the clouds, the oceans, the birds, the animals, by giving them energy—not just receiving energy from them. We look on them with Divine eyes, with reverence for all life and all of God's wonders. We call it "channeling"—"bird channels", "star channels", etc. Each aspect of nature manifests an aspect of God. A tree is upright, etc. So when you meditate on a tree, you try to develop this quality in yourself. This develops more of a rapport between nature and man and woman.

Be sensitive to right timing and to the organic growth process.

> The Dalai Lama told me in an interview that there were three conditions that would make it possible to accomplish my vision for the community here:
> —Great love
> —Great persistence
> —Great patience
> Patience is the hardest of all!
> > —Joan Halifax
> > Ojai Foundation

Patience is essential because things *always* go slower than you expect. Growth is slow and organic. It has its own timing. Any building on the physical plane always takes two to five times longer than you think it will. The mind works much faster than the physical body. Founders of communities are generally very good at grasping a vision far in the future and not realizing the timing involved—or realizing the hearts and minds that must be won over to the vision first.

> You shouldn't be too ambitious. Ambition will kill you—expecting things to happen.
> > —Swami Chandra Shekarananda
> > Sivananda Ashram

Relationships with people require infinite patience. This is the ultimate test: helping others to grow, to change, to take on more responsibility as they're ready. Patience is needed especially with one's own slow and sometimes painful growth process. There is always much to learn in a community, and it takes time.

> There's a tremendous guidance to this place, it's very strong, and we trust that. There's a perfect timing to everything. If many of the things had manifested at the speed we were asking for, we wouldn't have been able to deal with it.
> > —Linda Burnham
> > Center of the Light

Groups go through cycles of growth, development, and consolidation similar to those of individuals. It is important to recognize the cycle your group is in and be realistic about your expectations. Observation of the workings of the universal laws

Guidelines for Building Communities 327

of timing will do much to overcome the widespread human frailty of wanting to see everything happen right away. As the ancient wisdom of the *I Ching* points out, there is a time for action and a time for stillness and reflection. From this time of receptiveness, greater wisdom in action will later result. It's important to pay attention to cycles of inbreath and outbreath, of rest and action. Solid, deep spiritual roots in the ground of experience, and slow, organic growth, like a tree, are essential for sustained and balanced development in a community. Planning for the long term, rather than the short term, is essential.

A time for action, a time for stillness - slow, organic growth is essential for balanced community development

Francois Dusquesne of Findhorn remarks:

We realize that we are being called upon to root ourselves deeply both into the Earth and into Spirit, and that a new culture and civilization are not just born overnight. It is the work of several generations. So we can relax somewhat and let go of the sense of urgency and of the missionary impulse; we can get down to earth, get to know our neighbors, give time to raising our children, and think more about how we create culture and less about how we convert people according to our image of change.[27]

And Milenko Matanovic of the Lorian Association warns:

Many spiritual organizations have traded their quest for virtue and inner integrity for organizational power. They act out of the premise that in order to have impact on our...world, they themselves must become [like our world]. So they seek numbers and expansion (resulting in a "consciousness sprawl") and thus risk diluting or even losing their effectiveness as healers and harmonizers...By accepting limits and working through them, we can gradually and patiently transcend them. Like a growing tree extending both its roots and branches, season after season, we can inch our way into limitlessness. Transformation does not occur by transgressing or escaping boundaries, but by redeeming and blessing them.[28]

It's also important that the expansion of form in a community does not get ahead of an expansion of consciousness. They need to be kept in balance. One community we know began buying several large new buildings but neglected to make sure its spiritual roots grew deeper to balance all this growth of form. Members became too busy and too stretched in caring for all the new buildings and didn't have time to meditate or work on their personal problems. Soon people became burned out, more conflicts between members arose, and the community began having a lot of financial difficulties. When they realized this, they began to consolidate, to return to their spiritual focus and strengthen their group consciousness. Francois Duquesne notes:

> When the expansion of form outstrips the expansion of consciousness, when the life force is no longer backing the form...it becomes dead—full of inertia. And that's when disease sets in, because the life force doesn't flow to it...True expansion is when there is more vitality, an overflow, more life force that pushes the form and makes it move, and expand.

Most communities have started with a few people and slowly have added more members, more building projects, and more activities. There are a few examples of communites that started large, notably The Farm in Tennessee and The Abode in New York, but most haven't. Ananda Community in California is a successful community that started large and succeeded, but its founder recommends a slower and smaller approach to others, based on his experience.

> We had to start bigger than we wanted to. We would have liked to proceed slowly and comfortably and just gradually drawn the people we needed. But we were thrown into top gear from the very start-...that I just take as God's will. It's been, in a sense, the cornerstone of our success. It's forced us to think more in terms of income-producing businesses than we wanted to do. We would have loved to have a more meditative life, but instead we had to get out there and

hustle...We had to have a large number of people to make the operation work... But I would still recommend to others to start small . . . unless you get [spiritual] guidance to do otherwise. If God wants it, it happens. But as far as ordinary human advice is concerned, I think we have to go along with common sense and take a step at a time . . . I've always been careful to firm any position before attacking the next hill.

—Swami Kriyananda

Peter Caddy also recommends alternating periods of community expansion with periods of "pruning"—getting rid of dead weight. Pruning is good for trees and is also healthy for human organizations. Members who are not doing their share of the work or maintaining a generally positive view of the community should be gently asked to leave, for their own health as well as that of the rest of the community.

Develop an organism, not an organization.

To avoid the crystallized structures and bureaucratization of most large businesses and government, it's essential that the emphasis be placed on the human connections that create the community, keeping structures flexible and minimal. Good communication among members is the key for avoiding bureaucracy and rules. Instead of re-creating all the old forms of most organizations, a new age community needs to stay flexible and open to how it can best meet the real needs of the group in an innovative, simpler way.

For example, Esalen Institute has experimented with many humanistic growth techniques such as encounter groups, gestalt therapy, and even psychic guidance in its business management. Ojai Foundation keeps a flexible governing structure to respond to members' needs. Members of the University of the Trees Community cast the ancient Chinese *I Ching* to choose their leaders, instead of relying on traditional methods such as voting.

Order and organized rhythms of living are necessary to accomplish goals, but the real structure of a new age community is in the energies and consciousness of the group organism itself, which is a living, vibrating energy field. The most successful communities are those which are *flexible*—able to change and adapt to new input when the old and familiar ways of doing things no longer work.

Be realistic about manifesting ideals.

New age community people are idealistic. They're good at sensing a new vision and experiencing it as reality on the higher mental plane. Their problem is with *grounding* the vision on physical and emotional levels—making it real. Some people also seem to have trouble distinguishing between an ideal and the reality. What's required is a good dose of practicality, patience, and follow-through in order to make an ideal a reality.

Also needed is a good sense of balance. There is a subtle interplay between a community's ideals and what serves its real needs today. Ideals can generate the high spirits needed to overcome obstacles. They provide direction, giving inspiration to accomplish goals and achieve perfection. "Without vision, the people perish." But a people can also perish without a reality check! In the initial enthusiasm and energy of starting a community, you can get so carried away with the ideals that you push yourself and others and so create imbalance.

It's essential to be honest about where the community is really at, to have the humility to see it and admit it to yourselves, and to love and accept where you're at. You must be realistic about your own ability physically and emotionally to handle all the stress that the early years of a community can entail. It's important to stay balanced at all times, to take care of your health and your emotional well-being and that of your fellow members. Otherwise, it will affect the whole community and, in the end, will not serve the purposes of the community.

Idealism and unrealistic expectations are especially dangerous when they concern human behavior and presuppose a greater level of growth than is in fact the case. Members of a political community talked about how they *should* overcome "bourgeois" habits of material extravagance and break up monogamous relationships. But the reality was that no one was really ready emotionally to change overnight just because their belief system had changed. The *shoulds* became a real burden.

Changing behavior and habits is a slow process. In our community we sometimes hear people say, "We *should* all love each other, and we *should* be willing to live with anyone." But again, the ideal is not quite the reality, and we must have patience. Having unreal expectations of each other can oppress people and lead to resentments. Patience and gentleness are needed instead.

Another "should" concerns how hard each member should work. While it's important to establish minimum work requirements, the experience of most communities is that realistically, not all of the membership work really hard and are totally committed to the community. Some are content to create a cozy life for themselves, spending more time on personal development or socializing with friends while others carry far more than their share of responsibility for the whole.

> Let us not expect people to embrace a way of life too radically different from that to which they are now accustomed. This caution is important especially from the standpoint of enforcing "togetherness." A community of like minds cannot be forged on the strength of a theory. People must grow naturally to a sense of unity. The safest course for any new community would be to allow each person the freedom to meet others on his own terms...A common failing of new communities is the tendency to demand too radical a change of their members. In biology there is an axiom that nature never proceeds by sudden leaps. This is certainly true, with rare exceptions, of human nature. Leniency must be granted people, within reason, to grow at their own rate of speed...Often, unsuccessful communities were founded on too idealistic a view of human nature.[29]

Donovan Thesenga, founder of Sevenoaks Community, learned some similar lessons in his community.

> I think we were incredibly ambitious or not developed enough to pull off what we were trying to do...We were presuming an enormous degree of malleability of human beings, that there was no limit to how much they could change. In the ultimate sense that may be true, but in the practical situation we were pushing some people too far too fast (or they were pushing themselves) to keep up with some real or presumed group norm...Even though they felt they got a lot out of the experience here, their expectations were super-enormous, and they felt bitter in leaving...I feel somehow we were feeding those expectations. I'm now trying to learn some greater degree of carefulness about what we're doing so we don't have people leaving disappointed.
> —Donovan Thesenga

Develop ego detachment from the success or failure of the community.

This is the hardest principle of all for community founders. (Believe us; we know from experience!) The ultimate spiritual test is learning not to be attached to the fruit of our labors—to not be so overly identified with the community that its failure is our personal failure and its success is inflating to our ego. As Lama Community member Micha Abd-al Hayy Weinman comments,

> We residents are, after all, only caretakers of this place. In fact, we have the liability of personal identification which can blind us to the real purposes of the Foundation and the objective needs of those its serves.[30]

Swami Shekarananda advises,

> Don't be attached. If you're too possessive—have too much a sense of it being my [community], everything will be lost. No one will stay with you. Don't do it all. Surrender it and let others help. Allow them to do things. Be free enough to allow the thoughts of new people to influence the action, the product.

The founders of the community have a responsibilty on an inner level to hold the community in balance and be anchor points of the broader vision of the community so that it stays in alignment with its purpose. On the other hand, a community is also a joint creation of all its members on a day-to-day basis. Most things in a community are not the result of a single leader's inspiration or decisions but rather emerge out of necessary and self-evident directions of the whole group. And finally there is the overriding reality that if one is sincerely asking that the community be guided from a higher level, from God, for the good of the whole, then ultimately it's God's responsibility. Therefore, what any founder is ultimately responsible for is to do the best that s/he can in every situation and then release the rest to God or to the highest good. The most important thing is not whether the community as a form, a structure in itself, succeeds or fails but rather whether it serves the growth of the people who comprise it. Once it has finished fulfilling that purpose, it is no longer useful and its demise can release seeds needed for the development of other communites. And so the cycle continues...

Cultivate Flexibility

And lastly, communities which survive are those which do not become rigid or crystallized, but which are flexible and responsive to changes in members' needs and the needs of the larger society.

11 The Future of Communities

Let new communities arise as new springs in the desert. Around each spring tender grass will become green and the streams from the springs will eventually flow together in one current.[1]

The new communities live the future now. You can feel the spirit oı the new being born in their midst. There's an unmistakable optimism and vitality that you seldom find in mainstream society. This enthusiasm and creativity is the energy of the future visiting the present.

At times these communities are the leading edge of societal change—pioneering and experimenting with new social forms. Although there are always *individuals* who are ahead of their time, communities are often one of the foremost *collectivities* that innovate and explore new territories. As freer lifestyles, self-actualization, wholistic health, Eastern religions, organically-grown food—once solely the province of the hippie communes of the '60s—have gradually been adopted by much of the mainstream, communities of the future may pioneer the *next* step in social evolution.

As is true of any experiment or leading-edge phenomena, communities may never attract a majority of the population unless economic conditions worsen considerably. But they will undoubtedly continue to function as a catalyzing agent for society, like the yeast added to bread dough which makes it rise. And communities will also continue to grow in numbers to meet the increasing need for a sense of family in the alienating environment of our cities. Communities will continue to offer an alternative for those in crisis and transition and for those seeking a simpler and more economic lifestyle. And the sense of hope and a positive vision for the future found in communities will be increasingly magnetic to a weary world.

An unknown variable in the growth of communities in the future is whether the media will rediscover them, creating another sensational phenomenon, as it did in the '60s. But this kind of overexposure is always a mixed blessing, as the reality is often distorted and communities become a new form of entertainment rather than places to live, work, and build a new way of life. Often the carrying capacity of the communities is strained to the limit with too much publicity. On the other hand, moderate and favorable publicity can be very helpful in informing people about an option that they ordinarily might not come across in their daily lives. Communities, especially rural ones, are practically invisible to the mainstream today.

Evolution into "planetary villages"

Many communities are growing into villages with a planetary awareness, a sense of the connectedness of all life on the earth. "Planetary villages" are places where the presence of the planet as a whole is felt, where the cosmic embraces the mundane. Here the wonder of a new seed breaking up through the earth is simultaneously felt as one returns a withered plant into compost. Here, in the midst of chopping wood, the suffering and the joy of a fellow being halfway around the world is felt as if s/he were close. Here the rhythmn of kitchen sounds becomes the beating of the heart of Earth herself.

Francois Dusquesne sees the planetary village as including two important images: one from memory—the image of the sacred earth—and the other a promise from the future—the image of the heavenly city.[2] The sacred earth offers a remembrance of a state of innocence, the lost paradise, a sense of security, of intimacy with others and with nature. The heavenly city affords a promise of our creative power, of mastery, of freedom to create new cultural forms. It is the state of perfection that is the end result of evolution, the planetary impulse. The planetary village is an attempt to synthesize the sacred earth and the heavenly city, the past and the future—to learn nurturance on the one hand, and creative power and freedom on the other. Planetary villages inspire people through the beauty and healing power of nature to create new forms of governance and economics for a better world. Gardens are loved and respected as much as computers are.

Historian William Irwin Thompson's term for the new villages is "meta-industrial villages." Civilization has progressed from pre-industrial to post-industrial to "meta-industrial" (beyond industrial). The new villages are beginning to include aspects of all of these previous eras, expressing a union of culture and nature.

> If you want to be more poetic than demographic, then you can identify the meta-industrial culture as one in which the trees are counted in a census of the members of the community. Trees breathe what we exhale and exhale what we breathe; they are the very blood cells of the biosphere which nourish all parts of the planet...It is a culture in which death and life are seen together, and in which humans return to the trees what they take for their own needs...Trees die, and from their wood, human beings build homes and furniture, statues and Stradivariuses...The sacredness of food [is] re-discovered [and is] part of an individual's education...The students and teachers work in the fields as well as in the libraries.[3]

Planetary villages see themselves as a strategy for global change from the local level. Because of their awareness of ecology and the interdependance of all life on the planet, they are developing a sustainable way of life that is not dependent on non-renewable energy sources. They are working to reduce their level of consumption and to recycle used materials. Their community lifestyle encourages both the sharing of resources and, at the same time, the development of self-reliance. These communities are involved with local projects to promote inter-cultural understanding and planetary peace, and they also work to eliminate the cause of violence and war in the world by learning new forms of conflict resolution and creating inner peace through meditation. Findhorn, Chinook, High Wind, and Sirius are examples of communities evolving into planetary villages as they deepen their sense of interdependence with all life on the planet.

Terre Nouvelle - restoring houses in a French village to build a planetary village

Terre Nouvelle Community in France is another model of a planetary village, and it has members from several different countries. They have bought and restored houses in a nearly-deserted old village, seeing its possibilities for rebirth and development. "We are listening to the planet's heartbeat," members say, as visitors come from many different countries, bringing information and news. Community members also sit on the town council, practicing a commitment to "thinking globally, acting locally."

Some planetary villages such as Findhorn and Auroville are developing into truly international centers, showing that many diverse peoples from different cultures can live together in peace and cooperation. Auroville, for example, has members from over twenty countries, including a number of Third World peoples. Auroville's founding was attended by respresentatives from 121 nations, each bringing soil from his or her country to be placed in a central urn. The community received both formal recognition

The Future of Communities 337

*Listening to the planet's
heartbeat at Terre Nouvelle*

from the United Nations and development grants from UNESCO. In making the desert bloom and developing a center of transformation in one of the harshest environments in India—a country whose problems are some of the most difficult in the world—Auroville is showing that it is possible to create a planetary civilization anywhere.

But as David Spangler observes,

> A planetary village means more than a multi-cultural, inter-national community. Indeed, to my way of thinking, a planetary village could be made up entirely of people of a particular nationality or ethnic type. The distinguishing characteristic...is the nature of the relationship of the community to the wholeness and life of the earth...practicing in microcosm the qualities that make our world a living, evolving entity.
>
> I see these qualities as moving in four interrelated directions. The first is towards the development and enrichment of the individual as a focal point of evolutionary consciousness. The second is towards the development of mutually empowering relationships with other human beings...that enrich the species. The third direction...is the re-integration of human consciousness into the flow of nature. The fourth is the development of our attunement with the life, the pattern, the spirit that underlies and connects all of the preceding three levels into an evolving whole.[4]

Some communities are evolving into the traditional concept of village as they include more alternative services that take care of their members' needs, expanding into all areas of human life: agriculture, education, business, religion, therapy, health care, governance, art, music, entertainment, and science. Those communities which are the furthest along this path are often the oldest and largest communities: Findhorn, Auroville, Spring Valley, Sunrise Ranch, Ananda, Stelle, and The Farm.

The continued growth and expansion of community networks

Local and regional networks may eventually expand into a national association of communities, like the kibbutz movement in Israel, or even into an international association, consolidating political and economic power. Already, several networks of communities have been emerging in America: The National Federation of Egalitarian Communities (committed to egalitarian governance with income and resource sharing); The New England Network of Light (comprised of a number of regional spiritual communities and other groups we helped organize); and Earth Community Network, a West Coast network of communities (written about in Susan Campbell's book *Earth Community*, and including Ananda, Alpha, Chinook, The Bear Tribe, University of the Trees, and Living Love). Internationally, there is the International Communes Network (with communities in fifteen countries), the Alternative Communities Network in Britain, the Communes Network in Britain, the Japanese Commune Movement, and the Green Alliance Network in Australia. Laurieston Hall in Scotland has sponsored several international conferences on communities. There is also a growing world-wide network, started by *Tranet* in Maine, of appropriate technology centers like Farralones Institute, Windstar, and The New Alchemists. Like the New England Network and the Earth Community Network, networks in the future will probably evolve bio-regionally—based on regionally shared ecological characteristics.

The Federation of Egalitarian Communities (Appletree, Dandelion, East Wind, Sandhill, Twin Oaks, and Chrysalis communities) functions as an alternative support system for its members. The communities cooperate to produce material used in recruitment and/or public relations, such as brochures and slide shows. During economic shortages, they help each other with inter-community loans. As none of them hire help from outside but are dependent on a fixed labor pool, they often exchange workers when there are skill or labor shortages, and this has been psychologically beneficial as well.

*New England Network of
Light gathering at Sirius
Community*

Representatives from communities in the New England
Network (including The Abode, Renaissance, Mettanokit, Sirius,
Green Pastures, Fare-Thee-Well, Spring Hill, Merriam Hill, Temenos, Rowe, The Pathwork, etc.) meet quarterly at the Solstices
and Equinoxes to share their current issues, new directions, and
updates. A quarterly newsletter, with news of the communities,
is circulated, and a directory of participants is published by Sirius
Community.

The New England Network, in its evolving wisdom,
learned that "network" is essentially a verb, rather than a noun—
an on-going *process* of building personal relationships with people
in other groups. "The first level of networking is connecting people," says Betty Didcoct of Linnaea Community in British Columbia. "The second level is co-creative projects."

In our experience, networking among communities has
been very helpful in learning from each others' experiences.
There is a greater strength which results when each community
realizes it is not alone in trying to create something new, but others are doing related work and there can be a sense of support
and cooperation.

340 BUILDERS OF THE DAWN

Like individuals, all communities seem to go through a growth process. In its early years, each community experiences a necessary stage of self-centered consolidation and integration followed by an adolescent overconfidence in its own particular approach as being The Best And Only Way. Later a more mature attitude evolves which recognizes that there are many paths, each equally valid. The community recognizes its own focus as a valuable and unique part of the whole. From this awareness and sense of respect for others, communication links can be established with other communities. A growing recognition emerges of the power and potential of their combined work.

> Each community is different. Each can be likened to an organ in a body. Communities may have a similar consciousness, but each will be expressed in a different form and will have a different function...I found in networking that the only way to be successful is to work on the points of agreement, where you can unite, and ignore the differences. Otherwise, you can always see what's wrong, nitpick and find fault, but that won't unite. Make the links of the hearts, getting to love and know one another, so that with love comes understanding—and also a spirit of helping, of exchange. Findhorn has an exchange program with about sixteen other communities...Findhorn learned a lot from Esalen, and Esalen has learned a lot from Findhorn. We keep our uniqueness, but we learn from one another.[5]
>
> —Peter Caddy

Networking efforts have also been helped by meditative work on the inner levels, by visualizing lines of light and love uniting communities with each other and affirming a cooperative spirit. This was done for years at the Findhorn Community before any outer networking was undertaken, as Peter reports.

> Our early work here for three or four years was entirely on the inner planes, linking up through meditation and tuning in to these centers twice a day; receiving visions and telepathic tranmissions from 370 centers with which we connected...[6]

Ralph White adds that

> Scattered around the Earth are untold thousands of individuals, small groups and communities quietly creating a society based upon the unity of the human family and co-creation with the forces of nature. Part of our work at Findhorn is to link with a wide range of these

centers, organizations and individuals to reveal an emerging pattern that we call the "network of Light"...We now have a communications center with files listing over 6,000 individuals, groups and communities with whom we have had contact...There are many networks, from the telepathic to the electronic, and linking in Spirit continues to be a vital aspect of our work. At sanctuary gatherings and in smaller groups we continue to radiate light and love to many points and individuals thoughout the world by visualizing our interconnected energy fields in meditation.[7]

Communities in the New England Network of Light have also found it helpful to link up in meditation in their respective communities.

In addition to the more formal networks, there are many informal networks of communities around the world. Community members can travel from place to place, staying at fellow communities along the way, creating a vast information web— outposts of the new culture. These "light stations" can be found in every country.

A Twin Oaks member reports:

[T]here were days when I was on that commune when I felt as though at the crossroads of the world, when it seemed that emissaries from the entire planet were plodding up the driveway and it was urgent that together we find the answers to the world's problems right then and there. International travellers validated and enriched communal life significantly.[8]

The functioning of communities as transformative agents for society is dependent on the success of networking efforts, Robert Gilman feels. "It is much better to see each community as *part* of the laboratory [for social change], and to realize the juice won't really start to flow until the parts are connected."[9]

The future unfolds a growing network of points of light, places of hope and positive energy all over the earth. The number of lights keeps growing until a strong web of light is formed to hold the emerging new civilization and culture.

Providing ideas and tools for creating a sense of community in the cities and suburbs

Intentional communities are developing and refining useful ideas and systems that can be translated into urban and suburban living. Cooking, bulk food-buying, child care, and gardens can also be shared in non-community settings. Resources like tools and machinery, tractors, trucks, libraries of books and records, and household appliances, can be shared or even purchased together. In fact, Stelle in Chicago, Bryn Geveled in Pennsylvania, and Taormina in California, look like suburban communities, indistinguishable from any typical suburban neighborhood.

Some examples from our own and other communities may illustrate what could be applied to urban and suburban neighborhoods. Interestingly enough, our community is set up very much like a suburban neighborhood, even though we didn't plan it that way. Although we have a large piece of land, most of it is preserved as a nature sanctuary. Most community activities actually occur among the several suburban-style or newly-built solar houses which are on the front edge of our land or directly across the street. So perhaps we can serve as a model for what could happen in any neighborhood, if people want to create more of a sense of community right where they are.

One very popular and useful idea is the food co-op and meals-sharing system that our community has developed. It saves time and money and can be done anywhere. Residents of six houses on our street take turns cooking evening meals, and between twelve and thirty participants (not all of whom are community members) rotate from house to house for dinner, depending on whose turn it is to cook. Everyone cooks in proportion to the number of meals s/he wants to eat with the community. This system avoids the problem of the burned-out housewife cooking seven nights a week and feeling bored and uncreative.

We also buy our food staples in bulk together from a co-op warehouse, so we get healthy organic food very cheaply. Food-buying clubs are growing up all over the country in typical suburban and urban neighborhoods.

We share a garden with our neighbors. It's a lot more fun to garden with others than to do all the work yourself. We know of a number of neighborhoods where neighbors took down fences between yards or took over a nearby vacant lot to grow a neighborhood garden.

Enterprising members of our community at one time baked

The Future of Communities 343

bread and sold it to all the other members as a way to make some extra income. Everyone bought it, as fresh-baked bread is a treat, and not everyone had time to bake their own. By assessing what the needs of a neighborhood are, what products everyone buys elsewhere that could be produced at home and sold to neighbors, some good income-producing ideas may result in any neighborhood.

Sirius offers educational programs for the public in new age ideas as well as in practical skills such as building, gardening, and starting a business. Exchanging ideas and teaching skills could be done less formally in any neighborhood. We also at times have spiritual study groups, to study, meditate, and support each other's spiritual growth.

An urban community which we visited in San Francisco had a "tool library" where neighbors could borrow tools and check them out, promising to return them promptly in good working condition. As in communities, a neighborhood woodworking shop for home repairs could be maintained by neighbors sharing time, as most people don't need to use a shop and all the tools full-time.

Sharing child care at Renaissance Community - a good idea for the suburbs

Child care is shared at a community in Maryland where parents take turns watching each other's children in their home one morning a week, thereby freeing up their time on the other four mornings. This is another great neighborhood idea.

A community in the suburbs of New Mexico turned one room in each participating house on the block into a community space. A room in one house held the community library, another the community office, another the room for counseling, another the community meeting room, and another the meditation room. The rest of each house was reserved as private space for the resident family. Members could walk from one house to the other for community activities, so it was very convenient. From the outside, the community was invisible and the neighborhood appeared like any other block in the suburbs.

A swimming pool was put in by a community in Florida who bought land together, owning some in common and some privately. Those who wanted to use the pool contributed labor and money to build it. None of the familes could have afforded a swimming pool on their own, but a half-acre was paid for communally so all who wanted it could have access to the pool.

Fulfilling the American Dream

What is it most Americans want? A nice debt-free home (with low energy costs) in a quiet, safe neighborhood, with plenty of fresh air, trees, and flowers. A feeling of security and rootedness in the right place. Good, healthy, and plentiful food, safe drinking water. Lots of neighborhood kids for your kids to play with. Good schools nearby. A nearby park for taking walks and for the kids to play in. A pool or pond for swimming. Being able to support your family and live comfortably. Meaningful and fulfilling work. A job that is close enough to home that it's an easy walk, drive, or bus ride. Freedom to be creative and to express oneself. Good medical services at reasonable costs. A good church for Sunday services, to feed the Spirit. Nearby entertainment.

Believe it or not—The American Dream is alive and *real* in communities! Many community members are actually well on their way to living this dream—and probably in some ways much closer to it than most Americans! The difference, of course, is that they don't live the dream *alone*. It's *shared* with fellow members.

Intentional communities today are like small seeds that are keeping alive the spirit of community amidst the alienation and loneliness of our modern times. It is in these communities that experiences are being gained, lessons learned, and systems developed that can re-seed the community spirit when people realize their lack and look for ways to remedy it.

As America sees herself as a model for freedom, communities often see themselves as models for ideals such as love or equality or cooperation. Communities invite visitors to observe their experiment and hopefully be inspired enough to take it home and do it there. As Paul Kagan writes:

> The commune is a nation on a tiny scale—at least that is it's ideal...The commune, like America, starts as a *place*—an open space in which to experiment in living one's ideals. It is open-ended; it can go anywhere; there is faith in time. We may easily judge this faith as naivete—faith that there is time, that one has one's freedom...that man is naturally good, and that it is the function of the earth to support this goodness—but something similar seems to be believed by most Americans.[10]

Today's communities remind us of both the past and the future. They tap us into our past and our tribal roots as a people. We feel the sense of security and intimacy that comes from connectedness with others and with nature—instructing us in the art of relationship and how to think in terms of the good of the whole. And communities remind us of our future by inspiring us with a vision of a better world, sounding the harmonious notes that are blended together to build a more loving society. Amidst the networks of the new communities growing all over the world, we can begin to perceive the outlines of a new culture for humanity—a new planetary culture.

Society needs to have its "free" zones that communities provide, special enclaves where new adventures can be undertaken, new relationships explored, where the game of life can be played by different rules. In these free spaces you can explore who you really are, dying to the old and awakening to the new. Communities are places of renewal and becoming where personal change becomes a catalyst for societal change. Here everything is possible, as long as it is in harmony with the good of other people, as well as rocks, plants, and animals. These are places where the next evolutionary step can be taken seeing *all* the world as the *true* community. "Communities...flicker their unity across the night," writes Judson Jerome. "Already they are bathing the horizon in transforming fire," the welcoming Light of the Builders of the Dawn.

12   Community Resources and Addresses

"Communities are like small seeds keeping alive the spirit of sharing and connectedness - bathing the horizon in transforming fire"

Communities Featured In The Text (with page references):

1. The Abode 273-7
2. Alpha Farm 121-4
3. Alvastra 141-4
4. Ananda 134-8
5. Arcosanti 251-5
6. Auroville (India) 173-8
7. Bear Tribe 267-272
8. Center of the Light 221-6
9. Chinook 260-4
10. Esalen 211-216
11. Fare-Thee-Well 144-6
12. The Farm 199-202
13. Findhorn (Scotland) 178-186, 237-243
14. High Wind 248-251
15. Kripalu 226-231
16. Lama 282-5
17. Living Love 207-11
18. Movement for a New Society 162-8
19. Ojai Foundation 169-172
20. The Pathwork (Phoenicia) 158-162
21. Providence Zen Ctr. 277-282
22. Renaissance 124-7
23. Sevenoaks Pathwork 158-62
24. Shannon 138-141
25. Sirius 128-134, 26-7, 343-4
26. Spring Valley 231-7
27. Stelle 244-8
28. Twin Oaks 116-121, 193-8
29. University of the Trees 203-6
30. Yogaville 264-7

Communities Mentioned In The Text (with page references):

31. Alcyone 74, 318
32. Aloe 350
33. Appletree 339
34. Apprevecho 27, 53
35. Aurobindo Ashram (India) 57
36. Birchwood Hall (England) 305
37. Breitenbush 47
38. Bruderhof 19, 309
39. Bryn Gweled 19, 343
40. Camphill 53, 314
41. Centrepoint (New Zealand) 60
42. Christiana (Denmark) 43
43. Community for Creative Non-Violence 53
44. Chrysalis 339
45. Dandelion (Canada) 339
46. Eastwind 42, 339
47. Farralones Institute 46, 314, 339
48. God's Valley 19
49. Goodlife 19
50. Green Pastures 47, 340
51. Harbin Hot Springs 314
52. Hardscrabble Hill 188
53. Heathcote 19
54. Himalayan Institute 47, 48, 53, 314
55. Hohenort Hotel (So. Africa) 43
56. Hundred Mile House (Canada) 314
57. Insight Meditation Ctr. 258, 152
58. Kerista Village 188
59. Koinonia 19, 47, 59
60. Koinonia Partners 19
61. Krotona 15, 19
62. Lifespan (England) 81
63. Light of the Mountains 47, 257
64. Linnaea (Canada) 156, 340
66. Merriam Hill 340
68. Mettanokit 43, 47, 59, 192, 296
69. Monroe Institute 111
70. Mt. Madonna 47, 66, 257, 301, 303
71. Neve Shalom (Israel) 43
72. Pendle Hill 19, 297
73. Sandhill 339
74. School of Living (Deep Run Farm) 19, 218
75. Shantivanum (India) 43, 257
76. Sivananda Ashram 51, 58
77. Sparrow Hawk 4, 111
78. Spring Hill 42
79. Stardance 43, 299, 309
80. Sunbow 36, 55, 291, 303
81. Sunray 47, 59, 326
82. Sunrise Ranch 15, 19, 314, 339.
83. Taormina 343
84. Temenos 47, 259, 340
85. Terre Nouvelle (France) 39, 337
86. Traprock Peace Ctr. (Woolman Hill) 39
87. Yasodhara (Canada) 19, 258

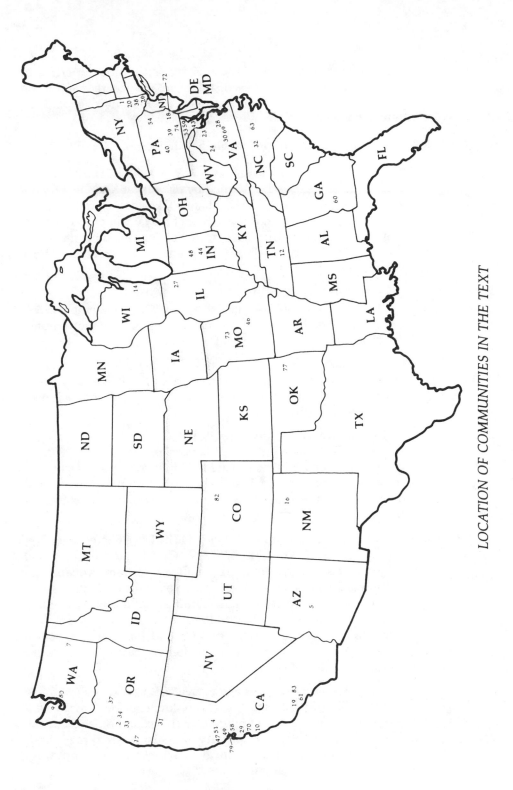

LOCATION OF COMMUNITIES IN THE TEXT

Community Resources and Addresses   349

Before visiting any of these communities, it's important to call or write to be sure these listings are still accurate and to be sure they have a visitors' program since communities experience rapid change.

Alvastra, Box 76, RD 3, Great Barrington, MA 01230

Abode of the Message, PO Box 300, New Lebanon, NY 12125—(518)794-8090—Established by Pir Vilayat Khan in 1974 on 450 acres in the Berkshire Mountains. Takes its inspiration from the teachings of the Sufi master, Hazrat Inayat Khan; sixty adults and twenty-five children; prayer, meditation, evening classes in Sufism, retreats, counseling, dance and music, and Universal Worship Service.

Alcyone, Box 225, Ashland, OR 97520 (503)482-0552, 482-0057—Established in 1979; six members, 360 acres, group meditation, consensus decision making, educational programs on new age spiritual themes.

Aloe, Rt #1 Box 100, Cedar Grove, NC 10950—Started in 1974, ten members, income from Tinnery Craft industry, decisions by consensus, vegetarian diet. Member of Federation of Egalitarian Communities.

Alpha Farm, Deadwood, OR 97430 (503)964-5102—Started in 1971, fourteen members on a 280 acre farm, all property and income are held in common as cooperative corporation, evening meals are taken together; produce much of own food and fuel, operate two stores in town; decisions by consensus.

Ananda Cooperative Village, 14618 Tyler Foote Road, Nevada City, CA 95959—(915)265-5877—One hundred adults and children on seven hundred acres, started by Swami Kriyananda. Disciples of Paramahansa Yogananda; yoga and meditation, seminars on healing, Yoga Teachers Training, etc. Industries include organic gardens, dairy, health food store and restaurant, gift store, construction company, incense and oils. Publish books, tapes, spiritual school for children. Retreat cabins available for visitors.

Appletree, Box 5, Cottage Grove, OR 97424 (503)942-4372—Established in 1974, six adults, belongs to the Federation of Egalitarian Communities, non-sexist, non-ageist, non-racist, nonviolent. Cooperative decision making, self-actualization, communal child rearing, income pooling, developing communal businesses.

Arcosanti, HC 74, Box 4136, Mayer, AZ 86333
(602)632-7135, 948-6145—Started in 1970 by architect Paulo Soleri to build a model city for five thousand people. Called an "arcology"—architecture and ecology working as one integrated process. Three-week courses to learn building process, working with concrete and solar greenhouse design. Bronze bells made in foundry for sale; visitors center, crafts building, music center, conferences.

Aurvoville, Auroville Cooperative, Matrimandir Office Center, Auroville 605101, Tamil Nadu, INDIA—Started in 1968 on eleven thousand acres, based on the teachings of Sri Aurobindo and The Mother; five hundred members from twenty-four countries; purpose is to create a spiritual and material environment to hasten humanity's evolution. Building spherical Matrimandir temple; large afforestation projects; governance by consensus.

Aurobindo Ashram, Pondicherry 605002, INDIA—Based on the teachings of Sri Aurobindo, an Indian philosopher and saint, and The Mother. Started in 1910; yoga and meditation.

Bear Tribe Medicine Society, PO Box 9167, Spokane, WA 99209—(509)326-6561—Ten adults striving to relearn proper relationship with the Earth Mother, the Great Spirit, and all living things. Based upon the vision of Sun Bear, a Cheppewa medicine man. Twelve years old, on forty acres. Share earth awareness and country-living skills, give seminars, lectures, Medicine Wheel Gatherings.

Birchwood Hall, Storridge, Malvern, Worcestershire, ENGLAND—(205)08864—Started in 1971; eighteen members; run a refuge for battered women; publish *Communes Network Newsletter*; share meals, cooking, cleaning, child raising; consensus decision making; ten-minute meeting system to build interpersonal unity.

Breitenbush, PO Box 578, Detroit, OR 97342
(503)854-3501—Twenty-five adults and children. Hot Springs resort facilities started in 1976 with healing mineral waters. Operate healing-retreat conference center where groups can come for meditations, healing workshops, etc. Run by consensus.

The Bruderhof, Woodcrest, Rifton, NY 12471
(914)658-3141—Started by Hutterites, a Christian society that began in Germany in 1920; currently three communities in the U.S. with 150 to four hundred residents each; produce Community Playthings, education play equipment and Rifton Equipment for the Handicapped; pool income; children's schools.

Bryn Gweled Homesteads, 1150 Woods Rd., Southampton, PA 18966—(215)357-3977 John Ewbank—seventy-five homes, each on a lot of about two acres, providing a neighborhood of cultural diversity, family autonomy, neighborliness, and honesty.

Camphill Village, Kimberton Hills, Kimberton, PA 19442 A 350-acre Bio-dynamic farm, based on philosophy of Rudolf Steiner, established in 1972, 110 people including some with mental retardation. The Kimberton Hills Agricultural Calendar is published annually; crafts workshops for the retarded.

Center of the Light, PO Box 540, Great Barrington, MA 01230—(413)229-2396—Eighty-four acres; twelve members; started in 1979; training for healers in wholistic techniques, herbs, Graf's Body Systems, etc. Herbal salve business.

Centrepoint, PO Box 35, Albany, Auckland, NEW ZEALAND—4159-468—Started in 1978 by Bert Potter, the community's spiritual leader, on thirty acres; one hundred members; focus on personal growth and therapy and on finding God within; believe in changing self first in order to change society. Workshops for public and several businesses support community.

Christiana, Christiana 1407, Copenhagen, DENMARK (01)546748—Started in 1971 in abandoned area of city; one thousand members with own governance and no police or taxes.

Chinook, PO Box 57, Clinton, WA 98236—(206)321-1884 Fifty acres, twenty-five covenanted members; started in 1972; educational programs offered on new age themes; bridging with traditional Christian Churches; attunement to nature; operates spiritual bookstore in town.

Chrysalis, PO Box 61, Helensburg, IN 47435 (812)988-6446—Walden II-type community, forty acres. Dairy goat business, conferences and workshops, children welcome. Modeled after several of the Egalitarian Communities in the Federation.

Community for Creative Non-Violence, 1345 Euclid St. NW, Washington, D.C. 20009—(202)667-6407—Fourteen-year-old community of resistance and service that is rooted in Christian spirituality. Share lives and resources with the poor. Soup kitchens and drop-in center.

Dandelion, RR 1, Enterprise, Ontario K0K 1Z0 CANADA (613)358-2304—Established 1975. A Walden II-inspired community of twelve adults sharing goods, income, and expenses on fifty acres. Own industries: tinnery, handwoven rope hammocks, and chairs. Operate a mail-order book service, hold workshops on communal living and social change. Raise children communally. Major decisions are made by consensus.

East Wind, Box CD 3, Tecumseh, MO 65760 (417)679-4682—Rural community of fifty people, started in 1974. Progressive political and social values, non-sexist, non-racist gentle culture, cooperation, equality, and environmental concern. On 160 acres of land, operate democratically, hold land, labor, and other resources in common. Own businesses, three industries: Casual Furniture, Rope Sandals, and new nutbutter industry.

Esalen Institute, Big Sur, CA 93920—(408)667-2335—Started in 1962 by Michael Murphy and Dick Price to offer programs in actualizing human potential, with speakers on themes from science and religion to therapy and body work. Thirty-five staff members; Gazebo School for children; mineral hot springs baths. Sponsoring citizen exchanges of scientists, psychics, and healers from USSR and USA.

Farallones Institute Rural Centre, 15290 Coleman Valley Road, Occidental, CA 95465—(707)874-2441—Founded in 1974 by California State Archietect Sim Van Der Ryn as a non-profit institute for appropriate technology. Classes in solar and wind energy, organic food production, permaculture, edible landscaping, composting toilets, etc. Also includes Integral Urban House model in Berkeley.

Fare-Thee-Well Center, Rt. 66, Huntington, MA 01050 (413)667-3027—Started in 1974 by Floyd McAuslan, a minister and healer, to help people connect with their own inner healing process. Seven families live on ninety-two acres in nearby Worthington. Services and classes for public.

The Farm, 156 Drakes Lane, Summertown, TN 38483—(615)964-3574—Has 150 people on 1750 acres. Founded in 1971. Outgrowth of Monday Night Class taught by Stephen Gaskin in the 1960s. Dedicated to making a difference in the planet for poor people, native people, animals, and the environment. All pacifists and vegetarians for spiritual reasons. Started PLENTY, a non-profit charitable organization to aid the Third World. Book publishing, whole foods company, midwifery school.

The Findhorn Foundation, The Park, Forres, SCOTLAND IV360TZ—Founded in 1962. Over two hundred people of all ages from many countries live and work in conscious awareness of the presence of God within all life, exploring the emergence of a new culture in the world. Extensive guest/education programs. Book publishing, performing arts, children's school, garden school, networking/resource center. Attunement with the forces of nature has grown remarkable gardens.

God's Valley (Pandamarama), R.R. 1 Box 478, Williams, IN 47470—(812)388-5571—Founded in 1966, two hundred members, economic base is sawmilling and log cabins. Own schools, kitchen, canning operation, craft shops. Spiritual orientation but non-denominational. Envisioned as a microcosm city of a new world order where people can live in oneness and harmony. Two thousand acres, with individual dwellings and common dining room.

Goodlife, 2006 Vine St., Berkeley, CA 94709 (415)525-0251—Established in 1968 as Harrad West. Ten members. Purpose is to live well and joyfully. Prefer "multi-lateral relationships."

Green Pastures, Rt. 3, Box 80, Epping, NH 03042 (603)679-8149—Intentional community of eighty residents; Emissaries of Divine Light; offer workshops in "The Art of Living"; run wholistic health center.

Harbin Hot Springs, PO Box 82, Middletown, CA 95461— (707)987-3747—Fifty members, 1,100-acre valley. Workshop and retreat businesses. Wide variety of beliefs and lifestyles represented. Home of Harbinger Center New Age Work Study Program, Niyama School of Massage, East West Center for Macrobiotic Studies and the Shiatsu Center. School, community food store, movies.

Hardscrabble Hill, Castine Rd., Box 62A, Orland, ME 04472—(207)469-7112—Feminist community offering workshops on personal growth, self-sufficiency skills.

Heathcote Center, 21300 Heathcote Rd., Freeland, MD 21053—(301)343-1070, 329-6041—Small intentional community on thirty-five acres. Founded in 1965. Placed in School of Living Land Trust in 1977. Host retreats. Creating an egalitarian environment, making decisions by consensus. Like an open expressive environment. Spirituality is explored.

High Wind, RR 2, Plymouth, WI 53703—(414)528-7212 Started by Lisa and Beldon Paulson, a professor at the University of Wisconsin, on forty-six acre farm; building "bio-shelter"—non-consuming micro-farm; solar showers and greenhouses; workshops on new age themes; bookstore in town. Twelve residents, consensus decision making.

Himalayan Institute, RD 1, Box 88, Honesdale, PA 18431 (717)253-5551—Founded in 1971 by Swami Rama to teach meditation and yoga and their application to wholistic health; biofeedback, stress management, nutrition also taught. On 442 acres, book publishing (forty titles, many used in universities); MSS. degree offered through the University of Scranton.

Insight Meditation Center, Pleasant St., Barre, MA 01005 (617)355-4378—Started in 1975 on eighty acres to provide retreat setting for Vipassana meditation practice—the moment-to-moment investigation of the mind-body process through calm and focused awareness. Retreats given with daily instruction in meditation and nightly Dharma talks. Fourteen members.

Kerista Village, 543 Frederick St., San Francisco, CA 94117—(415)566-6502 or 665-2988—A "neotribal," egalitarian community started in 1971. Pioneered many innovations in group living including Gestalt-O-Rama, an equalitarian economic system; multiple parenting of children; multi-adult home life without jealousy and possessiveness. Eighteen adults and six children. Publish a periodical quarterly and operate the University of Utopia/Storefront Classroom/Growth Co-op.

Koinonia, 1400 Greenspring Valley Rd., Stevenson, MD 21153—(301)486-6262—Established in 1951 as a nondenominational center for healing and growth. Thirty people. Provide residential programs and classes in health and new age themes. Waldorf School nursery for staff families; organic gardens.

Koinonia Partners, Route 2, Americus, GA 31709 Established in 1942, twenty-seven members. Christian service-oriented community and farm, 600 acres. Believe in nonviolence, reconciliation between nations, races, and sexes, and the sharing of the resources given by God.

Kripalu Center for Holistic Health, Box 774, Lenox, MA 01240—(413)637-3280—Spiritual community of 150 people sharing common goal of living holistically in keeping with yoga teachings. Founder and spiritual director is Yogi Amrit Desai, close disciple of Swami Shri Kripalvanandji. Residential preventative health care center.

Krotona Institute, PO Box 966, Ojai, CA 93023 (805)646-1139—Students of Theosophy, a philosophical system which brings together science and religion, East and West. Started in 1924 on 118 acres, forty residents. Classes and retreats, bookstore, press, extensive library on spiritual and esoteric subjects. Individual residences.

Lama Foundation, PO Box 444, San Cristobal, NM 87564 (505)586-1269—Founded in 1967, twenty-five members, of many spiritual paths. Summer programs, cottage industry products, work camps, visitors' programs and retreats. Decisions made by consensus. Ram Dass has been closely connected with it since beginning.

Laurieston Hall, Castle Douglas, Kirkcudbrightshire, SCOTLAND—**Phone:** Laurieston 275—Founded in 1971, Laurieston Hall is a huge mansion and the home of twenty adults and ten children. Two-thirds live in the main house and share income. Collectively own the buildings and 123 acres. Earn money by running summer conferences; also do variety of crafts. Decisions made through consensus and ideals are those of feminism, cooperation, and creativity.

Lifespan, Townhead, Dunford, Bridge, Near Sheffield, ENGLAND—Started in 1974; fifteen members; consensus decision making; nonviolence, sexual equality; printing business.

Light of the Mountains, Big Sandy Mush Creek Rd., Rt. 2, Box 166, Leicester, NC 28748—(704)683-3930—Sufi community based on the teachings of Hazrat Inayat Khan; prayer, meditation, Sufi dance, Universal Worship Services; healing work.

Linnaea Farm/Wilshire House, Mansons Landing, Cortes Island, B.C. VOP 1K0, CANADA—(604)935-6424—Raw milk dairy. Rural branch of Turtle Island Land Stewardship Society. Live with faith and attunement to indwelling spirit. Twelve members.

Living Love/Ken Keyes Center, 790 Commercial Ave., Coos Bay, OR 97420—(503)267-4821—Established in 1972. A training institute founded by Ken Keyes, Jr., author of *Handbook to Higher Consciousness*. Sixty residents, apprentices, forty to sixty students per month. Use the Living Love Methods based on those in the *Handbook* to keep loving and accepting others.

Matagiri Sri Aurobindo Center, Mt. Tremper, NY 12457 (914)679-8322—Established in 1968, practices Sri Aurobindo's system of integral yoga. Serves as a center for dissemination of information and products related to the teachings of Sri Aurobindo and Auroville. Regular collective meditations and readings.

Mettanokit, Another Place Conference Center, Route 123, Greenville, NH—(603)878-9883—Formed in 1978, an independent, self-sufficient, alternative society based on trust. Operate a new age conference center and have various sources of income such as making hand-made futons, baby carriers, and cradle-boards. Homeschool for their children. Started by Medicine Story, a Native American teacher.

Merriam Hill, 102 Merriam Hill Road, Greenville, NH 03048—(603)878-1818—Educational center to support the work of communities like Findhorn, Auroville, and Arcosanti by arranging visits and credit courses.

Monroe Institute (New Community), Rt 1, Box 175, Faber, VA 22938—(804)361-1252—Started in 1981 for "the enlightenment of man in his quest for communion with his Creator"; most members involved with Monroe Institute programs; individual homes and lots.

Mount Madonna Center, PO Box 51-BB, Watsonville, CA 95077—(408)847-0406—Educational institution on 337 acres. Inspired by Baba Hari Dass. Seminars in yoga, healing arts, and fine arts. Thirty-three adults.

Movement For a New Society (Philadelphia Life Center), 4722 Baltimore Ave., Philadelphia, PA 19143—(215)724-1464— Eighteen cooperative households using nonviolent, feminist strategy of direct action to bring about new society. Known for its democratic group process skills, conflict resolution, consensus decision making. Training programs, workshops.

Neve Shalom, D.N. Shimshon 99760, ISRAEL—Only cooperative Jewish/Arab settlement in Israel; Thirty-five members; includes Christians, Jews, and Muslims; started by Father Bruno.

Ojai Foundation, Box 1620, Ojai, CA 93023
(805)646-8343—Focus on principles and practices of sacred community. Offer workshops with spiritual leaders of many traditions. Fifteen resident members. Daily meditation. Started by Joan Halifax.

One Hundred Mile Lodge, Box 9, 100 Mile House, BC V0K 2E0, CANADA—Part of International Emissary Society. Allowing concepts and habits to fall away to consciously align with the inherent and true processes of life. Operate several businesses locally, publish *Integrity International* monthly and offer frequent "Art of Living" classes.

The Pathwork Phoenicia (Center for the Living Force), PO Box 66, Phoenicia, NY 12464—(914)688-2211—Started in 1972, three hundred acres; based on channeled writing of Eva Pierrakos and a therapeutic process called Core Energetics to transform the "lower self" and grow spiritually. Forty members; individual homes; workshops and conferences for the public.

Pendle Hill, Wallingford, PA 19086—(215)566-4507—Quaker educational center, founded in 1930; centered in daily meeting for worship; purpose is transforming of persons and society; thirty-five members; consensus decision making; workshops, conferences; publishing; work, study, meditation; "sojourners" program for short-term stays.

The Providence Zen Centre, 528 Pound Road, RFD #5, Cumberland, RI 02864—(401)769-6464—Traditional Zen training under the direction of Zen Master Seung Sahn; organic gardening, ecology, stone carving, retreats, meditation; forty residents.

Renaissance, Box 281, Turners Falls, MA 01376 (413)863-9711—Established in 1967; eighty adult members; to foster personal growth, creative expression, and growth of consciousness. Building an energy-efficient village with wind and solar design on eighty acres in Gill, MA; Businesses include construction and leasing of custom coaches; recording studio; varied contracting jobs.

Sandhill Farm, Route 1, Box 10, Rutledge, MO 36563 (816)883-5543—Established in 1974; sixty-three acres; eight adults. Make sorghum molasses and sell honey. Spiritual community, though not in a formal or structured way. Member of the Federation of Egalitarian Communities.

School of Living - Deep Run Farm, Route 7, Box 388, York, PA 17402—(717)755-2666—Founded in 1936 on the philosophy of Ralph Borsodi. Located on thirty-six community-land-trust acres, since 1976. Local adult education for New Age living, publication of *Green Revolution*. Self-sufficient homesteading lifestyle.

Sevenoaks Pathwork Center, Route 1, Box 86, Madison, VA 22727—(703)948-6544—Non-profit spiritual educational foundation. On 130 acres; twelve residents, and country retreat center for 120 adults living nearby. Conference center; two cottage industries. Approach to spiritual growth emphasizes work on mind, body, spirit, and emotions. Based on channeled teachings of Eva Pierrakos with Core Energetics therapeutic process.

Shannon Farm, Route 2, Box 343, Afton, VA 22920 (804)361-1180—Established 1974; five hundred acres; fifty-eight members; consensus decision making, equality, feminism; land owned in common, with individual houses; worker-owned businesses.

Shantivanam (Saccidananda Ashram), Tiruchirapalli, Tamil Nadu, INDIA—Founded by Benedictine priest in 1950; now headed by Father Bede Griffiths; creating a union of values of East and West; meditation and chanting of Hindu, Buddhist, and Christian prayers; a Benedictine "ashram."

Sirius, Baker Rd., Shutesbury, MA 01072 (413)259-1251—Established 1978 by former Findhorn Community members; eighty-six acres. Cooperative spiritual community, twenty-five members. Everyday life is the spiritual teacher; governed by group consensus and meditation. Offer educational programs in community living, spiritual principles,'and retreats. Several cooperative businesses and organic gardens. Lecture tapes and slide shows on new age communities; Publishes *New England Network of Light Directory.*

Sivananda Ashram, 8th Ave., Val Morin, P.Q., CANADA (819)322-3226—Based on the teachings of Swami Vishnu-Devananda and his master, Swami Sivananda; Hatha Raja yoga taught; meditation; Yoga Teachers' Training course.

Sparrowhawk Village, (Light of Christ Community Church), P.O. Box 1274, Tahlequah, OK 74465—(918)456-3421— Started 1981; on 332 acres (One-third nature sanctuary, one-third agricultural, one-third private homes); ecumenical church with Carol Parrish-Harra as pastor; classes in spiritual science, Agni Yoga; full-moon meditation.

Spring Hill, Box 124, Ashby, MA 01431—(617)386-2491 Seventy acres; New Age conference center, workshops, training programs, counseling service; musical performing group; gourmet vegetarian catering service. Decisions by attunement and consensus.

Spring Valley, 241 Hungry Hollow Rd., Spring Valley, NY 10977—(914)352-2295—Based on Rudolph Steiner's teachings. Book publishing; natural health care products; Green Meadow Waldorf school for children; Eurythmy School for adults; Bio-Dynamic gardening; nursing home for elderly; three hundred members.

Star Dance, 1531 Fulton St., San Francisco, CA 94121 (415)929-0671—Urban cooperative household; eight members; consensus decision making; share meals, resources; carpentry business.

Stelle, Box 12, Stelle, IL 60919—(815)256-2200—Founded in 1973 upon ideas in *The Ultimate Frontier*; One hundred twenty-five residents; forty-two homes on 240 acres; a factory, schools, cooperative market, greenhouses, holistic health center. Stelle, Illinois, is evolving into an ecumenical center. Health-related workshops, participatory democracy, seminars on various aspects of the human potential movement. Publishes *Communities Magazine.*

Sunbow, 14812 S.E. 368 Place, Auburn, WA 98002 (206)939-8824—Started 1980; forty-four acres; twelve members, business and professional people; committed to spiritual growth, service, ecology, and "living lightly on the earth".

Sunray Meditation Society, RD 1, Box 87, Huntington, VT 05462—(802)434-3685—International spiritual society dedicated to world peace. Founded by Dhanyi Yawhoo, Native American teacher, on ancient principles of the sacred unity of all being. Conferences with Native Elders, workshops on New Age themes, meditation, healing with color and crystals.

Sunrise Ranch, Loveland, CO 80537—(303)667-4675 Central headquarters of Emissaries of Divine Light, with two hundred communities around the world; headed by Lord Martin Cecil; workshops on the Art of Living and on Leadership.

Taorima, Krotona Hill, Ojai, CA 93023—(805)646-5322 Suburban community of retired people, connected with Theosophical Society at Krotona (next door to Taorima); one hundred or more residents; community activities and meetings.

Temenos, Box 84-A; Star Route, Shutesbury, MA 01072 Eighteen acres; retreats, workshops, daily life reflects convergence of Buddhist and Quaker practice; nonviolence, closeness to the earth, women's studies; small year-round staff.

Terre Nouvelle, BP 52-05300, Laragne, FRANCE—Eleven members restoring old village in French Alps, offering workshops on New Age themes, meditation, sacred dance; sell vegetables and cheese. Inspired by Findhorn Community.

Traprock Peace Center (Woolman Hill), Keets Road, Deerfield, MA 01342—(413)773-7427—Quaker activist community; peace education; anti-nuclear work, etc. workshops, conferences. Eight staff members.

Twin Oaks Community, R.R. 4G, Box 169, Louisa, VA 23093—(703)894-5126—Established 1967; sixty members; five hundred acres. Values of cooperation, nonviolence, and equality are central. Encourage women to lead and men to nurture. Economically self-sufficient; farm and garden provide close to 60% of food needs. Integration of work and play is a key to community life. Hammock business; communal income sharing; solar-design energy-efficient buildings.

University of the Trees, P.O. Box 644, Boulder Creek, CA 95006—(408)338-9362—Christopher Hills, founder and director of the University, teaches courses on meditation, "creative conflict" resolution, self-healing, etc. Members are engaged in running several cooperative businesses, including University of the Trees Press, Lightforce (Spirulina Company).

Yasodhara Ashram, Kootenay Bay, British Columbia, VOB 1XO—(604)227-9220—Founded by Swami Sivananda Radha in 1956. Eighty-three acres; retreat where people of all religions may come to find their centre, to pursue the goal of Self-realization. Teaching programs, yoga, meditation, bookstore, recording studio, printshop; publish a journal; operate small farm and orchard.

Yogaville (Satchidananda Ashram), Rt. 1, Box 172, Buckingham, VA 23921—(804)969-4801—Started in 1980 by Swami Satchidananda; 650 acres; fifty members; building L.O.T.U.S. temple to honor the religions of the world; classes in hatha yoga, meditation; own gas station, air strip; children's schools; vegetarianism, celibacy.

Institute for Cultural Affairs, 4750 N. Sheridan Rd., Chicago, IL 60640—(312) 769-6363—Grew out of ecumenical Christian movement to provide help and training in Third World Development. Members share large house in the city and work part of the year in the Third World.

NETWORKS OF COMMUNITIES

FEDERATION OF EGALITARIAN COMMUNITIES
Box 6B2, FS3
Tecumseh, MO, USA
(417) 679-4682

NEW ENGLAND NETWORK OF LIGHT
c/o Sirius Community
Baker Rd.
Shutesbury, MA 01072
(413) 259-1251

INTERNATIONAL COMMUNES NETWORK
Communidad
Box 15128
S-10465
SWEDEN

COMMUNES NETWORK
89 Ervington Road
Leicester
ENGLAND

ALTERNATIVE COMMUNITIES MOVEMENT
18 Garth Road
Bangor
NORTH WALES

GREEN ALLIANCE NETWORK
P.O. Box 23
Bellingen
New South Wales 2454
AUSTRALIA

KIBBUTZ-FEDERATION INTERNATIONAL
    COMMUNES DESK
P.O. Box 1777
Tel Aviv, ISRAEL

JAPANESE COMMUNE MOVEMENT
2083 Sakaecho
Imaichi-shi
Tochigi-ken 321-12
JAPAN

A slide or video presentation on thirty of the communities featured in this book is available for rental or sale, as well as lecture tapes on the ideas presented. For more information or if you would like to visit Sirius Community write for a brochure at the address below.

Corinne and Gordon have done extensive consulting with groups interested in building new communities, solving problems in existing ones or applying these ideas to suburban or urban settings. They have worked with government agencies, corporate executives and small businesses in applying the principles and techniques in this book to a wide variety of situations. They also travel to give lectures and workshops on new age communities and a variety of other themes, such as The Spiritual Destiny of America.

If you are interested in their work please write or call:
Sirius Community
Baker Rd.
Shutesbury, MA 01072
413-259-1505

Gordon Davidson &
Corinne McLaughlin

To order additional copies of this book, send a check for $17.95 plus $2.00 postage and packaging to:
Book Publishing Company
PO Box 99
Summertown, TN 38483

Recommended Books on Communities:

Seeds of Tomorrow, Cris and Oliver Popenoe, Harper and Row, San Francisco, 1984. (An overview of 21 new age communities around the world-with specific background information)

Earth Community, Susan Campbell, Evolutionary Press, San Francisco, 1983. (Innovative trends in new age communities on the West Coast—general overview, not specific communities)

Cooperative Communities: How to Start Them and Why, Swami Kriyananda, Ananda Publications, Nevada City, California, 1968 (Guidelines for starting communities from Ananda's experience)

Shared Houses, Shared Lives, Eric Raimy, J.P. Tarcher, Los Angeles, 1979 (An overview and guide to urban shared households)

The Group House Handbook, Nancy Branwein, Jill MacNeice, Peter Spiers, Acropolis Books, Washington, D.C. 1982 (How-to guidebook for group living)

The Best Investment: Land in a Loving Community, David Felder, Wellington Press, Tallahassee, Florida, 1982 (Guidelines for building communities and land trusts based on the experience of a Florida land trust)

Building Social Change Communities, by The Training/Action Affinity Group of Movement for a New Society, Philadelphia, 1979 (Relationships, conflict resolution, and decision-making in communal households)

The Community Land Trust Handbook, by the Institute for Community Economics, Rodale Press, Emmaus, Pennsylvania, 1982 (A practical guide to setting up community land trusts based on specific case studies)

Commitment and Community: Communes and Utopias in Sociological Perspective, Rosabeth Moss Kanter, Harvard University Press, Cambridge, Massachusetts, 1972 (Classic sociological study of communities of the 1800's and the 1960's—somewhat dated, but still of interest today)

New Consciousness Sourcebook: Spiritual Community Guide #5, Parmatma Singh Khalsa (editor), Spiritual Community Publications, Berkeley, CA, 1984 (Resource listings of communities and growth centers with short descriptions of each)

Communities Magazine, Sandhill Farm, Rt. 1, Box 155, Rutledge, MO 63563 (Articles by community members and directory of communities)

Communities Directory
    Sandhill Farm
    Rt.1, Box 155
    Rutledge, MO 63563
    (816) 883-5543

Books on Specific Communities:

Attempting an Alternative Society, Karol Borowski, Norwood
    Editions, Norwood, PA, 1984 (Renaissance Community)
Living the Dream: A Documentary Study of the Twin Oaks Com-
    munity, Ingrid Komar, Norwood, PA, 1983
The Findhorn Garden, by the Findhorn Community, Harper and
    Row, New York, 1975
Faces of Findhorn by the Findhorn Community, Harper and
    Row, New York, 1980
Arcosanti: An Urban Laboratory?, Paolo Soleri, Avant Books, San
    Diego, CA, 1984
Ananda: Where Yoga Lives, John Ball, Bowling Green University
    Popular Press, Bowling Green, OH, 1982
The Upstart Spring: Esalen and the American Awakening, Walter
    Anderson, Addison-Wesley Publishers, Menlo Park, CA,
    1983

Additional Resources:

Communes, Law and Commonsense, Lee Goldstein, New Com-
    munity Projects, Boston, MA, 1974 (Some useful legal infor-
    mation on setting up communities, although somewhat
    dated)
Awareness: Exploring, Experimenting, Experiencing, John
    Stevens, Bantam Books edition, New York, 1973 (A descrip-
    tion of more than 100 exercises that can be useful in creating
    closeness and connection in communities—used at Esalen)
Creative Conflict, Christopher Hills, University of the Trees
    Press, Boulder Creek, CA, 1980 (Description of a useful
    step-by-step process for resolving conflicts in communities)
New Age Community Guidebook, Harbin Springs Publishing,
    P.O. Box 82, Middletown, CA 95461 (Directory of 210 commu-
    nities in the U.S. and world, articles and resources on
    communities)

Notes

1
1. David Spangler, "From Strategy to Wholeness," p. 4, 25.
2. Daniel Yankelovitch, *New Rules*, p. 224.
3. Ingrid Komar, *Living the Dream*, p. 21.
4. *Ibid.*, p. xviii.
5. Benjamin Zablocki, *Alienation and Charisma*, p. 61.
6. Judson Jerome, *Families of Eden*, p. 3.
7. U.S. Bureau of the Census, *Household and Family Characteristics*, (March 1981): p. 4; and *Current Population Reports, P-20 #381*, (March 1982).
8. Judson Jerome, *Families of Eden*, p. 17.
9. Eric Raimy, *Shared Houses, Shared Lives*, p. 11.
10. *Washington Post* (October 23, 1982): p. 1, Section C.
11. Linda Hubbard, "Family Affair," *Modern Maturity Magazine* (January 1984): p. 46.
12. Dave Treanor, "Kokoo: Networking Alternative Denmark," *International Communes Network News* (July 1984).
13. Benjamin Zablocki, *Alienation and Charisma*, p. 20.
14. Rosabeth Kanter, *Community and Commitment*, p. 63-64.
15. Hugh Gardner, *Children of Prosperity*, p. 243.
16. Susan Campbell, *Earth Community*, p. 189.
17. Judson Jerome, *Families of Eden*, p. 188.

2
1. Agni Yoga Society, *New Era Community*, p. 68.
2. Eric Fromm, *The Sane Society*, p. 320.
3. Daniel Yankelovich, *New Rules*, p. 248.
4. Hugh Gardner, *Children of Prosperity*, p. 74.
5. Judson Jerome, *Families of Eden*, p. 63.
6. Da Free John, *Laughing Man Magazine*, Vol. 5, No.3 (1984): p. 67.
7. Lama Foundation Brochure (1979): p. 5.
8. *Ibid.*, p. 1.
9. David Felder, *The Best Investment: Land in a Loving Community*, p. 151.
10. "Interview with Two: Linda and Corb," *Leaves of Twin Oaks*, (Spring 1983): p. 11.
11. Ingrid Komar, *Living the Dream*, p. 195.
12. Agni Yoga Society, *New Era Community*, p. 189.
13. David Spangler, *Emergence: The Rebirth of the Sacred*, p. 116.
14. Theodore Roszak, *Person Planet*, p. 302.
15. Ron Jorgensen, "The Planetary City," *In Context Magazine* (Winter 1983): p. 46.
16. William Thompson, *Darkness and Scattered Light*, p. 92.
17. "Notes from Auroville," *In Context Magazine* (Winter 1983): p. 48.
18. Lawrence Veysey, *The Communal Experience*, p. 7.
19. Hugh Gardner, *Children of Prosperity*, p. 249.
20. Rosabeth Kanter, *Community and Commitment*, p. 236.
21. Alice Bailey, *Esoteric Psychology II*, p. 194.
22. Rosabeth Kanter, *Communes: Creating and Managing the Collective Life*, p. 5.
23. Danaan Parry, "The Dance of Male and Female in Intentional Community," *In Context* (December 1983): p. 23.

24. William Thompson, *Darkness and Scattered Light*, p. 97.

25. Chris Roberts, "Growing with Sunbow," *In Context Magazine* (Winter 1983): p. 10.

26. Roberto Assagioli, "The Balancing and Synthesis of the Opposites" (pamphlet), p. 4-6. Published 1972 by Psychosynthesis Research Foundation.

27. Satprem, *Sri Aurobindo: The Adventure of Consciousness*, p. 355.

3 1. Centrepoint Community Magazine (Spring/Summer 1984): p. 3.

2. Danaan Parry, "The Dance of Male and Female in Intentional Community," *In Context* (Winter 1983): p. 23.

3. The Findhorn Community, *Faces of Findhorn*, p. 35.

4. "Leaving Twin Oaks: A Conversation with Former Members," *Communities Magazine* #28: p. 20.

5. Rosabeth Kanter, "Communes in the Cities," in *Co-ops, Communes, and Collectives*, p. 128.

6. "Leaving Twin Oaks: A Conversation with Former Members," *Communities Magazine* #28: p. 20.

7. David Felder, *The Best Investment: Land in a Loving Community*, p. 89.

8. Eva Pierrakos, "Evolution in Terms of Individual and Group Consciousness," Lecture #225 (Nov. 20, 1974). Published as a study paper by The Center for The Living Force.

9. Robert Houriet, *Getting Back Together*, p. 208.

10. Taylor, "Reflections on Community Living," *Communities Magazine* #59: p. 36.

11. *Ibid.*

12. Bruce Hackett and Andrew Sun, "Communal Architecture and Social Structure," paper delivered at EDRA Conference, January 1972.

13. Dolores Hayden, *Seven American Utopias*, p. 45.

14. "Leaving Twin Oaks: A Conversation with Former Members," *Communities Magazine* #28: p. 20.

15. Judson Jerome, *Families of Eden*, p. 250-251.

16. *Ibid.*, p. 251.

17. Robert Houriet, *Getting Back Together*, p. 405.

18. Lewis Emanuel, "Growing Pains," *Communities Magazine* #59: p. 40.

19. Ingrid Komar, *Living the Dream*, p. vii.

20. Pat, Lifespan Community, "Do You Really Want to Live in a Commune?" *Collective Experience Journal* (June 1984): p. 51.

21. Rosabeth Kanter, "Communes in Cities" in *Co-ops, Communes, and Collectives*, p. 119-20.

22. Bob Matthews, "Jumping Off," *Collective Experience Journal* (June 1984): p. 36.

4 1. Theodore Roszak, *Person Planet*, p. 290-3.

2. Benjamin Zablocki, *Alienation and Charisma*, p. 33.

3. Julius Sachse, "The German Sectarians of Pennsylvania," *The Franklin Papers*, p. 323.

4. *Ibid.*

5. Thomas Bender, *Community and Social Change in America*, p. 65-67.

6. Rosabeth Kanter, *Community and Commitment*, p. 4-6.

7. Hugh Gardner, *Children of Prosperity*, p. 2.

8. Rosabeth Kanter, *Community and Commitment*, p. 4-6.

9. Paul Kegan, *New World Utopias*, p. 181.

10. Rosabeth Kanter, *Community and Commitment,* p. 226. •
11. *Kibbutz in Israel,* by the Israel Information Center, (October 1979).
12. Yaacov Oved, "American Communes and the Israeli Kibbutz," *Kibbutz Studies* (January 1983): p. 17.
13. Ingrid Komar, *Living the Dream,* foreword by Joseph Blasi, p. iii.
14. *Ibid.,* p. 9.
15. Bill Kovach, "Communes Spread as the Young Reject Old Values," *New York Times* (December 17, 1970).
16. Naomi Cutner, "Where the '60s Were Born," *Life* (December 1984): p. 142.
17. "Wish I Could Give All I Wanted to Give: Wish I Could Live All I Wanted to Live," a former member of COPS Commune, *Liberation Magazine* (Autumn 1970): p. 29-30.
18. Daniel Yankelovitch, *New Rules,* p. 34.
19. Ken Wilbur, *A Sociable God,* p. 103.
20. "Why People Join Cults," *Newsweek* (December 3, 1984): p. 36.
21. Bromly and Shupe, *Strange Gods,* p. 124.
22. Saul V. Levine, "Radical Departures," *Psychology Today* (August 1984): p. 23.
23. *Ibid.,* p. 27.
24. "Why People Join Cults," *Newsweek* (December 3, 1984): p. 36.
25. Ram Dass, *Journey of Awakening,* p. 125-6.
26. Arthur Deikman, "The Evaluation of Spiritual and Utopian Groups" and Frances Vaughn, "A Question of Balance: Health and Pathology in New Religious Movements" in *Journal of Humanistic Psychology* (Summer 1983): p. 8-41.

5 1. Kat Kinkade, "Standard of Living and Quality of Life in Community," *Communities Magazine* #63: p. 15.
2. Ingrid Komar, *Living the Dream,* p. 153.
3. *Communities Magazine* #28: p. 20.
4. Ingrid Komar, *Living the Dream,* p. 134.
5. *Ibid.,* p. 58.
6. Alpha Community brochure (1983).
7. Karol Borowski, *Attempting an Alternative Society,* p. 146.

6 1. Benjamin Zablocki, *Alienation and Charisma,* p. 251.
2. *Ibid.,* p. 152.
3. Susan Campbell, "Alternative Communities: Are They Working?" *Yoga Journal* (September/October 1981): p. 8.
4. William Rodamor, "The Secret Life of Swami Muktananda"; Katy Butler, "Events Are the Teacher," *Co-Evolution Quarterly* (Winter 1983): p. 104-129.
5. *Ibid.,* p. 118.
6. "Emptiness and Wholeness," an Interview with Jack Kornfield, *Inquiring Mind* (Winter 1984): p. 5.
7. Swami Kriyananda, *The Art of Creative Leadership,* p. 2-13.
8. Rosabeth Kanter, "Communes in the Cities," in *Co-ops, Communes, and Collectives,* p. 119.
9. Lama Community brochure (1979).
10. Ingrid Komar, *Living the Dream,* p. 79.
11. Susan Campbell, *Earth Community,* p. 52.

12. Virginia Coover et al, *Resource Manual for a Living Revolution*, p. 48-9.

13. *Ibid.*, p. 52.

14. *Ibid.*

15. Rod Hemsell, "On the Uses and Abuses of Money," *Auroville Review*, Vol. 6 (1982): p. 57.

16. Mary Inglis, "Auroville: Envelope Economy," *Onearth Magazine*, Vol. 3, No. 6: p. 20.

17. Rod Hemsell, "On the Uses and Abuses of Money," *Auroville Review*, Vol. 6 (1982): p. 56.

18. The Findhorn Community, *Faces of Findhorn*, p. 73.

19. *Ibid.*, p. 74.

20. *Ibid.*

21. *Ibid.*, p. 75.

22. Francois Dusquesne, "New Dimensions of Governance," *Onearth Magazine*, Vol. 1, No. 6: p. 13.

23. The Findhorn Community, *Faces of Findhorn*, p. 74.

24. *Ibid.*, p. 77.

25. *Ibid.*, p. 74.

26. *Ibid.*, p. 76.

27. William Irwin Thompson, *Passages about Earth*, p. 181.

7   1. Robert Houriet, *Getting Back Together*, p. 276.

2. James Ramey, "Emerging Patterns of Innovative Behavior in Marriage," *The Family Coordinator* (October 1972): p. 450.

3. *Time* (April 9, 1984): p. 74.

4. Susan Campbell, *Earth Community*, p. 138, 142.

5. Judson Jerome, *Families of Eden*, p. 138.

6. Rosabeth Kanter, "Communes in the Cities," in *Co-ops, Communes, and Collectives*, p. 118.

7. Daniel Yankelovitch, *New Rules*, p. 97-8.

8. William Rodamor, "The Secret Life of Swami Muktananda"; Katy Butler, "Events Are the Teacher," *Co-Evolution Quarterly* (Winter 1983): p. 104-129.

9. Rosabeth Kanter, "Communes in the Cities," in *Co-ops, Communes, and Collectives*, p. 121-6.

10. "Interview with Two: Linda and Corb," *Leaves of Twin Oaks* newsletter (Spring 1983): p. 8.

11. *Ibid.*, p. 11.

12. *Ibid.*, p. 12-13.

13. "Communal Life: A Haven for Some, A Way Station for Others," *Washington Post* (May 4, 1981): p. A2.

14. *Ibid.*

15. *Ibid.*

16. Ingrid Komar, *Living the Dream*, p. 194.

17. "Interview with Two: Linda and Corb," *Leaves of Twin Oaks* newsletter (Spring 1983): p. 7.

18. *Ibid.*, p. 12.

19. "Communal Life: A Haven for Some, A Way Station for Others," *Washington Post* (May 4, 1981): p. A2.

20. Ingrid Komar, *Living the Dream*, p. 204.

21. Kat Kinkade, "Standard of Living and Quality of Life in Community," *Communities Magazine* #63: p. 17.

22. "Communal Life: A Haven for Some, A Way Station for Others," *Washington Post* (May 4, 1981): p. A2.

23. Ina May Gaskin, *Spiritual Midwifery*, p. 11.

24. *Ibid.*, p. 382-3.

25. Farm brochure on *A Model Primary Health Care Delivery System*.

26. Ariel Bubissow, "The Farm," *Communities Magazine* (April/May 1982): p. 46.

27. Christopher Hills, *Creative Conflict*, p. 6-7.

28. *Ibid.*, p. 199-208.

29. Ken Keyes, *Handbook to Higher Consciousness*, p. 61.

30. *Ibid.*, p. 28.

31. *Ibid.*, p. 32-3.

32. Susan Campbell, "Alternative Communities: Are They Working?" *Yoga Journal* (Sept./Oct. 1981): p. 13.

33. Walter Truett Anderson, *The Upstart Spring*, p. 16.

34. *Earth Community Newsletter* (January 1983).

35. Walter Truett Anderson, *The Upstart Spring*, p. 296-7.

8
1. Duane Elgin, *Voluntary Simplicity*, p. 33.

2. *The Light Journal* (Spring 1983): p. 7; (July 1981): p. 19.

3. *The Light Journal* (July 1981): p. 15.

4. Mitch Seagrave, "The Crystal Connection," *The Light Journal* (Spring 1983): p. 6.

5. *The Center of the Light Summer 1983 Catalogue*, p. 13.

6. *Ibid.*, p. 35.

7. Rajendra, *Journey into the New Age*, p. 30.

8. Carolyn Delluomo, "Kripalu Hara Kinetics," *Kripalu Yoga Quest* (1984).

9. "Bio-dynamics: The 'Other' Organic Gardening Method," *Mother Earth News* (March/April 1984): p. 83.

10. *Ibid.*

11. *Anthroposophy: Summary Information on Agriculture*, brochure.

12. Rudolf Steiner, *Agriculture*, p. 70.

13. Busse Bruno, "Medicinal Herbs from Our Own Gardens," *Weleda News* #1 (1980): p. 2.

14. Herbert H. Koepf, *What is Bio-dynamic Agriculture?*, p. 25.

15. Busse Bruno, "Medicinal Herbs from Our Own Gardens," *Weleda News* #1 (1980): p. 2.

16. *Ibid.*

17. Rudolf Steiner, *Agriculture*, p. 47-8.

18. Robert Drennan, "Bio-Dynamic Gardening," *Natural Lifestyle* (September 1971): p. 60-4.

19. *Ibid.*, p. 65.

20. *Ibid.*

21. Busse Bruno, "Medicinal Herbs from Our Own Gardens," *Weleda News* #1 (1980): p. 2.

22. Robert Drennan, "Bio-Dynamic Gardening," *Natural Lifestyle* (September 1971): p. 68.

23. Paul Hawken, *Findhorn—A Center of Light*, p. 24.

24. The Findhorn Community, *The Findhorn Garden*, p. 59, 62.

25. Paul Hawken, *Findhorn—A Center of Light*, p. 19-20.

26. The Findhorn Community, *The Findhorn Garden*, p. 53.

27. *Ibid.*, p. 79.

28. Jill Wolcott, "Gardening at Findhorn," *Onearth Magazine* (November 1983): p. 9.

29. The Findhorn Community, *The Findhorn Garden*, p. 60, 73.

30. The Findhorn Community, *Faces of Findhorn*, p. 134.

31. The Findhorn Community, *The Findhorn Garden*, p. 138.

32. Michael Henretty, "Fuel Self-sufficiency for Stelle," *Stelle Letter* (March 1980).

33. Tim Johnson, "New Solar Greenhouse," *Star Newspaper* (April 26, 1984).

34. Jerome Clayton Glenn, *Linking the Future: Findhorn, Auroville, Arcosanti*, p. 109, 115.

35. Paolo Soleri, *Arcosanti: An Urban Laboratory?*, p. 27.

36. *Ibid.*, p. 35.

37. *Ibid.*, p. 21.

38. *Ibid.*, p. 57.

39. Sydney Beaudet, "Arcosanti," *Communities Magazine* (1979): p. 44.

9 1. Timothy Clark, "Consensus by Attunement," *The Chinook Letter* (Winter 1984).

2. Fritz and Vivian Hull, "Chinook, A Place of Vision," Chinook brochure.

3. Mimi Maduro, "Culture, Land and Education at Chinook," *Rain Magazine* (May/June 1984): p. 25.

4. Sun Bear, *The Path of Power*, p. 27.

5. *Ibid.*, p. 208-9.

6. Sun Bear, Wabun, Nimimosha and the Tribe, *Self-Reliance*, p. 32.

7. Sun Bear, *Path of Power*, p. 39.

8. *Ibid.*, p. 232.

9. *Ibid.*, p. 207, 223.

10. *Ibid.*, p. 122.

11. *Ibid.*, p. 204.

12. *Ibid.*, p. 183.

13. "The Abode Vision," *The Message* (October 1978): p. 3.

14. The Sufi Message, Vol IX, as quoted in *Bismillah* (March 1977): p. 20.

15. Donna Mattoon, "Abode in Its Sixth Year," *The Berkshire Eagle* (March 29, 1982): p. 8.

16. "The Abode Vision," *The Message* (October 1978): p. 8.

17. *Ibid.*, p. 9.

18. Jay F. Buters, "Zen Is Just Like This," *Sunday Providence Journal* Magazine Section (December 14, 1980).

19. Lincoln Rhodes, "Facing Your Karma," *Newsletter of the Providence Zen Center* (May, 1983): p. 2-4.

20. *Ibid.*

21. *Ibid.*

22. Lama brochure (Winter 1979): p. 1.

23. Mary Ann Matheson, "Lama," *Communities Magazine* (Spring 1982): p. 35.

10 1. Letters of Helena Roerich, Vol I, p. 100-101.

2. The Findhorn Community, *Faces of Findhorn*, p. 26-7.

3. *Ibid.,* p. 27.

4. Chris Roberts, "Growing with Sunbow," *In Context* (Winter 1983): p. 10.

5. The Findhorn Community, *The Faces of Findhorn,* p. 26.

6. Swami Kriyananda, *Cooperative Communities,* p. 19.

7. For further information on these options, see chapter 12 on Resources.

8. Benjamin Zablocki, *Alienation and Charisma,* p. 46.

9. Ram Dass, *Be Here Now,* p. 105.

10. David Spangler, *Emergence: Rebirth of the Sacred,* p. 127-8.

11. Kat Kinkade, "Selectors in a Community," *In Context* (Winter 1983): p. 26-7.

12. Benjamin Zablocki, *Alienation and Charisma,* p. 46.

13. The Findhorn Community, *Faces of Findhorn,* p. 27.

14. Chris Roberts, "Growing with Sunbow," *In Context* (Winter 1983): p. 11.

15. The Training/Action Affinity Group of Movement for a New Society, *Building Social Change Communities,* p. 20.

16. "The Alternative Way of Life," *Report on the First International Conference on Community Living,* Israel, 1982, p. 88.

17. David Spangler, *Anthology,* p. 52.

18. The Seven Rays, *A New Heaven and a New Earth,* p. 44-5.

19. Eberhard Arnold, "The Creative Pause," *The Plough* (November 1984).

20. Sun Bear, Wabun, Nimimosha and the Tribe, *Self-Reliance,* p. 51.

21. Carol Bridges, "Community as Business," *Earth Nation Sunrise* (Fall 1983): p. 23.

22. Agni Yoga Society, *Fiery World II,* p. 160.

23. Sun Bear, Wabun, Nimimosha and the Tribe, *Self-Reliance,* p. 48-9.

24. Bubba Free John, *The Eating Gorilla Comes in Peace,* p. 428.

25. Steve Leto, "Conscious Environments," *Crazy Wisdom,* Vol. 3, No. 7, p. 16-7.

26. Sun Bear, Wabun, Nimimosha and the Tribe, *Self-Reliance,* p. 48.

27. Francois Duquesne, "The Sacred Earth and the Heavenly City," *Onearth Magazine* (April/May 1983): p. 4.

28. Milenko Matanovic, "Growth and Containment," *Lorian Journal* (Summer 1982): p. 11-13.

29. Swami Kriyananda, *Cooperative Communities,* p. 18-20.

30. *Lama Views* (Autumn 1984): p. 6.

11 1. Agni Yoga Society, *New Era Community,* p. 205.

2. Francois Duquesne, "The Sacred Earth and the Heavenly City," *Onearth Magazine* (April/May 1983): p. 4.

3. William Irwin Thompson, *Darkness and Scattered Light,* p. 90-1.

4. David Spangler, "Stepping on to a Planetary Culture," *Onearth Magazine,* Vol. 2, No. 5 (May/June 1982): p. 4.

5. The Findhorn Community, *The Faces of Findhorn,* p. 172-4.

6. *Ibid.*

7. *Ibid.*

8. Ingrid Komar, *Living The Dream,* p. 65-6.

9. Robert Gilman, "The Village and Beyond," *In Context* (Winter 1983): p. 56.

10. Paul Kagan, *New World Utopias,* p. 176.